M000274871

A Norton Professional Book

Attachment-Focused EMDR
Healing Relational Trauma

Laurel Parnell
Foreword by Daniel J. Siegel

W. W. Norton & Company
New York • London

Copyright © 2013 by Laurel Parnell

All rights reserved
Printed in the United States of America
First Edition

For information about permission to reproduce selections from this book, write to
Permissions, W. W. Norton & Company, Inc., 500 Fifth Avenue, New York, NY 10110

For information about special discounts for bulk purchases, please contact W. W. Norton
Special Sales at specialsales@wwnorton.com or 800-233-4830

Manufacturing by Courier Westford
Book design by Paradigm Graphics
Production manager: Leeann Graham

Library of Congress Cataloging-in-Publication Data

Parnell, Laurel, 1955-
  Attachment-focused EMDR : healing relational trauma / Laurel Parnell. — First edition.
    pages cm
  "A Norton Professional Book."
  Includes bibliographical references and index.
  ISBN 978-0-393-70745-8 (hardcover)
1. Attachment disorder—Treatment. 2. Psychic trauma—Treatment. 3. Eye movement
desensitization and reprocessing. I. Title. II. Title: Attachment-focused eye movement
desensitization and reprocessing.
  RC455.4.A84P37 3013
  616.85'88—dc23
                              2013003374

ISBN: 978-0-393-70745-8

W. W. Norton & Company, Inc., 500 Fifth Avenue, New York, N.Y. 10110
                    www.wwnorton.com
W. W. Norton & Company Ltd., Castle House, 75/76 Wells Street, London W1T 3QT

2 3 4 5 6 7 8 9 0

To my granddaughter
Katya Laurel Kudrya
with love

Contents

Acknowledgments   ix

Foreword by Daniel J. Siegel   xiii

Introduction   xvii

PART I: OVERVIEW

Chapter 1   Laying the Groundwork   3

Chapter 2   The Five Basic Principles of   12
             Attachment-Focused EMDR

Chapter 3   Therapist Characteristics and Skills for   30
             Attachment Repair

PART II: HEALING RESOURCES

Chapter 4   The Four Most Important Resources   45

Chapter 5   Creating New Parents and Repairing   73
             Developmental Deficits

Chapter 6   Case Histories of Repairing Developmental   95
             Deficits

Chapter 7   Love Resources   107

Chapter 8   Additional Attachment-Repair Resources   118

PART III: USING EMDR

Chapter 9   Creating the Safe Therapeutic Container   137

Chapter 10   Case Example: *Preparing a Client with Severe*   160
              Attachment Trauma for EMDR, by Holly Prichard

Chapter 11   Creating Targets and Modifying the Protocol   174

Chapter 12   Reevaluation and the Pacing of Treatment   198

Chapter 13   Bringing an Attachment Focus to Desensitization   203

Chapter 14   Using Interweaves to Unblock Processing   216

Chapter 15   Five EMDR Sessions Demonstrating the Use   256
              of Interweaves to Repair Attachment Trauma

PART IV: CASE EXAMPLES

Chapter 16   Using AF-EMDR as an Adjunctive Therapist to   287
              Treat Lifelong Depression, Developmental
              Neglect, and Attachment Wounding,
              by Holly Prichard

Chapter 17   AF-EMDR With a Young Woman With Eating   321
              Disorders, PTSD, Anxiety, and Early
              Attachment Trauma, by Elena Felder

Chapter 18   Brief AF-EMDR With a Client Experiencing   341
              Panic Attacks, Depression, and Stalking
              Behavior, by Rachel Howard

References   373

Index   379

Acknowledgments

There are so many people I want to thank who have made this book possible. First of all, I want to thank all of the clients with whom I have worked over the years and those who so graciously provided their case material for inclusion in this book. All of these amazing individuals have contributed, through their courage and strength, to my understanding that it is possible to heal even the most unspeakable traumas and neglect. Thank you all from the bottom of my heart. With your contributions to this book, therapists and clients will have new hope for healing that for which there was previously so little remedy.

Special thanks to the three major contributors to this volume: Holly Prichard, Elena Felder, and Rachel Howard, all outstanding EMDR therapists who through their compassion, understanding of what is most important to heal attachment, and excellent clinical skills, beautifully illustrated for readers what attachment-focused EMDR looks like in clinical practice. Thank you also to the talented EMDR therapists Prabha Milstein and Nancy Ewing, whose case material on the development of the ideal mother and the repair of development deficits using imagination and BLS showed their creativity, attunement, and skillful application of this model in their clinical work.

I want to thank Daniel Siegel for his beautiful foreword to this book and for being such an important influence on my understanding of interpersonal neurobiology. His teaching has had a profound effect on the way I think about attachment and approach my clinical work. Not only is he an excellent teacher, but he demonstrates what he is teaching through the kindness, attunement, presence, and compassion in all his interactions.

I want to acknowledge Bessel van der Kolk for his invaluable contribution to my clinical work and teaching. A tireless educator, he has helped expand therapists' understanding of the effects of trauma on the brain, and of how to integrate this information into treatment.

I deeply appreciate Francine Shapiro, originator of this powerful therapy that has transformed my life and that of thousands of others.

I wish to acknowledge Allan Schore, who has taught me a great deal about attachment trauma and what is most important in its healing.

Thank you to Deborah Malmud, director of Norton Professional Books, for recognizing the value of this book, and to Sophie Hagen and Margaret Ryan for their excellent eye for detail and helpful suggestions in the line editing.

I appreciate my friend and colleague Maggie Phillips, who has made major contributions to the field of attachment, resource development, complex trauma, ego state work, and pain management.

Thank you to Diana Fosha, who added new ideas to how healing moments in the therapeutic relationship could be made explicit and "tapped in" as resources. Her AEDP is a major contribution to the field of attachment repair therapies.

I want to extend special thank-you's to my EMDR friends and colleagues, all of whom practice attachment-focused EMDR and are important resources for me personally and professionally: Harriet Sage, Susan Tieger, Alison Teal, Erika Masak-Goldman, Nancy Bravman, Pat Gallagher, Leah Leatherbee, Bruce Patterson, Sean Frankino, Ruth Ehrenkranz-Strauss, Linda Kocienewski, Sandy Shapiro, Caryn Markson, Debbe Davis, Rachel Howard, Susan Curry, John Prendergast, Dinah Weisberg-Tarah, and Meg Grundy. I want to acknowledge as well all of the talented EMDR therapists who have contributed to the growth and development of EMDR over the years; I also acknowledge the therapists, researchers, and authors who have added to our understanding of how an attachment orientation can be integrated into treatment of relational trauma.

I want to thank and acknowledge my dear friend Nischala Devi who has been with me through many ups and downs and whose friendship is one of my most precious resources.

I want to acknowledge my sons, Catono Perez and Etienne Perez-Parnell, and my parents, Helen McDonald and J. Dean Parnell, who I love dearly.

Wondrously, the writing of this book coincided with the birth and first two years of life of my granddaughter Katya, a special synchronicity. I am deeply grateful to Elena Kudryavtseva, Katya's mother, who has shown me that the love for one's baby is instinctual, and that the mother-infant bond can develop in a healthy way, even if the mother has had no experience of such a healthy relationship herself.

I am deeply grateful for my husband Pierre Antoine Blais, who has supported and loved me now for over twenty years and has taught me how a loving relationship can heal relational trauma.

Foreword

Daniel J. Siegel

Laurel Parnell's beautifully written book invites mental health practitioners to explore the idea that psychotherapy can provide deep growth for those who have experienced insecure forms of attachment in their early lives. Parnell writes in a directly accessible and clinically practical way, illuminating this helpful approach throughout the text with concepts, theory, and case vignettes. Our experienced and wise guide offers us a way to embrace two often separate worlds of knowing: the science of early attachment relationships and the practice of healing within a framework inspired by eye-movement desensitization and reprocessing (EMDR).

In this book you will find science-based ideas about how our early relationships shape the way the mind and brain develop from our young years into our adult lives. The "models of attachment" formed in the crucible of our communications and connections with our caregivers are states of mind—assembled brain activation profiles of neural circuit firings that persist throughout our lives, shaping how we think, feel, remember, and behave. These states of mind can be based on secure attachment experiences in which we feel seen, safe, soothed, and secure—the "four S's of attachment" that serve as the foundation for a healthy mind. From the perspective of the field of interpersonal neurobiology (IPNB), this security of attachment provides relational experiences that stimulate the neuronal activation and growth of the integrative fibers of the brain. IPNB views integration—the linkage of different parts of a system—as the basis of health and well-being, the core mechanism of healing.

Why is integration important? Integration is the fundamental mechanism beneath the adaptive and healthy regulation of affect, attention, memory, and social interactions. In these many ways, integration enables us to function well. Developmental compromises to attachment, in small and large ways, create various forms of persistent impediments to integration, both in the brain and in our interactions with others. Insecure attachment, including its more severe manifestation as developmental trauma, paired with suboptimal or overwhelming experiences in childhood, impairs the natural growth of integration within the individual, leading to difficulties in various forms of self-regulation. Psychotherapy that works, in this view, creates healing through cultivating integration.

This book reviews the various forms of insecure attachment and many examples of suboptimal regulation, such as difficulty balancing emotion, experiencing joy and ease, or focusing attention in a flexible and adaptive manner; challenges with painful traumatic memories; and unhelpful patterns of interaction with others that result in troubled relationships. Each of these challenges with optimal regulation can be viewed as deriving from suboptimal forms of neural integration. In fact, from an IPNB perspective, we envision the various forms of insecure attachment as not only linked to impaired integration in the brain, but also caused by non-integrated relationships that have stimulated neuronal sculpting toward non-integrated neural circuitry. An integrated relationship links two separate people into an integrated "we" by honoring differences and promoting compassionate communication. Relationships characterized by subtle forms of insecure attachment within avoidance or ambivalence, or by disorganized attachment and severe forms of developmental trauma, all represent forms of non-integrated communication.

Integrative relationships promote neural integration. In our early childhood, interpersonal experiences are vital in shaping healthy regulation. In psychotherapy, the therapeutic relationship and experience cultivate integration and the healing of insecure attachment and developmental trauma.

The attachment-based, EMDR-inspired framework of therapy that this book presents builds on basic attachment research and on the important work of Francine Shapiro's innovative EMDR approach. Utilizing aspects of the EMDR protocol, including resource cultivation and bilateral forms of stimulation, our author presents a powerful synthesis of innovative ways to adapt EMDR to cultivate secure attachment and health in the face of developmental trauma.

These early, prolonged, and sometimes severe relational experiences have a unique impact on the individual beyond a one-time traumatic experience, altering the epigenetic regulation of genetic expression, the hypothalamic-pituitary-adrenal axis (HPA axis) regulation of stress, and the growth of integrative fibers in the brain (including the prefrontal cortex, corpus callosum, and hippocampal regions). Treatment in this situation therefore needs to be tailored to these specific aspects of regulatory and integrative developmentally acquired issues. In the face of these foundational challenges to an individual's neuronal, epigenetic, and physiological capacities, blending a science-informed strategy to bring integration into an individual's life necessitates adjustment of standard approaches to focus on attachment models and the centrality of the presence, attunement, and resonance of the therapist.

In my own writings focusing on Francine Shapiro's work, I have suggested that IPNB views EMDR as a powerful approach to catalyzing integration in an individual or family across several domains, including memory, narrative, state, and vertical and bilateral integration. In Laurel Parnell's attachment-based modifications of the EMDR approach, the structural foundations of this integrative framework are adapted to further catalyze integration for this special population of individuals who have experienced non-secure attachment and developmental trauma. I hope that the wisdom of these pages will inform your work as a therapist, bringing deep and lasting integration and health to those who are so ready for it.

Daniel J. Siegel, MD
Executive Director, Mindsight Institute
Author, *The Developing Mind, Pocket
Guide to Interpersonal Neurobiology*

Introduction

Since my training in 1991, I have been dedicated to the development of the clinical application of eye movement desensitization and reprocessing (EMDR). In addition to practising EMDR with my own clients, as an EMDR consultant and trainer I have heard about and consulted on thousands of cases. All of this experience has helped me to learn and grow as a therapist and teacher so that my work is informed from a base of experience that has breadth and depth. I have written four previous books about EMDR or an EMDR-related technique I call Resource Tapping: *Transforming Trauma: EMDR, EMDR in the Treatment of Adults Abused As Children, A Therapist's Guide to EMDR*, and *Tapping In: A Step-by-Step Guide to Activating Your Healing Resources Through Bilateral Stimulation*. My thinking and clinical work have evolved over the years as evidenced by changes in my writing.

MY BACKGROUND AND INFLUENCES

I was trained psychodynamically with a developmental/object relation's emphasis. In my doctoral program we read Kohut, Mahler, Kernberg, and Masterson, and, most important to me, Alice Miller. Her book, *Drama of the Gifted Child* (1981), was revolutionary for many of us in my doctoral program. We eagerly read it, underlining passages throughout the thin volume. Miller described what many of us had experienced in our childhoods, but had never understood before: the emotional and psychological harm done to a developing child by parents who did not see, mirror, or value the child for him- or herself. In order to please the parents and gain their love, the child developed a false self, which seemed to function well, but was empty and devoid of vitality. I refer to Miller's work throughout this book because she has had a profound influence on my thinking and orientation to psychotherapy.

In addition to my psychodynamic orientation and background, I have also been influenced by Jungian psychology. I was drawn to study Jung because of my active dream life and spirituality. I did a predoctoral internship at the Jung Institute of San Francisco and had several years of Jungian analysis. I believe the free associative processing that EMDR clients do is much like Jungian active imagination. Jung's belief in the psyche's ability to heal itself also resonates with EMDR's adaptive information processing model. My Jungian background has helped me to stay open to the kind of exploration my clients do during their EMDR processing and to "trust the process."

My early training and experience included internships and work at community mental health clinics that served Spanish-speaking and low-income clients, most of whom suffered from trauma. This experience informs my sensitivity to the issues that clients of divergent backgrounds bring to EMDR therapy.

My doctoral dissertation as well as postdoctoral training were in the area of domestic violence. I have been working with family violence and complex trauma for over 34 years.

I was introduced to Buddhist meditation practices in 1972, when I was in high school. Buddhism fit my inquisitive personality well, as I learned that the Buddha instructed his followers not to believe what he said, but to "look within your own mind." I loved the idea of meditation as a laboratory within which to discover one's own truths. Over the years I have had extraordinary teachers, including Lama Thubten Yeshe, His Holiness the Dalai Lama, and Jean Klein, a teacher of Advaita Vedanta nondualism. I have also done many silent retreats with Vipassana teachers Jack Kornfield and Joseph Goldstein. Experiences and insights from years of meditation inform my orientation to life as well as the practice of psychotherapy. Tibetan practice has also influenced how I do EMDR, particularly the Resource Tapping work. Many Tibetan meditations use visualization and imagery to help cultivate enlightened qualities such as compassion, power, and wisdom. These qualities are within us already, but the imagery is utilized in order to evoke them so that they may be actualized. The Resource Tapping that I teach uses some of the same ideas. What do we wish to develop? And what imagery will help do that? The imagery and the bilateral stimulation together are a potent combination to activate and integrate information that is already within us to apply to a difficulty.

Jean Klein taught yoga in his retreats that emphasized body sensing on a deep, almost microscopic level. The yoga was very slow, bringing awareness to moment-to-moment experience. I believe this practice, along with the years of Vipassana or mindfulness meditation and retreats, helped me cultivate an awareness of my mind and body that I use when in sessions with my clients. When I feel something, I listen to it and wait to see what I am picking up. In this way I have developed an attunement to my body process. I experience what is coming up in me as information, rather than as something to be judged or discarded. I'll explain more about this in Chapter 10.

Other important influences on my work and understanding of trauma and attachment are the work of Daniel Siegel, Allan Schore, Bessel van der Kolk, Colin Ross, Maggie Phillips, Peter Levine, John Bowlby, Donald Winnicott, and Margaret Mahler.

WHY THE NEED FOR THIS BOOK?

I wrote *Attachment-Focused EMDR: Healing Relational Trauma* for EMDR therapists to present a new model of EMDR that I have developed over a period of 22 years that integrates the latest in attachment theory and research into the use of EMDR with clients who have relational traumas and attachment deficits. Clients who have experienced childhood traumas that have impacted their sense of safety and capacity to form close emotional relationships in adulthood require adjustments to the EMDR phases and procedural steps. These relational traumas can include childhood physical or sexual abuse, neglect, early losses, birth trauma, medical trauma, parental drug or alcohol abuse, caregiver misattunement, vicarious trauma or traumas that the child took into his or her *neuro networks*[1] from the parent's traumas. These traumas also include the narcissistic injuries to the development of a "true self," as described by Miller (1981). These clients were not allowed to experience their true

---

[1] This is a term Francine Shapiro uses in her text: "I use psychophysiological concepts by employing the term *neuropsychological* or *neuro networks*. This construct will subsume the way the term neural networks is currently being used by neuropsychologists and extend it to an additional state of cognitive/emotional processing. Using a term that does not have a precise neurophysiological referrent is particularly important to underscore the point that the efficacy of EMDR is not based on the validity of the physiological model being offered. This is relevant because we must remember that the physiology of the brain is not yet sufficiently understood to confirm the validity of the model at that level. However, the model does not appear to contradict anything known to be true, is congruent with the observed treatment effects of EMDR, and serves as a clinical road map for treating a wide range of pathologies" (Shapiro, 1995, p. 29).

feelings and to know themselves. In order to be loved, they adapted to the needs of their parents or caretakers, developing what Winnicott described as a "false self." These clients often present in therapy as depressed, with relationship difficulties or problems at work. They don't feel fully alive. In order for EMDR therapists to work most successfully with this population, it is important to incorporate an attachment-repair orientation to all phases of EMDR work.

I felt compelled to write this book to address the needs of therapists and their clients with relational trauma. I believe that these therapists need a guidebook to help them navigate the difficult and complex terrain of integrating EMDR into clinical practice with an attachment orientation. With this guidance I believe many more people can be helped to heal attachment wounds and go on to live fuller, more productive lives.

This book, like two of my other books (*EMDR in the Treatment of Adults Abused as Children* and *A Therapist's Guide to EMDR*), was written for EMDR therapists in a user-friendly way to help you better understand how to use EMDR in your clinical practices. The emphasis is on the practical, clinical application of EMDR with relational trauma. Case material is interwoven throughout the text, and Chapters 16–18 present in-depth cases that illustrate attachment-focused EMDR. These cases include history and background of the clients, actual EMDR sessions, attachment-repair interventions within these sessions and the rationale for them, and information about the effects of the interventions and the course of treatment. *Attachment-Focused EMDR: Healing Relational Trauma* includes information and ideas from the previous books with an emphasis on my work with clients who have relational trauma from an attachment-focused orientation.

I have been teaching and presenting the material in this book for many years, and I use it in my clinical practice. In fact, Daniel Siegel attended one of my EMDR trainings and after watching my demonstrations, called what I do "attachment-focused EMDR." This spurred me to ponder and then formulate a definition and basic principles for *attachment-focused* EMDR.

This book is meant as a guide, not as a manual. I outline basic principles of what I believe is important in attachment-focused EMDR and present case material that hopefully will stimulate your imagination and creativity. I believe that all good therapy is an art, not a technique, and that as we are able to drop into a place of silence and really listen to our own quiet voice and that of our clients, relational healing takes place. We are *being with* our clients. This right-brain to right-brain connection is nonlinear, timeless, felt in the body, intuitive, creative, and healing. When we connect with our clients in this way, they *feel* understood, without words.

Much has been written about trauma and neglect and the damage they do to the developing brain. However, little has been written or researched about the potential to heal these attachment wounds. In fact, some of the research makes one feel that there isn't much hope for healing damage from neglect or very poor parenting in early childhood. I have not found that to be true. I have been getting positive results with many of these clients, and so have my colleagues who use attachment-focused EMDR. The combination of Resource Tapping (building new neuronal pathways with imagination and bilateral stimulation) and targeting trauma memories via EMDR is showing promising results even with clients who have had years of psychotherapy with little progress. Though I have no research to support this claim, I have many clinical examples, which I include in this book. Clients with longstanding issues involving neglect and severe childhood abuse typically need longer-term therapy, with EMDR and Resource Tapping integrated into the work. I have found that it is hard to determine how quickly someone might respond to EMDR and Resource Tapping. Some clients experience very rapid change, with a large generalization effect throughout their neuro networks, whereas other clients may need many more sessions and more resourcing.

One might expect it to take longer with a client who has had severe trauma and neglect, but in some cases, even these clients make rapid progress that is almost incomprehensible, as in the case presented in Chapter 18. I believe that this rapid progress is often neurologically based. For some reason, these clients have brains that process information more rapidly. I have witnessed this in my trainings during the practicums, as well as in my private practice: There are some people who just process faster, process more material, and have greater generalization effects than other people. This characteristic doesn't seem to be associated with more insight or prior years of therapy. I am very encouraged by the brain's plasticity, a fact now well established by neuroscientific research. It is a remarkable organ, able to heal and change. It is important that we meet our clients with an open mind, and don't imprison them with our limiting beliefs about what their potential for healing is.

This is not to say that attachment-focused EMDR is a panacea. Many clients require longer-term psychotherapy that integrates EMDR and Resource Tapping, as well as other useful therapeutic tools. The therapeutic relationship is of utmost importance, helping to create a template of safety and trust from which these clients can learn to build other relationships. The sessions presented in this book do not demonstrate a one-session cure or even short-term therapy. Rather they show what attachment-focused EMDR looks like in a session. Though clients typically experience results that give them hope, this is not usually short-term treatment. There are many excellent EMDR therapists and teachers who have much to contribute to the use of EMDR in the healing of attachment trauma. This book is just one contribution to the ongoing development of this exciting area. The focus of *Attachment-Focused EMDR: Healing Relational Trauma* is on how to integrate an attachment-repair orientation into EMDR with *adult* clients who have attachment wounds and relational trauma. Though principles of this orientation should also be used with children, the information and cases described here involve adult clients and a few adolescents.

The cases in this book are from my private practice, from demonstrations in my trainings, and from clients of my EMDR colleagues. Though some are composites from several cases, most of the sessions presented are from actual client sessions. I am deeply grateful to all of the clients who have given their permission to use their case material. Without them, this book would not be possible.

THE BOOK'S ORGANIZATION

This book is divided into four parts. Part I, "Overview of Attachment-Focused EMDR," lays the groundwork and outlines the five basic principles that guide and define the work. Part II, "Healing Resources," provides information and many ideas for attachment-repair resources. This section can be used by therapists who are not trained in EMDR. Part III, "Using EMDR," teaches therapists how to use EMDR specifically with an attachment-repair orientation, including client preparation, target development, modifications of the standard EMDR protocol, desensitization, and using interweaves. Case material is used throughout. Part IV, "Cases," includes the presentation of three cases from different EMDR therapists who used attachment-focused EMDR with their clients. These cases illustrate information from the previous chapters, bringing it all together so that you can see what this looks like in clinical practice.

CONVENTIONS USED THROUGHOUT THIS BOOK

I have used fictitious first names for clients throughout the book. All of the identifying details of the cases have been changed in order to protect the privacy of the clients. I have changed names, professions, family constellations, races, and specific life events; and some cases represent composites of more than one client. I have used the word *client*, a term I prefer instead of *patient*. All clients are referred to by first names, which I felt created a more personal feeling about the people whose lives I describe.

The bilateral stimulation used in the cases presented includes auditory stimulation and tactile stimulation created by a device called the Tac/AudioScan, as well as alternate tapping on the hands or knees and eye movements directed by a light bar. In the book's transcripts you will see the ">>>>>" sign to indicate a set of bilateral stimulations (BLS). Unless otherwise indicated, assume that the client was directed by the therapist to focus on whatever material had just come up, and that at the end of BLS, the therapist asked the client a question such as, "What came up for you?" or "What do you get now?" to elicit information about the client's experience during the set of bilateral stimulation.

Attachment-Focused EMDR

Part I
OVERVIEW

CHAPTER 1

Laying the Groundwork

The Evolution of EMDR and Its Clinical Applications

EMDR was originally developed by Francine Shapiro to treat post-traumatic stress disorder (PTSD), particularly single-incident PTSD, with a population from Silicon Valley, California, a primarily educated group of clients. At the closing of my original training Dr. Shapiro instructed us all to "make it our own." She told us that it was "in our hands." She also told us that "EMDR is not a cookie cutter," meaning it is not meant to be used the same way with each person. Taking her instructions to heart, I began to find what worked and what didn't work with my clients. At the time of the training I was already an experienced psychotherapist with a decade of practice accrued. I have always worked with complex trauma, as well as with clients from divergent cultures and backgrounds. My early clinical work was in community mental health clinics working with a Spanish-speaking population. Many of the clients I have worked with experienced severe childhood sexual and physical abuse. I found early on that the standard protocol needed to be modified for these clients. I wrote about work with this population in my second book, *EMDR in the Treatment of Adults Abused as Children* (Parnell, 1999), which Francine Shapiro endorsed. Although she agreed that the procedural steps could be modified according to the needs of the clients, it was important to her that clinicians understand the rationale for the modifications and not just discard the protocol altogether. I agree with her on this. I believe it is important for therapists to understand the rationale for each of the steps in the EMDR protocol, and then to modify it intelligently. This is the stance I teach in all of my trainings, which I believe is respectful to the clinicians as well as to the intention of EMDR as it was originally designed.

EMDR as defined by Shapiro (1995, 2001) is an eight-phase model of treatment. Most therapists, aside from those of us who teach this or are on EMDR International Association (EMDRIA) committees, do not remember these phases. That's because they do not make a lot of sense. For example, history taking and preparation, phases 1 and 2, may not be sequential and may take days to months to accomplish, whereas installation and body scan, phases 5 and 6, may take only a few minutes. Most trauma therapies describe three phases of treatment—phases that are reasonable and are easy to conceptualize.

For many clients with severe childhood trauma suffering from complex PTSD, therapy may proceed over three phases. I described these phases in detail in *EMDR in the Treatment of Adults Abused as Children* (Parnell, 1999) and in *A Therapist's Guide to EMDR* (Parnell, 2007). Here I summarize them. The *beginning phase* includes assessment, preparation, and ego-strengthening (Shapiro's phases 1 and 2 of history taking and preparation). In this phase clients are assessed for appropriateness of the treatment and sufficiently stabilized; resources are developed and installed; the therapeutic relationship is well established; and coping skills are learned. The therapeutic container must be strong enough, which means that clients need to feel sufficiently safe with the therapist and be able to tolerate high levels of affect prior to beginning intensive trauma work. In the *middle phase,* trauma processing work and integration take place. In the *end phase,* creativity, spirituality, and integration are the focus, with less EMDR and more talking. Questions such as "Who am I?" and "What do I want to do with my life?" arise and need to be addressed. I have found that it is helpful to think in terms of these three phases when working with clients who have complex trauma histories. Talk therapy is typically integrated throughout the work, and transference and countertransference issues are addressed. EMDR is integrated into an overall treatment plan that can include many other therapeutic modalities.

But even these phases may not be appropriate for conceptualizing work with clients who have early attachment wounds. The primary work with some of these clients may involve the tapping in of resources that change their neuro networks. These sessions may not focus at all on trauma, but on clients' positive resources and the fruits of their creative imaginations. The work is subtler and more relationship-focused. *The therapy isn't so much focused on the traumas, but on the repair of the developmental deficits from what they didn't get*. When EMDR *is* done, imagination and resource interweaves are used more frequently and attention is paid to make sure that fragile clients are not retraumatized by leaving them too long in the trauma network as they process childhood abuse memories. EMDR and Resource Tapping are not just "front-loaded" in the beginning as preparation; rather they are interwoven throughout the therapy according to the needs of the client.

WHAT IS ATTACHMENT-FOCUSED EMDR?

Attachment-focused EMDR (AF-EMDR) is an orientation to the practice of EMDR. AF-EMDR is client-centered and emphasizes a reparative therapeutic relationship using a combination of (1) Resource Tapping (Parnell, 2008) to strengthen clients, (2) EMDR to process traumas, and (3) talk therapy to help integrate the information from EMDR sessions and to provide healing derived from therapist–client interactions. AF-EMDR can be used for clients with severe early attachment trauma, as well as *for all clients who require that the therapist attend to their needs as unique individuals*. AF-EMDR has five guiding principles that define it, which I discuss in Chapter 2.

Clients with attachment wounds require the modification and adaptation of the standard EMDR protocols. AF-EMDR addresses these issues by modifying the standard EMDR protocol, integrating resource-strengthening methods throughout the course of treatment, and emphasizing the centrality of the therapeutic relationship and healing derived from the right-brain to right-brain connection. In this model the therapist may utilize him- or herself as a "resource" implicitly or explicitly to help increase clients' feelings of safety and affect tolerance, which can then be integrated directly into clients' neural circuitry using bilateral stimulation. Simple touch (e.g., holding the client's hand), gentle eye contact, and the use of the therapist's voice providing caring support during abreactions are included as ways to build new neural pathways and heal attachment wounds. AF-EMDR is implemented in the treatment of clients with childhood trauma and neglect, as noted, as well as with those clients who require an adjustment to the standard protocol to increase their sense of safety, rapport, attunement, and empathy. AF-

EMDR is also used for clients for whom a manualized therapy would be injurious and could affect the creation and maintenance of the therapeutic bond.

DEFINITIONS

For greater clarity, in this section we consider definitions for key terms I use throughout the book: *relational trauma*, *Resource Tapping*, and *EMDR*.

Relational Trauma

I define *relational trauma* much more broadly than Allan Schore (2001), who uses this term for clients who have been abused or neglected in early childhood. For the purposes of this book, I define *relational trauma* as *trauma that occurs in the context of a relationship—either something that happened or did not happen (e.g., neglect) to the client that has caused him or her harm*. This trauma could stem from the treatment of a mother, father, siblings, other relatives, caretakers, or other significant relationships. The form of trauma might involve physical, sexual, or emotional abuse; neglect, abandonment, lack of mirroring and attunement; unconscious absorption of parents' traumas; early loss of a parent or caretaker; parent's mental or physical illness or drug and/or alcohol abuse. The trauma could include a parent's lack of response to an abusive situation, such as in the case of a client whose mother did not protect her from her father who was sexually abusing her. It can include the client who never had a father to provide guidance to him. There are many ways that clients can experience trauma from a relationship—be it a large *T* or a small *t* trauma—which will affect how they view themselves and their relationships. As you can see, by my definition *relational trauma* includes most of the clients we see in clinical practice.

EMDR and Resource Tapping

For the purposes of this book, I define EMDR as the use of alternating bilateral stimulation to reprocess emotionally charged memories, using a protocol that provides a structure for the session. Resource Tapping (Parnell, 2008) or resource installation is a method to strengthen and integrate internal resources by pairing imagined positive resources with alternating bilateral stimulation. Resource Tapping can be done as a treatment technique that is integrated into a therapy for relational trauma, or as a method for preparing clients for EMDR trauma processing.

ATTACHMENT STYLES AND THE USE OF EMDR

Mary Main (1992) developed the Adult Attachment Interview (AAI) as a way to categorize the attachment styles of adults. These styles reflect the way the mind, over time, has created a kind of template (Bowlby [1969] used the term *internal working model*) for relationships. People don't often fit neatly into one of these categories and may have some elements of several of them, as children often have relationships with different caretakers who have different styles of attachment. Even though there may have been several different caregivers, it appears that in adolescence, the brain integrates this information and develops a style of relating. The attachment styles reflect an implicit right-brain organization of neuro networks. Patterns of emotional responses, body sensations, and the beliefs associated with them operate beneath conscious awareness (hence, *implicit*). These patterns, developed through relationships with significant caregivers in early life, can be altered and changed through adaptive healing relationships in later life in a process called *earned secure attachment* (Main, 1992).

I have noticed that I avoid categorizing my clients. Upon reflection, I realized that the difficulty I have with these categories is that I believe strongly that we need to look at each of our clients as an individual, not as an attachment style. Reliance on the categories can be injurious to our clients if we fail to see them as individuals. For example, as soon as I think about the styles, I begin to try to see how my client fits into one of the categories. Then I realize I am trying to make him or her fit into a box, rather than perceive his or her full complexity. Our clients' ways of relating to others are the product of a combination of factors and can be quite complex. A female client can have close friendships with women, but have disastrous relationships with men. She has "holes" in her ways of relating that are in one specific area.

It is essential that we listen to and get to know each of our clients and adjust what we do according to each one's needs. In this way we help to heal clients through our attunement, connection, and caring, without reinjuring them through the imposition of a box or a label. Use these categories as guides, but not as a road map, and don't impose them on your clients. *The healing of attachment wounds emerges from the attun-*

ement and flexibility of the therapeutic relationship that is directed by the needs of the client. I worry when therapists want easy solutions to complex problems. The answer is in each client. What does this client need in order to create and repair attachment wounds? Use your intuition and your sense of your clients' attachment traumas and their needs for repair.

With these cautionary thoughts in mind, we now review the adult attachment styles as defined by Mary Main (1992) and associates (1986, 1990) derived from the AAI, along with suggestions for how AF-EMDR might be used.

Secure Attachment

These clients value relationships and are flexible and objective when speaking about attachment-related issues. They are able to integrate their past experiences with their present circumstances and their future aspirations, and they have made sense of their life histories. Even if they did not have a healthy attachment in childhood, a secure attachment can be "earned." Earned security is developed in adulthood via therapy or a healing relationship. These clients can then tell a coherent narrative of their lives that integrates the key elements and experiences of their past, present, and anticipated future with insight, relatedness, and emotional nuance. Those with earned security are able to use this understanding to create healthy relationships in the present.

Avoidant/Dismissing Attachment

These clients had parents who were unresponsive or neglectful, so they grew up with little interpersonal attunement or connection. They learned to give up and take care of themselves. They believe that they cannot depend on humans to meet their needs. These clients avoid relationships but may also desire them. They are not connected to their emotions or to their bodies and are therefore cut off from themselves and others. They typically don't recall their childhoods, except in the most fact-based manner—in linear, left-brain recollections devoid of emotional content. These clients have very little right-brain activity and do not perceive non-verbal signals from others. They rely on logical analysis and engage in little self-reflection.

In treatment, these clients need to integrate new relationship information, which means they need more right-brain involvement. Therapeutic techniques that facilitate right-brain activation and integration should be used with them. These include art, movement, psychodrama, guided imagery, body-based work, and Resource Tapping with imagery. It can be difficult finding EMDR targets with these clients because although they have attachment deficits aplenty, they also have little access to emotionally charged incidents. In these cases the work is to *add in* new relational circuits. The use of guided imagery with BLS that focuses on nonverbal signals, increased awareness of the body, and experiences that activate the right side of the brain can be helpful. Memories of being connected to another person and moments in the therapist–client relationship when they feel a connection can be made explicit and can be tapped in. The therapist might ask, "How was that for you when you felt seen by me? What did you notice in your body?" As the client responds to these queries, the therapist adds BLS to help the client take in this new information. If clients have difficulty accepting the resourcing, the therapist might say the following:

> *"Brain science suggests that new neurons, especially integrative ones, may continue to grow throughout our lives. That is why this resourcing work is so important—we are working to grow new neural pathways."*

Ambivalent and Preoccupied Attachment

These clients had parents who were inconsistent or unavailable, so they have anxiety about whether or not the other is available. In some cases their parents were overly intrusive. In either case they have a desperate need for the other, and at the same time, they fear that their needs can never be met in relationships or that they will be "taken over" by the other. They have an overactive right hemisphere and have difficulty self-soothing. They may feel shame, that "there is something wrong with me" because their needs were not met consistently.

These clients may or may not have significant large traumas; EMDR can also be done on the smaller traumas. When EMDR is employed in the presence of a compassionately attuned therapist, clients take in relational healing along with the healing of the original trauma memory. In other words, they integrate the therapist's compassionately attuned presence into their right-brain neural nets. This is a corrective emotional experience in which the client is seen, heard, and attuned to by a caring person.

These clients also need tools to calm their anxiety and sooth their self-criticism and shame. They need to develop positive self-talk to counter the negative thoughts that undermine them in their daily lives. EMDR resourcing is an important tool with which to calm the right hemisphere and develop new neural pathways. As noted, EMDR can be done on traumas large and small to help clients develop a coherent narrative and a cohesive sense of self.

Disorganized and Unresolved Trauma or Loss

These clients had parents/caregivers whose behavior was overwhelming, frightening, and/or chaotic. They therefore suffered from significant childhood traumas, including physical or sexual abuse and/or loss, which has caused internal fragmentation and disconnection from themselves and others. They may have flashbacks, frightening body memories, problems with social communication, and problems with reasoning (because the left hemisphere is offline), and they dissociate. Their unresolved, unprocessed traumas leave their memories, emotions, and body sensations in an unintegrated and chaotic state.

This attachment style is also found in clients whose parents did not physically abuse them, but whose behavior was frightening or disorienting to the child, such as in families with drug and alcohol abuse and where parents raged, but did not hit, the children.

For these clients, their source of comfort (i.e., their caregivers) was also their source of terror. This impossible situation is too much for children to integrate so they fragment or compartmentalize. For example, for one client, "daytime daddy" —loving and warm, safe and fun—was in one compartment, and "nighttime daddy"—who touched her in bed, smelled bad, and was terrifying—was in another. For her they were two different daddies. Because of this child's dependence on her father for her survival, realizing that daytime daddy and nighttime daddy were both the same man could overwhelm her with anxiety. Her dissociation allowed her to function.

For many of these clients, memories, emotions, body sensations, and other lived information is fragmented, like shards of a shattered mirror. These clients have a difficult time with emotional regulation. *Dysregulation* is the inability to manage an emotional balance and maintain connection to others. When a parent is abusive or frightening, it creates a state of disorganization and disrupts the safety of attachment to that person for the child. The child empathically becomes dysregulated as he or she both attunes to the parent's state and continues to experience his or her own fear. These feelings are difficult to resolve, which creates a state of inner chaos.

These clients require stabilization before doing EMDR trauma processing work. They need the development of a stable, secure therapeutic relationship and may take longer than clients with the other attachment styles before they are ready to do EMDR trauma processing. Trust may be more difficult to establish and may be challenged by the client repeatedly throughout the therapy. Resource Tapping is very important with these clients because it adds in new neural pathways and gives them tools for coping between sessions.

EMDR is done on the traumas using distancing techniques and resources, as needed, to create a sense of safety for the client prior to beginning processing. These clients may dissociate during EMDR processing of childhood traumas. Work with these clients requires a high level of skill on the part of the therapist because they tend to have intense abreactions, especially when processing childhood sexual abuse. Therapists need to help to regulate clients by staying grounded, spacious, and compassionately attuned to them, but also aligned with their wholeness and their capacity to heal the trauma.

CHAPTER 2

The Five Basic Principles of Attachment-Focused EMDR

As I explained earlier, Daniel Siegel, a renowned expert in the neuro-biology of attachment, is responsible for calling my work "attachment-focused EMDR." He attended my EMDR Advanced Clinical Workshop and Refresher Course at Esalen Institute and witnessed a live demonstration I did with a workshop participant who had early relational trauma. Upon hearing my work described in this way, I began to wonder, what makes this application attachment-focused? What am I doing that is different from what other EMDR therapists are doing (especially since most of my close colleagues who are EMDR consultants work in much the same way I do)? In fact, I have been teaching from an attachment-focused orientation since I began providing EMDR training in 1995, but I just didn't think of it in that way. Frankly, I just thought I was following what I always believed were the fundamental tenets of EMDR: Work in a client-centered way, trust the inherent wisdom within the client, and follow the process with minimal intervention.

A division has developed within the EMDR community between those who adapt the protocols for the benefit of their clients, and those who are rigid adherents. For the adherents, protocol trumps the individual needs of the client (Marich, 2011). Research forms the basis for clinical decisions, rather than what is best for the individual. Yet, this view is not in keeping with the guidelines set out by the American Psychological Task Force (2006), which state: "Evidence-based practice in psychology (EBPP) is the integration of the best available research with clinical expertise in the context of patient characteristics, culture, and preferences" (p. 273). Furthermore, they state:

> There are many problem constellations, patient populations, and clinical situations for which treatment evidence is sparse. In such instances, evidence-based practice consists of using clinical expertise in interpreting and applying the best available evidence while carefully monitoring patient progress and modifying treatment as appropriate. . . . Research suggests that sensitivity and flexibility in the administration of therapeutic interventions produces better outcomes than rigid application of manuals or principles. (p. 278)

According to these guidelines, *modifying the EMDR protocol to adapt what we do with our clients according to their needs would constitute evidenced-based practice.*

Many EMDR therapists have published research that includes adaptions of the EMDR standard protocol. For example, Russell (2008) reported modifying elements of the standard protocol with war veterans. Wesselmann and Potter (2009), in their research on clients with attachment trauma, did not use the Validity of Cognition Scale in their study. Ahmad, Abdulbaghi, Sundelin-Wahlsten, and Viveka (2008) used child-adjusted modifications in the original adult-based protocol, when EMDR was used in a randomized controlled trial (RCT) on thirty-three 6- to 16-year-old children with post-traumatic stress disorder (PTSD). In addition, three groups of researchers (Zaghrout-Hodali, Ferdoos, & Dodgson, 2008; Jarero, Artigas, López Cano, Mauer, & Alcalá, 1999; Jarero, Artigas, & Hartung, 2006) have written about their EMDR group protocol for children that represents a significant modification of the standard EMDR protocol.

Furthermore, most of the research on EMDR has been done with simpler cases of PTSD, not the kinds of cases involving complex relational trauma that I present in this book. As Debbie Korn (2009) noted in her review of using EMDR with complex PTSD, "While EMDR and other trauma treatments have been proven efficacious in the treatment of simpler cases of PTSD, the effectiveness of treatments for more complex cases has been less widely studied" (p. 264). According to Marich (2011):

> The studies that protocol advocates generally cite to support the efficacy of established EMDR approaches do not often apply to the complex clients. . . . In the randomized controlled studies that

support EMDR, participants/clients with complex issues (e.g., substance abuse, psychosis) were typically excluded due to concerns with confounding variables. Confounding variables exist in real-world clinical settings, and that is a reality to which we must be attuned when working with the complex client. . . . [Presently, the standard protocol] only applies to single-incident PTSD, if we are using a strict interpretation of the research. (pp. 42–43)

Clients who have attachment trauma, as well as those from a range of different educational and cultural backgrounds, need modifications so as not to shame, humiliate, or disrupt the therapeutic alliance. I first wrote about the need to make modifications in my second book, *EMDR in the Treatment of Adults Abused as Children* (Parnell, 1999), which was endorsed by Francine Shapiro. At that time she said that it was important for clinicians to think about what they were doing and to modify "intelligently." She never intended to apply a "cookie cutter" protocol to each and every client.

I have identified five basic principles that define AF-EMDR and help guide the work we do with clients who have relational trauma. Though many EMDR therapists already work this way, I believe it is helpful to provide a framework and rationale for modifying the way in which we use EMDR that informs our thinking and interventions. The five basic principles of AF-EMDR are:

1. Foster client safety.
2. Develop and nurture the therapeutic relationship to facilitate healing.
3. Use a client-centered approach.
4. Create reparative neuro networks through the use of Resource Tapping.
5. Use modified EMDR whenever client needs indicate.

CLIENT SAFETY

It is essential for the success of any psychotherapy, but especially when doing attachment-repair work, that the client feels safe. Most of our clients with attachment wounds did not feel safe growing up. Whereas some who were abused or neglected as children did not feel physically safe, many others did not feel emotionally safe. When we create a safe environment in which our clients can be themselves, they can more freely explore the places that have heretofore been forbidden or too frightening.

Safety is created in many ways, both explicitly and implicitly by the therapist. *Explicitly* we assess clients for appropriateness of EMDR utilization, making sure that they are not so emotionally fragile that they cannot handle the intensity of EMDR trauma processing work. We install or tap in resources to assess their ability to connect to these resources and establish a resource safety net (more about this in Chapter 3). All of these safety issues are covered in more detail in *A Therapist's Guide to EMDR* (Parnell, 2007) as well as in Shapiro's texts (1995, 2001). We also establish a metaphor for creating distance so that if the processing becomes too intense, we can utilize the imagery from the metaphor to remind clients that they are safe in the present. It is important that clients feel safe in the present as they process the past.

I tell my clients, "You don't have to reexperience what happened to you." In this way we can use distancing techniques such as projecting the distressing memory onto a screen like a movie or placing a glass wall between the client and the incident. I might hold my client's hand or encourage him or her to bring in a safe object, a favorite dog, or even a family member.

Implicitly we help our clients feel safe in many ways too. We address any fears or concerns they have before beginning EMDR trauma processing work. If they communicate, verbally or nonverbally, that they don't feel safe, I will ask them, "What do you need to feel safe?" Together we work to come up with a solution to the problem.

We implicitly create safety when we attune to our clients nonverbally by exhibiting a nonjudgmental, empathic attitude and reassuring them when necessary. Whatever is coming up for them is fine; we don't need to control or judge them. This attitude is especially important when working with issues of shame.

We help our clients feel safe when we are comfortable with strong affect and the thoughts and feelings that clients are expressing. We help to regulate our clients' strong emotions by remaining grounded, present, and confident that they can move through them. Schore (2009) and Hughes (2007) also describe the importance of the therapist as a regulator of the client's experience: The therapist helps to create a safe context for the reexperiencing of the trauma in a way that the feelings are less intense and so can be more easily integrated. We help our clients to contain the pain. We hold it with them, thereby increasing their sense of safety and their capacity to process their experience in a new way.

I also believe that when we ally ourselves with the part of the client that is already whole—the part that has never been touched by the trauma, the part that is the silent witness—we provide him or her with the strength to move through even the worst pain. But if we are fearful of strong affect and not confident in our client's capacity to heal, that too is communicated and can make him or her feel unsafe.

When we are attuned to our clients, they don't feel alone like they did when they were originally hurt. One client told me that part of what was so healing for her about our EMDR work was that she had been alone when she was abused, and no one ever believed her when she reported it. During our EMDR work, I was a compassionate witness to her story, giving it validity and creating a feeling of safety she'd never experienced before. I understood that my presence with her during her processing provided an implicit relational resource that changed her neuro networks. Clients attune to and "borrow" our courage and confidence, which helps lessen their fear and shame so that they can work through painful experiences in a new way. When we are attuned to our clients while they reprocess painful memories, they integrate into their neuro networks the experience of feeling safe.

THE IMPORTANCE OF THE
THERAPEUTIC RELATIONSHIP

The development of a safe, secure therapeutic relationship in which there is trust and rapport between client and therapist is important in all therapies, but especially so when working with clients who have relational trauma. The underlying assumption of many attachment-focused therapies is that the therapeutic relationship provides an opportunity to rework attachment difficulties, or, per Bowlby's theory (1969), to revise *internal working models*. I think of the therapeutic relationship as a foundation upon which the therapy builds. If the foundation is shaky and insecure, the therapy will not progress. For some clients this relationship is built more quickly than with others. With clients who have had extensive physical and sexual abuse and early childhood neglect, it may take longer for trust to develop and a secure relationship to form. Sometimes the therapeutic relationship develops, but then is disrupted for some reason. The repair of any breaks is essential and an important part of the healing. Navigating through the hurts, misunderstandings, and therapist errors in a healthy way creates new neural pathways in the client that allow him or her to begin to develop healthier relationships with others.

I believe it is important to explore and repair the breaks before resuming EMDR trauma work. Without a firm foundation, the client does not feel safe enough to descend into the pain and allow uncensored free associative processing. *Trusting the therapist* and *trusting the process* are the keys to successful EMDR treatment.

With this principle in mind, if what we are doing in our EMDR therapy threatens to create a break in the therapeutic relationship, then we must make adjustments to the protocols and procedures to maintain the integrity of the alliance.

WHAT DOES RESEARCH TELL US?

Research shows that the therapeutic relationship is crucial in determining the effectiveness of therapy (Lambert & Barley, 2001; Orlinski, Grave, & Parks, 1994). According to the American Psychological Association Presidential Task Force on Evidence-Based Practice (2006): "Psychotherapy is, at root, an interpersonal relationship between psychologist and patient" (p. 277). Furthermore, "Central to clinical expertise is interpersonal skill, which is manifested in forming a therapeutic relationship, encoding and decoding verbal and nonverbal responses, creating realistic but positive expectations, and responding empathically to the patient's explicit and implicit experiences and concerns" (p. 277).

The Corrective Emotional Experience

I believe that crucial to the healing of relational trauma is the corrective emotional experience the client has with a compassionately attuned therapist. According to Alexander and French (1946):

> In all forms of etiological psychotherapy, the basic therapeutic principle is the same: To re-expose the patient, under more favorable circumstances, to emotional situations which he could not handle in the past. The patient, in order to be helped, must undergo a corrective emotional experience suitable to repair the traumatic influence of previous experiences. (p. 46)

Freud believed that in order to resolve trauma, the patient needed to access the memory, express it emotionally, and work through its effects in his or her life. Franz Alexander (Alexander, 1961; Alexander & French, 1946) made an important contribution to psychoanalytic theory, emphasizing the significance of the therapeutic relationship in the healing of the trauma. Alexander believed that once the childhood memories were uncovered, in the context of a safe therapeutic relationship, patients could reexperience the event differently than they had originally. Because they experience the trauma in the context of a therapeutic relationship, which differs significantly from the experience they had with their parents as children, they are able to experience the events in a less traumatic way and express feelings they were unable to express without being punished or censored. Clients are able to experience themselves as adults rather than as helpless children. Alexander called this type of emotional experience in treatment a *corrective emotional experience*: "Merely remembering an intimidating or demoralizing event does not change the effect of such an experience. Only a corrective emotional experience can undo the effect of the old" (Alexander, 1946, p. 22).

When using EMDR with clients who have relational trauma, it is essential that we develop a therapeutic relationship that fosters a corrective emotional experience for them. When we create a safe, bonded, attuned relationship in which we hold the shame, hurt, trauma, and repressed or dissociated feelings and impulses without censoring our clients, we facilitate a corrective emotional experience for them. I believe that we are thereby adding in neural pathways that include our compassionate, nonjudgmental presence. As they reprocess old traumas, they feel us with them, and that sense of support or scaffolding is added into the mix of their experience. The corrective emotional experience adds new relational information, new neuro networks, that change the inner experience of our clients. According to Schore (2011), "The corrective emotional experience of psychotherapeutic change process is not just cathartic discharge but right brain interactive regulation of affect" (p. 140). When we align with our clients, emotionally attune with them, they no longer feel all alone. This right-brain to right-brain connection—this interpersonal neurobiological connection—changes our clients' brains (Amini et al., 1996).

CLIENT-CENTERED ATTACHMENT-FOCUSED EMDR

Client-centered therapy is an orientation to the work that makes the needs of the individual client central to any intervention that is used in the treatment.

Clinical experience led Shapiro (1995) to the foundational EMDR theory that within each person is a natural ability to heal that is disrupted after a traumatic experience, but which BLS helps to reactivate and move toward an adaptive resolution. This is the *adaptive information processing* (AIP) model. This theory helps guide our EMDR work, teaching us to trust the wisdom inherent in our clients and their ability to heal. Processing naturally moves in a positive direction. Hate, anger, fear, and grief all clear away as the client moves toward wholeness. Therapists learn to stay out of the client's way and to trust the process.

With AF-EMDR, the client is the focus of the work. We adapt what we do in relation to the needs of the individual. We follow our clients' process and intervene as little as possible. We trust that the wisdom lies within our clients and ask questions to help them make the links rather than making our own interpretations. As therapists we facilitate our clients' process. We are guides, but we do not tell them where they need to go. We help them get out of stuck places by helping them link networks that are not linking up and untangle tangled networks, and we add in creative solutions or resources that come from their imaginations. We ask our clients what they need, and we strive to accommodate those needs, including what they need to feel safe: the type of BLS that feels most comfortable to them, the length of sets of BLS, where the therapist sits, what they feel comfortable targeting, how often EMDR processing is used, and so on. The relationship is collaborative and respectful of each client's individual needs. For example, no one is forced to do eye movements if they are not comfortable doing so or if they prefer another type of BLS, and they are not forced to comply with a protocol that doesn't feel right for them or isn't helpful. Clients' needs are central throughout all phases of the work.

THE DEVELOPMENT OF REPARATIVE NEURO NETWORKS THROUGH THE USE OF RESOURCE TAPPING

In the early days of EMDR we discovered that bilateral stimulation could also be used in a focused way to activate and strengthen resources (Leeds & Shapiro, 2000; Parnell, 1997, 1998, 1999, 2007, 2008; Shapiro, 1995, 2001). This has been called *resource installation*. However, I prefer to use the term *Resource Tapping* instead. I have long had difficulty with the word *install* or *installation* because it sounds very mechanical, as if we are installing software or a car battery. I am concerned that by using terms in our work that are mechanical, we are dehumanizing our clients. In addition, the term *install* does not accurately describe what we are doing. We are not taking something from outside our clients and putting it into them. In fact, what we are doing is *activating* their own imaginations—*stimulating* their own neural pathways—and then adding BLS to integrate the information more fully into their mind–body circuitry. *We are not putting something into our clients.* I prefer the phrase *tapping in* resources, which I developed for my book *Tapping In: A Step-by Step Guide to Activating Your Healing Resources Through Bilateral Stimulation* (Parnell, 2008).

We "tap in resources" when we activate a positive resource via imagination, and then add BLS. It is a play on the words *tap in.* Clients tap into their own healing resources by using their imaginations, and then they literally "tap them in" using BLS. I find that I often use the words *tap in*, whether I'm using my hands to tap a client's knees or hands, or if I'm using auditory or tactile stimulation, or even eye movements. To say to a client "Let's tap that in" sounds much better than "Let's install that," which can sound like mind control—or machine repair!

In the early days of EMDR, the safe place was the principle resource that was tapped in to clients. Guiding clients to imagine a place where they feel safe and comfortable had been used for many years by psychotherapists to help reduce anxiety. We found that by directing clients to focus on a safe place and then adding short sets of BLS worked even better than the imagery alone to calm them down and provide them with a sense of control over their distress. In order to help highly traumatized clients feel safer, EMDR therapists began to tap in a safe place prior to beginning EMDR sessions. Later we found that we could tap in many different kinds of resources—nurturing figures, protector figures, and inner wisdom figures to help strengthen and stabilize clients who had been severely traumatized in childhood. Resource Tapping is an important tool in helping to prepare clients for the difficult work of EMDR trauma processing.

Over the years Resource Tapping has expanded and developed considerably. Many positive resources can be tapped in, including inherent qualities and positive memories, experiences, images, or people to whom we can connect to that comfort, lift spirits, or empower. I have found that Resource Tapping can be used as a stand-alone therapy. *Some clients never need to do EMDR to target their traumas* and reduce or even clear their symptoms. They derive sufficient benefit from Resource Tapping and do not require the more intense, potentially destabilizing EMDR. New applications for tapping in resources are being discovered every day (Parnell, 2008).

Tapping in resources is related to EMDR but is an essentially different model. With EMDR we focus on the trauma memory, add BLS, and follow a protocol that allows for the unfolding of a free-associative processing. In contrast, when we tap in resources, we focus on the positive resource and only allow a short amount of BLS. We keep the work focused exclusively on the positive, healing resources. Unless the client is following a completely positive network of associations (which can sometimes happen when we do developmental repair work with imagination and BLS), we do not allow a free flow of processing that can unleash trauma networks.

Resource Tapping (or installation) can be used to prepare clients for EMDR as well as throughout the course of treatment. Some clients have experienced such severe neglect that they cannot find EMDR targets because they have no access to a trauma memory to target. They report only an *absence* as the trauma. For example: "There was no one to take care of me. That is just the way it was." The report of this absence is often given with no charge, no negative affect. In these cases and others where there has been severe neglect or very damaging early attachment relationships, it is most therapeutic to build in new neural pathways through the use of imagery, body sensing (i.e., detecting and identifying bodily sensations), the current rapport in the therapist–client relationship, and BLS—in other words, Resource Tapping. In many cases Resource Tapping is the treatment of choice. I believe this shift in orientation can be helpful to EMDR therapists and clients alike who have felt like failures because they had not done the EMDR work. *The Resource Tapping is the work*.

Tapping into the Imagination

In my book *Tapping In* (Parnell, 2008) I describe how we can combine imagination with BLS. The imagination is a very powerful resource. Techniques that evoke imagination and visualization are used to heal physical and psychological problems in many forms of therapy. Brain research has shown that when we imagine doing something, the neurons in the brain are activated as if we are actually doing it. For example, if you imagine moving your right arm, the region of your brain that is activated when you actually move your arm registers the same when it is only imagined. *Clinical experience has shown that tapping strengthens this process even more*.

When you ask your clients to imagine a resource that you want to help them cultivate, they can bring to mind a memory of when they experienced it, an image that evokes it, or someone or something that represents it for them. Activating the imagination in this way, in its greatest capacity, brings in as many of the senses as possible and can be very powerful. The more detail that can be "fleshed out," the better, the more alive the image is for them.

If you wish to help your clients feel less anxious, for example, you might ask them to think of a time when they felt calm and peaceful. Perhaps a client remembers a time she was at a cottage by a lake. She can imagine sitting on the porch, looking out at the light sparkling on the water, birdsong punctuating the stillness. As she imagines this scene, she feels at peace. When she can feel the peaceful feelings strongly, she has activated the resource you wish to tap. She has used her imagination to locate the stored positive information. Once her resource has been activated, when she has a strong feeling for it, you add the BLS. Clients can tap on their own knees (right–left, right–left, or vice versa, it doesn't seem to matter), or you can use any other kind of BLS, including eye movements or auditory stimulation. It is recommended (Parnell, 2008; Shapiro 1995, 2001) that you use short sets of BLS—6 to 12 times, right–left, right–left. The BLS helps the client to *feel* the resource more fully. Using the imagination brings it up, but the BLS does something more; the resource experience seems to become more *embodied*.

Tapping in resources seems to facilitate their assimilation into the person's whole experience, making these resources more accessible. Tapping in seems to *integrate memory networks*. When we use the BLS, we help the brain process and integrate information that is stored in different compartments. I use the analogy of a large house with many rooms. Only a few rooms are used on a daily basis, many of the best rooms are rarely used, and some are entirely forgotten. When we bring our focus to resources we wish to cultivate and then add BLS, the doors to the forgotten rooms open and are made accessible to the rest of the house. Instead of just using a few rooms, more of the house is available (Parnell, 2008). You can also think of the mind–body circuitry as a system of interconnected neuronal webs. The circuits have been firing in a particular pattern over and over again. Hebb's law states that neurons that fire together, wire together—which is the mechanism that causes our clients (and ourselves, at times) to become stuck in unhealthy patterns. Information that is positive, resourceful, and healthy is also stored, but is in the dark, not lit up, and not integrated into the overall circuitry. The Resource Tapping *lights up* the healthy circuits, and the BLS enables this information to link in with the other circuits.

Many of our clients who have been traumatized in childhood have experienced *synaptic pruning* in the orbital frontal cortex (Schore, 2003), which creates a disturbance in the sympathetic–parasympathetic system. Their nervous systems become more reactive, they have a difficult time with self-soothing, and they are more prone to PTSD and depression. They even feel more physical pain. These clients need tools to help them feel safe and enable them to calm their nervous systems. I believe that the tapping in of healthy resources—by pairing imagination and BLS—creates new neural pathways that repair damage from childhood trauma and neglect.

Moreover, traumatized people do not attend to neutral stimuli; their brains are geared to detect and protect against traumatic stimuli (McFarlane, 1992). According to van der Kolk (2001): "We see that in our neurophysiology studies, traumatized people have very low P300 on the EEG to neutral stimuli. So they can't concentrate on, take in, and process information, but they actually get hyperaroused to the old trauma. So the problem with trauma is that no new information can come in and they start looping through the old misery."

With this information in mind when working with our traumatized clients, I believe it is important that we add in new information, or light up positively stored experiences and resources that have not been integrated, and add BLS. These clients tend to be hypervigilant, taking in, over and over again, a negative view that the world isn't safe and that they aren't safe in it. They notice what is wrong, potentially dangerous, but they don't take in the beauty of the spring day, or the kindness they just received from a stranger. *For some of our clients the work is to develop and build positive neuro networks.* This can be done by purposely searching for positive memories or experiences in clients' lives: a time when they felt seen and understood by someone, a time when they experienced beauty or awe, a memory of loving or being loved. Even looking for experiences in daily life that don't have any conflict in them and tapping those in can help build a new view of themselves and their world. If the client's schema or belief is that he is unlovable, focusing and tapping in experiences of when he loved someone or something can change how he feels about himself.

Cultivating Resources to Tap In

I have found that clients can be directed to cultivate positive resources and, with the help of BLS, thereby develop a firmer foundation that relieves their anxiety and hypervigilance (Parnell, 1999). You can give your client homework assignments to look for positive experiences and then tap them in. For example, you can ask them to look for beauty.

What is beautiful to them? It might be a place in nature such as a mountain, a garden, art, snow falling, a child's smile. When they find, let's say, five things, they bring them to their imagination, notice how they feel, and then tap right–left, right–left on their knees or sides of their legs or do the butterfly hug (described below). In this way they can begin to intentionally incorporate positive experiences. You can also do this exercise using gratitude as the focus. Clients are asked to write down five things for which they feel grateful, then tap them in before going to bed at night and again when they wake up in the morning. In this way you can facilitate the rewiring of the nervous system.

Instructions for Resource Tapping

Tapping in resources is relatively easy to do. As we've discussed, it begins with the imagination. You might want to begin by having your client tap in one or more of the most commonly used resources: safe/peaceful place, nurturing figures, protector figures, and inner wisdom figures (I discuss these resources more fully in Chapter 4). By tapping in the most commonly used resources, a resource toolkit is created that will be available to use when you or your client needs to access it. It is like having your basic household tools in a handy place where you can find them and use them to repair things that are not working in your home. These resources will be your basic tools that can help you and your clients with most situations that require resources.

When tapping in a resource, it is important to encourage your clients to use their imaginations to enhance their sensory experience of the resource as much as possible. They have to *feel* the resource in their bodies. Just thinking about it, at a purely mental level, is not enough.

For example, one way to elicit the resource of love is to ask clients to think of someone for whom they care. To begin, they can bring an *image* of the person to mind or just think of the person. If they have difficulty visualizing, ask them to just *imagine* the person through whatever images or sensations arise. We create mental images all the time without realizing it. They don't have to "see" an image of the person to access the power of the resource. What is most important is that they have the *feeling* of the resource they are evoking.

For example, if you want to tap in a beloved grandmother, ask your client, "When you think of her, what image comes to mind?" Sometimes it is easier to find the resource by locating a specific memory: "Do you have a memory of her that could help in this particular instance?" Perhaps your client responds that he imagines her in the kitchen with her apron on baking a cake, her hands covered in flour, a welcoming smile on her face. As he imagines this scene, what does he feel? "Now as you imagine your grandmother, let yourself feel her love for you. Feel your heart becoming soft and warm." When your client can feel the quality you are trying to elicit, the resource is activated. This is when you begin the BLS.

Tapping in resources can include many forms of BLS. You can (1) use the Tac/AudioScan (comes with small roundish objects or *pulsers* that vibrate, and which clients can hold in their hands, put in their pockets, or place under their legs, as well as headphones through which clients hear bilateral tones or other sounds); (2) tap on your client's legs or knees (like drumming); (3) instruct him or her to do the tapping; or (4) use eye movements or other forms of BLS. Clients can even tap their feet on the floor or march in place. It is important to tap one side and then the other. In this way both sides of the brain are stimulated. They can also do the *butterfly hug*. For this hug, instruct clients to cross their arms across their chest and tap either shoulder. The butterfly hug is helpful to use when clients want to feel comforted.

Following is a summary of Resource Tapping instructions:

1. Ask clients to close their eyes, go inside, and bring their attention to a quiet, still place within. You might begin by asking them to take full, deep breaths, slowly exhaling.
2. Ask clients to bring to mind the resource you have chosen to work with: a positive memory, an inherent quality, an experience, or an important person or animal.
3. Ask clients to imagine the resource as well as they can. Open their senses: "Notice what you are seeing. Notice what you are hearing. Notice what you are smelling. What sensations do you feel on your skin? What do you taste? What do you feel?" Suggest that they take the time they need to elicit this information and fill out/enliven the resource.
4. When they have a strong sense of the resource—when they can feel its quality—begin the BLS. Do 6 to 12 right–left, right–left sets, then stop and check in with them. If they report positive feelings and the resource is strengthening, you can do more BLS.
5. You can continue the BLS as long as it feels positive. If other memories or resources come to mind that feel good to clients, you can tap them in also.

You might want to begin the BLS at a slow, rhythmic pace and then find the pace that feels best to your client. Some people prefer longer rounds of BLS. This is fine as long as the resource remains positive. If the positive feelings increase, and they are linking to more resources, you can keep the BLS going. Some clients drop into very positive associations of reparative resources. For example, they may recall a series of memories of being loved and cared for by their grandmother, followed by memories of love from other people they hadn't thought of in years. They may also begin to fill in their resource with more sensory details. This elaboration helps to more fully develop the resource and make it more available to them. If this is happening, I let the BLS continue as long as it remains positive.

However, it is common for highly traumatized clients, after short amounts of BLS, to begin free-associative processing that links to memories that are upsetting. Sometimes a resource will flip to the negative or become contaminated in some way (e.g., they remember that their loved one is deceased and become sad, or a dangerous person threatens their peaceful place). For this reason it is best to do short sets of BLS and monitor how your client is doing. If you have found that the resource is no longer entirely positive, you should stop it immediately and try one of the following approaches:

1. After you have stopped tapping, see if they can think of another, different resource that is fully positive. It is important that the resource feel completely positive. If clients can find another one, tap it in, this time using BLS for a shorter duration.

2. If a distressing memory has arisen, clients can imagine placing it in a container that can hold it for them. This container can be made of anything they can imagine that can safely hold the material that has come up. They might imagine a safe, a treasure chest with a good lock, or a vault. It is important that the container have a strong lid. This imagery can help them consciously compartmentalize information that is too much to integrate. It is a skillful way to handle material that does not feel manageable. If they want to address the memory at another time, they can take it "out of the container" to work on it.

3. When you feel that the memory is sufficiently contained, you can return to the resource you began with, or bring up another one that has only positive feelings and associations. This time, use BLS for a very short time.

4. You can ask clients to imagine returning to their safe/peaceful place.

When tapping in resources, you must be careful that you do not activate the reprocessing of traumatic memories. BLS can stimulate connection to all kinds of networks, lighting up old memories, including ones that are distressing. *For clients with a lot of trauma in their backgrounds, be very careful with the tapping of resources.*

THE USE OF MODIFIED EMDR

When working with clients who have relational trauma and attachment wounds, it is important that we modify our application of EMDR according to their needs. I have described these modifications in my other books (Parnell, 1999, 2007) and provide a more detailed rationale for the modifications in Chapter 11. I have been using a simplified version of the standard EMDR protocol in my clinical work for 20 years that works best with clients who have relational trauma. Although there is no research yet demonstrating the efficacy of the modifed protocol with PTSD, it is currently being researched.

As of this writing there are two ongoing research projects on the efficacy of the EMDR modified protocol (EMDR-M) for PTSD. One of them involves female soldiers who were sexually assaulted in the military, and are the focus of the Oscar-nominated film *Invisible War*. The Artemis Rising Foundation, which was founded by Regina Kulik Scully, sponsored the recovery program developed by Joanne Mednick and Karol Darsa; the emphasis of the program is on non-pharmaceutical healing modalities for trauma. Six of these women received intensive EMDR-M over a two-week period in a retreat setting. This research is being conducted by Mylea Charvat. Preliminary results of this study are very promising. Heath "Hank" J. Brightman, Linda Curran, and I are conducting other research on EMDR-M in our study "Exploring the Efficacy of Parnell's Modified Eye Movement Desensitization and Reprocessing Protocol for Participants Diagnosed with Posttraumatic Stress Disorder." We are currently in the data collection phase of the study.

With the modified protocol, the creation of safety is paramount, as is the connection between client and therapist. Clients must feel that the therapist is attending to *their needs* and not imposing a technique on them that is objectifying. After the focus of the work is established and safety is created through the use of Resource Tapping, the therapist helps clients activate the memory network where the trauma is stored as quickly and smoothly as possible. Instead of taking them into right-brain activation and out into left-brain assessment and thinking, as is done with the standard protocol, the therapist helps clients activate various elements of the trauma that are stored in the right-brain implicit memory network, then add BLS and begin to process. The positive cognition and Validity of Cognition Scale are eliminated in the assessment phase altogether, as they are an impediment to the activation of the memory network and the processing of the trauma. A positive cognition or alternatives (e.g., new insights or understandings) are installed at the end of the session. The body scan is done after the Subjective Units of Distress Scale (SUDS) in order to be certain that the body is clear of unprocessed information prior to the installation of the positive cognition.

In *A Therapist's Guide to EMDR* (Parnell, 2007) I outlined what I call the *essential EMDR protocol*: Create safety, stimulate the memory network, add BLS and process, end with safety. These are the steps I found common in EMDR therapists' work with children, which required modification of the standard steps and, I believe, are essential to all successful EMDR processing. When we smoothly and seamlessly activate the memory network and then begin to process, clients feel attuned to; we drop into the network with them. It is quick, often as little as 2 or 3 minutes. It eliminates discussion about which cognition fits the best, which takes the client out of the trauma network. With the modified protocol, clients get rapidly into the network and begin to move toward healing and out of the emotional pain in which they have been living. It is an efficient use of the therapy time. I am often able to do productive work and have completed sessions within a 50-minute time frame. Figure 2.1 summarizes this modied EMDR protocol.

FIGURE 2.1.
MODIFIED EMDR PROTOCOL (EMDR-M)

**Safe Place and Resources Installed or
Evoked for Support (Optional)**
Tap in safe or peaceful place, nurturing figures, protector figures,
inner wisdom figures, and/or inner support team.

Picture
"What picture represents the worst part of the memory?"

Emotions
"What emotions do you feel?"

Body Sensations
"What do you notice in your body?"

Negative Cognition
"What do you believe about yourself?" or "What negative belief do
you have about yourself?"

**SUDS (optional: Take if it is clinically useful to know;
skip if it takes the client out of the process)**
"How disturbing does that feel to you on a scale from 0 to 10, where 0 is
no disturbance or neutral and 10 is the most disturbance you can imagine?"

Desensitize
Add BLS and process until the SUDS is a 0 or 1.

Body Scan
"Scan your body and see if there is anything there that you notice." This can
be repeated again after the desensitization and before installation.

Installation
When the SUDS is 0 or 1, ask, "What do you believe about yourself now?"
Install the positive cognition, insight, or understanding.

Close and Debrief
Be sure to do thorough closure. Always leave enough time to debrief.

CHAPTER 3

Therapist Characteristics and Skills for Attachment Repair

There are certain therapist's capacities that are important to the development of a secure, healthy, therapeutic relationship. In this chapter we explore some of the most important ones that I have culled from the attachment literature as well as from my clinical experience.

ABILITY TO LISTEN

It is important that we learn to listen, and listen well, to our clients using more than our ears. Listening involves using our bodies as instruments. What does my body tell me about what is happening? Listening involves being present to all that is going on in ourselves (each of us should ask ourselves, "What is going on in my mind and body?") as well as in our clients. When we really listen to our clients, they feel seen and heard. This is an important part of the healing of relationship wounds. I believe it is also important to listen purely, dropping all of the theories, so that we can experience our clients freshly. Let go of the categories, even the types of attachment style, and listen to what this person tells you.

According to the experts in attachment-repair work (e.g., Schore, Siegel), the healing takes place in the right-brain to right-brain connection that ideally occurs between therapist and client. The intuitions the therapist picks up also come from the right brain and are not connected to a sense of linear time or reasoning. These are the flashes of insight we have, the interventions that come to us without thinking them through, the feeling that we need to ask a question or suggest a particular interweave. These intuitions bypass the left hemisphere and arise spontaneously. Pay attention to this information. As we become better at attunement, and listening, we want to listen to our intuitions and follow them. Some of the best therapeutic interventions come from a therapist's intuition. We can explain the reason for what we did afterward, but the intuition came in a flash, faster than we could think about it.

ABILITY TO BE PRESENT

When you are present, focused, and undistracted, your clients feel seen, listened to, and calmed. Because your mind states (e.g., sad, happy, depressed, anxious) affect your clients, when you are present and listening, your clients take this into their neuro networks and feel valued. Presence is communicated through gentle eye contact, a soothing voice, and a sense of peacefulness. When you are present, your clients do not feel so alone in their distress. Presence can be cultivated and developed through mindfulness practices such as mindfulness meditation and some yogic practices (e.g., Goldstein, 1976; Kabat-Zinn, 1990; Parnell, 1996, 1999). In addition, therapists should receive their own EMDR treatment to clear issues that interfere with their ability to be present.

CAPACITY FOR EMPATHIC RESONANCE
OR ATTUNEMENT

EMDR therapists who do attachment-focused work should have a strong capacity for empathy. Essential to the healing of attachment wounds is the nonverbal attunement between the therapist and client. According to Hughes (2005):

> *Nonverbal attunement* refers to the frequent interactions between a parent and infant, in which both are sharing affect and focused attention on each other in a way such that the child's enjoyable experiences are amplified and his/her stressful experiences are reduced and contained. . . . This is done through eye contact, facial expressions, gestures and movements, voice tone, time, and touch. (pp. 4, 9)

Also called *limbic resonance* or *empathic resonance*, *nonverbal attunement* is a complex and rapid exchange of information that takes place between two people about their own inner state as well as their adaptations to the other's state. Empathic resonance facilitates a deep, personal connection that is below the level of consciousness and is a meeting of minds: a right-brain to right-brain connection. It is like when you pluck the strings of a harp: You feel the vibration from the instrument resonating inside of you. In this way, we resonate with the experiences of our clients, and our own bodies are our instruments to feel what is happening in them.

When we resonate with our clients, and they resonate with us through facial expressions, tone of voice, and emotions, it draws us into congruence. An example of empathic resonance is the calming influence a secure mother has on her baby by gazing into her baby's eyes or by cradling her baby so that it can hear her heart beating. This is the mechanism that provides the "bonding" between mother and infant, and also that which creates a healing bond between therapist and client. When we have an empathic connection with our clients, we resonate with what they are feeling. We can feel what they are experiencing inside, nonverbally. We *feel* with them. I can often follow what my clients are feeling by listening to what I am sensing in my body. This deep empathic connection is very healing for clients. When they see my face responding to their feelings, they feel seen and cared for.

This limbic or empathic resonance has been linked to the mirror neuron system, which, according to Chartrand and Bargh (1999), seems to monitor the interdependence and intimacy that come out of social interactions. The concept of limbic resonance was first described by three professors of psychiatry at the University of California at San Francisco: Thomas Lewis, Fari Amini, and Richard Lannon, in the book *A General Theory of Love* (2000). They defined *limbic resonance* as the capacity for empathy and nonverbal connection that is present in both nonhuman and human mammals (i.e., people). Limbic resonance creates the basis of social connections and is foundational for therapy and healing.

Hammer (1990) describes the receptive state for sensitively resonating with the client's unconscious nonverbal communications:

My mental posture, like my physical posture, is not one of leaning forward to catch the clues, but of leaning back to let the mood, the atmosphere come to me—to hear the meaning between the lines, to listen for the music behind the words. As one gives oneself to being carried along by the affective cadence of the patient's session, one may sense its tone and subtleties. (pp. 99–100)

This sounds very much like the receptive awareness that is cultivated in mindfulness practices and that is important in all of our EMDR processing. In *A Therapist's Guide to EMDR* (Parnell, 2007), I described the therapeutic stance as one of spacious, grounded attunement:

> *The clients feel the therapist's caring, sensing that whatever arises in their experience is accepted unconditionally. The therapists are able to be present with the clients without becoming overwhelmed by the client's process. When the therapists are able to feel with the clients, without fear and interference, it provides the client with a feeling of safety and confidence in the process. (p. 225)*

ABILITY TO SENSE ONE'S OWN BODY EXPERIENCE

Freud (1913) stated: "Everyone possesses in his own unconscious an instrument with which he can interpret the utterances of the unconscious of other people" (p. 320). Essential to attunement is the ability to sense the signals coming from one's own body. Our bodies are our instruments for receiving information emanating from our clients. When we listen to the information we are *feeling*, it can guide us in our work. For instance, if my client is laughing as she is describing something, but I feel a pain in my heart, I am picking up some kind of information. I may not know if it is coming from her or if it is triggering something in me. I will often put it aside as information that I may use later. If she is processing during EMDR, I might ask her what she is experiencing in her body as a way to discern if it is coming from her. She might say, "I feel sadness in my heart." And then I tell her to "go with that, " processing the feelings and body sensation I had been feeling and of which she had not been conscious.

I am often directed by my internal cues as to when to stop the BLS during EMDR processing sessions. I feel a subtle release that indicates to me that the client has finished a wave. I also follow my body sense when I *feel* that the processing is stuck or looping. It can feel like a kind of congestion in my body. I listen to this and ask my client if he is stuck, even if he hasn't been looping very long.

During the processing of the desensitization phase, it often feels like a dance of attunement. As I track my client's experience, I often seem to know when to stop the BLS based on the release I feel in my own body, often without an obvious sign from my client. Clients love how this synchrony feels because it is intimate, attuned, and connected in a way many have never felt before. When working in this way, there is a loss of time; I am fully present in the moment. This is an indication of the right-brain to right-brain connection that has no sense of chronological time.

If we are cut off from our bodies, we are cut off from a large source of information. Information coming from our heads, left-brain information, is often limited by thoughts and theories that interfere with a more direct perception of what is going on. When we are attuned to our bodies, we are more aware of nonverbal communication that underlies the words we are hearing.

Many of our clients dissociated during the abuse they suffered as children. When we are attuned to our own bodies, we can feel when our clients dissociate and help them return to themselves, center, create safety, and learn to sense their bodies without the need to disconnect. I can often tell that my clients have dissociated because I feel spacey, lightheaded, or sleepy. Instead of criticizing myself for not being more alert, I try to pay attention to what might be happening with my client. The information I'm picking up can aid me in making a helpful intervention for my client, such as using a distancing technique or an interweave.

Just as many of our clients need tools and techniques for learning to sense their bodies, so do therapists. As I said earlier, our bodies are our instruments for perceiving nonverbal communication from our clients. There are many methods for developing body sensing, including different forms of mindfulness meditation, yoga techniques that emphasize body sensing, and body-based therapies such as Hakomi (Kurtz, 1990) and Somatic Experiencing (Levine, 1997), as well as EMDR. The better we get at inhabiting our own bodies, listening to what they tell us, and bringing an attitude of open curiosity to the exploration to these experiences, the better we will become at facilitating the healing of our client's relational trauma.

Case Example of a Client's Experience of Empathic Resonance and Its Lasting Effect

"Monica" was a woman in her 40s who sought EMDR therapy to help heal the physical and sexual abuse she had suffered as a child. She had been given up for adoption as an infant and had no secure attachment growing up in her abusive adoptive family. Her EMDR therapist asked her for a nurturing figure to install prior to EMDR processing of the early traumas. Monica immediately came up with a social worker she had met briefly for an evaluation in a treatment center when she was a teenager. She described her as kind, loving, and caring of her. "She really listened." When Monica told the social worker about her life at that point, the social worker gently patted her back and a tear ran down her cheek. She told her that she was a good person and that what was wrong with her came from what had been done to her, not who she was. Monica *felt* the social worker empathically resonating with her pain. She felt seen, met, understood, and valued for herself. This momentary experience made such an impression on Monica that she was able to recall it 20 years later with the feelings of connection she felt at the time. Like a child being soothed by her mother, Monica had taken this experience of empathic resonance into her nervous system and it had made a lasting impression. She was able to use this kind social worker as a nurturing figure in her EMDR work.

ABILITY TO ATTUNE AND RESPOND TO NONVERBAL COMMUNICATION

It is important for a therapist who is doing attachment-repair work to be able to listen and attune to nonverbal communication. What are you picking up under what your client is saying? You might be picking up information from the way in which she holds her hands, the tone of voice, the look in his eyes. This nonverbal communication helps to guide us in any interventions we might initiate. Nonverbal communication is implicit right-brain communication. According to Allan Schore (2005), much of the healing and repair that occur within the context of therapy involve the right-brain to right-brain attunement and connection between client and therapist. Schore and Schore (2008) note: "The sensitive clinician's oscillating attentiveness is focused on barely perceptible cues that signal a change in state, and on nonverbal behaviors and shifts in affects" (p. 17).

It is important for us as therapists to be adept at processing nonverbal communications that come from implicit right-brain primary processes. This capacity to attend and respond to these nonverbal communications is more important than explicit left-brain communications. In other words, it is more important for us to be able to tune into and respond to what our clients are communicating behind their words. The information that we pick up quickly, intuitively, that we *feel*, is most important in the repair of attachment wounds. Many times I know something without knowing how I know it. I have a sense, perhaps coming from something I pick up somatically, or it is like a flash of knowing, and then I respond to it. This implicit level of communication is referred to as *intersubjectivity* (Siegel, 2001, 2002). It is an empathic, participatory experience we have with our clients in which we resonate with them. It can be experienced as a sharing of minds. This intersubjective experience is much like a mother's implicit ability to read her baby's nonverbal communications and respond to them.

ABILITY TO BE INTIMATE, AUTHENTIC, AND REAL

It is also important that those of us who work to repair attachment deficits have the capacity for true intimacy, that we are able to be authentic and real. As we are working to clear the traumas and early painful experiences that impede the expression of our clients' true selves, we must also be able to go there with them. There are times when we must be able to hold a client's gaze as he or she drops into deep, terrifying places that are raw. As we hold the client with our eyes, we must be present, authentic, and intimate with him or her. If we block or defend against the intensity of the feelings, the client will pick this up and pull back, feeling unsafe. Our clients resonate with our authenticity, our humanity, and our courage to descend into the depths. When I hold my client's gaze, I'm communicating my compassionate presence to him or her. Nonverbally, I'm conveying that the client is safe and I am with him or her. I have often felt that EMDR is the most intimate work I have ever done. What are your blocks to intimacy? Do you want to pull back and defend against your clients' strong feelings? This work compels us to continue to work on ourselves so that we can be intimate, authentic, and even transparent facilitators of our clients' unfolding process.

Therapists who do AF-EMDR should be able to be comfortable with simple touch, such as holding a client's hand or placing a hand on a knee, if this is what clients wish and what feels safe to them. We need to have healed our attachment wounds to the extent that we can emotionally connect to our clients. This may require that we sit closer to them, if they need us to, and hold their hands so that they don't feel all alone as they did when they were traumatized as children. We have to be flexible, available, and open. Many therapists may not be comfortable with this level of authentic connection. Although it is intimate in the sense of the meeting of minds and hearts, it is also well "boundaried." We are not using our clients to fulfill our unmet developmental needs.

ABILITY TO LOVE AND FEEL COMPASSION WHILE MAINTAINING APPROPRIATE BOUNDARIES

I believe it is essential that we have the ability to feel love and compassion for the clients with whom we are working. When we can love and accept them as they are, when we can connect with them and feel compassion, we are providing a corrective emotional experience. One of my consultees, who was working with a young woman who had never been loved by her family and had experienced years of physical and sexual abuse, told me, almost apologetically, that she loved her client. Not only did she love her, but she fantasized about taking care of her and providing the love she had never received growing up. She added, "But of course I would never do that—I have good boundaries." I am convinced that the progress her client had made derived from the love she felt implicitly from her therapist. As this therapist conveyed to her client through her tone of voice, soft caring gaze, and gentle encouragement that she cared about her, she also communicated that the client was therefore worthy of love, and not bad as she had always believed.

Along with our caring and compassion, it is important to have appropriate boundaries. Many clients who were violated as children don't have good boundaries in their personal lives. Some of our clients were hurt by those who provided the most nurturing for them, such as the father who read them stories and tucked them in, but snuck in later to molest them. These violations can be the most destructive as our clients have linked nurturing and abuse in their nervous systems. By showing our caring in the context of healthy boundaries, we are creating a safe environment in which clients can process their traumas, as well as providing a new experience for them that can change how they relate to others.

ABILITY TO BE PLAYFUL, ACCEPTING, EMPATHIC, AND CURIOUS

Daniel Hughes's (2007) model for healing attachment trauma involves four components—playfulness, acceptance, empathy, and curiosity (or PACE, for short)—which are integrated into all aspects of the therapeutic work. I have also found these qualities to be essential for AF-EMDR. We are playful and accepting of our clients. We are curious about what things mean to them, and we explore the possibilities with them. In doing so, we create more distance from their identification with the painful feelings and negative self constructs. Experiencing the elements of PACE decreases the sense of shame with which many of our clients live. Our clients' beliefs, emotions, and behaviors come from somewhere, but neither they nor us may yet understand their genesis. What is often called *resistance* indicates a blocking belief or an early schema that may be active. I might ask: "What belief is up for you right now? What are you afraid of?" By exploring what is happening, instead of judging our clients to be resisting us or the therapy, we connect with them and with whatever is happening for them. Their reactions can be targets for EMDR, using the bridging technique to find the early roots.

When we are curious and accepting of our clients, we are also modeling these healthy behaviors for them. Rather than feeling shame and shutting down or acting out their own reactions and inner experiences, they become curious about them. As I explain in Chapter 11, even transference can be used as an entry into the bridging technique to find the origins of a client's reaction.

I have found that it is important to bring a light touch to our work with clients. In that regard it can be beneficial to spend time focusing on clients' favorite activities and the things that make them happy, using BLS to reinforce and integrate the information. Spending time recalling successes they have had, both in and out of therapy, can be useful.

We should convey optimism and hope to our clients in an honest and open way. We must not imprison our clients with a limited view of what is possible for them to heal. "Let's explore and see what is possible for you." I remain curious and open. I really don't know what is possible. When I read some of the literature on attachment theory, especially with regard to critical periods, it leaves me pessimistic about the prospects for healing to occur in many of my clients. Yet what I have *seen* in practice is altogether different. I have seen clients complete therapy and move on to have happy, full lives despite terrible histories of abuse and relational trauma. EMDR and Resource Tapping are changing clients who, before, were unable to realize the kinds of gains they are now experiencing. You will read some examples of these kinds of changes in Chapters 16, 17, and 18. When clients ask me about their prognosis, I tell them that I don't know, but will do my best. I convey optimism that some things can change, and that I don't know what the limits are. I believe in the plasticity of the brain and its ability to create new neural pathways. My suggestion is, "Let's work together and see what we can do."

Therapists who are happy and at peace with themselves convey their state to their clients. How does it feel to work with an unhappy, grim, depressed therapist versus a therapist who is happy and optimistic, at peace with him- or herself?

The ability to be playful, flexible, and creative is also important. I am especially playful with my clients when they are stuck and/or looping in their processing and need an interweave. Together we come up with a solution to the problem in a way that is often playful and creative. For instance, a woman was looping and stuck when recalling trauma from a cruel dentist. I stopped her and asked, "What do you need? What would help you?" She said, "I'd like to torture the dentist!" My face brightened and I smiled gleefully, and said, "What would you like to do to him?" Together we came up with a plan that was reminiscent of a Bugs Bunny cartoon—it was playful, funny, and violent at the same time. She imagined tying the dentist to the dental chair, injecting him with needles, drilling his teeth relentlessly, and then finally, blowing him up with TNT in his dental chair. She imagined doing all of these things and more with the BLS. She loved imagining this, and as we laughed together, it helped to connect us even more. This playful creativity joins the minds of therapist and client like two children engrossed in imaginative play during which there is a loss of time. This is another example of right-brain to right-brain connection so essential in attachment repair.

ABILITY TO BE COURAGEOUS AND COMFORTABLE WITH STRONG AFFECT, AND HAVE THE WISDOM OF INSECURITY

I have found that the best EMDR therapists are courageous. Courage doesn't mean that you aren't afraid; it means that you feel the fear, but continue forward. Especially when working with clients who have severe early trauma, the emotions that they process during EMDR can be quite intense. Calling on our trust in clients' inherent wisdom, and in their ability to heal, we go into the eye of the storm, and while connecting with them and assuring them that they are safe in the present as they process the past, we encourage them to keep going. EMDR with highly traumatized clients is not for the faint of heart. It requires courage, confidence and the ability to remain grounded, spacious, and compassionately attuned as the client processes the traumatic memories. Not only do *clients* have to be able to tolerate strong affect in order to do EMDR, but so do the *therapists.* If we are too afraid, if we cannot handle our client's strong emotions, we communicate to them that their feelings are too much for us. We shut them down, in response to which they may experience shame. They won't want to go there again. Our ability and comfort with strong affect creates a safe container within which clients can process all the disparate thoughts, feelings, and body sensations that arise for them, without censorship. At times an EMDR session feels like getting on a scary roller coaster ride with our clients that will terrify us, but we hold on tight, ride the ups and downs, our stomachs lurching, our hearts racing, knowing that we will end in safety. The more we do EMDR, the better we get at trusting the process, our own intuition, the wisdom of our clients, and our ability to move through strong abreactions with our EMDR tools.

Along with the courage it takes to work with strong emotions and terrible traumas, the best EMDR therapists have what Alan Watts (1951) called the *wisdom of insecurity.* When we develop inner confidence in our ability to be with what arises, moment to moment, in ourselves and in our clients in the intersubjective field, we let go of having to control this information. We are better able to bring an open, curious attitude to the process. A client's willingness to go blindly into unknown territory in therapy requires that the therapist be comfortable with the prospect of not knowing exactly what will happen next in the session. Often this is the case in my practice. I believe, however, that I can facilitate the continuation of the processing and guide the client through the blockages, relying on the inherent wisdom in the process that what needs to happen next therapeutically will occur. As Miller (1981) noted over three decades ago:

> *If we want to do more than provide patients with intellectual insight, or—as may be necessary in some psychotherapies—merely to strengthen their defense mechanisms, then we shall have to embark on a new voyage of discovery with each patient. What we discover will not be a distant land but one that does not yet exist and will only begin to do so in the course of its discovery and settlement. It is a fascinating experience to accompany a patient on this journey— so long as we do not try to enter this new land with concepts that are familiar to us, perhaps in order to avoid our own fear of what is unknown and not yet understood. The patient discovers his true self little by little through experiencing his own feelings and needs, because the analyst is able to accept and respect these even when he does not yet understand them. (pp. 76–77)*

THERAPISTS MUST BE ABLE TO MANAGE THEIR OWN COUNTERTRANSFERENCE RESPONSES

Therapists must be able to manage and explore their own countertransference responses, without acting them out, shutting down clients' emotional expression, or responding in a way that is more about what is triggered in the therapist than the client's psychological needs. What arises in the therapist is information. It might be about what is going on in the client or in the therapist's own unprocessed emotional reactions. Many of our clients with severe attachment trauma, especially those with a borderline diagnosis, can be very challenging, evoking a myriad of feelings in us. This is also important when there has been an attachment disruption in the therapy. It is essential that we handle our own psychological reaction so that we can engage in relational repair with our client. Because many of our more difficult clients tend to elicit strong countertransference reactions in us, it is very helpful to receive continuing consultation, or even our own EMDR therapy.

Therapists must also feel competent enough with their EMDR skills and understanding of what is required of them to do attachment-repair work. If therapists are insecure, when transference arises they may not feel comfortable enough to explore the meaning and reprocess the roots. I've consulted to therapists who avoid doing EMDR with clients who could benefit from it because they are afraid of the emotions the clients might express. The therapist and client can collude to avoid doing EMDR because both are affect averse. This is a disservice to clients who could be helped with EMDR. Often therapists keep their clients from healing wounds they themselves have yet to heal. They don't believe it is possible to go there, because they lack the confidence of their own healing.

It's important to be able to feel what our clients are feeling, and also to be able to differentiate what is theirs from what is ours. Are the feelings you are having coming from something that is arising in your client—for example, unexpressed anger—or is something being triggered in you that belongs to your unprocessed childhood traumas? Sometimes it isn't clear until later what you are experiencing. According to Miller (1981): "Feelings that belong to the countertransference are like a quick flash, a signal, and clearly related to the analysand's person. When they are intense, tormenting, and continuous, they have to do with oneself" (p. 78). The capacity to be open and curious and to explore information that we are picking up in session, rather than judging and dismissing it, is important to understanding our clients. Miller (1981) notes: "I always assume that the patient has no other way of telling me his story than the one he actually uses. Seen thus, all feelings arising in me, including irritation, belong to his coded language and are of great heuristic value. At times they may help to find the lost key to still invisible doors" (p. 77).

KNOWLEDGE OF HEALTHY CHILD DEVELOPMENT

In order to help with attachment repair, it is crucial that the therapist have a good working knowledge of child development. When we add in new neural pathways by guiding our clients through the developmental stages during sessions of Resource Tapping, it is important that we have the information to add in for them (more on this topic in Chapter 5). This knowledge is also essential to creating interweaves that are age-appropriate for the developmental phase in which the client is working. We must know what is required of a healthy mother to ensure attachment through each phase of development. We also model healthy attachment in the way in which we interact with our clients.

Part II

HEALING RESOURCES

CHAPTER 4

The Four Most Important Resources

In this chapter I introduce you to the four most important resources, those most commonly used and accessible:

- Safe or peaceful place
- Nurturing figures
- Protector figures
- Inner wisdom figures

I find it helpful to install/tap in the first three resources with all of my clients, regardless of their presenting problems, and use the fourth for my most traumatized clients. By doing so I get a picture of clients' inner capacity, resilience, areas of strengths, and areas that need strengthening. I am able to assess readiness to begin EMDR trauma processing work. I am often surprised at the resources clients come up with, even those with severe trauma and neglect in their histories. I can also be taken aback by a client who seems stronger than he or she is, and who struggles to find any kind of nurturer or protector. In these cases it may be that the client has always coped on his or her own, without help from others. By locating and tapping in these resources before you need to utilize them with the client, you are consciously developing and placing these most important and useful tools where you can find them. In some cases you may want to summon one of these resources as an interweave if your client is stuck and looping. I tap in the resources for very traumatized clients before beginning EMDR each time, as a way of creating a safety net that helps them feel more contained. They can even imagine their resource figures with them as they process the traumas. Tapping in these essential resources creates a foundation of safety and stabilization for the work. For some clients with severe trauma and neglect, much time can be taken developing and tapping in these resources.

I have found that installing imagined safe/peaceful places and nurturing and protector figures in the beginning of treatment helps to create a stronger container for the trauma processing work. I believe that because we have stimulated the memory networks where these resources reside, the client has easier access to them, and can even sense them in the background when he or she begins the trauma processing work. Some clients require only a few minutes identifying and installing these resources during one session. If a client is able to easily locate and install them, we may only need to do this one time. That way I know he or she has the ego strength and the resources readily available if an interweave is necessary. We may never refer to their resources again for many clients because the processing moves along without the use of interweaves. For other clients, because these resources have been installed, they come up in their processing and link up as interweaves the client does him- or herself. For example, a client might "pull in" his best friend to protect his child self.

THE SAFE/PEACEFUL PLACE RESOURCE

Part of the client preparation before beginning the reprocessing work is to help clients establish a place where they can go in their imagination to feel comfortable and relaxed . . . a place they can imagine that evokes a feeling of safety and peacefulness. In the early years of EMDR, and in my earlier writings, I described the use of a *safe place*. However, I have found that for clients who have had extensive childhood trauma and neglect, the word *safe* evokes just the opposite: the absence of safety. For most clients these days, I use the term *peaceful place* as an alternative to *safe place*. The point is to identify a place that when evoked imaginatively, creates a sense of relaxation and a decrease in sympathetic activity in the nervous system. If your client responds well to the term *safe*, use it; if not, find alternatives. Many EMDR therapists mistakenly believe that if their clients cannot find a safe place, they cannot use EMDR with them. I have done very successful EMDR with clients who could not find a safe place, but *could* imagine peaceful, relaxing, calm places, or conflict-free images.

We may begin sessions with the safe or peaceful place, use it as a place our clients can go to during difficult processing to take a break and regain a sense of control, or use it to close down incomplete sessions. For clients who need to develop more of a sense of self-constancy, each EMDR session can begin and end with the peaceful place. This repetition increases the sense that they are the same person in different situations and can hold onto the peaceful place at home between sessions. Clients can also practice going to their safe/peaceful place between sessions as a means of self-soothing, and can even use it before going to sleep at night. The safe/peaceful place can also be imagined as the gathering spot for the client's resource figures to add extra safety and support.

You and your client work together to develop the safe/peaceful place. You adapt the safe/peaceful place instructions for each client's unique needs. What is important to achieve? Do you want to create a place of peace and calm where your client can turn off the outside world and the triggers to emotional upset? The safe/peaceful place can be a real-world location or a completely imaginary place. Many people choose a place in nature, such as a beautiful beach or mountain lake. One client chose the arms of a large mother bear as her peaceful place. The therapeutic relationship and the therapist's office can also be used as the safe/peaceful place. In addition, art can be used to create or enhance the safe/peaceful place. Clients can draw the place and then tap it in with BLS.

Before beginning the safe/peaceful place experience, you can help your clients enter a state of general relaxation by using a variety of known relaxation exercises. Or, they may have their own way to relax. Some people can contact an image and feeling of a safe/peaceful place easily, requiring little preparation. This is very individual and the time necessary for relaxation depends on the emotional/bodily state of the client.

It is helpful to activate the senses associated with the safe/peaceful place imagery. You might ask your client, "What do you see? What do you smell? What do you hear? What do you feel?" Then I'll ask, "Do you have a good sense of it now?" Or I'll simply comment, "Let me know when you can really feel your peaceful place." When the client signals yes, I begin a short sequence of BLS, maybe 6 to 12, to install this. I might ask, "Is it getting stronger?" If it is, I might go a little longer with the BLS. I watch my client for signs of deepening relaxation or increased agitation. If the client's breathing increases, I will stop immediately and ask him or her what is happening. Though for many clients, the BLS works quite well to install the feeling and imagery more securely, for some clients, the BLS opens up processing of traumatic material. Clients who have had many *unsafe* experiences may begin to associate to those experiences if the word *safe* was used. If this happens, stop the BLS and explore with the client what he or she is experiencing. You may need to develop another safe place using imagery only or use the word *peaceful* or *comfortable* instead. I have worked with some clients who flipped to the negative so quickly, I could never use BLS to install the safe or peaceful place. With them, I use imagery only. As with everything in EMDR therapy, stay closely attuned to your clients and accommodate what you do according to their needs.

You may want to focus even more attention on making their safe/peaceful place feel secure for clients who have been traumatized or are anxious and stressed. If you feel the need for extra safety, you can ask your clients to imagine putting a protective barrier around their safe/peaceful place, made of anything they wish. They might imagine a protective shield around it, like from *Star Trek*, or imagine fierce protectors guarding it.

Shapiro (2001) recommends the use of a cue word with the installation of the safe place. For example, if the client's safe place is a beach, she can imagine the beach and say the word *beach* as she receives the BLS to install it. Then between sessions she can practice using the safe/peaceful place imagery and cue word during times of anxiety or distress. For instance, if she has to make a speech and is anxious about it, she can say the word *beach* to herself and imagine her safe place.

In the next box is a summary of what a therapist might say to a client during the process of creating and tapping in a safe/peaceful place resource.

The following material is a script for developing a peaceful place for clients who need more guidance (see Parnell, 2007). Begin this script after the client is in a relaxed state.

> *"With your eyes closed, imagine yourself now in a beautiful, peaceful place. . . . This might be somewhere you've visited before or somewhere you just make up in your imagination. . . . Just let the image of the place come to you. . . . It really doesn't matter what kind of place you imagine as long as it's beautiful, quiet, peaceful. and serene. . . . Let this be a special inner place for you . . . somewhere that you feel particularly at ease . . . a place where you feel safe and secure . . . at one with your surroundings. . . . Maybe you've had a place like this in your life . . . somewhere to go to be quiet and reflective . . . somewhere special and healing for you. . . . Or it could be a place you've seen in*

TAPPING IN THE PEACEFUL PLACE*

1. "Close your eyes and go inside. Do deep, slow breathing or use another method to calm yourself and come to the present moment."
2. "Now that you are relaxed, imagine a place where you feel peaceful and comfortable, a place where you can feel relaxed and at ease."
3. After finding the place, enhance it using the senses:

   "What do you see?"
   "What do you hear?"
   "What do you smell?"
   "What do you feel?"
4. "When you have a strong positive feeling, I'll begin the BLS."
5. "If you feel distress or experience the intrusion of negative imagery, signal me, and we will stop the BLS immediately."
6. You can use a cue word as you tap in the peaceful place. For example, if your client's peaceful place is a beach, he or she can imagine the beach with the associated feelings of relaxation, and say to him- or herself *beach* as you add the BLS. When you do this, the cue word becomes linked with the feelings of relaxation and comfort that the peaceful place evokes. During times of anxiety or distress, you can instruct your client to use the peaceful place imagery and the cue word. For instance, if you have to make a speech and are anxious, you can say the word *beach* and imagine your safe/peaceful place to elicit a feeling of calm.
7. "Remember that this is *your* peaceful place. You can contact it whenever you would like. All you have to do is close your eyes and imagine your special place. You can repeat your cue word to yourself as you imagine your peaceful place and tap to access and strengthen your connection to it."

*Reprinted with permission from Sounds True, Inc.

---

a movie . . . read about . . . or just dreamed of. . . . It could be a real place . . . a place you know . . . or an imaginary place . . . .

"Let yourself explore and experience whatever quiet, imaginary place you go to as if you were there now. . . . Notice what you see there . . . what sounds you hear . . . even the smells and aroma you sense there. . . . Notice especially what it feels like to be there, and immerse yourself in the beauty, the feelings of peacefulness . . . of being secure and at ease.

"As you explore this special inner place, find a spot that feels particularly good to be in . . . a spot where you feel especially calm . . . centered . . . safe and at ease. . . . Let yourself become comfortable in this spot. . . . Let this be your safe place. . . . Let this be your power spot . . . a place in which you draw from the deep sense of peacefulness and safety you feel here. . . . Now just let yourself experience what it is like to be in this place. . . . (Wait a few moments before beginning again, keeping your voice lower than usual because the client is in a deeper relaxed state.)

"Keeping your eyes closed . . . would you describe this place? (At this point begin BLS. Depending on the response, ask a few questions to help strengthen the imagery. The therapist can use short sets of BLS after the client responds to questions.)

"What season of the year is it? . . . What time of day is it? . . . What aromas do you smell? . . . What sounds do you hear? . . . How are you dressed? . . . How are you experiencing your safe place?

"As you relax and are aware of how it feels to be here . . . tell yourself you can return anytime you wish. . . . This is your special place . . . a place where safety, rest, and peace are always available at your own choosing. . . . If you like, you can choose a cue word that will help you to remember your safe place. (Therapist adds more BLS as client says cue word to him- or herself.) *In the future you can say this word to bring back the feelings of your special place.*

"When you are ready, slowly open your eyes and come back to the room."

Using Art to Enhance the Peaceful Place

Art can be used to create or enhance the peaceful place. Drawing the peaceful place can give it more substance for your clients. This is their special place and they can make it any way they wish. When they draw, the connection to it may strengthen, and they can add details to their picture to make it even more secure.

If they have difficulty finding their own safe/peaceful place, suggest that they draw a "safe island." Find a piece of paper large enough for them to stand in the middle of it. Butcher-block paper can be used. They can stand in the center of the paper and draw a large circle around themselves. This is their safe island, which they can create in any way they would like. They can put anything and anyone they want on the island.

They can make it as safe and peaceful as they want. If they like, they can put a protective barrier around the island and encircle it with guardians.

Some people find that their sense of comfort increases when they draw the safe/peaceful place. Afterward they can use their drawing as a reminder of their safe/peaceful place that they can tap whenever they feel the need.

TAPPING IN THE SAFE/PEACEFUL PLACE THROUGH DRAWING

1. Get a piece of blank paper and use markers, crayons, pastels, or whatever medium you wish to use.
2. Say to your client: "Close your eyes and go inside. Imagine a place where you feel safe and secure, a place that is serene and peaceful."
3. "When the image comes to you, begin to draw it. Don't censor yourself or judge your artistic skills. Just allow what comes to be expressed on the page. It is most important to create some kind of visual representation, even if it looks like a drawing a child would make. What do you need to make it as safe as you would like?"
4. "Now, when you have completed the drawing, take a look at it and take in the feelings it evokes. Add whatever else you would like to it, even guardians to make it more protected."
5. "Close your eyes and hold the image in your mind. I'm going to begin the BLS now. I'll continue as long as it strengthens your positive feelings."

The main purpose of the peaceful place is to help clients find a means of calming the nervous system, a self-control technique. There are many other ways to accomplish this same purpose.

A Sacred Place Variation

A variant on the safe/peaceful place resource is the sacred place (see Parnell, 2008). Instead of focusing on the sense of safety or peacefulness, the emphasis is on the feeling of sacredness in the space, a place where there is a feeling of spirituality. The sacred place can be a place clients have been to or a place they can imagine. In this place they feel peaceful, but also a sense of something larger than themselves. Examples of sacred places are the Chartre Cathedral, the Hopi mesas, a Navajo kiva, a meditation cave in the Himalayas, sitting in a meditation hall with a spiritual teacher, or a sacred landscape, such as the Grand Canyon.

Positive Memories or Conflict-Free Images as Variations

Clients can bring up memories of doing something that they find comforting or relaxing that bring them pleasure as an alternative to the safe/peaceful place image (see Parnell, 2007). The idea is to find images of doing things that will help clients relax their nervous systems. Many people who have experienced early traumatization develop nervous systems that are attuned only to potentially dangerous stimuli, thus totally missing, or not registering in their memories, ordinary, nontraumatic daily life experiences that would counter their perception of the world as an entirely dangerous place (McFarlane et al., 1993). For that reason, the development of positive images and mindfulness practices catalyzes new neural pathways in the brain and serves as an important ego-strengthening method.

Phillips (1997a, 1997b) suggests that clients install *positive, conflict-free images* derived from experiences in their everyday life when they felt present and whole. It can be a real experience from the person's daily life, such as gardening, stroking a cat, or walking in a park. The image is strengthened by asking for sensory details and then installing them via BLS. It is important to emphasize the somatic component of the imagery. You want clients to feel free of anxiety and fear. The conflict-free image helps to create a sense of wholeness and increased feeling in clients that their life is not *all* terrible. It helps with self-soothing and affect regulation. The following are examples of images clients have used: the memory of baking bread, hiking in the mountains, sitting at a sushi bar, riding a horse, having a meal with a friend, playing with a kitten or puppy, watching baby ducks on a lake, walking among spring flowers, playing a musical instrument, cuddling with their children or grandchildren, or playing a musical instrument. Installing positive memories and images can be helpful for clients who are chronically depressed or have histories of serious abuse or neglect. As I mentioned earlier, many of these clients do not attend to positive or neutral stimuli. They have developed a kind of tunnel vision. Installing conflict-free images can help these clients begin to broaden their perceptual field, adding in new neuro networks.

NURTURING FIGURES

I have found it to be very helpful for clients to identify nurturing figures to use as resources before beginning EMDR processing. These inner allies can include real or imaginary figures from the present or

---

STEPS TO DEVELOP AND USE POSITIVE, CONFLICT-FREE IMAGES*

1. Help the client identify the conflict-free image by asking questions or making statements such as the following: "Where in your life do you feel wholly yourself? Is there an activity in which you feel entirely free to engage? Think of a time in your everyday life when your body felt most like just the way you want it to feel. You do not have any fear or anxiety. This should be a time when all of your energy is engaged in a positive manner and you experience only positive (or neutral) feelings about yourself and in your body."
2. Help the client select an image that represents a conflict-free area of functioning and evokes *completely* positive feelings. Install this image, using BLS, with the associated body sensations.
3. The client must be able to hold this image in a consistently positive manner and actually strengthen the image throughout the sets. If this does not happen, return to the second step.
4. Listen for and identify positive cognitions that emerge.
5. Have the client practice using this technique between sessions to manage distressing affect related to his or her symptoms. For example, the client may want to bring up the image before going to sleep, making a public presentation, and so forth.

*© Maggie Phillips. Reprinted with permission.

---

past, inner guides, and animals that have a nurturing quality. With all the resource figures that we tap in, the idea is to evoke imagery that activates the desired qualities in the client's own nervous system. When we imagine something, the nervous systems "lights up" in a particular pattern. When my client can imagine a loving mother, she *feels* those qualities in herself, whether she is conscious of that process or not. It's as if that loving mother is within her (which she is, because it is her imagination that has created her). We aren't taking an outside mother figure and putting her into our client; rather we are activating those qualities of a loving mother in our client's own nervous system by the use of imagination and BLS. When we add BLS to these imagined figures, we are integrating this healing imagery more fully into their neuro networks.

During the history taking, you can look for those people from the client's past who were loving, safe, nurturing figures for them. There may be a parent or stepparent, sibling, grandparent, nanny, aunt or uncle, teacher, coach, doctor, counselor, friend's parent, or clergy person who was an important source of caring for the client. Sometimes it's a one-time experience of being seen and understood by someone (as occurred for Monica, in the case example with the social worker in Chapter 3), or it can be a vicarious experience of someone else receiving nurturing from this person. Occasionally the client will want to install you, the therapist, as nurturer. I find this to be an honor and an indication that the client has received and internalized my caring. In these cases, in order to decrease the dependency on me, I try to get other resources as well. Often when I'm doing adjunctive work, clients choose their primary therapist as a nurturing or protector figure, or both. I encourage this as it decreases the likelihood of splitting and helps the client to incorporate the other therapist into his or her work in a healthy way.

If clients choose their mother or father, I may discourage them from that choice if I suspect that the parent will be involved negatively in some way in the trauma network, such as when I know that the parents were neglectful or abusive. Sometimes clients feel loyal to their parents, or they dissociate the abuse to the extent that they will try to use them as resources. We need to protect clients from using someone or something that is not healthy. If I allow the parents to function as resources because I believe that they may be appropriate, I try to have additional resources as back-ups because of the possibility that the parents will be associated with the trauma or with a disappointment of some kind. For example, a client may want to use her mother as a nurturer, but her mother did not protect her from her father's abuse. In this case her mother failed her as a nurturer— information that is probably not integrated into the client's neural nets.

There may be people from clients' current lives who are important resources for them, such as a current spouse, partner, friend, or lover. They can even use figures from movies, TV, or books, historical figures, or people from popular culture. Clients have chosen Atticus Finch (Gregory Peck), the father in the film *To Kill a Mockingbird*, as a nurturing figure, and Aibileen (Viola Davis), the nanny in the movie *The Help*. Spiritual figures can also be used as nurturers, such as Quan Yin, Tara, Mary, Jesus, Moses, a Native American elder, or an angel. The same figure can be used as a nurturing figure, a protector figure, and a wise figure.

For clients with significant attachment trauma from neglect or abuse, and those who never experienced attachment to a healthy caregiver, I work with them to create and tap in an ideal mother. This is the mother they wish they'd had, a mother who can love and care for them in a consistent, healthy way. I explain more about this important resource figure in the next chapter.

The adult self can be used as a nurturer too. Schmidt (2002) recommends installing a nurturing adult self for clients who have unmet developmental needs. She has created a protocol for enhancing this ego state in which the client connects with his or her innate qualities of empathy, compassion, confidence, courage, strength, and so on. She asks clients if they have, or can form, a mental picture of that part of themselves. My clients often use their nurturing adult selves as one of their figures. I can evoke this part in my clients by asking them to recall a time when they nurtured someone or something. It can be caring for their own children, a relative, a friend, or even a pet. I'll say: "This is your nurturing adult self." Once clients have a strong sense of this inner component, we add the BLS.

For clients who have always taken care of themselves, and have never had anyone take care of them, I try to find another nurturing figure in addition to their adult self. It can be anyone or anything that has nurturing qualities.

Animals can be valuable resources for some clients. These can be pets from the client's present or past (e.g., a loving dog) or animals for which the client has a special affinity. Many clients have used their past or present dogs or cats as nurturers. Sometimes an affectionate dog was the only source of comfort and nurturance the client had as a child. Sometimes people have a special connection with an animal (e.g., wolf, bear, lion, panther, coyote, eagle) that may carry the numen of a power animal (Harner, 1980). Some have used mythological creatures such as dragons as resources.

I try to find more than one figure for clients with histories of abuse or neglect, as each figure has a different feeling and fills a different need. If my client is working on memories from childhood, I will ask him to find a nurturing figure or figures that can comfort and care for his child self.

Together we compile a list of nurturing figures and then tap them in one at a time. I begin with the first one, asking the client to close her eyes and bring up the image as strongly as she can. "See your grandmother in her nurturing aspect. When you can feel that, let me know." At that point I begin the BLS. I might ask the client to tell me when it feels complete, when she feels the sense of nurturing more deeply. I then move on to the next one on the list and ask the client to imagine her dog, for example, in his nurturing aspect. When she has a good sense of the dog's unconditional devotion, I add the BLS.

I have found it challenging for many clients who have been neglected to come up with nurturing figures. I need to work with them to come up with someone or something that has a nurturing quality. I help these clients by offering suggestions. In one case the woman came up with the actress Meryl Streep as her nurturing figure. She could imagine her as a loving mother who could provide her infant self with the love and attention she needed to develop in a healthy way. Another woman struggled to find anyone at all. We searched through her history, current relationships, and even figures from movies. Finally we came up with a figure from *The Secret Life of Bees*, by Sue Monk Kidd, a book that has a powerful, nurturing woman named August as one of its primary characters. This woman had the capacity to nurture her child self. When we found this figure, it was as if a light had come on inside of her. The image of August became essential to our EMDR work. Not only did the sense of her presence create a stronger container, but she was used in interweaves to nurture the child self.

A woman I worked with in a live demonstration at a master therapist workshop I taught demonstrating AF-EMDR (Cassidy Seminars, San Francisco, 2010) told me, when we attempted to find nurturing figures, that there were none—she had never been loved or nurtured in her life. Undaunted by what she told me (I am always sure we will find something, somehow), together we scanned through her life looking for any experiences she might draw from of being loved or nurtured, any examples of observing this, or even giving love or nurturing herself. Finally, she said, "The only thing I have is a memory of an experience of God as a loving presence." I told her that was great, and to bring up the memory as strongly as she could, and when she had it I would tap on her knees. As I tapped on her knees she had a powerful experience of love and light suffusing her entire body. She seemed to glow. She felt full of this love. I could feel it too. I kept tapping for several minutes as the feeling kept getting stronger. After we finished and took a break, a woman from the audience who was inspired by what she had witnessed came up to her and asked her if she could give her a hug. She said yes and received this woman's warm embrace. After the embrace they gazed at one another and chatted for a short time. I could see something special transmit between them. When the client and I resumed our work for the next part of the workshop, I reviewed the resources. Along with God as a loving presence, she now wanted to tap in the woman who had embraced her. This woman became a nurturing figure, a physical manifestation of the loving God for her that was easily accessible and very real for her.

For clients who have difficulty finding nurturing figures, I think it is key to let them know that they don't have to imagine the figure nurturing *them. What is important is that they can imagine someone or something that has a nurturing quality.* It is just too much of a stretch for our most neglected and abused clients to imagine that they can be nurtured, when they never have. It can bring up strong feelings of failure and amplify the feelings of neglect. I believe that by imagining someone or something that *has* a nurturing quality, and thereby activating that quality within *them*, they will have more access to this resource and will eventually be able to use it as a nurturing figure that can provide this for them. Initially, however, I just want them to imagine a figure that has that quality.

However, if they *can* imagine the nurturing figure nurturing them, that is excellent—use it, install it. I think we need to begin where we can with our clients and help them to feel that they are successful wherever they begin. You might suggest that the client imagine himself being held by his nurturing figure. As he holds that image and feels himself being held, add BLS.

I have seen clients come up with nurturers I would not have thought of. For instance, several clients have chosen their adult children as nurturing figures. They told me that they could imagine calling on their sons or daughters to nurture their child selves. In another case the client chose her parents when they were older adults as nurturers. When she was a child and they were young adults, they did not do such a good job of nurturing her. But over time they matured and developed into wise, kind people she could imagine caring for her child self. In another case, the client's mother was dysfunctional when the client was growing up, but got therapy and became a close confidante and support in her life. She was able to install her mother in her present aspect as a nurturing figure.

Sometimes tapping in the nurturing figure or figures can bring up feelings of grief and loss for what they didn't receive as children. I believe it is important to validate these feelings and to provide comfort to our clients with our compassion. I also tell them that even though they didn't get this as children, they can change the way it feels inside by using their imagination to create what they need and want *in the present.*

With some clients who could think of no one to be a nurturer, I asked them if they could remember times when they were able to love and nurture another person or even a pet. In this approach I am attempting to access the nurturing quality within the client and then install that so that they could bring that in for themselves if necessary. For example:

THERAPIST: Can you remember a time when you held or comforted your daughter?

CLIENT: Yes.

THERAPIST: Bring up a memory of doing that. What do you see?

CLIENT: I see my daughter around 3 years old, cuddled on my lap, and I'm rocking her in the rocking chair and singing her a song.

THERAPIST: Can you feel the feelings of love and nurturing towards her?

CLIENT: Yes.

THERAPIST: Focus on that while I tap on your knees.

In this case the adult self could be used as a nurturing figure.

TAPPING IN NURTURING FIGURES*

1. Ask your client to "spend a few moments going inside and quieting your mind."
2. "Think of a figure or figures from your present or past that you associate with nurturance. This can be a person or animal, real or imagined, a spiritual figure, or even someone from a book or movie. When you imagine the figure, *feel* the nurturing quality in your body."
3. "After finding your nurturing figure, enhance the image as strongly as you can. What do you see? What do you hear? What do you smell? What do you feel in your body?"
4. "When you have a strong sense of the nurturing quality of the figure, let me know. Now I'll begin the BLS." (*Use the BLS for 6–12 right–lefts sets. Then stop and check in with your client.*) "How was that for you? How do you feel?"
5. If the nurturing quality is continuing to strengthen, you can do more BLS if you sense that it would help your client. Continue the BLS as long as your client feels the figure and the nurturing quality strengthening and integrating.
6. If there is more than one resource, suggest that the client bring the next nurturing figure to mind and then tap it in also.
7. Repeat this process, tapping in one resource at a time.
8. When the client is through, he or she might want to imagine being held by the nurturing figure or figures. As he or she imagines that, add some more BLS to strengthen and deepen the feeling of being nurtured.

*Reprinted with permission from Sounds True, Inc.

You can spend considerable time working on developing the nurturing figures and cultivating these inner resources. You can do this in four different ways, as we've seen in the above discussion and examples. All four provide healing. You can begin where it is easiest for the client. It is important to begin wherever the client can begin with the most comfort. Here is a summary of the four perspectives:

1. Clients imagine a figure that has a nurturing quality.
2. Clients imagine themselves as the nurturing figure providing nurturance to someone or something.
3. Clients imagine the nurturing figure nurturing them.
4. Clients imagine viewing a scene in which one figure gives nurturance and the other receives it.

Child Self and Adult Self Relationship
Assessment and Development

As I wrote about in *EMDR in the Treatment of Adults Abused as Children* (Parnell, 1999) and in *A Therapist's Guide to EMDR* (Parnell, 2007), very often during EMDR processing with an adult traumatized as a child, the client suddenly accesses the child self in its separate memory compartment and begins to process the past from the child's perspective. Commonly, clients become caught in looping or stuck processing and need help from the therapist in the way of interweaves. I have found it useful, in the preparation phase of treatment, to have the client access the child self before EMDR processing begins in order to evaluate the state of the relationship between the child self and the adult self. Sometimes one will find that the child does not like or trust the adult or that the adult does not like or trust the child. This is important information because during the processing of a traumatic event with EMDR, the therapist may find that the adult has turned on the child self or that the child cannot depend on the adult self to act as a protector resource. It is better to know of this possibility ahead of time. Having a good, strong, loving relationship between the client's adult and child selves is useful for interweaves and aids tremendously in the healing process.

The following is a description of how the adult self–child self relationship can be accessed and evaluated:

Begin by guiding your clients in finding their safe/peaceful place. After the safe/peaceful place has been established, you can ask them to invite their child self into a protective circle that they imagine surrounds them. You can then begin a dialogue between the adult and child selves to evaluate the nature of their relationship.

Generally, clients keeps their eyes closed and the therapist asks questions directed either to the adult self or to the child self. For example, the therapist might ask the child how old he is and how he is feeling. What does he need? How does he feel about the adult self? What is happening in his life? The client might respond, "I am 3 years old. I feel scared 'cause I know my daddy's in the house somewhere and my mommy's not home." The answer to any of the questions can lead to more questions as the therapist gathers information. At some point the attention can shift to the adult self to get his opinions and impressions of the child self. "How do you feel about him?" and "Do you think you can meet his needs?" are possible questions. You are attempting to find out what the child is like, his current emotional state, and the quality of the relationship between the adult and the child. If there are problems between the two (e.g., the child may feel betrayed by the adult), the therapist must seek a way to remedy the problem. It is like doing inner family therapy. A whole session or sessions may be taken up with trying to heal hurts from the past and developing a caring bond between the adult and child selves.

When a caring relationship has been established, you can ask the client to imagine holding his child self on his lap, playing with him, or engaging the child in some positive nurturing way. This feeling can also be installed with BLS. Once the relationship has been established, the adult can serve as a resource for the child self during times of blocked processing and to help create an increased sense of safety for closing sessions.

PROTECTOR FIGURES

Protector figures are allies that can be summoned in your clients' imagination to give them strength and to help them feel protected. I believe that protector figures are a very important resource for clients who have been abused, as they feel so helpless and unprotected. These figures can be used to reduce anxiety and to empower clients. Protector figures can include people (from their childhood or from their present life), animals, or imaginary figures from books, movies, TV, or dreams. Clients might even choose their protective adult self. It is most important that when they think of their protectors, they can *feel* their protective quality. Who would they like to summon that is strong, powerful, and protective? If they can't think of a real person, is there someone from a movie or book? Action figures can make good protectors. The client's spouse or partner can also be a protector figure. For instance, a client who had no one in her childhood who protected or defended her, but was currently in a loving marriage, chose her husband, a man who would defend her ferociously if needed. After tapping him in as a resource, she was able to bring him in whenever her child self felt threatened by the perpetrator during EMDR processing. Memories of positive interactions with these protector figures can be installed with BLS.

For clients with abuse histories who were powerless as children, I insist that they tap in strong, powerful protectors. In this way I am helping to advocate and protect my clients and helping them to access the neural circuitry that is associated with power in their own bodies. For example, if the client imagines an elephant as a protector, she can feel the power of its body, the strength in its legs, its size, and its capacity to move large obstacles. In a sense, the client embodies the elephant, which becomes a powerful and effective protector for her. This resource then can become available to her in daily life, during the processing of the trauma memory, and for interweaves.

As with the nurturing figures, your client does not have to imagine the figure protecting him or her, specifically. It can be enough to imagine the figure in his or her protective aspect, displaying the quality of protection.

Many clients choose large animals as protectors, such as bears, tigers, lions, panthers, wolves, and elephants. Spiritual figures from many traditions can also be invoked, including protective angels and deities. Memories of positive interactions with protector figures can be tapped in. You might find that the figure the client uses for nurturing also serves as a protector. One woman's dragon served as her protector, nurturer, and wise figure. Examples of protector figures people have used include parents, grandparents, friends, partners, spouses, dogs; figures from movies and TV such as James Bond, Spiderman, Superman, Superwoman, Xena the warrior princess, and Rambo; mythic figures such as Hercules; and even the genie Mr. Clean from a TV commercial.

The *adult self* can also be a protector figure. This is the part that we can contact to protect ourselves or those for whom we care. You can help clients find their adult protective self by getting in touch with a number of skills and traits that they already possess, and then use BLS to strengthen and integrate these qualities.

Schmidt (2002) recommends installing a protective adult self for clients who have unmet developmental needs, particularly those who have been neglected and have had disruptions in early attachment. As with the nurturing adult self, Schmidt asks the client to get in touch with a number of skills and traits that she tells the client he or she already possesses and then names them as the client feels them inside. They include attributes such as the ability to be protective, courageous, strong, logical, confident, grounded, and so on. After the client feels all of these qualities within herself, she is asked to bring all of them together into a single sense of self that is then installed with BLS. If the client has an image that represents the protective adult self, that image is installed. It is important that the client accesses a body sense of the resource. As I said with regard to using the adult self as a nurturing figure, for some clients it is important to install other figures as backups.

HELPING CLIENTS FIND AND TAP IN THEIR PROTECTIVE ADULT SELF*

1. "Close your eyes and go inside. Take some deep breaths and slowly let them out. Relax and release with your exhalation. Bring yourself to the present moment. When you feel yourself present, see if you can find a time when you were protective. Can you think of a time when you defended someone you cared about? Be aware of whatever memory or image comes to mind."

2. "When you find the memory, notice what you see. What are you hearing? What do you notice in your body? When you have the image and can *feel* the quality of protectiveness let me know." (*Do short set of BLS.*)

3. "How are you feeling? Can you feel the sense of protectiveness? If you wish, we can add BLS again as long as it remains positive and the feeling of protectiveness strengthens."

4. "Now think of a time when you were courageous. What picture comes to mind?"

5. "As you bring up the picture, notice what you feel. Notice what you hear, smell, sense. What do you feel in your body?"

6. "When you have the image and the feeling of courage strongly activated, let me know." (*Begin BLS, 6–12 times or more if client wishes and tolerates it well. Stop BLS and check in with the client.*) "How do you feel? If you want to go longer to continue to strengthen the quality of courage, tap some more."

7. "What other qualities are associated with protectiveness? Strength, confidence, groundedness, and others. Continue to think of times when you felt these qualities." (*Add BLS to strengthen and deepen them.*)

continued on next page

8. "After you have felt all of these qualities within yourself, bring all of them together into a single sense of self." (*Add BLS to strengthen and integrate them.*) "An image might arise that represents the protective adult self. Let any image arise that feels like it captures all of the qualities of protectiveness that you have tapped. It is important that you have a bodily sense of the resource."

*From Parnell (2008).

TAPPING IN PROTECTOR FIGURES

1. "Can you think of someone or something that has a protective quality? It can be real or imaginary. It can be someone you know from the present or past, an animal, or even a figure from a movie, book, or TV. It can be a spiritual figure that is protective. It can be your adult protective self. It can be helpful to have more than one." (*Write down the list of protectors your client comes up with, then go through and install them one by one.*)

2. "Close your eyes and go inside. Bring up an image of ___[the first protector figure on the list.] Feel the protective quality. When you have a good sense of it, let me know. Good, now I'll begin the BLS." [It is most important that the client have a body sense of the figure's protective quality.]

3. Keep the BLS going 6–12 times, right–left. Now stop and check in with your client to ask how he or she feels. If the sense of the image is getting stronger, or the client wants to go longer, continue with the BLS as long as it remains positive. Stop the BLS when the client feels that the protector resource is strongly anchored within.

4. Now bring up the next protector. Be sure that the client is experiencing its protective quality. When the client indicates a strong sense of the protector, begin the BLS.

5. Repeat this process of imagining and tapping in of protectors as long as the experience is positive for the client.

6. It can help to strengthen the feeling of the protectors by drawing them.

As with the nurturing figures, you can help clients access and integrate protection from four different perspectives:

1. *Imagining a figure that has a protective quality.* Clients imagine a figure, real or imaginary, which has a protective aspect. It can be a figure from a movie or a book, a person from their family, or even themselves. They bring the figure to mind, feel the protective quality of the figure, and then add BLS. The idea here is to activate the neuro network of protection; they feel this quality in themselves even if the protector is a character from a movie or a book.

2. *Imagining themselves as the protector figure providing protection to someone or something.* The client is the protector figure, bringing up a memory or a fantasy of providing protection. For example, the therapist might say: "If someone should threaten your son, what would you do?" Client: "I'd stand up to the bully and make sure he didn't harm my son." In this case you want to activate the imagery, body sensations, and emotions associated with the act of protection. "What do you notice in your body as you imagine doing this? How does that feel?" Add BLS if the feelings are positive. "Notice how your son looks when he is being protected." If it is positive, use BLS to integrate that too.

3. *Imagining the protector figure protecting them.* This is from the point of view of the child or adult receiving protection. Many of our clients have never had an experience of being protected by someone, or seeing someone stand up for them. As with imagining receiving nurturing, this can be much harder to do for many of our clients with attachment trauma. They first imagine and tap in the protector figure, and then imagine the figure protecting *them*. "Imagine your friend John in his protecting aspect. Good, can you feel it? (*If affirmative, add BLS.*) Now can you imagine him protecting you if you are under some kind of threat? What do you feel in your body when you imagine this?" Be sure to add in the senses to more fully activate the right hemisphere, asking, "What do you see? What do you hear? What do you feel emotionally?" Then ask, "How was that for you? How did it feel to be protected?" If it was positive, add BLS to enhance that experience.

If they had imagined protecting someone or something earlier, clients can then imagine themselves in the position of the one receiving the protection. As in the above example: "Now imagine you are your son being protected. Put yourself in his position. What are you seeing? What are you feeling? What do you notice in your body?" If it is positive, add BLS. Then you could ask, "How was that for you to imagine being protected?"

If they give a positive response, you can ask them to "take that in," and add BLS to more fully integrate it.

4. *Imagining viewing the scene of protecting and receiving protection.* In this version clients imagine seeing the scene of a protector figure protecting a child. This is an objective view. "How does that feel to imagine that, to see that scene? How do you think the protector figure feels? How do think the child feels receiving the protection?" You can add BLS as they imagine this from any of the positions.

You can increase the feeling of protection by imagining a circle of protection comprising all your client's protector figures (see box). This can be used during times when your clients feel vulnerable and afraid and wish to feel their protectors more fully.

TAPPING IN THE CIRCLE OF PROTECTION*

1. "Close your eyes and go inside. Take some deep breaths in and slowly let them go. Relax with the exhalation. Bring yourself to a quiet place inside."

2. "When you are more relaxed, imagine yourself surrounded by your protector figures. Look around the circle. Look at each protector, one at a time. Feel all of their protection for you. If you would like to, you can enhance the details of the imagery and the sense of protection. It is important that you *feel* the sense of protection from your protector figures."

3. "When you have a strong sense of them, signal me and I will begin the BLS (BLS 6–12 times, then stop and check in with your client; if it is getting stronger, continue BLS). You might suggest to your client that he or she "take in the feeling of being surrounded by protection. Take in all the strength of your protectors. Let in their courage. Receive their determination to protect you."

4. "You can also draw your circle of protection. Take the time to draw yourself surrounded by your protectors. Drawing can serve to reinforce the feeling of protection. Viewing it can provide you with comfort when you need it." The therapist can add BLS as the client looks at it.

*Reprinted with permission from Sounds True, Inc.

INNER WISDOM FIGURES

For most of my clients the peaceful place, nurturing, and protector figures are sufficient resources to begin the trauma processing work. But for clients who are more fragile or more traumatized, I add in inner wisdom figures to supplement the resource team. These are wise figures such as teachers, parents, grandparents, or helpers of any kind that they have known personally; spiritual figures, ancestors, or historical figures from movies, TV, or books. For some clients the easiest way to initiate this version is to simply ask them to compile a list of wise figures they would like as resources. Once they have provided a list of wise figures, tap in one at a time. For example, a client might choose the Dalai Lama, his grandfather, and Einstein as wise figures. I would ask him to close his eyes, go inside, and bring up the image of the Dalai Lama, along with the sense of the wise quality. When he indicates he has a sense of it, I begin the BLS. I do a short set and then check in with him. If he tells me it is getting stronger, I will do more BLS until he tells me it feels complete to him. I then ask him to recall his grandfather, to imagine him there with him in this moment, to get the sense of his wisdom quality, and use the BLS again. I repeat this process with the figure of Einstein. I find that each figure has a different quality that is evoked with the installation. He can access these inner resources any time he needs help or advice.

Another way to develop wise figures as resources is to use guided imagery and invite an inner advisor or wise figure to arise in that place. I described this process in three of my previous books (Parnell, 1999, 2007, 2008). I have found that developing and installing the inner advisor or wise self is particularly powerful and helpful, as it arises directly from the client's unconscious mind. The inner advisor or wise figure is an aspect of the ego that represents wisdom and offers a balanced perspective (Parnell, 1999, 2007, 2008; Rossman, 1987). It can be a very valuable ally during EMDR processing and between sessions. The inner advisor can be called on in times of difficulty or if the processing becomes stuck. When they develop the inner advisor, clients can derive a greater sense of connection to their own inner resources. Many clients light up with surprise and awe at the wisdom that comes out of their own mouths. The development and installation of the inner advisor provides clients with another tool and assures the therapist that clients can access their own source of wisdom and creativity.

When beginning this process of finding the inner advisor, guide your client to the peaceful place first. Let him know that you will do short sets of BLS when he finds the advisor. After your client is settled in his peaceful place, tell him that he is going to meet his inner advisor or wise self, an aspect of himself that is wise and can offer him guidance when he asks for it. When the inner advisor appears, ask your client what the advisor looks like and if he or she has any advice to give him at this time. You may choose to install the feeling of the inner advisor with BLS. Tell your client that the inner advisor is available whenever he needs him or her and can call on him or her when he feels a need to do so. Inner advisors appear spontaneously to clients during the guided imagery and take a variety of forms that have included fairies, wise women, grandfathers, trees, waterfalls, elves, wizards, Jesus, hawks, snakes, Native American elders, goddesses, older versions of the client, and so on. It is important that the client not judge what comes up and that he accept the advice that is given as long as it is compassionate. The most critical and important function of the inner advisor is to *empower* the client. The advisor can also be present as a source of support and comfort.

INNER ADVISOR SCRIPT*

"As you relax in your safe place, invite your inner advisor to join you in this special place. . . . Just allow an image to form that represents your inner advisor, a wise, kind, loving figure who knows you well. . . . Let it appear in any way that comes and accept it as it is. . . . It may come in many forms—as a man, woman, animal, friend, someone you know, or a character from a movie or book.

"Accept your advisor as it appears, as long as it seems wise, kind, loving, and compassionate. . . . You will be able to sense its caring for you and its wisdom. . . . Invite it to be comfortable there with you and ask it its name . . . accept what comes. . . .

"Keeping your eyes closed . . . describe your inner advisor and tell me its name. (At this point begin the BLS. Do short sets and check in to see how the client is doing. If it continues to be positive, do longer sets.) When you are ready tell it about your problem . . . ask any questions you have concerning this situation. . . . Now listen carefully to [name of advisor's] response. . . . You may imagine [name of advisor] talking with you, or you may simply have a direct sense of its message in some other way. . . . Allow it to communicate in whatever way seems natural. . . . If you are uncertain about the meaning of the advice or if there are other questions you want to ask, continue the conversation until you feel you have learned all you can at this time . . .

continued on next page

INNER ADVISOR SCRIPT *(continued)*

(After a long pause, ask the client what is happening. After he or she tells you, begin BLS again.) "As you consider what your advisor told you, imagine what your life would be like if you took the advice you have received. . . . If you have more questions, continue the conversation. (If the client continues the conversation with the advisor again, pause, then ask what is happening. Resume BLS.)*

"When it seems right, thank your advisor for meeting with you, and ask it to tell you the easiest, surest method for getting back in touch with it. . . . Realize that you can call another meeting whenever you feel the need for some advice or support. . . . Say good-bye for now in whatever way seems appropriate, and allow yourself to come back to the room."*

At the end, spend time debriefing the experience. Take care that the client is fully back in the room before ending the session.

*Adapted with permission from the "Inner Advisor" script developed by Martin L. Rossman, MD, and David E. Bresler, PhD, for the Academy for Guided Imagery.

Clients can use their inner advisor to help them in a number of ways. If they have a question, problem, or don't know what direction to turn, they can take a moment and go inside themselves. They can bring up their inner advisor and ask him or her for guidance. Then they can tap themselves and listen for the response. In this way their inner wisdom figure can be there to provide guidance and support for them in their life. These figures can be used as interweaves when the processing is stuck. "What advice would your inner advisor give you?" Listen for the advice, and then say "Go with that" or "Imagine that" and add the BLS. Clients can have more than one inner advisor, and they can change each time you do the exercise. They may require a different inner advisor for different problems in their life, or at different times in their life.

TEAM OF INNER HELPERS

I ask many of my clients if they would like to imagine the resources they have tapped in as a team of support. Some clients take to this immediately and love the idea. They imagine all of their resources surrounding them, providing them with the support they need. "Now that we have tapped in your basic resource figures, would you like to imagine them together surrounding you and providing you support? They are your inner support team." When they have imagined or have a good sense of this team, I add the BLS. Sometimes clients want to imagine all their figures assembled in their peaceful place. I let them choose whatever feels best for them.

Some clients do not like this idea. They can't imagine how their grandmother could fit with their mother grizzly bear. That's fine. I just move on. For those for whom this image works, it can be a wonderful resource. When they can feel a circle of support, clients don't feel so alone. They can draw upon their team for help whenever they need to during their EMDR processing, and also during daily life. Later you can suggest to clients: "You can imagine taking your circle of inner helpers into your life. They can be called upon and tapped in to help you whenever you need them." As clients discover more resource figures, they can be added to their team. A guided imagery that you can use to enhance the team of inner helpers is provided in the box.

TAPPING IN CIRCLE OF INNER HELPERS

1. "Imagine yourself surrounded by your inner helpers. You are in the center of a circle of support. Spend a moment and look at each one of your inner resource figures. Feel their support for you. Take in this support; feel it as strongly as you can in your body." (Add BLS.)
2. "Now feel the combined support from your inner helpers. Feel their caring and the qualities they provide as you tap in this entire team of inner helpers. When you can feel the sense of support strongly in your body, let me know." (Add BLS as long as it feels positive.)
3. "You may imagine more inner resource figures joining your circle, or some may arise spontaneously, adding even more support for you." (Add BLS.)
4. "Imagine taking this feeling of support with you into your life. When you have an image, picture, or sense of doing this, let me know." (Add BLS.)
5. Remember that your circle of inner helpers is always there. All you have to do is think of them. You can tap on your own knees or do the butterfly hug."

EXAMPLE OF INSTALLING RESOURCES WITH A CLIENT WITH RELATIONAL TRAUMA

Following is a transcript from a session I did that was videotaped from my class at the New York Open Center ("Attachment-Focused EMDR for Social Anxiety," available through www.emdrinfo.com). The client was a woman in her early 50s who presented with issues of having difficulty in group situations. She was highly anxious and told me that she had often been scapegoated as a child. She'd had insecure attachment with her mother who was not loving or nurturing of her. An orthodox Jew, she was currently married to a man she loved. I will present this case in more detail in Chapter 15. In this session I am installing the four resources outlined above. Because this client was highly anxious, she needed a lot of reassurance from me as we went along.

LAUREL: So, do you have a place that feels peaceful and relaxing to you?

MIRIUM: Yeah, well, the western wall in Jerusalem.

LAUREL: So, it's being there?

MIRIUM: Yeah, or just visualizing it.

LAUREL: OK. Great. So just take a moment and imagine that wall . . . and when you have a sense of peacefulness, let me know.

MIRIUM: Yes. >>>>> (*installing or tapping in peaceful place*)

LAUREL: OK, how's that?

MIRIUM: Good.

LAUREL: Great, OK. Now, do you have nurturing figures, real or imaginary?

MIRIUM: My husband.

LAUREL: OK, anyone else? [I want to have some backups in case he isn't enough.]

MIRIUM: Nurturing . . .

LAUREL: Yes, it could be an animal, it could be a spiritual figure, someone from the past …

MIRIUM: I guess our dog growing up . . . I really didn't have much nurturing, except for since I got married.

LAUREL: It doesn't have to be from your childhood. It could be from any time. It should have that nurturing quality.

MIRIUM: I guess that the last time I picked you actually.

LAUREL: Oh, OK.

MIRIUM: The way you look when you're doing this work! It's very nurturing.

LAUREL: Oh, OK, so let's go to your husband and feel his nurturing quality.

MIRIUM: (*Closes her eyes and focuses on the image and feeling.*) OK . . . >>>>> (*Opens eyes when done.*)

LAUREL: OK, great, so you got it ... so now imagine me and feel my nurturing qualities.

MIRIUM: Hmmm . . .

LAUREL: Great, you got a sense of it, OK.

MIRIUM: >>>>> OK . . . (*Opens eyes when done.*)

LAUREL: Can you think of protective figures, real or imaginary?

MIRIUM: Ok, hmmm, again my husband. . . . I really have trouble with this . . . hmmm . . . I mean, there are lots of protective figures in movies but . . . I picture King David (*laughs nervously*) from the Bible (*anxious and unsure of herself*).

LAUREL: Great, he's a powerful figure!

MIRIUM: Yes.

LAUREL: OK, that's good, you feel a resonance with that image?

MIRIUM: Yes.

LAUREL: So imagine your husband and imagine his protective quality now.

MIRIUM: OK. (*Closes eyes.*) >>>>>

LAUREL: OK, got it?

MIRIUM: Yes.

LAUREL: OK, and then King David . . . OK?

MIRIUM: Yeah. >>>>>

LAUREL: OK, that's great! . . . Good, now, wise figures—are there any wise figures?

MIRIUM: Wise figures . . . well, weird that this should come up, because one of my problem figures is my mother, but she's in this whole thing, but she is a wise figure also, but we're not going to use her . . . ha-ha!

LAUREL: Nooooo . . . (*laughs*).

MIRIUM: Hmmm . . . I don't know, I feel so stupid but, no, I'm going to say again, I'm going to say Moses (*laughs nervously*).

LAUREL: Well, great, you're resonating with these figures and that's what's important.

MIRIUM: Yes, well . . .

LAUREL: OK, wonderful, so just feel his wisdom quality.

MIRIUM: >>>>> OK, great.

LAUREL: Wonderful. Do you want to imagine them as a team?

MIRIUM: Well, right now it would take too much work to get every-
         body and put them together (*chuckle*) . . . yeah . . .

LAUREL: OK, not a problem.

The rest of the session, which includes the EMDR processing, is presented in Chapter 15.

CHAPTER 5

Creating New Parents and Repairing Developmental Deficits

In this chapter you will learn how to use Resource Tapping to install an ideal mother and ideal father for the repair of attachment wounds and developmental deficits, as well as how these resources can be used as interweaves. Cases are used to illustrate the process so that you will gain a sense of what this work might look like in clinical practice.

DEVELOPING AND TAPPING IN AN IDEAL MOTHER

The ideal mother is a resource figure that can be developed and tapped in to help repair early childhood attachment deficits. When taking a client's history and hearing a story of a mother who was abusive, neglectful, mentally or physically ill, abusing drugs or alcohol, or simply absent, I begin to think that perhaps it might be helpful to the client to construct an ideal mother—the mother she wishes she'd had growing up. In these cases, it is not one or two instances of the mother not being there or being misattuned; rather, it is a pervasive pattern that the client experienced over a prolonged period of time. In many cases clients do not experience emotional charge related to the neglect—it was simply the way it was for them.

Some clients spend more than one session constructing this ideal mother. They take pleasure in filling out the details of the kind of mother they wish they'd had. Sometimes you can help your client construct the mother, offering suggestions about what you believe to be qualities important to healthy mothering. I feel that tapping in the ideal mother begins to create a healthy alternative to the unhealthy attachment pattern that clients experienced growing up. With the use of imagination, clients create alternate realities that seem to develop new neural pathways that change the way they feel about themselves and how they relate to others.

In working with clients to create the ideal mother, I want to keep in mind the kinds of qualities that activate the right hemisphere where early attachment processes are registered. Eye contact, tone of voice, smell, touch, qualities such as calmness, stability, compassion, love, confidence, happiness—these are all primarily right-brain processes. If the real-life mother was an alcoholic or drug addict, the ideal mother will be sober. If their real mother was depressed, bipolar, or psychotic, the ideal mother will be mentally healthy and stable. I typically explain this creation process to clients in the following way:

> "Can you imagine an ideal mother? You can create the mother you wish you'd had. She can be any way you would like her to be. What would she feel like? What would her body feel like? What qualities would she have? Bring in the senses. What would it feel like to be in her arms? What would she smell like? Her breath, her skin? Feel her softness, the relaxation and calmness she exudes. You can construct her from someone you know, from aspects of people you know, from neighbors, friends, your actual mother, from characters in books, movies, and from aspects of yourself."

If the client is having difficulty, and you know he or she has children and has loved and nurtured them, you can try to draw on their own nurturing self to construct this mother: "Can you remember nurturing and loving your own children? You can take aspects of your own nurturing self to construct this mother."

Some clients do not have an image of an ideal mother, but they can get a sense of her. That works fine. Sometimes an image comes to them as you use the BLS. Sometimes clients and I make a list of the qualities together, and then with their eyes closed and the BLS, I read back the list to them. I may even make the suggestion that an image may form of their ideal mother. I worked with one woman from a very deprived background who was not able to come up with any image before I began the BLS on her list of ideal mother qualities. But as she became immersed in the sense of what this mother would be like, a very strong image arose that had previously been in a dream. This mother had a very distinct look to her; she was very tall and strong. The client resonated with the felt sense of what it would be like to be loved and cared for by this mother. After the session the client reported feeling safe in her everyday life in a way she had never felt before.

For clients who don't have their own children or who weren't particularly good parents, you can ask about a pet from their childhood or adult life. "Do you have a pet you have loved and cared for?" If they are able to remember loving and caring for a pet, then use those feelings to help construct the ideal mother.

Once the client has created his or her ideal mother and has a strong felt sense of her, add BLS to tap her in. If clients continue to elaborate on the imagery and feelings, let them go as long as the process remains positive. If it should turn negative, stop and return to only positive imagery and feelings. What is most important here is to construct this ideal mother and develop a strong felt sense of her nurturing quality.

For many of our clients it is enough initially to be able to create and imagine a loving mother figure. It is too big a step for them to then imagine having such a mother and being nurtured *by* her. I go where my client can go. If this is what he or she can do, we will focus on only this for the time being. When the client can go forward, I will see if he or she can imagine being in the arms of such a mother. Imagine being the baby receiving this love, nurturing, and adoration. It can help to encourage a state of relaxation, so that the client can enter into active imagination.

First the client creates the ideal mother and taps her in. Then the client imagines being the baby in the arms of this mother. Often the client will choose the age he or she wishes to be in the interaction. Sometimes the client can easily imagine this, and at others, I will fill in the sensory right-brain information I know is important for attachment:

> *"As you are in your mother's arms, see how happy she is to gaze at you. She adores you. Feel the softness of her arms, and the security. She smells good and her voice is soothing to you. Feel her stroke your soft head and rock you in her arms. You feel loved and at peace."*

As the client takes in this loving scene, add the BLS. Some clients prefer continuous BLS as they do this imagination. Others like shorter sets. Some clients really get into this imagery and drop into a deep reverie with the BLS going. They can feel themselves as the baby being loved. When you stop for a break, ask your client how that was, or what's coming up for him or her. If it is positive, say, "Go with that," and add BLS to take it in.

You can also suggest that clients imagine the scene from the *point of view of the mother*. What might she be feeling as she holds and gazes at her baby?

> *"Imagine you are this loving mother holding your sweet baby in your arms and looking at her [him] with love. Can you imagine this? Good."*

Then add the BLS as the client imagines this. When you stop the BLS, ask the client how that was for him or her. If it felt good, say "Go with that," and add the BLS to enable the client to more fully integrate it.

If it doesn't feel good or something comes up, ask the client what is needed to make it better. I tell my clients that they can make it any way they want—it is *their* imagination. This instruction can be quite freeing.

This whole process is fluid and creative. It is important to be flexible and to go where your client wants to go. For some, it is easier to begin with the ideal mother and then imagine nurturing the child from her perspective first. For others, it works better to begin with the child's perspective of being nurtured, and then do the mother's. Many clients don't want or need to do the mother's perspective. I believe part of the attachment repair comes from the therapist–client interaction and the fluid, creative way in which this work is done. By attuning to our clients' needs in the present, we are creating in vivo new adaptive, healing neural pathways related to healthy relationships.

Clients who have difficulty with this process can:

1. Think of a time when they were nurturing to someone or something, even one time. Can they evoke that feeling of caring for another? If they can, tap in that memory.
2. Now take that feeling and use it to construct a mother figure.
3. Then, if they can do it, ask them to imagine themselves in the position of receiving the nurturing they gave. For example, if they evoked a memory of holding and rocking their own daughter in their arms, tap that in, then ask if they can imagine themselves as the baby receiving that loving. If they can, ask them to imagine it with the feeling and tap it in. This can be difficult for many clients with relational trauma. Go easy with it. I find it is most important that they can imagine and tap in an ideal mother.

4. You can give your clients homework assignments. They can search for pictures of loving mother–infant interactions and examples of healthy bonding. They can compile these pictures from the Internet or from magazines and create a collage. The pictures can help stimulate their imagination and help them create what they wish they'd had. The collage is a physical representation of what they want in their mother. They can also compile developmentally chronological pictures of mother–child interactions. For example, they can select pictures of healthy, happy pregnant women; then mothers who have just given birth bonding with their babies on their chests; mothers suckling their newborns, gazing lovingly at the babies; mothers with babies, then toddlers, then children at different ages, doing different activities, and growing up in a happy home.

5. They can look at videos of healthy mother–child interactions to get ideas, as well as read books.

Roadblocks to Creating the Ideal Mother

Several roadblocks can come up for clients that make it difficult for them to imagine and tap in an ideal mother. What follows are some of those roadblocks and suggestions for working with them.

"But This Isn't What Happened to Me"

Some clients will protest to the therapist, for example, "But I never had such a mother! What good will this do me? This isn't the reality of what happened to me." I think it is important to acknowledge the pain and truth of what they didn't get, and at the same time let them know that it is possible to change how this information is held in their nervous systems. I tell clients:

"You didn't have a loving, caring mother. That is the truth, but you can change how this truth is held in your nervous system. You are no longer a child living with your parents, are you? But you still feel like you are, don't you? This is because you have developed memory networks that light up in a particular pattern, making it feel as if you are still a child. This isn't reality, is it? Well, we can change the way in which you feel by using your imagination and BLS and adding new neural pathways. You

*won't forget what happened to you, you just won't feel like it is impor-
tant to you now. You will have new ways of responding to situations that
used to upset you."*

Most clients can accept such an explanation.

Disloyalty

Another roadblock to creating an ideal mother can be a feeling of disloyalty: Clients feel that they are being disloyal to their mothers by
imagining an ideal one. I might say, "What you are creating is only in
your imagination—you aren't really replacing your mother." Or "This
is a mother who is there for you. Can you allow yourself to have what
you have always wanted?" Some clients don't want to give up the good
things they got from their mothers. I explain that they don't need to give
up those good things—that we can find a way to preserve those positive
experiences.

Sometimes what can help is to ask if clients want to imagine someone
who can *help* their mother be a better mother. In this way you aid clients
in constructing a good *adjunct* mother who can teach their *real* mother
how to parent. In some cases clients are open to creating a "co-mother"
who provides nurturing and care the mother couldn't offer. For example, perhaps her mother was a good cook and made delicious meals, but
was unable to attend to and listen to the needs of her children. The co-
mother can fill in the needs her own mother couldn't provide.

Grief

Sometimes clients experience grief when imagining and tapping in an
ideal mother. It is often the realization of what they never got, and always
longed for, that brings the tears, and for some it is also the loss of hope
that their own mother could somehow change. It can be difficult for clients to give up hope that their mother will ever be good enough—even if
their mother is deceased. It can be healing to acknowledge this and help
them grieve. I often suggest that they imagine their ideal mother holding
them as they grieve the loss of hope, with the BLS going on, so they can
process this material.

Using the Ideal Mother in Interweaves

The ideal mother can be used in interweaves (discussed in more detail in
Chapter 13). When the client is stuck or looping, the therapist asks the

child self what he or she needs. When the client responds as the child self with something to the effect of "I need nurturing or protection" and the therapist asks "Who can provide that for you?" the client can bring in his or her ideal mother to do the job.

One client who created an ideal mother was able to use her to help with her insomnia. As a child from a very young age she'd had to put herself to bed without comfort or transitions. During her EMDR session she asked her therapist about bedtime rituals for children. She was then able to use her ideal mother and create a ritual for her child self. She imagined her ideal mother reading to her and singing to her as she fell asleep. She couldn't allow her mother figure to touch her yet (she had been sexually abused), but she could imagine her ideal mother sitting right next to her in a rocking chair. She was later able to bring up this image, tap herself, and go to sleep.

Sometimes an ideal mother figure is needed but has not been created ahead of time when the client is looping and stuck during EMDR processing. When this happens, the client can create the ideal mother then and there. The sequence might go something like this:

THERAPIST: What does the child need . . . what does your little girl [little boy] need?
CLIENT: I need a new mother!
THERAPIST: Would you like to create a new mother? You can create the mother you wish you'd had.

At this point the client can imagine the mother he or she wishes to have had and then use this figure in the interweave—which can be quite long, elaborate, and creative.

REPAIRING DEVELOPMENTAL DEFICITS

After you have tapped in an ideal mother, and perhaps an ideal father (I describe this experience later in this chapter), clients can use these resources to repair developmental deficits anywhere in their histories. They can imagine the development that they wanted and needed, using BLS to integrate the desired qualities and experiences. They can also use these resources and imagined repair as interweaves during EMDR processing sessions. Entire sessions can be devoted to creating and tapping in an alternate birth, infancy, childhood, adolescence, and even adulthood. Sometimes clients need to spend more time in a particular developmental stage, repeating the reparative scenarios many times. This is what occurred with therapist Holly Prichard's case of Maria in Chapter 16. Interestingly, this client, as an imagined baby, seemed to get a little older each time they returned to a scene in the baby's crib. Sometimes you begin with the conception and birth, and the client spontaneously progresses through his or her life, filling in the developmental gaps. Many people prefer continuous BLS as they do this. While some clients wish to imagine and tap in an ideal mother, then an ideal father, and then reimagine their developmental stages with both parents, others do not. Some clients emphasize the importance of the attachment repair with their mother. This seems to be the choice of most clients with whom I have worked. In all cases I follow what is needed for each client, and we adapt things as we go along.

Repairing Attachment Wounds from Conception and Birth

For many clients the attachment wound occurred at birth, perhaps because the birth was traumatic (e.g., mother and child nearly died, they were born premature, death of a twin, medical problems); there were medical complications that separated them from their mother or she was anesthetized; their mother was physically or psychologically unwell, drug addicted, or unable to bond with them; or they were given up for adoption. I have worked with clients who were born with Rh blood type incompatibility and nearly died at birth, as well as others who experienced life-threatening birth trauma. Some clients were not wanted or loved and were either kept and neglected or given up for adoption. In some cases the child was wanted but the mother was young, overwhelmed, or had lost other babies before this child and was afraid of another loss and so did not attach.

Sometimes we find these birth traumas from bridging back from a current symptom or problem (see Chapter 11), or the client discovers the links during processing, or we purposely target the birth by asking for an image that represents it and has emotional charge (e.g., "When you think of your birth, what picture represents that for you?").

I have found that clients with birth traumas or attachment trauma that originated at birth benefit from reimagining their births in a way that is healing. As they reimagine their birth, with BLS, often beginning with conception and the womb experience, they can use their ideal mother and even an ideal father that they create. They can have the family they always wished they'd had. This imagination with BLS changes the way they feel inside, and thereby changes symptoms and relationship patterns.

In order to help your clients reimagine conception, birth, and early infancy, you need to educate yourself about healthy development. Then as your clients imagine themselves growing up, you can provide informed support and fill in information they lack.

Suggestions for Guided Imagery and BLS to Repair Womb and Birth Experiences

You can begin by asking clients to imagine their ideal mother, evoking the sensory feeling as strongly as possible. Then ask them to imagine being conceived by this mother. Perhaps they might want to imagine that their mother is in love with their father, that they are conceived in love and joy. The mother learns of the pregnancy with great happiness. She welcomes the new life and takes good care of herself emotionally and physically. Allow clients time to imagine what an ideal pregnancy would be like, and what it would be like to be in the womb of such a mother. As they imagine this amazing process, add BLS. Some clients like short amounts of BLS, and some longer. Some will be silent in their imaginings, and some will speak aloud, describing their experience. You can offer suggestions to fill out the experience, or you might ask questions such as "What else would make the baby feel safe and loved? What might you want to experience if you could imagine the best womb experience?" You might suggest:

> *"Imagine you are floating in a warm bath, surrounded by love. You are totally at peace and know you are wanted. You can hear your mother sing to you and are deeply contented with your being. She is peaceful and you can feel it. You feel safe, as she feels safe."*

Some clients will want a lot of time in this stage, some very little. Follow what feels most natural for your client.

When they are ready, ask clients if they want to imagine their birth. They can imagine it any way they would like. They can imagine their mother safe, supported, and secure, ready to welcome them into the world: "Your mother is surrounded by loving people who welcome you into the world. You are put on her chest and you can see the love in your mother's eyes. You can feel the warmth and security of her soft body." Again, sensory details are important: the smell of the mother's skin, the warmth of her body, the feeling of being held and supported, the soft look of love in her eyes, the tone of her voice. Remember that this experience involves a process of right-brain repair. As clients imagine their birth scene, add BLS. You can go back and forth, imagination and BLS, stop and check in with short sets, or go long sets with continuous BLS if clients do better with this and you know they are not shifting to negative associations. This process is very much like what Jungians call *active imagination* (Jung, 1961). Clients are allowed to drop into a process of free-flowing imagination that is augmented by the use of BLS.

Moving forward with the imagination, you might continue: "Do you want to imagine nursing? See yourself being placed on your mother's breast to nurse. You can feel the connection to nurturing and safety." Give clients permission to imagine whatever they want to, repairing what was not adequately present at their actual birth. Allow clients time to embellish with any details they want. You can assist clients in activating their imagination by asking questions or offering suggestions that may deepen the experience. Use what you know about early infant attachment to help clients imagine those experiences. For example:

> *"What do you see in your mother's eyes? How does it feel to be so loved and welcomed? Your mother gazes at you with so much love; you see her loving you and you take in that love. Can you feel it? Good."* (Now add BLS.) Or: *"Remember how much love you felt when you held your son for the first time? Now imagine that you are the baby receiving that love. Good."* (Now add BLS.)

Your tone of voice, gentle encouragement, eye contact, and love also go into the client's nervous system. Our clients use us as resources that are tapped in *implicitly* as part of the process. We can also be tapped in *explicitly* by asking the client, "How did that feel to have me here at your birth with you?" If the client says, "That felt good, that felt meaningful," tap in the positive response as well.

You might do this womb and birth experience repeatedly, with clients adding in more sensory detail. Your clients can imagine and tap in their ideal mother, and remember the love and positive sensory information. Ask if your clients want to move this process forward in time. Is their mother ready to bring the baby home? What would they like that experience to be? What kind of a home would their ideal mother have? Do they want to create an ideal father? What other resources would they like to add in? What would their room be like? Would they like to sleep in the parent's room, in the family bed?

I have found this process also helpful for gay and lesbian clients who want to repair damage to their self-esteem due to parental rejection or lack of attunement. These clients can be invited to imagine parents who accept and love them for who they are. They may even want to imagine same-sex parents providing them with what they needed to grow up in a healthy way. This can be very healing to clients who have felt that they are not ok for who they are.

Some clients may want to imagine and tap in an ideal brother or sister, or even a new family—one that is loving and supportive of who they are. Anything they needed for healthy development can be imagined and tapped in with BLS.

DEVELOPING AND TAPPING IN AN IDEAL FATHER

Sometimes some of the client's developmental trauma is associated with the absence of a father or father figure. This is the case with many men as well as women today whose parents divorced and fathers disengaged or even disappeared. What are the emotional wounds associated with the absence of a father? There are many, and they vary from person to person. If you suspect that some of your clients' problems are linked to the lack of a father or father figure, you can tap in an ideal father, and then have them imagine this father in their life from the beginning, using BLS and active imagination to add in new, healthy neural nets. You can ask clients to imagine such a father from conception and go forward from there, as was done with the ideal mother, or you can ask clients to pinpoint the first time they were aware that they lacked a father, and then bring the ideal father into the scene in an interweave. If clients wish to imagine this father in their life, through all the stages and major events, they can do this in conjunction with the BLS. Some clients will do short sets of BLS, and others long sets, wishing it to go continuously. The case that follows is an example of the latter.

CASE: REPAIRING BIRTH TRAUMA WITH EMDR

The client was a therapist in her 40s from my training at the New York Open Center who wanted to work on a lifelong belief that was limiting her life and causing her anxiety (*Repairing Birth Trauma with EMDR*, DVD available at www.emdrinfo.com). In this session we bridged back her belief, "I'm not safe in the world," to her birth and her mother's loss of babies before her. She reprocessed the trauma and creatively reimagined her birth with the qualities and experiences she needed.

The client easily installed resources: Walden Pond was her peaceful place; her husband, along with two female friends, was her nurturing figure; and an ex-boyfriend was her protector figure. (Note: The sign ">>>>>" signifies that BLS has begun. In this client's case, I tapped on her knees, right–left/right–left, as she processed.)

LAUREL: So, tell me, what do you want to work on?

CLIENT: OK, it's not real clear but, well there is a real core belief that I am not safe in the world, and I would love to get a taste, to at least get on the other side and have a peek at that.

LAUREL: OK.

CLIENT: And some of that manifests as feeling anxiety a lot, but when I try to get a clear picture of it, it's like, *poof*, it's really hard to grasp onto.

LAUREL: [I decide to use the bridging technique, to find the link between the negative cognition and the roots of this problem.] Just take a moment, close your eyes, and say to yourself, "I'm not safe in the world." Now what emotions do you feel?

CLIENT: Fear, terror.

LAUREL: What do you notice in your body?

CLIENT: I think I want to cry.

LAUREL: OK, OK, just stay with that, you are doing great, and trace it back in time. "I'm not safe in the world." Welcome these feelings and go back as far as you can without censoring it.

CLIENT: (*silent for a few minutes*) I have two thoughts. I think the first one is about being born.

LAUREL: OK. OK.

CLIENT: You can't go much earlier than that!

LAUREL: So what comes up with this?

CLIENT: It's just that I know, I don't know, I don't have a . . . it's just that my mom had two miscarriages before she had me.

LAUREL: Uh-huh.

CLIENT: And she had a stillborn baby before me and I just, I know, because she was just terrified. Probably about would I be OK, would I be born alive?

LAUREL: OK.

CLIENT: I just feel, talking about this, the generational trauma. I just feel this is in my nervous system. It was just passed on, whether it's through the Holocaust or my mom's personal experience or just something . . .

LAUREL: OK . . . let's go to your birth. So just close your eyes and go inside. When you think of your birth, what picture do you get?

CLIENT: I don't know, I don't remember.

LAUREL: Just anything, just create a picture. [I'm looking for an image that will tap into the neural net of her birth.]

CLIENT: OK. Ah, my mom being scared in the delivery room.

LAUREL: [This picture tells me so much about the trauma. It symbolizes the issue perfectly.] OK. That's it. So as you see that, what emotions do you feel? [I'm using the modified protocol.]

CLIENT: I feel sad, I feel scared.

LAUREL: Yeah. What do you feel in your body?

CLIENT: Shaky.

LAUREL: What do you believe about yourself?

CLIENT: I don't know (*insecure and self-conscious*).

LAUREL: [She is in a regressed state and can't come up with a negative cognition, so I skip it in order to keep her in the neural net. I give her encouragement all along as she often becomes self-conscious, believing that she isn't doing it right.] That's OK, just go with the feelings and go with the picture you have of your mom. OK? I'm going to tap and let whatever comes up come up without censoring it. >>>>>

CLIENT: I'm getting this image of her, you know, in the delivery room with the sheet, some doctor on the other side, and she is so terrified. She told me that day, you know, that they put her out (*laughs nervously, then cries*). So now I feel blank.

LAUREL: That's OK. [Again, I'm reassuring her she is doing it right and is OK. I believe she is at the end of a channel so I direct her to return to target.] So now go back to the picture of your mom. What's happening now?

CLIENT: Just that she is terrified . . .

LAUREL: OK, let's go with that. >>>>> (*Client begins to sob deeply. I provide gentle encouragement as she cries.*) That's it, you're doing great.

CLIENT: (*deep, deep sobbing*) What I'm thinking is . . . I feel bad for her because I think she was alone. You know, she didn't have any, like when I was born, she didn't have anybody . . . she was probably scared and really alone.

LAUREL: Yeah, OK, go with that. >>>>> (*Client resumes deep sobbing. I provide more encouragement through her abreaction as I tap on her knees.*) That's OK . . . what's coming up?

CLIENT: (*smiles, then looks up*) What is coming up, a little bit, like some other thoughts, just like, hmmm, I'm really pleased to be doing this with you . . . so often I can't even get this far (*nervous laughter*).

LAUREL: OK, great. [I'm acknowledging receiving the compliment and her appreciation. I feel happy that she is happy, but want to keep her processing, so I return her to the target.] So let's go back to the picture with your mom again. Tell me, what comes up?

CLIENT: I think we're still in the hospital room. I see that she, the atmosphere, is really—it's not the atmosphere for a baby, of joy, happiness; there's a lot of fear—at times it feels gray and cold.

LAUREL: [She sounds stuck to me, so I use a resource interweave for her mother. This is an example of the child taking her mother's experience into her neural nets. By bringing in a resource for her mother, we are actually helping to heal the trauma in her.] OK, so what does your mom need?

CLIENT: (*sobbing deeply*) She needs a nurturing presence, a nurturing figure, and probably a protector too.

LAUREL: Do you want to bring somebody in? Some figures for your mom?

CLIENT: Yeah!

LAUREL: Who would you like to bring in?

CLIENT: I'd like to bring in her mother.

LAUREL: OK, great. So just imagine that for your mom. >>>>>

CLIENT: (*sobbing deeply for several minutes*) I remember a story my mother told me as an adult, that after she had two miscarriages, her mother said to her, well maybe next time you'll have a boy. But my mom talks about her mother with, you know, that she misses her, that they had a good connection.

LAUREL: Great! Do you want to follow that or is it just . . .

CLIENT: I don't know.

LAUREL: [It feels like we are at the end of a channel so I direct her to go back to target.] Let's go back to the birth again. So bring up the picture. Tell me what you notice now.

CLIENT: I don't know. Maybe it feels a little bit warmer, a little more colorful.

LAUREL: OK, let's go with that. >>>>>

CLIENT: She just needed somebody to tell her it was going to be OK. I'm trying to think who else I could bring in to help her. I'm not sure. Maybe her sister.

LAUREL: [She's doing her own resource interweave.] Uh-huh, somebody there to hold her hand, to comfort her, to tell her "you're going to be fine." [We are co-creating the needed resources.]

CLIENT: You're safe.

LAUREL: [She adds to what I have just suggested.] Would your nurturing figures help your mother?

CLIENT: I was thinking I could help her.

LAUREL: You want to help her?

CLIENT: Yeah (*laughs nervously*).

LAUREL: Great. OK, get in there and you help her. >>>>>

CLIENT: (*Begins to sob; waves of deep crying as she does a long set of processing for about 5 minutes.*) I was having a thought, which is like, we live, you know, waiting for the other shoe to drop. It hasn't dropped. She has been saved pretty much all of her life. It's so sad, you know, it's awful. [She is having an insight.] I get confused, this is what happens. I get that the world isn't safe. That all these bad things happen. Like I don't know, yeah.

LAUREL: [It seems like she is at the end of another channel. I want to check our work, so I go back to target again.] OK, let's go back to the birth again and tell me what comes up now.

CLIENT: It does feel warmer, like it's more colorful, like it's not gray. I'm seeing some flesh tones.

LAUREL: [It seems she is in the same scene, still in the birth canal and hasn't been born yet. I decide to have her go forward in time.] OK. So do you want this to go forward in time? Can you imagine being born?

CLIENT: Yeah, yeah, yeah! I have a sense, a welcomed sense. It feels safer.

LAUREL: OK, imagine that. >>>>>

CLIENT: (*Opens her eyes after a short time; I stop the BLS.*) I think I need more resources around.

LAUREL: OK, who would you like to bring in?

CLIENT: My husband (*begins to sob deeply*).

LAUREL: OK, so he's in there too. >>>>>

CLIENT: (*long abreaction with deep sobbing for about 10 minutes of BLS*) It's a nice image. It's an image of my whole team in the delivery room, I think, including myself, just telling her, "You can do it, you can do it. It's going to be all right, you're safe. You're going to have a healthy baby."

LAUREL: Great, great. So what are you noticing now?

CLIENT: I don't know. (*She gets embarrassed and remarks on how when she opens her eyes and looks at me, it takes her out of the experience. I reassure her that it's OK, then redirect her to the target.*)

LAUREL: So let's go back in again and see what's there as you think of the birth . . .

CLIENT: Yeah, I want to imagine it happening and appearing just joyous and happy and safe . . .

LAUREL: OK, go with that. >>>>>

CLIENT: I feel welcomed, relaxed. (*beginning to sob*) I'm feeling stuck, like I can't quite get that picture.

LAUREL: [I don't know if the processing is stuck or if she has completed a channel of associations.] OK, what's coming up now?

CLIENT: I don't know.

LAUREL: Well, are you still there [meaning, in the picture of the birth]? Have you progressed? Has she brought you home? [I'm trying to determine where she is in the processing.]

CLIENT: I'm with all those resources, like they're all in the room encouraging her and cheering her on. I'm waiting to see myself born, but I'm not getting that picture.

LAUREL: [I can tell from what she's telling me that the process is stuck, so I do an interweave.] What do you need in order to be born? Check in with the baby.

CLIENT: I'm going to have my mom be awake! [The mother had been drugged and unconscious during her birth.]

LAUREL: OK, OK! So she can push.

CLIENT: She's not awake. She's out. They put her under. She's going to be welcoming and she's going to be happy (*laughs with delight to imagine this*).

LAUREL: Great, OK, so redo it. >>>>>

CLIENT: (*begins to sob deeply*) I feel like I'm almost there. >>>>>

LAUREL: (*I soothe and comfort her as she sobs, great heaving sobs, with the BLS going for several minutes.*) Take the time you need. Just tell me when to stop. You're doing great.

CLIENT: (*She opens her eyes as a signal to stop the BLS and begins to report, blowing her nose and wiping her eyes.*) So I imagined being born and like in the movies, the doctor holds me up in the air, and they pat you or something like that, and he said to my mom, "You've a healthy baby girl." And I imagined my mom taking that in and wanting to hold me and just be, "Oh my God, I've got a healthy baby," and just taking that in . . . and then I actually had her telling me that I was safe.

LAUREL: That's great, that's great. So how are you doing right now?

CLIENT: I'm good, I'm good. It's like part of me thinks it's time to wrap it up. [She thinks she is out of time and needs to finish her session, so I reassure her again.]

LAUREL: No, no hurry you're doing great.

CLIENT: I feel like it is moving. I don't feel totally there yet.

LAUREL: [I want to check the target again for progress.] Let's go back to the birth and just check and see what's still there. What do you notice?

CLIENT: It's much warmer now! I love this imaginal stuff! I think I've gotten hung up 'cause I can't remember what happened, and I'm feeling like I have to know what happened, and so this is very freeing to be able to just imagine.

LAUREL: Yes, so go back and see what comes up when you think of the birth.

CLIENT: It definitely feels like there's more color, and it feels warmer. I think I'm a little bit hung up in really believing that my mom could experience safety and communicate that to me.

LAUREL: Don't get hung up on reality! (*laughing together*) [Next I do a Socratic interweave to more fully link in the truth of her safety.] Let me ask you this: Was she safe? Were you safe?

CLIENT: Yes!

LAUREL: Go with that. >>>>>

CLIENT: (*begins to breathe heavily and to sob deeply, releasing the old belief from her system*) I was thinking that yes, she was safe, and I was safe and just trying to take that in.

LAUREL: Do you want to take that in some more? Take as long as you need to take that in, 'cause that was the truth, wasn't it?

CLIENT: It was the truth, yeah. I mean, that birth before me, it wasn't safe.

LAUREL: Right . . .

CLIENT: But I was.

LAUREL: You were.

CLIENT: I was, it went fine, yeah. She was OK, and I was OK. That's reality.

LAUREL: Yeah. You can just put that in. That is reality. >>>>>>>

CLIENT: Yeah (*tentative smile*).

LAUREL: What's coming up now?

CLIENT: I don't know (*smiles*). Maybe nothing!

LAUREL: OK, go back and check the birth and see what comes up.

CLIENT: I keep having the image of that white sheet below the knees or something. That's still in the picture. It feels like something that's dark, that's still hanging around. But it also feels warmer and with more color. That piece is still true. And there's another part of my mind that's starting to question, did I do it wrong. [Self-doubt comes up again, and I reassure her that she's doing fine.]

LAUREL: Do you want to make it go forward now? Out of the hospital and taking you home?

CLIENT: Yeah!

LAUREL: And now you're a healthy baby and your mom is taking care of you. Do you want to do that?

CLIENT: Yeah.

LAUREL: OK, so let's just do that. Imagine going forward.

CLIENT: OK, I'm going to go back to the part about being born and start there and go forward. >>>>> (*She begins to sob deeply. I use my voice for support and encouragement: "It's OK, you're doing great." She processes and cries for several minutes as I tap on her knees. She then stops, blows her nose, and reports.*)

CLIENT: So, that was me picturing my dad meeting me. He just loved me. That was really sweet. I remember him telling me that when they took me home from the hospital, that it was a beautiful spring day. They lived in New York City. They took a taxi, so that's where I was going. I was picturing being in a taxi with my mom and my dad and going home.

LAUREL: OK, so you want to keep going forward a bit?

CLIENT: Yeah. >>>>> (*begins to sob deeply again*) I just pictured being in a taxi with my mom and my dad, a yellow taxi. It was a beautiful April, spring, flowers, tulips, sun, and just being bundled up in the back seat and going home.

LAUREL: [I am very moved by her new narrative. It is full of color and love.] Great!

CLIENT: Oh, and I was thinking, "All is well, all is well."

LAUREL: Ah, beautiful! So now just go from the beginning to the end and see if there is any charge.

CLIENT: I keep coming back to the sheet. It separates us. [She is speaking of the sheet that separates her mother from the baby.]

LAUREL: Do you want to take it down? [This is an imagination interweave.] Take the sheet down. There's no need for the sheet. >>>>>

CLIENT: Yeah, it feels much better.

LAUREL: So is there anything there when you think of the whole thing? Is there any charge? Anywhere?

CLIENT: I don't think so.

LAUREL: On a scale from 0 to 10, how would you rate it now?

CLIENT: I think it's 0.

LAUREL: When you think of your birth now, what do you believe about yourself?

CLIENT: I was safe!

LAUREL: So hold that belief as you play the whole movie again. >>>>>

CLIENT: (*begins to sob again*)

LAUREL: [Her sobbing is more a releasing of old patterns than it is a sign of distress.] What's coming up?

CLIENT: Just nice positive pictures. The cheerleading team is in the hospital room. The sheet's down for my mom. She's got this team of people telling her she can do it and the baby's safe and it's fine. Everything's good, and then when I'm born, she wants me and holds me. And she tells me I'm safe. I meet my dad, and he's just in love with me and . . . yeah, he's happy and everyone's happy and I'm swaddled in the taxi riding home and it's spring (*smiling radiantly, happy and at peace*).

LAUREL: [I feel very moved. I wipe tears from my eyes. We laugh together, both moved.] Wow, That's so beautiful! It's so beautiful. So how's your body feeling now?

CLIENT: Good, yes, yes.

MOVING THROUGH DEVELOPMENTAL STAGES

After re-creating their conception, womb experience, and birth, some clients begin to go all the way through their lives, repairing the damage they experienced, re-creating a happy, healthy childhood, adolescence, and adulthood. I let them go where they want to go as long as it remains completely positive. If it should become negative, I'll do some kind of interweave, or direct them back to a place where it was positive. As clients reimagine their lives, they are laying down new tracks, new neural pathways, filling in the deficits.

I usually suggest that my clients progress chronologically, from birth forward, filling in what is needed as they go. Sometimes they move quickly through certain stages that were not as painful, spending more time repairing the ones where the most damage was done. Where did your client have the most harm? Perhaps he had a loving mother, but she died or became too ill to care for him. He can imagine bringing in a mother who could provide what he didn't get during those years. Sometimes clients linger in a particular stage of life, using their imagination to add in what they needed to repair. Encourage their open imagination. They can have anything they need. They don't have to limit themselves. In a way this is like make-believe games children engage in, playing house, building forts, creating fantasy lives. You play together with your clients to co-create what they need, letting them take the lead in their fantasy. This whole process can be fun and light, further helping to heal their attachment wounds as well as to bond you and your clients through your reparative therapeutic relationship.

Case Example

"Cassie" came to see me because she had a history of chaotic relationships. A professional woman in her late 40s, she functioned well in many areas, but could not seem to sustain a healthy, long-term relationship with a man. She wanted to change the old pattern and be able to have a healthy relationship. When I took her history, I learned that her mother was unhappy to conceive her and rejected her at birth. Cassie believed that her mother rejected her because she resembled her grandfather who had abused her mother when she was a child. Her mother never did attach to her. However, Cassie did feel loved and wanted by her father.

Cassie chose both auditory and tactile stimulation, placing the pulsers under her legs so that her hands would be free. Cassie was easily able to tap in resources. She chose her father as both a nurturing and a protector figure. In order to repair the early attachment wound, I believed it was important to tap in an ideal mother. When I asked her if she could imagine an ideal mother, a mother she wished she'd had who could be loving and nurturing to her, she came up with Meryl Streep. She said it was not Meryl Streep in any particular role she had played, but who she imagined Meryl Streep to be as a mother. I asked her to *imagine* Meryl Streep as a mother figure, and when she told me she had a good sense of her as "strong, loving, capable, intelligent, attentive," I began the BLS. After a short time, Cassie opened her eyes and said she had a good feeling for Meryl as a nurturing figure.

Because Cassie had such extensive attachment wounding from her rejecting mother, I asked her if she wanted to imagine being in the womb of Meryl Streep as her mother. She said she wanted to do that. As soon as I felt she had created the imagery and the feeling associated with that imagery, I again began the BLS. I was amazed by what followed. As the BLS continued, she began to narrate her experience. She provided vivid imagery and sensory detail on her own, without my prompting. I kept the BLS going as she was in the experience and seemed to be integrating it. She reported:

"I am happy in my mother's womb. She loves me, and I feel at peace. Then I am born to her. It is an easy birth. I come out and am placed on her chest. She looks at me with love. She is so interested in me, so welcoming. My mother never did that for me (silence for a short time). *Now she is bringing me home. I'm placed in a crib, but when I cry she comes and picks me up. She holds me and feeds me. She gazes at me as she nurses me. She is interested in everything I do. I look at her and she looks at me. I feel connected to her. I feel welcomed and wanted. My father is there too. He is looking at me too, and there is love in his eyes. He always loved and wanted me."*

Cassie's detailed reparative narrative continued for 40 minutes. Though she had never had children of her own, she seemed to know instinctively what a baby needed for healthy attachment.

When the session was over, she reported feeling good. She had a sense of well-being she had not known before. We did more sessions like this, imagining her birth and early infancy with Meryl Streep as her mother. She made rapid progress and felt hopeful about having better relationships.

CHAPTER 6

Case Histories of Repairing Developmental Deficits

What follows are two case examples of using an ideal mother and an ideal father in AF-EMDR. In the first case, the therapist, Prabha Milstein, helped her client create and tap in an ideal mother and then use this mother to repair early developmental deficits. The client continued this work in subsequent sessions, imagining herself progressing through different ages with different needs. In the second case, the client was a student therapist who volunteered to be in a class demonstration at my Advanced Clinical Workshop and Refresher Course, given at Esalen Institute. After tapping in an ideal father, he began an elaborate, creative imagination incorporating this father into a new alternate history as I tapped on his knees.

CASE EXAMPLE: CREATING AND USING AN IDEAL MOTHER TO REPAIR DEVELOPMENTAL DEFICITS
Prabha Milstein

"Susan" was a 40-year-old unemployed artist who sought treatment for symptoms of severe depression and anxiety. She lived with her boyfriend of 10 years, with whom she was having problems. She reported that he was secretive and was constantly looking at pornography on the Internet. Susan was very isolated and had lost friends due to her preoccupation with her partner. Raised in rural Kentucky by an alcoholic father and a cold, submissive mother, she had been physically, emotionally, and sexually abused as a child.

Over the course of our work together, it became clear that Susan wanted to address the abuse. Because of the level of deprivation and the lack of nurturing and secure attachment she had experienced as a child, I felt that she did not have the internal resources in place to do EMDR with regard to the childhood abuse. Instead we began by focusing on attachment repair, to which she was agreeable.

We used both the earphones and the vibrating paddles of the Tac/AudioScan. I asked her to imagine the mother she wished she'd had, the mother that would have fit her needs. Susan was a very bright woman with a vivid imagination. She began to create her ideal mother and used the entire session to fill in all of the details going through developmental stages. *I began the BLS at the beginning and left it on the entire time.* I was amazed and deeply moved by what she said. This was a woman who had not been nurtured by her mother as a child. I don't know where she got all the detail she reported here about healthy development. It was quite remarkable and ultimately healing for her. The following is her account of her ideal mother. *Please note that I prompted her when she seemed to have completed a stage of development.*

THERAPIST: Can you imagine an ideal mother, the mother you wish you'd had? You can make her any way you like.

SUSAN: Yes. >>>>> (*The BLS begins; the therapist prompts the client from time to time, but leaves the BLS on continuously.*) I'm filling in the parts of her—auburn, shoulder-length hair, kind face, twinkly eyes, mouth upturned. She's very wholesome, in tune with her baby. She looked forward to her pregnancy and giving birth. She had a mother who was available, and her friends supported her, were happy for her. All through her pregnancy, she sang and hummed to me, as an early welcome. She is married to someone who loves her and me, and whom she loves. I'm a newborn. She holds me close and smiles. I see love in her face and familiarity. She and I are one; she's never far away. I can always smell her, feel her, or hear her. She says my name. She touches me. She rocks me, walking me, dancing with me in her arms. It feels like perfect love. The noise level is calm and serene. She anticipates my needs, is very responsive. If I cry, she never lets me cry for long. She's always ready to make me comfortable. She planned to have me. I feel happy and giggle a lot.

THERAPIST: What happens at 3 months?

SUSAN: I'm making eye contact. It's great to lock eyes with the one you love. I cannot imagine not having this connection. I can see love, tears of joy, concern, laughter, so much is communicated. I start to process these expressions. I'm taking it in because I can.

THERAPIST: What happens at 6 months?

SUSAN: I'm cuter, active, I flail around, roll over onto my tummy, say *Mommy*, *Daddy*, and more. It gets better. I make a lot of sounds, mimicking Mommy. I love to let my mouth make sounds. I'm encouraged. I always feel safe, warm, well fed, rested.

THERAPIST: Nine months?

SUSAN: I feel strong, I can do everything. I'm able to say words. I'm crawling, trying to stand up. I'm not scared, because Mom will be there if I hurt myself. She encourages me. It's very important. My mom wants me to explore and try things. She's a confident person, and I feel that, and it rubs off on me. I have friends my age who come over and we play. It's fun to hear the laughter.

THERAPIST: One year?

SUSAN: I can see myself. I'm walking, stumbling. I like to dance in my diaper for Mom and Dad. They laugh and it encourages me. It's fun to be naked. My hair is growing long. My mom likes to brush it. It's an evening ritual. I can play by myself. I like to play with blocks, paints, crayons. I like to get my hands into that stuff.

THERAPIST: Two years?

SUSAN: I'm speaking in sentences. I like to use the word *mine* and *want*. I have needs. There's a shift going on. I love my mom but I need some independence. I need to venture. I'm developing and learning. I do it for spurts and then run back for reassurance and a hug and kiss. She's still there, watching and encouraging me.

THERAPIST: At 3 years?

SUSAN: I'm happy, growing, taking a ballet class for little ones. I'm a little shy, but Mom's always there. We have play dates with the girls in my class. This helps my shyness. I like that.

Mom wants to keep an eye on my friends. She loves me and spends a lot of time finding things to do together. I'm a big focus of her life. There's so much to do and see. I love to go outside and go to the park and the beach. We have a dog, and we run together. We have fun.

THERAPIST: At 4 years?

SUSAN: I'm in preschool. It's more structured than my days were before. She drops me off and picks me up. I love my teacher and my class. I'm happy when I see my mom at the end of the day. When I see her face, I feel better. She has a pretty face that's symmetrical. She lets me pick out my own clothes. I love showing her different outfits. I sometimes want to wear a tutu to school. She lets me. She helps me feel secure. She lets me express myself.

THERAPIST: Five years?

SUSAN: Kindergarten. I look forward to it. Mom is giving me a pep talk for big kid school. She'll miss me until she gets used to it. I hug her. I tell her she can come to school and sit next to me. My first day was a good day. I'm not stressed at home either. It makes a big difference. I love school. I love all the different stations. I love learning to read and learning the numbers. I soak it up. I love to draw most of all. When it's time for parent–teacher night, my mom goes. My teacher tells Mom how advanced my drawings are for my age. My mom remembers this.

THERAPIST: Six years?

SUSAN: First grade. It seems scary at first. I feel like a big kid. We have productive workdays in the classroom. I like my teacher. She has pictures of her kids in the classroom. I have friends, boys and girls. I don't shun anyone or exclude anyone.

At this point, we were close to the end of the 2 hours. I asked Susan how she was doing. She said that she felt very peaceful. She described feeling as if she were floating (in a good way). I suggested that she pay attention to her dreams and thoughts over the next few weeks.

Susan reported a great sense of peace at the end of the reattachment session. In subsequent sessions, she recalled her high school years, wanting to move toward fashion design, and the many obstacles in her path. I supported her, focusing on her dreams.

CASE EXAMPLE: CREATING AND USING AN IDEAL FATHER TO REPAIR DEVELOPMENTAL DEFICITS

"David" was a handsome man in his 50s who volunteered as a client for a demonstration session in my EMDR Advanced Clinical Workshop and Refresher Course at Esalen Institute. He said he wanted to repair the psychological damage he had experienced because of the abuse, neglect, and general chaos to which he was subjected as a child. He said that the trauma and neglect from his childhood had affected his self-esteem, self-confidence, and basic sense of safety in the world. In his previous EMDR sessions in the class practicum, he had developed an ideal mother that worked well to repair wounds from his emotionally unstable, abusive mother. He was feeling much better after these sessions and wished to create an ideal father to continue the healing. In the session described below, he created an ideal father that he used, to great effect, to heal the absence of a good father growing up. After creating this father, he imagined him as his mentor and guide throughout all the stages of his life.

This session took about an hour and a half, including the debriefing. Because this session was so meaningful and healing for him, and he knew I was writing a book about EMDR and attachment repair, David offered to let me use it for my book. After the session, he recreated the dialogue himself with as much detail as he could recall. As you will see, his memory for detail is quite remarkable, especially since he gave long, elaborate narration during the BLS. Because I was busy tapping on his knees, I only took notes on the resources and target at the beginning of the session, and then added to what he recalled to the best of my ability. What follows is our best attempt to recreate the session.

History and Background

David was the second child born to his 18-year-old mother. He described his father, who was 21 years old when David was born, as a career criminal who was sent to prison when David was a year old. He visited him once in prison when he was 4 years old, but never knew him or spent time with him, because his father spent his life in and out of prison. David's grandfather—his mother's father—was the family patriarch who sexually abused his mother and her sister. David's mother divorced his father and remarried a man who was withdrawn and violent. She was violent and abusive toward her son. David had difficulty thinking of any positive male role models or mentors from his childhood years. He did

remember a man whom he described as a "cool dad" who taught his Boy
Scout troop mountain climbing.

David had been married and divorced and had a daughter now in
college. He said that he had raised his daughter himself as a single dad.
When he spoke of his daughter his face lit up, the love and pride he had
for her obvious. I could tell that he was a strong, nurturing father—
a resource he would call on when he constructed his ideal father. He
was presently married and employed, doing work he enjoyed. Despite
his traumatic childhood, he was functioning well, but not as well as he
believed he was capable of.

The Session

We began by tapping in his basic resources, which he did easily. He
requested that I tap on his knees, instead of using the pulsers, as he
wanted the physical contact. His peaceful place was a beach at Mauna
Kea on the Big Island of Hawaii. His nurturing figure was "Mom in the
blue dress," the ideal mother he had created the previous session. His
protectors were Fancy, a collie he'd had as a child, and a wolf. For his
wise figure he chose the father of a friend, named Stanley, and himself as
the father he was to his daughter "Chloe." To construct an ideal father I
asked him to close his eyes and go inside.

LAUREL: Take a moment to quiet your mind. Now, can you imagine an
           ideal father, the father you always wish you'd had? You can
           make him any way you'd like. What qualities would he have?
DAVID: He'd be affectionate and fun. He'd have good boundaries.
           He'd read to me in his lap. We'd play at the beach. He'd be
           cooking and bring me into his world. I could lie against his
           strong body and feel safety and support around struggles
           without judgment. I'd feel acceptance by him.
LAUREL: (*When I could tell he was into the imagination and was actively
           creating this ideal father, I began tapping on his knees. I tapped
           as he spoke out loud.*) How was that for you?
DAVID: That felt great. I have a good sense of him.

I could see that David had a strong, active imagination and easy
access to resources. What I wanted to do now was find the earliest time
he could remember when he first felt the lack of a father and go up from
there. I wasn't sure how we would access this, but I was going to see what

we could find. My goal for this session was to create a father figure that could be used to repair the wounds in his life up the developmental line. I realized that this might be subtle work, and finding entryways might be difficult, especially since the *absence* of a father was all he knew.

LAUREL: Take a moment and close your eyes and go inside. See if you can connect to the feeling of lack, or to the longing for a father. Do you have it? (*David nods.*) Good, now go back to a time when you first felt the absence of a father. Go back as far as you can.

DAVID: (*silent for a few moments*) My mother, grandmother, brother, and I are in our Oakland apartment. There are no men. I am 2 or 3 years old. There's a table to eat at, with a box of corn flakes. I feel danger, instability, uncertainty, but I feel good about myself. I'm a stout little presence. I feel separate from all of them.

At this point I felt that his memory network was activated, so I began tapping on his knees. I tapped continuously as he narrated his experience. He gave quite a detailed account of his imagined repair. He brings in the ideal father he created spontaneously, with no direction from me. I am following him and allowing his imagination to do the healing. The dialogue that follows is how he narrated his experience, using the voices of the different people involved.

DAVID: I lock myself in the bathroom—good, separate. I look up to the window—too high, I could never manage that. [He is imagining trying to escape.] Mom is banging on the door— "Davey, open this goddamned door!" Gram's voice, Johnny's voice, unintelligible. More banging—I like being separate, I don't care if I'm in trouble. I hear a man's voice—my Dad. [This is his ideal father, the father he created and tapped in earlier.] He tells Mom and Gram to get back—he has to raise his voice and repeat himself. I have a floating, split view; I can see/feel a point of view of him on his side of the door, and I am on my side. I feel good that he's there, not surprised, not relieved.

LAUREL: [David now begins a dialogue between his "Dad" and his child self, "Davey." This dialogue is poignant and reparative. I continue tapping on his knees throughout this dialogue.]

DAD: Davey, are you in there?

DAVEY: Yes, I'm here.

DAD: Good, I'm out here. I'm going to sit with my back against the door. Would you like to do that?

DAVEY: OK.

DAD: I'm going to stick my arm out and put my hand against the door. Can you feel that?

DAVEY: Yes, I feel it. (*I have my back against the door and my left hand out to match his.*) This feels good.

DAD: You don't have to open the door until you want to.

DAVEY: OK. (*I open the door, come out and sit on my dad's legs, facing him with my legs on his sides. He hugs me gently, then holds me in his big hands and looks at me.*)

DAD: Come on, let's get out of here.

DAVEY: OK (*happy, feeling special*).

DAD: Wait, you're in a diaper. Let's get some pants on you.

DAVEY: (*My dad dresses me in jeans, a shirt, and shoes and socks, then picks me up and we head out the door. Mom, Johnny, and Gram are present but very background, grumbling. We ignore them. Dad and I are outside on the bright Oakland street. Dad picks me up and sits me on his shoulder, facing out. My left arm is around his head. His right hand holds me securely to his ear and the side of his head. I feel very peaceful and safe. He is big. I am high in the air.*)

DAD: Let's go to my place.

DAVEY: OK. (*We are at his place in San Francisco, up Russian Hill, lots of stairs, great view of the Bay Bridge, the lights of the city, the lights of Oakland. His place feels narrow, multileveled, masculine, tasteful, lived in, solid, warm, but sparely furnished. He is reading to me in a big chair with a light above it. The rest of the living room is in the dark. I am in his lap, but I see us from a point of view that is across the room and to the left of us. From my point of view, I feel the view off to my right. He looks up.*)

DAD: You live here now. That's Oakland (*referring to the view out the window*)—you don't live there anymore.

DAVEY: (*This feels good to me. Dad is putting me to bed in my room; my bed is against the wall in the corner, the view off to our left. He turns out the light, kisses me, then sits down just past my feet with his back against the wall. He puts his hand lightly on my chest and holds me and caresses me.*)

DAD: I'll just sit right here with you until you fall asleep. (*I slip imme-diately into sleep feeling absolutely safe, secure, and solid with my father.*)

DAVEY: (*Now we are at Gram and Grandad's house. I am with my dad; Mom, Gram, and Johnny are vaguely in the room. Grandad gets up from a chair and stalks toward my dad to hit him. He tries to bully my dad, who is much bigger and maybe a head taller. My dad pushes Grandad with his finger on Grandad's left pectoral muscle, and onto the brown leather couch Grandad plops.*)

DAD: Sit down, Ed. (*Grandad tries to push to get up to hit Dad, but Dad pushes him back down onto the couch with his finger again.*)

GRANDAD: You sonofabitch! Nobody tells me where to go!

DAD: You are never going to do that to anybody again! I have called the police.

MOM: (*approaching, afraid*) But what's going to happen?

GRAM: The whole thing is going to fall apart.

DAD: It's going to be fine—he's going to get help.

DAVEY: (*Grandad starts to cry and gets even smaller and younger. There's a knock at the door— it's not the police but an ambulance. The two attendants take Grandad away on a stretcher.*)

GRAM: (*suddenly very chipper*) Good! I was tired of him anyway.

JOHNNY [Davey's brother]:   But what's going to happen to Mom?

DAD: I know someone to help her. She's going to be OK.

DAVEY: (*The confused scene settles some.*) So are you and Mom going to be together?

DAD: No, Johnny will be with her and Gram, and you're going to live with me and they'll come visit.

DAVEY: (*This feels right and good, and it is what I want. I don't want to be with them and all that craziness.*)

At this point we take a short break and check in. Then David goes back inside and continues with his imaginative narrative while I tap on his knees. He begins to get older, bringing his "dad" into his life to repair more of his development. His father brings him into his world, the world of men. First, David narrates and I begin to tap on his knees again. I keep tapping continuously as he speaks aloud:

"The movie shifts to San Francisco again, by the docks. My dad works in shipping. He is an executive of some kind, administrating huge ships. He wears normal clothes at work, not suits. I am walking with

*him at work. I sense his pride and love in me as his colleagues and
workers encounter us.*

*"Next, I am at school in San Francisco, up in the hills. There are
trees. My dad helps me with my homework. He comes to my class to
read out loud every week. We make lunch in the morning. Johnny is
not part of this picture.*

*"My dad and mom are friendly and she does have a visiting pres-
ence. I feel her support (blue dress love) but she is not central. I
imagined a woman in Dad's life briefly, but she got no traction. [The
mom he is imagining is not his "real" mom, but the ideal mom he
created and used in the previous session, the mom in the blue dress.
Now he gets even older. I am not directing him; he does all of this
spontaneously.]*

*"I am in college at UCSB [University of California at Santa Barbara].
Dad is visiting me and we are body surfing naked off campus point.
I see us walking into the ocean with our untanned butts—genetically
similar. We are both big. Then we are at Mauna Kea playing tennis—
Court 1, first court to the right as you walk in. We are competitive, but I
beat him."*

DAD: Fucker, you aced me four times in a row. I can't believe it! No
          one has ever done that to me. God, I must be getting old!
DAVID: Those would have been aces even when you were young.
DAD: Not a chance!

David resumes his narration:

*"'Linda' [his wife] is down at the shore looking for shells. We see her
and go down to her and join in. She is a part of this family.*

*"Next we are on the beach at Mauna Kea with Chloe [their daugh-
ter]. She is young, maybe 3 or 4. My dad is delighting in her, holding
her up in the air and lightly tossing her the way I would. She giggles,
loving it. I am filled with love for them both. Chloe trundles over to me,
slaps both her little hands on my chest and declares 'Daddy!' as she
climbs into my arms. Then my dad holds Chloe out in the water. He
puts her on his back and says 'Hold onto my hair,' and they ride a wave
all the way into the shore, with Chloe laughing the whole way.*

"Next we are on the golf course at Mauna Kea, at the sixth hole, the over-the-water hole. Dad drives to the green easily. I hit ball after ball into the drink. Dad comes up behind me, puts his arms around me and says, 'Close your eyes. Feel the grip (his hands on my hands). *Now just let it happen.' I drive the green and my dad says, 'See, you can do this with your eyes closed.'"*

At this point David begins to sob. He is overcome with grief at not having had this dad in his life. I keep tapping his knees and saying things like, "It's OK, let it go, you're doing great," as he continues his narration.

"I imagine my mom [blue dress, ideal mom] there again wryly whispering to me, 'You do have this. Not having this never happened.' Suddenly I imagine being much older, and I'm spreading my dad's ashes at Mauna Kea—on the beach, a pinch on the tennis court, and down on the shore where the shells are. I think I'm done."

David cried as he imagined his dad's death. He said it felt like a good kind of grief, the kind of grief you have when you have been loved well and had a fulfilling relationship. "You always have the person within you. It is not a grief of lack or longing."

At the end of the session we returned to the scene in the Oakland apartment. It felt completely different: David wasn't there; he was with his dad. He no longer felt alone. He said that he felt a new kind of completeness. He felt whole and loved.

In the days that followed, David described feeling different, like he had been "rewired." His whole history felt different. He no longer felt fatherless. The ideal dad felt real, even though he knew he wasn't. The developmental holes that had always been there because of the lack of a father felt like they had been mended. He felt more present, secure, and solid in himself.

I had created a compassionate, steady presence for David so that he could do his own work. He trusted me to stay out of the way, yet to provide guidance as needed. From time to time he would open his eyes and meet my caring gaze. I was with him. The physical tapping also provided the sensory experience of my presence for him. I believe that was an important resource for him. With his eyes closed, he could *feel* me present for him.

The following is an excerpt from an e-mail I received from David:

Dear Laurel,

Wow, what a week. My nets are still abuzz. Here is the session to the best of my recollection. [He sent me his notes.] I wanted to hurry it up to you while you may still have some recall. You may have had a couple more interweaves in there, but for me, it was all so seamless and of a piece that I can't separate them out. Writing this up has relit the pathways. I feel very grateful to you, me, and my dad for the gift that this is. To suddenly have a dad after 57+ years, especially one this cool and deep—well, it is nothing less than a chunk of my identity, always defined by void or anti-dads, finally come home . . . finally completing that internal sense of home for me. Thank you.

Yours truly,

David

CHAPTER 7

Love Resources

L ove is an antidote for shame, anxiety, and fear. Because love is profoundly healing, it can be used as a powerful resource that can be
activated and tapped in for the repair of relational trauma and attachment wounds. Researchers have found that love can activate areas in the
brain responsible for emotion, attention, motivation, and memory and
help with stress reduction (Esch & Stefano, 2005). According to Selhub
(2009), "Love carries with it an ingrained biochemical function that creates bonding, attachment, and pleasurable sensations. Certain physical
processes occur in the body and brain when you feel love and you give
and receive affection" (p. 33). Furthermore, when one feels love, the
body releases peptides and hormones (e.g., endorphins, oxytocin, dopa-
mine, vasopressin, nitric oxide) that help turn off the sympathetic nervous system fight-or-flight response and evoke the relaxation response
(Selhub, 2009). It appears that certain circuits in the brain, along with
the release of these hormones and peptides, influence the attachment
created between parents and between parents and their infants. Because
love and affection release these hormones and peptides, it helps to create
a circuit by which the pleasurable feelings enhance the desire for more of
that contact. This process, in turn, helps people to bond, stay together,
and support one another (Selub, 2009).

Though they may not be aware of it, many of our clients have had
experiences of love. They may have been loved by someone during their
lives, and they may have loved someone or something. By drawing from
the reservoir of love in their lives and tapping it in, we can help many of

our clients with attachment trauma heal and better manage life's challenges. Contained in this wellspring are all the memories of loving and being loved, experiences with cherished family and friends from their past and present life. Even though they may lose contact with it, the love they have received is never lost. It continues to abide in their hearts. This reservoir of love can be tapped so that our clients are better able to make use of the gift. These resources can be tapped in, used as interweaves, and also used for session closure.

What follows in this chapter are many ideas and scripts you can use for tapping in/installing the resource of love (Parnell, 2008).

THOSE YOU LOVE

One of the easiest ways to help your clients tap into love is to think of the people whom they love. By accessing these memories and images, you can help your clients contact their soft, open hearts, which can help when they are feeling anxious, unsupported, sad, lonely, and in need of an infusion of comfort. It is also a powerful antidote to shame. Many of our clients feel bad about themselves. If they were unloved as children, they believe that somehow they were not worthy of love. They feel unlovable. But when they are able to contact memories of loving, they feel themselves to be loving people. The belief that they are bad is not so compelling. How can they be bad and loving at the same time? I have found that for many people, it is easier to develop the feelings of love by first focusing on those they love, and then, if they can, bring in memories of being loved. I believe that this process activates the mirror neuron circuitry.

What follows is a script for guiding your clients in tapping in those they love. You can direct the BLS using equipment, eye movements, or by tapping on clients' knees, or clients can tap themselves using the butterfly hug or tapping on the sides of their legs.

For example, your client might begin with her son, then bring in her husband, best friend, and then her cat. You can suggest: "Bring up the image of holding and rocking your son in your arms. Let me know when you have it." Then add BLS. Continue the BLS until she reports that the experience feels strong, integrated, and complete. "Now bring up an image or memory of loving your husband. Maybe it was when you were together on vacation walking hand in hand on the beach. When you feel that strongly, let me know." Then add BLS. Continue until the experience feels complete, more fully embodied. Then, "Think of a time when you were close to your best friend. Maybe it was having lunch together at

TAPPING IN LOVED ONES

"Take a few moments to go inside and quiet your mind. Find that still place within yourself and rest there a while.

"Now think, who are the people and/or animals from your past and present that you have loved? You can go all the way back to your childhood, to parents, grandparents, nannies, friends, teachers, or pets you had. Did you have a pet as a child with whom you felt a special bond? You can focus on those who are alive and special to you now. Think of your children, grandchildren, nieces and nephews, your dog, cat, or horse. Do you have a close friend you love?

"If the people or animals are deceased and you feel sad when you think of them, see if you can put these feelings aside and focus only on your love for them. Remember that this love never dies. What they gave to you continues to be a resource for you throughout your life.

"You might want to imagine a container made of something strong into which you can put your grief or sadness, or any other painful thoughts or feelings. The container can be a treasure box with a strong lid that you can open when you would like. In the meantime, putting these feelings in there will allow you to focus on the good feelings.

"Now bring up an image of a person or animal you love or have loved in the past. Bring the person or animal to mind as strongly as you can. The image should evoke only positive feelings. For example, you might imagine your daughter as a little girl sitting on your lap as you read her a story. As you bring this image to mind, let yourself feel your love for her. Let the feeling of love fill your heart as much as possible.

"When you can hold the image and the loving feelings, begin to tap. Tap 6–12 times, or longer, right–left, right–left, provided that the feelings strengthen or remain positive.

"If it should become negative in any way (e.g., sad memories, regretful feelings, and so on), stop tapping. Bring up the image you began with again and try to find the loving feelings. If you find them, tap again, but only a short time. If you cannot find the positive feelings, look for another being for whom you have loving feelings and evoke the image and feelings with tapping again. This time only tap a short while.

"You can repeat this process with many beings for whom you have loving feelings. Bring each one to mind, feel the feelings of love and affection, then tap to strengthen them."

your favorite Italian restaurant listening to one another, offering support and advice." Add BLS. Finally, "Imagine your cat sitting on your lap purring as you feel an upwelling of affection for her." Again, add BLS.

THOSE WHO LOVE YOU

You can also direct your clients to think about all those who love them, or have loved them (i.e., now deceased) and tap in this resource. They can think of people or animals from their current life or all the way back to their childhood. You can ask your clients to do a review of their life beginning with infancy, thinking of all those who have loved them. Then, focus on each one and stimulate the sensory memories, including remembered eye contact, tone of voice—anything that helps activate the feeling and its underlying right-brain activation.

What follows is a script to help you guide your clients in tapping in those who love them. You can do the BLS or clients can do it for themselves.

TAPPING IN THOSE WHO LOVE YOU

"Find a quiet place to be. Close your eyes and go inside. Bring your attention to your breath. Take some deep breaths and slowly let them out, relaxing and letting go with the exhalations. Do this for a few minutes, until you feel yourself present.

"Now bring to mind someone who loves you. It can be someone from your life now, or someone who has loved you in the past. They can be alive, or they can be friends or family members who are deceased. They can include parents, children, grandparents, aunts, uncles, brothers, sisters, friends, teachers, caretakers, counselors, and others. You might bring up a memory of being with that person when he or she was expressing his or her love for you or imagine the person expressing his or her love in some way, such as holding you or gazing at you with warm, tender eyes.

"As you imagine your loving resource person, you can increase the memory by activating the senses. What are you seeing, smelling, hearing, feeling? Take in this person's loving presence. Feel it in your body. Remember what it feels like to be loved, to be seen. Focus only on positive imagery and feelings. Put aside any memories or feelings of disappointment or loss.

continued on next page

> *"When you have a strong sense of your resource person's love for you, begin to tap on your knees or, using the butterfly hug, on your shoulders. Tap 6–12 times, right–left, right–left, strengthening the feeling of being loved. Really let yourself take in the feeling of being cared for. Let the feeling permeate your cells, bringing warmth and well-being to all of you. If the feeling keeps getting stronger, you can tap longer.*
>
> *"If anything negative should come up while you tap, stop tapping and return again to the positive image. Try to stay with only positive feelings. If you cannot do this, bring up another memory of being loved by the same resource person, or think of another person and then tap to strengthen that one.*
>
> *"After tapping in the first image, bring another loving resource image to mind—a friend, child, partner, or other person. When you have a strong image of being loved by that person, tap that one in to strengthen it.*
>
> *"Continue bringing up images of loving resource people and tapping them in as long as you like."*

CIRCLE OF LOVE

The *circle of love* uses the loving resources you have tapped in to give your clients even more comfort and support. The loving resources are imagined in a circle surrounding them, sending love. Clients can use this resource when they are feeling low, alone, and in need of support. The image of the circle of love can also be tapped in before going to sleep at night. As with any of these exercises, this one can bring up strong emotions. If this happens, stop the BLS and check in with your client. You may wish to focus just on the positive feelings again or even stop the installation. On page 112 you will find a script for the circle of love.

One woman reported that she included in her circle people she was loved by but also with whom she felt angry. She realized that she had closed her heart to these people who loved her. As a result, she opened her heart and felt grief. The grief felt healing, not bad, and she continued BLS on herself at home to process through it. I have found that grief can open the heart and that often people close their hearts to the love as a defense against grief. The use of BLS can help them process through the grief more quickly, and come to a heart that is open and feels cleansed. You can do the BLS or your clients can do it themselves.

TAPPING IN THE CIRCLE OF LOVE

"Imagine yourself surrounded by the loving resource people you have tapped in. Look around at these people who love you. Feel the sense of support of being encircled by their love.

"Now, focus on each loving person one at a time and imagine a ray of warm light of the color you associate with love coming directly from each person and entering your heart center. Focus on one person at a time, seeing and feeling his or her love light radiating into your heart center.

"Open to each one, until you are receiving love light emanating from multiple sources, radiating from each of them into your heart center.

"When you can feel the love, begin to tap, right–left, right–left. Continue tapping as long as the feelings are positive. You are the center of a wheel of love; your resource people and their love light are like the spokes. Take in this love light. Let it enter your heart and then permeate, radiate, throughout your body, until you are filled with the love light.

"Now, bring your attention back to your loving resources. Look at each of them and feel your love for them, one at a time. Now see and feel your heart radiating love light back to each of them. The love light goes from them to you and you to them as a continuous circuit of blissful energy. Stay with this image and the feelings associated with it as long as you can. Bathe in it. Soak it in. Let it support and nurture you. Continue to tap as long as it feels positive.

"Realize that this love is in you, always available. Feel the connection to those you love and who love you also. Let this connection support you and bring you comfort when you need it. Remember, it is always there. If you would like, you can imagine taking the love and support with you into a future situation.

"Tap as you imagine it."

THE HEART AS A PLACE OF REFUGE

Your clients can use their heart center as a place of refuge, a kind of safe place. Their heart center can serve as a gathering place for their loving resources. They can focus on their heart center and then evoke and tap in each resource, one at a time. You can direct them to imagine the resources in their heart, or just the feeling of them there. By focusing on their heart center and tapping in loving resources, clients are creating a resource to which they can return during times of difficulty.

I first used this exercise many years ago with a client who had such severe trauma, we couldn't find any kind of safe or peaceful place for him. His nervous system was highly reactive, and he was having surges of panic and adrenaline rushes. I knew that he loved his children very much, and that he seemed to calm down whenever he spoke about them. I could see that love calmed his sympathetic nervous system response. Using this information, I directed him to breathe in and out of his heart center. He was easily able to do this. Then I asked him to imagine his children, one by one, and feel his love for them. When he indicated he could do this, I began the BLS. I could see that he quickly calmed down, the tension in his face relaxed, and his breathing eased. With this resource installed, we used it throughout our work, and he could use it on his own to calm himself down between sessions.

TAPPING IN THE HEART REFUGE

"Bring your attention to your heart center. Let your heart become soft and warm. Breathe easily, in and out of this center, very relaxed.

"Imagine your heart as a place of refuge, a sanctuary, a place of safety and repose.

"Now bring to mind someone you love. As you think of that person, feel the love in your heart. If it feels right to you, you might even imagine holding the person in your heart center. Or you might experience in your heart the feeling of love that person evokes for you.

"When you have the image and feeling, begin to tap. Tap right-left, right-left 6 to 12 times. Tap longer only if it strengthens or remains positive.

"Now think of someone else you love. As you think of that person tap. Feel your heart center radiating love and warmth. You might experience a string of positive memories or associations. That is fine. Tap to strengthen the positive feelings."

LOVING-KINDNESS MEDITATION

I first learned *metta*, or the loving-kindness meditation, from Sharon Salzberg at a Vipassana meditation retreat she was co-teaching with Joseph Goldstein in 1976. From the Tibetan Buddhist teacher Lama Yeshe I also learned meditations that served to develop love toward self and others. I have written about them in several of my other books (Parnell, 1999, 2007, 2008), have taught many therapists these practices in my EMDR trainings, and have used them with my clients. Over time, I have combined elements from these various meditations and have adapted them according to the needs of different practitioners.

Many years ago I led a meditation group for women who had been sexually abused in childhood. It turned out that all of the group members had the diagnosis of dissociative identity disorder (DID). With their input, I adapted the meditation instructions in a way that was most helpful to all of their inner parts. (The child parts, in particular, needed to know how much longer they had to sit.) I have found that BLS can be added to these meditations to further strengthen and integrate the healing feelings they generate.

You can ask your clients to begin their meditation by sitting quietly and relaxing as they inhale and exhale deeply. This breathing can be followed by guided imagery to their safe or peaceful place, putting a protective boundary around themselves, and bringing in nurturing or protector figures, if needed. (The clients with DID needed the protective barrier during the meditation, as they didn't feel safe without it.) The loving-kindness meditation can then be done within the safe or peaceful place. You can record this script for your clients to listen to later.

What follows are several variations on this meditation, which can be used according to the needs of the client. You can use BLS continuously throughout the meditation, beginning as soon as the client experiences positive feelings, or use BLS intermittently in short sets. Clients can also tap on their own knees or, if they prefer, cross their arms across their chest and tap on either shoulder in the butterfly hug.

LOVING-KINDNESS MEDITATION BEGINNING WITH ONESELF

"Close your eyes and feel yourself sitting. Be aware of the places of contact: your bottom on the cushion and your feet on the floor. Be aware of your breathing, in and out. Feel the breath in your body. Let yourself relax into the present moment.

"Now bring your attention to the area of your heart. Breathe in and out from your heart. Let the breath be gentle and natural. In and out . . . in and out. Feel your heart becoming soft and warm. Mindfully observe your breath until you are calm and your awareness is focused on the here and now. Now begin to send loving-kindness to yourself, repeating phrases such as May I be peaceful . . . may I be

continued on next page

happy . . . may I be free from suffering . . . may I be filled with loving-kindness. *Find the words that work best for you.*

"Let the sound of your voice be gentle, with a cadence rhythm. Think of a parent gently rocking and soothing a child. The idea is to generate a feeling of warmth and tenderness toward yourself. As you send loving-kindness toward yourself, feel your heart becoming soft, warm, and receptive. When you can feel some warmth in your heart, begin to tap. Tap right–left, right–left. Continue tapping through the meditation as long as the feelings remain positive. If for any reason negative thoughts or feelings should arise, stop tapping and return to generating loving-kindness toward yourself. Begin to tap again when positive feelings return.

"Now think of someone you love. As you think of this person, allow your natural good feelings for this person to arise. You might imagine your love as a warm, bright light that is glowing in your heart. Now begin to extend loving-kindness to this person. May you be peaceful . . . may you be happy . . . may you be free from suffering . . . may you be liberated. *Use the words that work best for you to send loving thoughts to this person. As you do so, you might imagine light radiating from your heart to your loved one. Imagine this warm, luminous energy filling your loved one's heart with a feeling of well-being and loving-kindness. When you have the positive feelings, tap right–left, right–left. Continue tapping as long as it feels positive.*

"Now let your love flow out to others for whom you care. Let it extend to your family and close friends. You might even imagine them sitting near you. May you be peaceful . . . may you be happy . . . may you have ease of being. *Imagine the warm, luminous energy radiating from your heart, touching them and filling their hearts. Tap as you feel and see the love energy going out to others.*

"Continue to send your loving thoughts and energy out to all the other people around you . . . letting this feeling expand to include your community . . . town . . . state . . . country . . . continent . . . world . . . finally, the whole universe. Know that the source of this love is infinite, so as you send it out to others, you are continually replenished.

"At the end of this meditation you can imagine sending loving-kindness to all sentient beings in the universe. May all beings everywhere be happy, peaceful, and free from suffering. *When the meditation is over, sit for a few minutes longer and take in the feeling of love and expansion in your heart center. If it feels right, continue to tap as it expands. When the meditation is complete, remind yourself that you can always contact this feeling—it is your true nature, your warm, loving heart."*

Many people have difficulty beginning this meditation by generating loving- kindness toward themselves. It can be easier to begin by thinking of someone they love or care about first, and then sending the love toward themselves.

LOVING-KINDNESS MEDITATION BEGINNING WITH SOMEONE YOU LOVE

"After relaxing and breathing through your heart center, imagine someone you love in front of you. As you imagine this person, begin to send him or her loving-kindness. May you be peaceful . . . may you be happy . . . may you feel joy . . . may you have ease of being . . . may you be free from suffering . . . may you be filled with loving-kindness. *Imagine that warm light radiates out from your heart center into the heart of your loved one. When you feel your heart expanding, begin to tap. Tap as long as it continues to be positive. You might tap a little and then stop, check in with how you are feeling, and then begin again if it feels good.* May you be peaceful . . . may you be happy . . . may you know freedom from fear . . . may you feel joyful . . .may you be liberated.

"Now, bring up another person toward whom you have loving feelings. As you imagine this person in front of you, begin to send him or her loving-kindness. Tenderly send your loved one your loving wishes for him or her. When you feel the good feelings, begin to tap. Continue in this way, generating loving thoughts and feelings toward those you love and tapping when you have the loving feelings.

"After you feel your heart expanding, begin to include yourself in your generation of loving-kindness. May I be peaceful . . . may I be happy . . . may I be free from suffering . . . may I be filled with loving-kindness . . . may I have ease of being . . . may I love and receive love . . . may I be free from fear. *When you feel loving-kindness toward yourself, begin to tap. Continue tapping as long as it feels good, as the warmth emanates from your heart."*

If you wish, you can continue the meditation by expanding the feeling of loving-kindness further, as described above, suggesting to your clients that they expand it to their community, state, country, world, universe, and all sentient beings.

The loving-kindness meditation can be adapted to send loving-kindness toward the inner child self. This meditation can be especially helpful for clients who were abused or neglected as children and are frequently frightened, lonely, distressed, or triggered. If you and your client have done inner child work or you are familiar with their child parts—those aspects that hold memories from a child's point of view—the loving-kindness meditation can be adapted to help bring comfort to those parts.

INNER CHILD LOVING-KINDNESS MEDITATION

"Begin by relaxing comfortably. Close your eyes and go inside. Feel yourself sitting, your bottom on the seat, your feet on the floor. Take some deep, relaxing breaths. As you exhale, let go and relax. Let go into the earth. Let your body relax, easing into the present moment.

"Now bring your attention to your heart center. Letting your breath be soft and relaxed, begin to breathe in and out of your loving heart. Imagine your heart as a safe place, a sanctuary. Now imagine your inner child in your heart. . . . Your loving heart is a safe place for your tender child. . . . Begin to send loving-kindness to this child self. (In a soft, gentle voice repeat with pauses between phrases): May you be peaceful . . . may you be happy . . . may you be filled with loving-kindness . . . may you be free from fear . . . may you be free from suffering . . . may you be joyful . . . may you feel free . . . may you love and be loved. *Use the words that work for you. Repeat them silently to yourself as you send loving-kindness to your child self.*

"When you can feel warm, tender feelings, begin to tap. If it feels right, you can do the butterfly hug. Tap right–left, right–left. Continue as long as it feels good. Stop tapping if it does not feel good and return to thinking loving thoughts without tapping. May you be peaceful . . . may you be happy . . . may you be free from suffering . . . may you be free from fear . . . may you be safe.*"*

Continue in this way, repeating words of loving-kindness to their child self. You may want to ask your clients to imagine their adult self holding their child self in their lap as you repeat the loving phrases, and other nurturer resources may also be in the space sending them loving-kindness. The meditation can focus completely on the child self or it can expand to include others. This meditation can be adapted as needed.

CHAPTER 8

Additional Attachment-Repair Resources

In this chapter I describe additional resources that can be developed and tapped in for attachment repair. Many of our clients who experienced severe early neglect or abuse lack the early foundation upon which to draw during EMDR processing of traumas. Some of these clients have chaotic present-day lives, in which they lurch from one crisis to another. Many arrive late to sessions or don't come regularly enough to do EMDR. Because of the lack of stability, their therapists keep postponing EMDR trauma processing work until these clients are sufficiently stabilized. In some cases they will never be able to do EMDR because the clients remain too erratic.

I have found that the resource work can be very beneficial for these clients. It can be done in a short amount of time, and clients leave feeling better, not more stirred up. Many low-income clients from abusive backgrounds with unstable present-day lives do well with resource work. The resource work creates a foundation upon which the rest of the therapy can build. Some of these clients *never do EMDR trauma processing*, yet they derive great benefit from the tapping in of resources and the use of the resource protocol I outline in this chapter. What follows are more ideas for resourcing your clients.

THE THERAPEUTIC RELATIONSHIP

There are moments when our clients experience the therapeutic relationship as healing. We may have teared up when a client spoke of emotional pain, or he or she may have felt us present as he or she processed some deep material during EMDR processing. These moments of contact, connection, attunement, and rapport can be made explicit by the therapist, and then added BLS to more fully integrate them. Diana Fosha's *accelerated experiential-dynamic psychotherapy* (Fosha, 2000; Fosha, Siegel, & Solomon, 2009) makes use of these moments to help heal attachment wounds. After Diana attended my EMDR Advanced Clinical Workshops and Refresher course at the New York Open Center, she told me that what she would add to my AF-EMDR work was to make explicit those moments of contact, connection, resonance, and healing, and add the BLS to strengthen and integrate them.

I have long been convinced that our clients take us into their nervous systems as healing resources during EMDR. As compassionate, attuned therapists we help our clients feel safe as they process their traumas, and in the process, they experience the past in a new way. They are not alone; we are with them validating, witnessing, and supporting them through it. All of that is healing, and I believe that the BLS that we use in EMDR helps to more fully integrate the healing presence of the therapist and the therapeutic relationship. These corrective emotional experiences are essential to the healing of early attachment wounds in therapy. What Diana added, however, was that it can be even more potent to make these moments of connection explicit, and then to add BLS to install them. In other words, therapists can highlight the moments of connection, attunement, and empathy that the client experiences in the therapy, and then add BLS to integrate them more fully as a resource.

I have found that the explicit tapping in of the positive therapeutic relationship can be done most easily at the end of the session, at a time of reflection on what you went through together, and also during a talk therapy session when we are not doing EMDR. For example, when debriefing the session, say your client tells you how meaningful the session was for him. You might ask, "How was that for you when you saw me seeing you, or when you felt understood by me? How does that feel to you right now to be understood?" If the client responds positively, say, "Just take a moment, feel that, and then just take that in." You then add the BLS. As you make these moments explicit, you want to be aware of your use of eye contact, your tone of voice, and the feeling of empathy and connection as you add the BLS. Here is an example of what this process might look like:

CLIENT: It meant a lot to me that you didn't leave me in that scary place. I could feel your caring for me.
THERAPIST: Can you take a moment and let yourself feel that? Take in what it felt like for me to help keep you safe and care about you.
CLIENT: Yes.
THERAPIST: OK, great. (*Then add the BLS.*) How was that for you?
CLIENT: It felt good. This is very new for me. You are there for me.

You will be able to read examples of what this looks like in an EMDR session in the case presented in Chapter 16.

MEMORIES OF HEALTHY RELATING AS RESOURCES

Our clients have had many experiences in their lives of healthy relating that can be tapped in as resources. These may include memories from long ago of being loved, cared for, and seen by someone, as well as experiences from their present life. Times when they have coped well can also be tapped in to help strengthen them.

Memories of Feeling Cared for, Loved, Nurtured, and Seen

It can be helpful, when working with clients who have attachment wounds to go through their history and focus sessions on their *memories* of feeling cared for, loved, nurtured, and seen. When you focus on positive memories during their earlier years, it helps them to change how they feel about their life: It changes their life narrative from one that is trauma-focused and deficit-oriented to one that is much broader and includes positive life-affirming memories. You can ask your clients to review their lives with a focus on memories of receiving support, nurturance, or guidance from parents, siblings, grandparents, aunts and uncles, other relatives, neighbors, teachers, tutors, coaches, clergy people, friends, and lovers or partners. As they find something positive to recall, add BLS to more fully integrate it into their nervous system.

You might ask the client to run a movie of his or her life from birth forward looking for those kinds of experiences. There may be moments, brief experiences, which are valuable. As I said earlier, clients with childhood trauma don't attend to the positive or neutral experiences because they are busy scanning and taking in the bad things. So for them to purposely look for the good things is new. Clients might compile a list of these experiences and you can tap them in with them. Begin with the earliest memories and tap them in chronologically. These memories can be enhanced with BLS, which can bring out more sensory details and fill out the experience.

Some clients, when tapping in positive memories, will begin a string of positive associations and memories that further enhance the resource. For example, a client might recall a kind neighbor woman, the mother of one of his friends. As he taps her in, he remembers how much time he spent at her home as a child and how loving she was to him. He recalls that he always wished that she was his mother, and how important she was to him throughout the years. As the positive associations process, continue with the BLS. In many cases the connection with the resource is a wonderful new discovery. She was always there, but hidden away somewhere in another compartment of his mind. As he recalls her and the kindness she showed him, he doesn't feel as unloved or worthless. If you would like to enhance the resource, you could ask this client, for example, to bring up any sensory information he can about her—the perfume she wore, the smell of her house, the clothes she wore, the feeling of her hug when she greeted him. Beginning with one of the sensory details and then adding BLS can help others to be recovered and available. In this way the resource is stronger and more "real" to clients.

Let's say a client recalls being listened to and cared for by a certain teacher in grade school. Ask the client to bring up the memory, with the emotions, body sensations, and other sensory components, if possible. Then add the BLS. This processing of positive memories breaks up the client's old story of never being listened to or cared for, and new associations may arise of other times a significant person listened to the client. Suddenly, she may see that she has created an erroneous assumption about herself and her life. EMDR processing of the positive life experiences can dissolve the solidity of the negative self-concept, as BLS strengthens what is positive and adaptive.

"Sally," a client with an early history of physical and sexual abuse and the traumatic loss of her mother as a young child, struggled with chronic depression. We focused several EMDR sessions on fragments of memories of being loved by her mother. Part of Sally's trauma was the loss of the *memories* of her mother; this loss resulted in Sally's difficulty in providing nurturing and comforting to herself. We began the bilateral knee tapping while she focused on body memories (she had no visual memories) of her mother holding her in her lap, and she could feel her mother's comforting embrace as I tapped on her knees. Visual memories emerged during the sets of tapping that strengthened the feeling. Prior to the resource installation, she believed that she had not been loved and was therefore unlovable. After strengthening the positive memory of her mother loving her, she felt that her mother *did* love her and she could assert that she was lovable. Later, we used the memory of her mother during the processing of traumatic memories to help with interweaves and session closure.

Experiences from Present Life of Connection, Attunement, and Nurturing

You can tap in experiences from your clients' present life of connection, attunement, nurturing, and any other experiences of healthy relating. They may have had a tender experience with their own children, their partner, or a friend that can be emphasized and tapped in. You can review their week and highlight any of these types of experiences and tap them in. Perhaps your client had an abusive childhood, but is currently in a loving relationship. Memories and experiences of the current relationship can be tapped in. It can be as simple as the time the client came home from work upset, and her husband gave her a hug. Healthy interactions with their own children can be tapped in—those times when they provided the nurturing and care for their children that they themselves didn't get as children. The times when they loved, protected, defended, listened to, and cuddled their children can be tapped in.

Memories of Positive or Neutral Experiences and Adaptive Coping Efforts

Memories of positive or neutral experiences and adaptive coping efforts can also be tapped in. You can ask your clients to do a review of their lives, beginning at conception, and to find one or more things each year that were either positive or neutral. When they locate the experience, add BLS. You can progress from conception and birth to the first months, the first year, second year, and so on. If, when you add the BLS, they associate in a positive way remembering good things, go longer with the BLS. If it should become negative, stop and refocus on only positive or neutral memories. In this way they are changing the internal narrative or schema of their lives, adding in new neural pathways. You can also ask clients to contact their adult self, or a witnessing self, that then observes the life story as the BLS is employed. This part can also remind them that they grew up and they survived.

One man with whom I worked had a terrible history of emotional neglect. He suffered from a chronic low-grade depression and diminished self-esteem. His early childhood was quite bleak and included sexual abuse. We began our resourcing by focusing on any positive memories he had of his childhood. We focused on these positive memories and added BLS to allow him to associate to them and install them. As a result of this work, his depression and the global feeling that his whole life was miserable lifted, and he felt lighter and more hopeful.

HEALTHY BOUNDARIES

Clients who had intrusive parents may have difficulty with the nurturing or connecting resources. They may need help developing and tapping in healthy boundaries. What do healthy boundaries look like? What do they feel like? Once clients answer these questions, you can help them use their answers to construct a barrier or boundary. It can be as light as a bubble or a more formidable barrier. This boundary work can stimulate a very energetic process. The client creates the image, articulates the feeling that goes with it, and then you or the client adds BLS. How did that feel? For example, if the image of her mother sitting next to your client makes her feel awful, yucky, you can ask her, "What do you need to feel safe?" Perhaps she needs to create a boundary. "Where would you like your mother to sit? How far away?" The client can create an imaginary boundary or she can imagine putting her mother at a distance where she feels more comfortable. When the client can imagine that boundary and can feel it, tap it in. Ask her, "How does that feel?" If it feels good to her, say, "Pay attention to that," and add BLS. You can also help your client discover where she feels comfortable with you in the room, and setting a physical boundary with you. In our example, I would move my chair increasingly closer to the client until she signals me to stop, noticing the signals in her body that indicate where her sense of safety ends. Then we would add BLS. You can also tap in memories of setting boundaries, and examples of others who are good models of setting boundaries and saying "no." You can give your clients homework to practice setting boundaries and also to notice how they feel when they are around different people.

One of my clients had an engulfing mother whom she was always taking care of. When her mother was near her, she reported feeling "dirty and violated." Her mother was needy, helpless, and highly emotional, and she used her daughter for her own emotional regulation. This client needed boundaries, so we worked with this area in our session.

LAUREL: Imagine your mother next to you. What do you feel? Now imagine creating a boundary around yourself that keeps your energy in and your mother's out. It can be made of anything you would like. It can be a force field, a wall, a bubble. When you have created the boundary, and can feel your own energetic integrity and your mother outside of it, let me know.

CLIENT: I've got it. >>>>>

I told her that she could practice using this boundary on her own.

RESOURCES FOR DIFFERENT ATTACHMENT STYLES

You can work on developing the resources your clients need to repair their attachment deficits. What is their attachment style? What do they need to develop a healthy way of relating? You can add in resources that fill in the gaps. For example, if the client has a need for connection, then add in memories, experiences, fantasies, and any recent experiences of connection, using BLS to install them. If they have a need for more emotional regulation and calming, add in resources that help to soothe them. If it's a need for safety, add in those.

Case Example

A 36-year-old woman came to treatment with anxiety and depression. She was married and had a 6-year-old daughter. She was a highly intelligent professional who functioned well at work, yet dissociated easily in relationships. Her trigger for dissociation was around her fear of loss of connection. She identified no big traumas in her life. It seemed that her dissociation and symptoms were linked to the lack of emotional connection she experienced growing up.

When her therapist tried to find a target for EMDR by bridging back from her triggers, she was unable to find a target with any emotional charge. In fact, they had difficulty finding *any* targets with charge for EMDR. This was because her symptoms of dissociation were associated with a *lack* of attachment, a deficit trauma—she was like a balloon that could just float away. Even though she had been taken care of materially as a child, she did not receive validation, reflection, attunement, or connection from her parents.

In order to begin to heal these deficits, the therapist looked for moments of connection in the client's present life and installed them. She made explicit the times of connection between herself and her client, and directed her client to tap in moments of connection in her life now. These included times when she felt connected to her daughter, and times when she felt connected to her husband. What does she feel in her body when she feels connected? What does she feel emotionally? The therapist asked her to "take it all in" and then added the BLS.

SCENES OF HEALTHY RELATING FROM BOOKS, MOVIES, TELEVISION, OR YOUTUBE

You can focus on and tap in scenes from books, movies, television, or even YouTube that show healthy relating between people. You can purposely direct your clients to read certain novels or watch movies or DVDs that illustrate healing relationships. In the novel and film *The Help*, there is a tender, nurturing relationship between a maid and a little girl Mae Mobely. The maid, Aibileen, recognizes that the child is not loved by her mother who is obviously not attached to her, and so attempts to repair the damage as much as she can by holding the child on her lap and telling her as she rocks her, "You is kind. You is smart. You is important" (Sockett, 2009, p. 443).

Aibileen makes an excellent nurturing figure, or ideal mother, and many clients have used her as such. If clients resonate with this scene, you can ask them to imagine it, to feel the comfort, nurturing, and well-being, and then to add the BLS. They can imagine the scene from the point of view of Aibileen as the nurturer, from the perspective of the child, or from "outside" as an observer of both.

The same can be done with other media. If the client has seen something lately that touched him, the scene can be imagined with BLS to further install it. You can find anything on YouTube these days, and scenes of healthy mother–infant bonding, healthy relating between father and child, and so forth, can be found and installed. The idea here again is to activate, through imagination, the imagery and feelings associated with them and then add the BLS, which helps to create new neural pathways.

Other attachment-repair resourcing protocols you might want to explore to augment your toolkit are Shirley-Jean Schmidt's (2002, 2009) *Developmental Needs Meeting Strategy*, April Steele's (2007) *Develop-*

ing a Secure Self, Phillip Manfield's (2010) *Dyadic Resourcing*, Katy O'Shea's *The EMDR Early Trauma Protocol* (2009), and Peggy Pace's (2012) *Lifespan Integration*.

SPIRITUAL RESOURCES

Spiritual resources can be evoked and tapped in to provide support for the work. Evoking spiritual resources can create a larger context within which our clients can view their lives and their problems. I have found that for some clients, tapping in spiritual resources gives them courage and support to go into difficult places with me, and can be the most powerful of all the resources we install. These resources are often used in interweaves, to provide comfort, to speak words of wisdom and advise, and to protect them.

Spiritual Figures

Spiritual resources can include spiritual figures such as Jesus, Mary, Moses, God, Kwan Yin, the Buddha, angelic beings, spirit guides, or images from nature. These figures are imbued with a power that feels numinous and suprahuman. After clients identify the spiritual figure, you can ask them for more sensory detail to fully evoke the experience. As clients hold in mind the image and feeling of the figure, add BLS to install the resource.

If the spiritual figure had appeared in a dream or had been called on in the past for support, memories of these times can be recalled and the positive images and feelings further strengthened with BLS.

An example of installing a spiritual resource with a client occurred with "Molly," who felt a strong affinity with Kwan Yin, the female Buddha of compassion (Parnell, 2007). Molly brought up the image of Kwan Yin and as she held the image of the goddess and the feeling of compassion and strength in her mind, I tapped on her knees. She felt the image strengthen and experienced a more intimate relationship with Kwan Yin. Afterward, when Molly felt overwhelmed by the terrible memories of abuse she was processing and the excruciating physical pain she felt in her child's body, she would take a break and imagine being held in Kwan Yin's loving arms. I would tap on Molly's knees to install this feeling of warmth and safety from a power that felt infinitely compassionate and untouched by abuse. After feeling renewed energy from the experience, she would return again to the disturbing memory and process it to the end. Her ability to shift from being in the midst of a traumatic memory to the experience of love and safety gave her a sense of increased control and confidence in the therapeutic process.

Another client contacted a figure she referred to as her childhood "spirit guide." We spent time bringing up memories of help she had gotten from her inner guide. I knew that her spirit guide could be a resource when and if she needed it. It helps to remind our clients that their spiritual figures are always close at hand; they need only focus inward, recall them, and tap them in to increase their felt connection with them. In this way clients can do their own resourcing at home when they need to call up the support from their resources.

Spiritual Experiences

Clients can also process and strengthen spiritual experiences. These might be experiences they had in nature, a peak experience during an athletic feat, or an experience during meditation or prayer. Some clients had spiritual experiences in childhood that were significant to them. After installing these experiences, they can be recalled to bring strength and comfort. One of my clients had a visionary experience as a child that involved Jesus. By recalling this experience from childhood and adding the BLS, she was able to reevoke it, along with the feelings of awe and compassion. She was able to use Jesus as a resource during EMDR, and if she needed, to connect to her spirituality to bring up the childhood experience and add BLS.

Spiritual figures are part of an inner support team for some of my clients. In any event, after the installation of resources, traumatized clients will feel more support; they are not alone, as they were when they experienced the trauma.

The Essential or Core Spiritual Self

I use the term *essential spiritual self* to refer to the essence of who we are, a core of goodness that has been there since the moment of conception. This is the part of our clients that has never been touched by any of the bad things that have happened. It has always remained in the background. I described this concept in *A Therapist's Guide to EMDR* (Parnell, 2007) and *Tapping In* (Parnell, 2008) and have used it with many clients. The essential spiritual self remains conflict-free. It is the silent witness behind all experience. It is the part that knows that the child is innocent and that the parents are the ones who are responsible. It is a kind of higher self, a deeper self. It is the aspect of our clients that is whole already, and with which, as therapists, we align and resonate to help them actualize this wholeness. No matter how damaged our clients may seem as a result of their childhood trauma, this part remains undamaged and whole. The essential spiritual self can be used as a resource that strengthens clients and gives them a sense of hope, and it can be used for an interweave. It is a helpful antidote to shame, as what was done to clients does not affect this essential self.

Maggie Phillips talks to most of her clients about this core essence: "You have an experience, an energy inside, a self, if you will, that when you are whole, when you're fully connected, then you are connected with the essence of who you are, of who you were created to be" (Parnell & Phillips, 2012). The language you use with your clients in describing this core spiritual self depends on the belief system of your clients. Some clients will recognize this part of them immediately and feel seen by you, whereas others will struggle with it or even reject it. I believe that even if they reject it, we as therapists need to remember this essential wholeness about our clients, and, in a sense, hold it for them. They then will feel us seeing them in this way, resonate with it, and begin to recognize it.

The question is, how do you find the essential spiritual self? One way is simply to talk about it, and if clients recognize this notion, then you can ask them to bring up a memory of a time when they experienced it, and then add BLS. You might say: "Can you think of a time when you recognized that there was a part of you that was untouched by what was happening to you? This could be like a wise, dispassionate witness to your experience that knew that you were essentially OK." If clients answer affirmatively, ask them for the memory or their sense of that part of themselves and add BLS. You could tap in many experiences they might have had with this part of themselves.

You can also recognize moments in the therapy when the client has an experience of the core spiritual self—perhaps during EMDR processing when a wise perspective emerges, or even at the end of the session. Clients commonly connect to this part of themselves at the end of EMDR sessions. They say, "Who I am was never touched by what happened to me." They recognize this core essence in those moments. You can make explicit this aspect of the higher self and thereby help to integrate it by adding BLS. You might say: "I want you to take a moment and connect with that part of you that sees, yet has never been touched by, what happened to you. This part of you that has always been there, and is whole." When they can connect, add BLS. In this way we are helping to integrate this information. Then, if you would like, you can add a future template: "You can contact and tap in this part of yourself and then use it as a resource for wisdom and support when you need it." The essential spiritual self can also purposely be contacted through the use of guided imagery, like the one in the box that follows.

TAPPING THE ESSENTIAL SPIRITUAL SELF

"Find a quiet place to sit where you won't be disturbed for a while. Close your eyes and go inside. Feel yourself sitting. Take some deep breaths in and slowly let them out. Relax and let go with the exhalation. Take another deep breath, breathing up from the center of the earth, filling you, and then releasing your breath back down into the earth. Let go of all the tension in your body and mind as you exhale. Take some more deep breaths, relaxing with the exhalation.

"When you feel relaxed, imagine going to your safe or peaceful place. Take as much time as you need to go there. Look around—what do you see? What do you hear? What bodily sensations are you aware of? How do you feel in your special place? When you feel good and relaxed, tap a few times to increase the feeling.

"Now, in your special place, allow yourself to connect to your essential spiritual self. This essential part of yourself was there before you were born, and has been there all your life. This is the part of you that has been with you through all you have experienced in your life, yet has not been touched by any of it. This part of you is pure, good, innocent, wise, and resilient. This is the core of your being.

"When you have a sense of your essential spiritual self, tap 6–12 times and then stop to check in with yourself. If the connection and feeling are strengthening, tap some more. Tap as long as it feels positive.

"If a name for your essential spiritual self comes up, take note of it and tap it in.

"If it seems right, allow an image to arise of your essential spiritual self. If no image comes up that is fine. If you have an image and would like to, you can tap to strengthen your connection to the image. Remember that your essential spiritual self is always with you. You can contact it whenever you need to. All you have to do to contact it is to imagine it, say its name, and tap. Or simply think of it and tap."

Higher Power

Many people relate to the concept of a Higher Power. Some might call this God. This Higher Power is seen as providing wisdom, guidance, and a broader perspective. Clients may have had an experience of a Higher Power. It may have come during a time of great duress, while in nature, or during meditation or prayer. Contact with a Higher Power provides comfort and a sense that there is something much greater than oneself directing the unfolding of one's life. Learning to listen and attune to the wisdom expressed through the Higher Power provides a foundation for healing work. All the 12-step programs draw from this understanding.

Clients can contact memories or a sense of their Higher Power and tap it in to strengthen the feeling and make it more accessible. In so doing clients can call on this internalized Higher Power to provide wisdom and direction and it can be integrated into EMDR work as a resource and used as an interweave.

TAPPING YOUR HIGHER POWER

"Close your eyes and go inside. Take a few moments to find that quiet place inside yourself. You might take some long, deep breaths to calm your mind. When you are quiet inside, imagine going to your peaceful place. This is your special place where you are at ease and can be fully who you are. Spend as much time as you need in your peaceful sanctuary.

"Now open yourself to experiencing your Higher Power. You may have a direct experience of it in the moment, or you may recall a time when you had a strong feeling of it. Allow yourself to experience it in whatever form it takes.

"When you have a sense or feeling of your Higher Power, tap 6–12 times. If you would like to tap longer, you may continue as long as it feels positive and the contact with your Higher Power strengthens.

"If you have a problem for which you need guidance, a request, or a question, you can speak to your Higher Power.

"Now listen for the response. Be open to receiving it in the way in which it comes. You may receive it in words, pictures or feelings.

"When you receive the message, begin to tap. Tap as long as it feels positive.

"Imagine what your life would be like if you followed the guidance of your Higher Power. Tap as you imagine it.

"Remember that you can contact your Higher Power at any time. It is always with you. You are never separate from it."

RESOURCE INSTALLATION FOCUSING ON A CHALLENGING CURRENT LIFE SITUATION, BLOCKING BELIEF, OR MALADAPTIVE SCHEMA

Leeds and Korn (1998) presented a protocol for the identification and installation of resources that focuses on helping clients come up with the resources needed for current life difficulties, blocking beliefs, and maladaptive schemas. This protocol is helpful for clients who do not have the ego strength to do EMDR, who cannot handle the emotions and distress EMDR might stir up for them in their current life. It is also used for clients with good ego strength for performance enhancement. The following is a modification of the Leeds and Korn protocol that I have found helpful (Parnell, 2007).

1. You can begin the identification of the needed resource by asking the client to focus on a current life situation that is difficult for him or her, a blocking belief, or a life issue.

2. Next ask your client what quality or qualities he or she would need to better deal with the situation, belief, or issue. Explore with the client times when he or she had that quality or qualities. If unable to think of one, the client can think of someone else who dealt effectively with this type of situation. The person could be someone he or she knows personally, someone from a movie, TV, book, historical or religious figure, or anyone else. It could even be a symbolic representation of this resource.

3. Next ask your client to describe the image or memory in more detail. Have the client provide sensory detail: What does he or she see, hear, feel, smell, or taste? What emotions and sensations does he or she feel and what does he or she feel in the body?

4. You can ask your client to say a cue word or phrase with the resource he or she wants to amplify. The installation of the positive resource may or may not be done, depending on the client. Some clients will flip to the polar opposite when the BLS is used or may begin processing traumatic memories. For others, the addition of the BLS will enhance the client's felt sense of the resource.

5. The installation of the positive resource is done much like with the standard protocol for traumatic memories: The client is asked to focus on the image, feelings, and the cue word or phrase (if one is used), and the therapist adds the BLS. A short set of BLS is used: 6–12 passes or taps initially (one right–left sequence equals one pass). Watch the client

for changes. If he or she looks distressed, stop immediately. Otherwise, after the set ask the client what comes up for him or her. If the client reports that the positive feelings have gotten stronger, continue for more sets of BLS. Stop the BLS when you feel that the resource has been strengthened. If the processing has become negative, stop immediately and consider choosing another resource.

6. You can repeat this process for many different qualities that the client wants to develop and strengthen. A future template can be added, in which the client imagines using the resource in different situations.

For example, a client comes in for treatment because she is having difficulty at work. She feels intimidated by her boss and does not know why. Whenever he comes up to her desk, she becomes speechless, feels stupid and small, and can hardly think. She is puzzled by her reaction because he is a nice man and has done nothing to cause her current feelings. This is a pattern she has experienced in relationship to many men. When you take her history, you learn that she was physically and sexually abused by her father, a tyrant who controlled everyone in the family. Because her symptoms are troubling her in the present and interfering with her ability to do her job, you want to give her relief as soon as possible. Because of the number of abuse incidents, she is afraid that opening them up will make it harder for her to function. She is not ready for the intensity of EMDR trauma work. The issue she identifies is having difficulty feeling her own power and standing up for herself with men.

THERAPIST: When you think of the situation with your boss at work, what picture is most disturbing to you?

CLIENT: It's when he is standing next to my desk looking down at me.

THERAPIST: When you bring up that picture, what emotions do you feel?

CLIENT: Fear.

THERAPIST: What quality or qualities would you need to handle the situation the way you would like?

CLIENT: I would need strength and power.

THERAPIST: Can you think of a time when you had strength and power?

CLIENT: Yes. A couple of weeks ago my daughter came home from school and told me that her teacher had humiliated her in front of the class. I immediately called the principal and teacher and arranged to meet with them. I told them that this was wrong and that it could not happen again. The teacher apologized to my daughter and me.

THERAPIST: When you think of that situation, what picture comes to mind that represents the moment when you felt the most strength and power?

CLIENT: I see myself facing the teacher and principal in the class-room. I feel strong.

THERAPIST: Good. Now I want you to close your eyes for a moment and really feel what that feels like in your body, the strength and power. When you have a good sense of it, let me know and I will tap on your knees.

CLIENT: (*Takes a moment, nods her head. Therapist begins BLS. Therapist notices a relaxation in the client's face.*)

THERAPIST: What do you notice now?

CLIENT: I feel strength in my legs and arms.

THERAPIST: Focus on that. >>>>>

THERAPIST: What's happening now?

CLIENT: I'm remembering another time when I was strong and stood up for myself.

THERAPIST: Go with that. >>>>> (*Continues following the client's positive associations until they finish, then returns to the picture with the boss.*) When you bring up the picture with your boss, what comes up for you now?

CLIENT: I feel bigger, more in my adult self.

THERAPIST: Are there any other qualities you might need?

CLIENT: Yes, self-confidence.

THERAPIST: Can you think of a time when you were self-confident?

CLIENT: No, I can't think of any times.

THERAPIST: Can you think of someone you know, or even someone from a movie or book?

CLIENT: Oprah. She has self-confidence.

THERAPIST: Close your eyes and go inside. Bring up an image of Oprah displaying self-confidence. As you see that image, what do you feel in your body?

CLIENT: I feel energy in my legs, and my back feels straighter.

THERAPIST: Focus on the image and feeling in your body. >>>>>

THERAPIST: What's happening now?

CLIENT: I feel better, it feels good.

THERAPIST: Let's return to the picture with your boss we started with. What comes up for you now?

CLIENT: It feels OK. I feel more like an adult now.
THERAPIST: Go with that. >>>>>
CLIENT: It feels better. He's a nice man. I really like my job.
THERAPIST: Can you imagine yourself at work in the future?
CLIENT: Yes.
THERAPIST: Imagine that. >>>>>

They then close and debrief. The cue word *Oprah* can also be installed with the resource. To do this ask your client to repeat the word *Oprah*, along with the image she has and the associated feelings and body sensations; add BLS. Then, when she wants to summon the feeling again, she says *Oprah* to herself, which should elicit the positive feeling of the resource.

You can also anchor a physical act with the resource. This is done by adding a physical act, such as pressing the thumb and middle finger together, as the cue word, image, and feelings are activated; then add BLS. As in this example, the client would (1) imagine Oprah and the feelings of self-confidence she experiences in her body, (2) say the word *Oprah* to herself, (3) press her thumb and middle finger together, and then (4) add BLS. Later, if she is in need of self-confidence, she can say the word *Oprah* silently to herself and put her thumb and finger together to elicit the feeling.

Part III
USING EMDR

CHAPTER 9

Creating the Safe Therapeutic Container
Preparation for EMDR

This chapter explores ways to integrate an attachment-repair orientation into the preparation phase of EMDR with clients who have had relational trauma. These ways include the development of the therapeutic relationship, how to gather history while maintaining a connection with your clients and helping them to feel safe, and assessing readiness for EMDR. Suggestions are provided on how to introduce EMDR; the choice of BLS; the seating arrangement; and the use of safe touch, eye contact, and safe objects. You will also learn about distancing techniques, the use of an imaginal container, and the importance of reinstalling resources before the processing of traumatic childhood incidents.

DEVELOPING THE THERAPEUTIC RELATIONSHIP

Before beginning the use of EMDR in the treatment of clients with relational trauma, you want to develop a safe, connected therapeutic relationship. I think of the therapeutic relationship as the foundation of the therapy. Everything you do builds on this foundation. Like the secure base a child enjoys with a healthy parent, a good therapeutic relationship provides a foundation of internal support from which the therapy can build.

The therapeutic relationship begins to develop from the first contact you have with your clients. This may be the first phone conversation you have with them, or when you see them the first time. These early impressions can be significant to clients, causing them to feel safe or unsafe with you. Most people feel anxious when they first come into therapy with a new therapist. Clients who have had significant traumas or are anxious may feel particularly vulnerable and uneasy with a new person. We want to be sensitive to these issues and help our clients feel at ease with us. Everything you do should help your clients feel safe in your office. Safety is foundational to the therapeutic relationship, and to the therapy, especially with clients who have attachment trauma. Even the way we greet our clients in the waiting room makes an impression on them. Do we meet them with a smile, with a distracted face, or with a blank face? One client remarked that it made her feel happy and valued that I always seemed glad to see her.

FOCUS ON SAFETY AND ATTUNEMENT RATHER THAN INFORMATION GATHERING

Everything we do and say makes an impression on our clients. With that in mind, we want to be sure that our focus is on our clients, rather than on how "perfectly" we apply any protocol or procedure. We want to help our clients feel comfortable and cared for. When my clients are settled in, I ask them what brings them to therapy with me. I listen to how they tell their story. I ask them about their symptoms and try to get specific information. For example, if the client says he has anxiety in social situations, I might ask him to give me examples of this: "Do you have difficulty at parties? Do you have difficulty when you know the people well? Can you give me an example of when this happened?"

Often in the beginning I let the client tell me his or her story and listen carefully. As I listen I am attuning to my client and feeling with him or her. I am picking up the level of anxiety, the places in his or her story where there seems to be more emotional charge, any negative beliefs that stand out, and the way he or she relates to me. The connection between us begins right away. Does my client keep eye contact, or does she look away from me as she speaks? Is there an easy rapport, or is he suspicious and withholding? In the first session, I am gathering information about the presenting problem, getting a history of the presenting problem, and developing goals for treatment. I may even take a good developmental history and install resources. It all depends on the client. However, with everything I do, I am integrating an attachment-focused orientation. I am attuning to my clients and feeling with them. I am listening to their words, and listening for what is under the words, the feeling that they may or not be aware of. I am connecting and empathizing with them. I am conscious of the need to help them feel safe with me in my office. *The focus is on safety and attunement, rather than on information gathering.* I am also optimistic about clients' capacity to heal, but I do not make any promises or guarantees.

As with standard EMDR, I explain what EMDR is and how it seems to work. I explain how I think EMDR may be useful for them in particular. For example, if my client has severe social anxiety rooted in childhood trauma and neglect, I will explain that EMDR can work on reprocessing the traumas so that they lose their emotional charge, and that we can use imagery and BLS to fill in some of the deficits that occurred in response to the neglect: "EMDR can be used to clear the traumas you have, and we can use positive imagery with bilateral stimulation to fill in the areas that didn't develop because of what you didn't get as a child." I might also explain about neuroplasticity and how the brain is able to change, as well as the power of imagery to create new healthy neural pathways.

TITRATE INFORMATION GATHERING

As noted, in the first sessions you want to find out about the presenting problem, what the symptoms are, the history of the problem, the goals for treatment, and what clients have tried in the past to address these problems. I wrote about these steps in more detail in *A Therapist's Guide to EMDR* (Parnell, 2007). Instead of two separate phases, I think of phase one (history taking) and phase two (preparation) as one phase. Trauma therapy is described by many, including myself (Parnell, 1999, 2007; Herman, 1992), as a three-phase treatment: The beginning phase focuses on stabilization, the middle phase on trauma processing, and the end phase on integration. In this first phase we are preparing our clients for the intensity of the trauma processing work. While many of our clients don't need as much preparation as others, those with complex trauma, or those who have disorganized attachment, require more preparation and stabilization work. I have described this extended process in detail in *EMDR in the Treatment of Adults Abused as Children* (Parnell, 1999) and in *A Therapist's Guide to EMDR* (Parnell, 2007). One caveat in this stage: With these clients, you must be very careful in the history taking that they do not become flooded or retraumatized by giving you too much of their trauma history.

After I have gathered information about the presenting problem, I ask my clients to give me a history of their life, beginning from birth. *They don't have to give you details.* I want to get a kind of outline so that I know generally what is in their history. The history provides me with a sense of my clients: how they are organized, potential targets linked to the presenting problem, their early attachments, and something about the coherence of their personal narrative. I want to get their life narrative and hear how they are able to tell it.

As we know from the AAI protocol (Main, 1992), we can learn a lot about our clients from how they tell their story. Are they able to tell their story? Do they have a coherent narrative that holds together, makes sense, has insight, and is integrated? A narrative that is coherent is correlated with a secure attachment. Though their childhood may be rife with trauma and neglect, the narrative may be coherent, indicating that the attachment may be one that was "earned" through reparative relationships. Are there big holes in their narrative—big gaps where they lack information or have no memories? Such gaps may indicate either trauma with dissociation or neglect in childhood with no mirroring or validation from parents or caregivers. Do they jump all over the place as they tell their story, going from the past to the present? How do they relate to you as they tell you their story? Do you feel connected, or do they keep you at a distance? What is their affect as they recall their history? Are they emotionally overwhelmed, crying, or disconnected?

As far as content, I want to get the history of their lives from birth (or conception) to the present time. I want to know about their early attachment relationships with mother, father, siblings, or any other significant people in their early years. This can include nannies and extended family. For many clients, their parents were not the primary attachment figures in their early years. Sometimes it is the grandparents or nannies who raised them and to whom they are most closely bonded. What was the quality of these attachments? I want to know if there were any losses or disruptions early on. In one case, already mentioned, the client had loving parents, but her mother had lost three babies before her birth. The client's relationship with her mother was profoundly affected by these early losses. In another case, which I wrote about in *Extending EMDR* (Manfield, 1998), the client was having difficulty bonding with her own baby in part because her baby resembled her sister when she was a baby. The client had been very close to her mother until her baby sister was born and took her place on her mother's lap. Her anger at her mother for her displacement caused her to reject any overtures from her mother and to disconnect from her. Later, she had difficulty bonding with her own daughter. Ask if there were any traumas during the early months and years of their life. Were there any medical procedures, separations, or losses? I try to get a picture of what their life was like.

For some clients who have difficulty recalling their childhood, I'll do a guided imagery to try to fill out the picture for myself. I might guide them to a peaceful place and then invite their child self there. I might ask, "How old are you? What do you look like? How do you feel? Tell me a little about your life. How do you feel about your daddy? How do you feel about your mommy?" In this way I am contacting the child network and learning some of the information stored implicitly in the right hemisphere. You can do this for any age for which you want more information. If a scene or an image pops into their awareness, invite clients to fill it in with more information. You can even use BLS to help enhance and fill in the history. I have found that this approach provides me with a kind of snapshot of their childhood.

A range of problems can occur in early childhood that can affect attachment, many of them not related to the mother's capacity to bond, but to other circumstances such as the following possibilities:

- Being born prematurely and being separated from the mother
- Loss of a twin in utero or at birth
- A mother's postpartum depression
- A mother's illness following the birth of the baby or afterward
- The birth of a sibling
- The client's development of an illness early in life
- A mother's PTSD
- A mother's experience of a loss, such as loss of a husband, parent, or someone close to her
- The primary caregiver, such as a nanny or grandparent, leaving or dying
- Being given up for adoption
- Mother's emigration to another country and inability to take her children
- Mother's need to work to survive and inability to provide the care her children need
- A mother with too many children to care for without enough support
- A mother's addiction or abuse of alcohol and/or drugs.

I have learned to keep an open mind with regard to parents. I have often seen that a parent may have experienced something that affects the bond that was not the parent's fault, such as a loss experienced at the time of the birth or a medical condition. I have also seen that some parents are better with their children at different ages. Some parents improve as they get older and more mature, or they receive medication needed to manage their depression or bipolar disorder, get into recovery, or leave an abusive relationship. In addition, there may be one parent who is more stable and nurturing than the other, who is dismissing or abusive. One client had a very nurturing mother who was married to a violent man who terrorized the two of them. The client's internal settings were disorganized because she couldn't depend on her mother to keep her safe, and she was regularly sent into high sympathetic response because of the terror her father inflicted on them. In later childhood her mother escaped her father and was able to create a safe environment for her daughter. But the emotional damage had been done to my client. As an adult, her nervous system was easily dysregulated, and she had difficulty in relationships because she couldn't trust anyone to care for her consistently.

After learning about their infancy and early childhood, I ask clients about their school years. How did they do in the classroom, and how did they do on the playground? Some children are secure until they get to school. They may have learning disabilities, attention-deficit disorder (ADD), attention-deficit/hyperactivity disorder (ADHD), or separation anxiety. Many children who are abused or traumatized look like they have ADD or ADHD and are misdiagnosed. They are anxious and have poor attention spans because of unprocessed trauma. Traumatized children have difficulty concentrating. Many depressed children act aggressively and then become labeled behavior problems. This label compounds the esteem issues that originated in their unsafe home environment. They believe they are bad, stupid, and worthless. Because they may have been misdiagnosed, they often don't get the help they need to learn to regulate their nervous system and develop inner resources. I also ask how they survived their childhood. What did they like to do? The answers to these questions help me learn about their resources, inner strengths, and capacities.

How did they do in adolescence? Did they use or abuse drugs or alcohol? How did they relate with peers? What was their sexual development like?

What were the significant events of their adult life? I inquire about relationships, marriages, children, losses, jobs, health issues, substance use/abuse, and any traumas they might have experienced. I inquire about the important events and people in their life. Along with the traumas, I want to learn about any experiences and people who served a resourcing function.

If I see that my client is becoming distressed in the process of telling her story (there are too many traumatic experiences), I will ask her about positive experiences from her past or her present. We need to be sensitive to helping our clients remain emotionally balanced and feeling safe in everything we do with them. So if a client has just told me something that brings tears to her eyes, and she is beginning to feel overwhelmed or to dissociate, I can "change the channel" and ask her about what she liked to do as a child: "What were your favorite things to do as a child?" When she begins to tell me about how she loved to sing in the choir, I can ask her to pay attention to how she feels as she thinks about that, and suggest that she tap the sides of her legs to increase and integrate that feeling. If she has difficulty thinking of anything positive from her childhood, I can ask her about her present life. "Tell me about things you like to do now. What brings you pleasure now?" When she tells me about going to her daughter's soccer games and rooting for her, I can ask her to focus on that and I add BLS to help install those feelings and sensations.

As with all clients I see for EMDR, I assess for affect tolerance, ego strength, coping skills, mental illness, stability of their current life, substance use/abuse, and their general health. Do we have a connection? Do we have a rapport? Do I feel I can work with this person? If I assess that the client is too fragile, I do more resource work to strengthen and build in new neural pathways of positive resources. If I feel a client needs medication, I refer him for a medication evaluation and wait to do EMDR trauma processing work. If I suspect that the client has DID, I will refer her out to a therapist who specializes in working with this diagnosis. (See *A Therapist's Guide to EMDR* [Parnell, 2007] for more information on assessing for readiness for EMDR.) The box on page 144 provides a basic template for assessing EMDR readiness in an outpatient setting.

THERAPEUTIC CONTAINER

The therapeutic container is a nonlinear way in which I get a feel for whether or not my client is ready for the processing of highly charged material. If I don't feel the container is strong enough, I do more resourcing, or work to fill in the "holes." Sometimes the client has some areas that are quite strong and others that are not, and I just feel that we need

---

QUICK ASSESSMENT OF READINESS FOR EMDR

1. Do we have rapport? Do I feel I can work with this person?
2. Is he or she committed to safety and treatment?
3. Can the client handle high levels of affect? Can he or she install a peaceful place, other resources, and respond to guided visualizations?
4. How is the client currently functioning? Does the client have support via family, friends, community?
5. Does the client have a medical condition that may require a physician consultation to assess safety issues with EMDR utilization?
6. Is the client abusing drugs or alcohol? Does the client have other self-harming behaviors?
7. Does the client have a mental illness that would contraindicate the use of EMDR until he or she is stabilized? Does the client need a medication evaluation?
8. Does the client have DID?
9. Is the client involved in an active legal case?

---

to do more ego-strengthening work, whereas there will be clients who seem to have deficits in many areas, but my sense of their container is that they can handle the work. This is more of an intuitive way of assessing a client's readiness for EMDR. Figure 9.1 represents this "container."

FIGURE 9.1

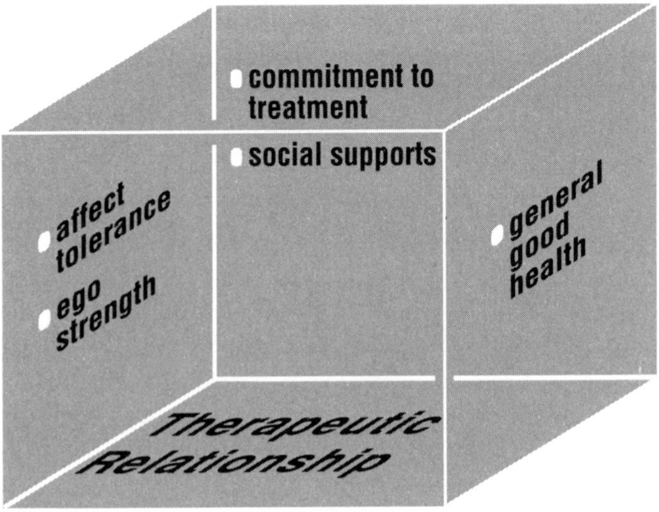

Beginning Resource Tapping/Installation in the First Session

You can begin resource installation/tapping in the first session. I might do this with a client who has become activated in the history taking and needs to calm down before he leaves. I can guide him to a safe or peaceful place, and then add the BLS. I can show him how he can do this for himself if he should become distressed before I see him next. In this way my client has a tool he can use to help regulate his own nervous system.

I want my clients to feel empowered, and to experience my office as a safe place. Clients appreciate receiving tools they can use immediately. A man I saw had been traumatized from war and also had an abusive stepfather and an unloving mother. After telling me about some of what happened in war, and about his troubled childhood, I could see that he was upset. I immediately taught him about the peaceful place and the nurturing and protector figures he could access within. He responded very positively to the resourcing. He left my session feeling balanced, at peace, and optimistic about his ability to be helped by me.

PREPARING THE CLIENT FOR AN EMDR TRAUMA PROCESSING SESSION

In this section you will learn some suggestions for how to prepare your clients for a trauma-processing session of EMDR including suggestions for how to introduce EMDR, choosing the type of BLS, creating signals for continuing or stopping, and using safe touch and eye contact. You will also learn how you can include safe objects, support people, or animals in sessions, using distancing techniques, creating an imaginal container for affect management, preventing memory chaining and flooding, and reinstalling resources.

Introducing EMDR

I often introduce my client to EMDR beginning in the first session. I explain what EMDR is, some of the theories about how it works, and why I think it might be helpful to him or her. I might, as I mentioned earlier, teach clients resource tapping in the first session so that they experience how the BLS can calm them down and can use it as a self-regulating tool. I direct them to things they can read about EMDR, including some of the books for the general public, such as *Transforming Trauma: EMDR*

(Parnell, 1997), *EMDR Made Simple* (Marich, 2011), *EMDR Essentials* (Maiberger, 2009), and *EMDR* (Shapiro & Silk-Forrest, 1997). There are also DVDs available showing what EMDR sessions look like, such as those I have produced and that are available through my website (www.emdrinfo.com).

Along with explaining EMDR and the basic procedure, I also explain about resource tapping. I explain that it can be helpful to create new neural pathways in the mind and body to fill in areas that were not fully developed. I explain that the resources can be used to calm down, decrease anxiety, and to make one feel stronger and more resilient. The resources can also be used to create a safety net before we begin the trauma processing, and will be available to use if the processing should become stuck.

Type of Bilateral Stimulation

I introduce my clients to a variety of types of BLS and ask them to see what feels best for them. I tell them that what it is most important is that they feel comfortable with whichever modality they choose, and that they can change it at any time. Though there has been some research (Andrade, Kavanagh, & Baddeley, 1997; Kavanagh, Freese, Andrade, & May, 2001; Sharpley, Montgomery, & Scalzo, 1996; van den Hout, Muris, Salemink, & Kindt, 2001) indicating that the eye movements may be more effective for diminishing the vividness of memories, these studies only used eye movements versus tapping and not the full EMDR protocol. I question the validity of any research that compares eye movements to tactile or auditory stimulation if subjects' eyes were not immobilized in the comparison groups. I say this because I have often observed clients' eyes rapidly moving under their eyelids while receiving auditory or tactile BLS, very much resembling the eye movements seen in rapid eye movement (REM) sleep states. How can eye movements be compared to other types of BLS if the researchers haven't kept the comparison groups from moving their eyes? As far as I know, this has not been done and therefore the comparison is not a "clean" one.

I am not convinced that this research is significant enough to direct clients to use eye movements (EMs) if they are inclined to choose another form of BLS. There are many problems with the use of EMs. For example, many people feel assaulted by the sight of a therapist's fingers in front of their face, and they don't feel comfortable with someone sitting so close to them. Some clients don't want to keep their eyes open because they cannot connect to themselves and their feelings with their eyes open. Furthermore, it is difficult to move one's eyes back and forth while crying, which clients often do through an abreaction. Clients with eye problems, eye injuries, or blindness should not or cannot do EMs. Clients who tend to become easily hypnotized may go into trance with EMs. Clients who have a history of seizures should not do EMs. I have found that clients "resist" doing EMDR more when EMs are used because they complain of feeling tired, and they don't want to exert the physical effort it takes to do EMDR with EMs.

There is yet another factor that causes many clients to reject EMs. It is what I call a *weirdness* factor. It is weird to follow someone's fingers with your eyes. Even using equipment, which allows directed EMs, is somehow weirder culturally, than, say, holding little pulsers in your hands or listening to auditory stimulation. Clients are more likely to accept the use of BLS, other than EMs, if they feel comfortable using it.

The argument that recommends EMs because closed eyes lead to dissociation is also inaccurate. Clients can open their eyes while receiving tactile or auditory stimulation in order to create more distance and reinforce dual-attention processing, or close their eyes to go deeper into the memory network. In fact, clients have more flexibility in their regulation of the intensity of their processing with the other types of BLS. When they wish to close their eyes for more privacy or when crying, they are able to do so instead of being forced to keep their eyes open moving back and forth through their tears.

I believe it is most important to discover what works best for each person. This is the client-centered approach that is reparative. It is the most humanizing and compassionate way of working and communicates to clients that they are most important and that you are attending to their unique needs.

I typically introduce clients to the Tac/AudioScan, which has tactile pulsers clients hold in their hands or put under their legs, and head phones through which they hear alternating bilateral tones or other sounds. I let the clients adjust the speed of the alternating sounds or pulses, the intensity of the tactile stimulation, and the volume of the sound. I have found that clients have their own preferences, with some liking it very slow and soft, and others loud and fast. I assure them that there is no "right" or "better" way to do it. I explain that they want the BLS to be in the background and not to be a distraction or interference.

Some clients cannot tolerate technical equipment. Their nervous systems may be very sensitive, or they require a human touch because of their attachment wounding. These clients may prefer that I tap on the sides of their legs or on their hands. One client, who had been physically abused as a child, had a very sensitive nervous system and could not tolerate the machine. I offered to tap on her knees. She directed me to tap very lightly and very slowly. Because of how soft and slow the BLS was, I wondered if it would even work. But it did, and she was able to install resources and process with EMDR to the same degree that occurs when I go at a faster pace. I believe that this slow, soft BLS helped her feel safe with me, enabling her to feel that I was attuning to her needs.

When introducing touch, you need to be aware of all of the issues it may bring up. I am particularly careful with a client who has been sexually abused, especially if the abuse was by someone female. I would never suggest using touch with some clients because it would be too triggering and feel too unsafe to them. You, yourself, must be comfortable touching your clients. If you are not comfortable, your client will feel this and take this discomfort into his or her neural nets in a way that would not be healing. If you or your client are not comfortable, do not do it. The use of tapping on your client's knees, hands, or sides of legs should be discussed first, of course, before doing it. If you both feel comfortable, you can go ahead with the understanding that the client can ask you to stop if at any time he or she doesn't feel comfortable, and you can do something else.

When I tap on my clients, I scoot my chair up so that I am sitting in front of them. I prop my wrists on the sides of my legs, lean forward, and tap the sides of the client's legs. I do it this way to put as little stress as possible on my wrists, which get tired from the repetition of the movement. Some clients like to go long sets of BLS, which can be hard on my wrists if I tap on their knees without support for my wrists. I ask my clients how fast they like it, and what pressure they prefer. I then set up a rhythm, which I keep during most of the processing, but I tend to speed up while they go through an abreaction. I prefer not to tap on their hands (but it can be done) because it requires clients to keep their hands on their knees, which inhibits them from moving them if they wish to express something with gesture, or to even be able to wipe their eyes or blow their nose. (See DVDs of my work that demonstrate this at www.emdrinfo.com).

The bilateral tapping is very intimate. I have found that the attunement between my clients and myself is enhanced by the physical contact. We seem to drop into a deep state in which I feel what they feel as they process. There is a kind of merged experience in which I am with them in their past as well as in the present, aware that they survived and are able to get through what they are processing. Clients report that the physical tapping helps them feel physically connected to me as they process painful material. *The touch seems to provide a somatic resource.* They don't feel alone in their pain because they feel the connection to me as they process the past.

Because it is physically difficult for me to tap on a client's knees for long periods of time, I have found that by offering to hold their hand or hands as they process, while the equipment provides the BLS, clients are able to feel connected to me and derive benefit comparable to my tapping on them.

Signal for Continuing or Stopping

As is standard in EMDR, I like to set up a signal for *stop*. Clients might raise a hand as a stop signal, say the word *stop*, or open their eyes if they have been using BLS other than EMs. The signal can be used as an emergency brake, "I want to stop now!" or, as is usually the case, simply a signal that clients have completed a wave of processing and wish to report their experience. Even if a signal hasn't been set up initially, clients usually find a way to communicate that they are done with something and wish to report. I have found that a hand signal for *keep going* can be helpful to establish too. Sometimes we stop the BLS while our clients are still processing. The hand signal gives them a means of communicating to us without further disrupting their processing.

Seating Arrangement

Along with the type of BLS you use, you want to determine where you and your client will sit. Clients who have had intrusive, engulfing mothers may want you to sit quite a distance from them, whereas a client who has craved contact may want you to sit much closer. One client was very fearful about beginning EMDR with me. She projected her intrusive mother onto me and was easily triggered. I often needed to apologize and repair misunderstandings so that she could feel safe. When she was ready to begin EMDR, she asked that I sit as far from her as possible, and she wanted to use the light bar. She also instructed me to watch her all the time, let her use long sets of EMs, and not stop her until she said she wanted to. She needed all the control to enable her to feel safe. This worked quite well, and after a few weeks she no longer needed me to sit so far from her, and she was much more relaxed.

Another client who had not been well nurtured by her mother, asked that I sit next to her on the couch and put my arms around her shoulders when processing a memory of being burned as a baby. This level of closeness and touch brought comfort to her that she had not felt at the time. Not only could she not be held because she was burned on her back, but she said that her mother blamed her for the incident and did not comfort her.

I believe it is important to be flexible and adapt what we do according to the needs of the client. Chairs with wheels can be helpful for accommodating client's needs for closeness and distance. I watched a video of Daniel Hughes working and saw that he sat close to his clients when doing attachment-focused work and also incorporated safe touch. It is important that clients have control over both the degree distance and the use of touch to enable them to feel safe and regulate their nervous systems.

Safe Touch

Many years ago I worked with a client who had been terribly abused and neglected as a child by both of her parents. This client taught me the power and benefit of using safe touch during EMDR. I have always been cautious about using touch with clients, and I still am because of all that it can elicit in the transference. But I have also seen how beneficial it can be for some people. This client had already had years of therapy and knew what she needed to feel safe in EMDR. She told me that the resources we installed were not sufficient. She said that she lacked the resources to feel internally safe and contained while she processed. If I would sit close to her and hold her hand, she told me, she would be better able to tolerate the intensity of the work. Following her lead, we developed a way of working together that was healing and reparative.

This is what we would do: After deciding what she wanted to process, based on her triggers, we would install her resources. She would place the tactile pulsers under her legs so that her hands were free. She had a spiritual nurturing figure, as well as animals, and strong protector figures. Then I would bring my chair close to hers and take her hands in mine. She would meet my gaze, and then close her eyes. Sometimes she would process the entire session with me holding her hands. Sometimes she would release them at the end of a set and then hold them again when she would process, while at other times she would hold them in the beginning, and through the worst trauma abreactions, and then let them go when she felt calmer. On occasion she would grip my hands tight, feeling me there with her. It was important to her to *feel* me there with her.

She told me that she would not have been able to do the work without this touch. Over time she needed the handholding for less time in the session, until she no longer required it at all. She had processed the traumas sufficiently and had internalized the resource I had provided by my touch.

I learned a lot from this work with her and have applied the lessons learned with other clients, with good results. I believe that the physical contact creates a somatic resource that adds in the creation of new, reparative neural pathways for the client. At the time of the trauma, she was hurt and all alone. This time, as she reprocessed the trauma, she was connected to a caring person. I believe that she literally took the safety and support of my felt presence into her nervous system, and she would describe it that way too. *The imaginative resources were not enough for her.* She had very strong, loving resources, but she still did not feel safe enough to process the childhood traumas.

I asked Daniel Siegel (2007) about what might be occurring with handholding. He told me that there was research that showed that holding a person's hand decreases his or her experience of pain (Field et al., 2008). Indeed, researchers have found that hand-holding decreases the stress hormone cortisol and lowers blood pressure and heart rate. It also increases the release of oxytocin, which affects behaviors such as trust and bonding (Field et al., 1992; Hertenstein & Weiss, 2011). The vagus nerve, which controls the parasympathetic nervous system, is also activated by pleasant touch (Rolls et al., 2003). I believe that what was happening for my client, in part, was that I was helping to regulate her pain and stress level, decreasing it to a point where it felt manageable, within her window of tolerance (Ogden & Minton, 2000). The hand-holding created a somatic resource that provided her what she needed: stronger walls for the therapeutic container.

I might also add that it was very important to her that I listened to her needs and accommodated them. I was not bound by a theory that kept me from discovering what worked best for her. The very process by which we discovered the power of handholding in EMDR was reparative.

I have used this approach with other clients in different permutations—perhaps putting a hand on their knee—or have used someone else, such as a friend or partner, to provide the physical contact. One client who'd had severe physical and sexual abuse asked that I sit with my knees touching her knees and then tap on the sides of her legs. Though this may seem very intimate, it is what she needed and requested to feel safe, more grounded, less dissociated, and connected to me as she processed. (See "Attachment-Focused EMDR with a Client with Severe Early Sexual Abuse," DVD, www.emdrinfo.com.)

Use of Eye Contact

The use of eye contact can also create right-brain to right-brain healing of attachment wounds. Clients can keep their eyes open if they wish, meeting the therapist's soft, caring gaze. This contact goes directly into their nervous systems. Sometimes a client will close her eyes, and then open them during the processing, meeting my eyes. It is soothing for her to see me seeing her. She is not alone. The client in the above example would open her eyes at times, and at others she would close them. She could regulate the intensity and the connection to me in this way. One man who'd had a mentally ill mother kept his eyes locked with mine the entire session. He needed to take in my calm, grounded presence to counteract the "craziness" to which he had been subjected as a child. He also did not feel safe enough to close his eyes. For the client to see you seeing him can be very reparative. So many of our clients with attachment trauma were not seen or connected to by their caregivers.

There are also clients who do not feel comfortable with eye contact. Allow them to do what they feel most comfortable doing, and meet them there. One man avoided eye contact because of the shame he carried inside. Over time he became comfortable with more eye contact. This gaze aversion can also be a cultural issue; people from some cultures are not at ease with eye contact.

Therapists working in this way must feel at ease with eye contact and soft gazing, which can feel exposing and quite intimate. It can help to imagine that you are gazing at your baby, grandchild, or beloved niece or nephew. While my clients are processing, I try to feel love for them and connect to an inner source of strength and confidence that they can get through this. They can feel or intuit this energy coming from me as they go through some of the hardest material. Through my eyes I tell them, "You can do it, I'm here with you, you are good, you are kind, you are valuable."

Using Safe Objects, Support People, or Animals in Sessions

For clients who are especially fragile or insecure, you can suggest that they bring a *safe object* or *person* into the session. This object can be something like a teddy bear, blanket, or something associated with a safe person in their lives. One young girl I worked with brought her dog to the session. His presence helped her feel much safer. When she wanted to take a break from the processing, she would put her arms around him. Other clients have brought their partners, parents, or friends to sessions. They can sit next to the client, hold his or her hand, or just be a safe presence in the room offering support. When doing adjunctive EMDR for a client who has a primary therapist, I have done EMDR with the other therapist in the room providing support. Some couple therapists work with one partner supporting or witnessing the other work in session. It is important that the person observing and providing support be capable of doing so. Sometimes the material the client processes can be difficult to hear and the abreactions intense and painful to witness. We don't want to traumatize the support people. You want them to be a help, not a hindrance, to the person working.

Using Distancing Techniques

You and your client may be concerned that the memory to be processed with EMDR is too charged. Your client might be hesitant to begin EMDR. It is a key concept in EMDR that there needs to be charge in order for successful processing to occur. Yet too much charge can cause the client to dissociate and stop the processing. For that reason we try to modulate the intensity of affect so that it does not overwhelm the client. Several distancing techniques drawn from hypnotherapy can be used prior to beginning EMDR processing of a traumatic memory. These same techniques can also be used in the middle of a processing session to help clients gain distance if they are overwhelmed, dissociating, or request more distance from the memory. Following are some suggestions for helping your clients create more distance when processing emotionally charged material.

1. *"Imagine that you are watching it as a movie."* Ask the client to imagine that he is in a safe place, perhaps in his home, and that he is going to watch a movie of the traumatic event. He can have

whomever he wants with him as he watches. His protectors and nurturing figures can be there. He can put the movie in a DVD player and watch it on his TV. He can hold the remote control in his hand. He has control. He can start or stop the movie whenever he wishes. He can put it on pause and go to his safe place or take a break if he wants to. He can fast-forward it. He can make it a still picture, make it black and white, and he can take the sound out of it. What is important to emphasize is that *the client is in control.*

2. *"Imagine that there is a glass wall between you and the image."* The client can imagine watching the scene with a wall separating her from it.

3. *"Imagine that your resource figures are there with you."* The client can imagine his nurturing and protector figures there with him as he goes through the event.

4. *"Feel the support of [name of partner, parent, or friend] next to you, holding your hand."* The client is not alone and can feel the support in the present as she processes the past. The therapist can also hold the client's hand.

5. *The use of a metaphor*: With my most traumatized clients I'll set up a metaphor for creating distance that I can use if they get overwhelmed during processing and need a reminder that they are safe in the present as they process the past. The purpose of the metaphor is to create a feeling of being grounded and present as the process moves by. There is *flow* as well as *distance*. This has worked well at times when clients need the distance and to keep things moving along. The metaphor is not installed with BLS. Here are some of the metaphors that I use: "Imagine that you are sitting on the banks of a river and watching the water flow by"; "Imagine that you are on a train watching the scenery pass by"; "Imagine that you are lying on your back watching the clouds in the sky float by."

A client's trepidation about beginning EMDR processing indicates to me that I will need to use distancing techniques. My typical question to the client is, "What do you need to feel safe?" If the client says, "I'm afraid of being overwhelmed, that it will be too much for me," I offer distancing techniques and see what appeals to him or her.

Creating an Imaginal Container for Affect Management

Omaha (2004) recommends creating an imaginal container. This container serves to limit pressures and feelings and helps clients to not become overwhelmed. It is used to contain distress, emotions, and problems, both in and out of sessions, and provides clients with control over emotions that feel too great for them. It can help minimize disruption to clients' daily life as well as hold material that emerges during EMDR sessions that is not directly related to the target but is affecting the client's ability to process, such as distressing memories. The container can also be used to close incomplete sessions. Clients can be instructed in this way:

> *"Bring up an image of a container that is large enough to hold every disturbing thing, but do not focus on any particular thing or image. Be sure it has a lid that is secure. You can label the container. Imagine a valve on it that allows you to take out what you want and to put in what you want a little at a time. It can be opened only when it will serve your healing. If you want, you can arrange for a place to store the container. Make sure no part of you is in the container. Then imagine these things passing into the container. Now seal the container."*

The imagery can be installed with short sets of BLS, or not (see Omaha [2004] for more information).

Some therapists ask their clients to imagine a book with all their issues in it. Clients can open or close the book whenever they want, and they can keep it wherever they want. Clients can also create a container for sounds. They can be asked to imagine putting disturbing sounds or words on a tape or CD and putting them in a case that is stored securely until they are ready to open it.

For clients who are afraid of being overwhelmed by a memory, I have suggested that they work on only one part of it. The rest can be put aside in a container. In this way clients can gain a sense of control. I have also used a container for clients who want to preserve the good memories or good parts of a perpetrator who was also an attachment figure: "Would you like to put the good memories of your father in a container where we can keep them safe so that you can work on the disturbing part?" In this way the client can focus on reprocessing disturbing memories without censoring him- or herself.

Preventing Memory Chaining and Flooding

Clients who have multiple early traumas often have a difficult time completely reprocessing a single memory because the memory they begin with links into another memory, which then links into another one and another, with none of them resolved during a session. These associated memories are like links in a long chain. Clients can become overwhelmed by the memories unlocked during EMDR processing and can feel as if multiple doors have swung open and all the horrible skeletons in the closet are escaping at once. There are a number of suggestions for preventing this chain reaction from occurring.

In the beginning of the session, you can use guided imagery to help your client go to her peaceful place. When she is there, surrounded by her nurturing or protector figures, you can suggest that she bring up the memory she wants to work on and imagine it on a movie or video screen. *Tell your client that she will work on one memory only. It will have a beginning, middle, and an end. If she wants to take a break, she can do so at any time and return to her safe or peaceful place. A signal for stopping is agreed upon. When the client is ready, the memory can be brought to mind and the EMDR processing begun.* This technique has been very helpful for clients who have a tendency to chain. It comforts them to know that they have control and will only work on one memory at a time. This process can be done with the client in the safe or peaceful place projecting the memory on a screen, or leaving the safe/peaceful place, knowing he or she can return there as needed and bring up the memory to be worked on.

Later, when the client is processing a traumatic memory and another linked memory that is overwhelming surfaces, the client can signal you to stop. You then stop the BLS, and direct her to return to the target memory. For example, if she is processing a memory of being abused by her father as a 3-year-old and another memory comes up of being abused by her uncle, she signals you to stop. You stop the BLS and say, "Let's return to the scene with your father when you were 3—what comes up now?" In this way the client feels contained and is able to complete the memory with which she began. She has a feeling of control and accomplishment. The work done on the target memory generalizes to other memories and incidents. At the end of the session during closure, the client can imagine putting the memory that surfaced in a container with a strong lid on it.

Reinstalling Resources

For highly traumatized clients it is helpful to have them reinstall their safe/peaceful place along with their resource figures prior to beginning their EMDR processing session. I might also suggest that the client imagine the whole team of resource figures together and tap them in. Beginning the session with the resources creates a safe base from which to begin. Some of my most traumatized clients need this extra security to help them feel safe, and to create the feeling that their resource figures are close at hand, ready to provide support and help if needed. I also believe that reinstalling the resources creates a neural net of safety for the nervous system that keeps the abreactions from going over the top, and the client from feeling the aloneness and powerlessness of the original trauma.

For some clients it is sufficient to recall the resources before they begin their session without BLS, and many clients don't need to bring up resources at all prior to beginning sessions.

PUTTING IT ALL TOGETHER

Here's what it might look like to use all of the elements I have described above. Imagine you have a client who has a history of severe neglect and abuse as a child. Her parents were drug addicted, and she was sexually abused by her father and his friends. She was removed from her home and placed in foster homes, where she was abused by older foster children. Her entire childhood was fraught with neglect, abuse, and mismanagement of her case by professionals. She managed to find a stable foster home in late adolescence, finish school, and, after several failed abusive relationships, find a man who cares for her. They have two small children she is struggling to raise in a healthy way. Though her life is currently stable, she is triggered by her husband and her children. She has nightmares and flashbacks from her abuse, and worries that she is a bad mother.

You help her feel comfortable with you. You answer her questions and concerns, and explain about EMDR and how it might be helpful for her. You ask her about her history and background, and when seeing her anxiety escalate with her description of her early abuse, you ask her about what she liked to do as a child. What were her favorite things? You also ask if she has a sense of something larger than herself, and about anyone who has been kind or nurturing for her in her life. She perks up when she talks about a neighbor, in whose home she spent a lot of time as a respite from her crazy family. You get her to talk about her children and how she loves them. You see that when you "change the channel" on the trauma, she can easily find resources and calm down. You might direct her to tap on her legs as she focuses on the good things. If you have time, you could ask if she can imagine a peaceful place, and tap it in. You might teach her how to do it for herself so that she has a tool she can use at home.

In the sessions that follow you continue with the history and install resources. You introduce her to the different forms of BLS and discover together what works best for her. Because of the seriousness of the neglect and the lack of a stable mother throughout her childhood, you decide that along with the other resources, it will be important to create and install an ideal mother.

When she is ready to do EMDR, she tells you that she wants you to sit close to her, and she wants the pulsers under her legs. She wants you to hold her hands and to be present with her. She wants to imagine her resources and tap them in each time, and to end with them too. She is frightened to begin EMDR, but feels better doing it this way. She knows that she can stop whenever she wishes, and she has the signal to let you know. She knows which memory she wants to start with; it's the one that haunts her in her dreams. Because she is afraid that all the other terrible memories will come up and flood her, you add the instructions about processing one memory at a time.

You direct her to her peaceful place, then invite all of her resource figures to be there with her. You might tap in each, one at a time, and then have her imagine them as a team. Then you tell her:

"Imagine that you are going to watch this video of abuse by your father. You have your support team with you. I am going to hold your hand. You can stop it at any time. You have the remote control in your hand. You can take the color out of it, the sound, or put it on pause and take a break. You are in control. You are going to work on this memory only. It has a beginning, middle, and end. If it should start to link to another memory you don't want to process, you signal me to stop, and we will stop the BLS and return to this movie only. Let me know when you are ready."

When she signals me, I bring my chair up, take her hands in mine, and gently gaze into her eyes before she closes them. We activate the memory network using the modified protocol, and then turn on the BLS. As she processes the memory, she squeezes my hands and opens her eyes from time to time. I let her know with my voice that I am there, and that she is safe.

At the end of the session, she returns to her peaceful place, brings in her resources, and puts the things that came up that she didn't want to process in a container. We then debrief the session.

CHAPTER 10

Case Example
Preparing a Client with Severe Attachment Trauma for EMDR

Holly Prichard

Holly Prichard is a marriage and family therapist practicing in Sonoma County, California, specializing in the treatment of trauma. She has worked in multiple treatment settings, including a residential crisis center, a low-fee counseling clinic, the mental health unit of the county jail, and private practice. She worked with the client she discusses over a period of 3 years. In this chapter, Holly presents the background, case conceptualization, resourcing, and preparation for the middle phase of treatment. The rest of the course of treatment with this client is presented in Chapter 16. This case is an excellent example of AF-EMDR conducted by a very skilled and compassionate EMDR therapist.

THE CLIENT

"Mary" was single and 60 years old. She came to see me based on the recommendation of a friend who had experienced a positive outcome with EMDR. Mary's lifelong friend knew that she had struggled with depression for many years and felt that EMDR could offer her some much-needed relief.

Mary presented as an attractive, articulate, bright-eyed woman who appeared happy to meet me, with hopes of exploring a new process that would finally get to the root of her problems. She was a well-educated practitioner of yoga and meditation and had spent many years as a teacher to others. Because I had come highly recommended by her trusted friend, she came into the initial session with a built-in, positive transference toward me. She was eager, attentive, relational, and made eye contact with me from the start. It felt like she was open and ready to explore using EMDR. I immediately liked her and felt my heart opening to the possibility of working with her.

PRESENTING ISSUES

Mary began by describing a longstanding, painful pattern. She had never been married and over the course of her life had had a series of relationships with unavailable men. She reported that she stayed in relationships longer than was good for her; her current relationship had been on and off for several years. She seemed to accommodate to her boyfriend's needs but had trouble identifying and voicing her own. She often felt paralyzed to act on her own behalf.

She wanted to specifically work on getting to the root of a recurring, longstanding set of somatic and emotional problems that occurred whenever she felt rejected, in any way, by her boyfriend(s). She described this problem dating back many years and said that it was being activated in her current relationship. She was in a relationship with a man who, she said, wasn't able to "meet" her. He was not emotionally available to her, and she was being triggered into negative beliefs about herself on an ongoing basis. Mary had a deep need to be "met" by her boyfriend, and his apparent inability to do so was causing her severe suffering.

She explained that when she felt rejected or not important or valued by her boyfriend, her body took her to a very dark place. Rejection for her could mean not getting a phone call from him when expected or receiving a disapproving look. Her belly would contract and knot up, her throat would clinch, her breathing would become restricted, and she would feel faint. She described "spiraling down" into an endless pit and becoming immobilized with fear. At times she had even stayed in her house, in this place of immobilization, for long periods of time. In the past, it may have taken her several months to come out of her dark funk. The beliefs that accompanied these somatic reactions were, "I'll be alone forever. I think I'm going to die." Fear of loss and abandonment took her into this very lonely and entrenched place of feeling like she was dying. She described her biggest fear as going to the place where there was a sense of "falling and there is nobody there. When I'm in that place, all I want is someone to be there." She had experienced numerous depressive episodes and felt that she had never been truly happy in all of her 60 years. She had taken medication off and on for years.

Mary was in the midst of a 4-year period of chronic fatigue and had not been able to work much during that time. Her energy was depleted and she described having "flare-ups" that would put her out of commission for days. She was tired of living this way and wanted to try anything to get her life back to some sense of normalcy. She told me, "I want to not be afraid. I want to feel OK in myself, so I don't go to such aloneness and darkness." When I heard about the dramatic nature of her symptoms, I felt certain that the origin of her problems was rooted in very early, attachment-related wounding.

Mary had done a lot of therapy over the years. When she presented to me for EMDR, she had been seeing a wonderful, loving therapist for 5½ years and had done a good amount of work on attaching to her in a positive way. They had established a close connection on which Mary relied, especially during times when she descended into her fearful place. Over the years, Mary had increased her ability to receive comfort from her therapist and had successfully internalized her soothing and caring presence. As positive as this relationship was and as deep as the work had been, Mary intuitively felt that she needed an alternative way of working that would get to the root of the intractable feeling states that plagued her. While she had experienced improvement in her life, she was still going to the deep, immovable, painful places when she felt rejected. She wanted to heal this painful pattern once and for all, and she had high hopes that EMDR would lead her to that healing. When Mary came to see me, she was still in therapy with her therapist, who thought that EMDR would be a good idea for Mary.

I was faced with the possibility of working as an adjunctive therapist, which was new territory for me. I didn't usually work with clients who were already in therapy with a primary therapist. I think most therapists, including myself, have been trained to actively avoid such setups. Didn't it go against conventional wisdom that a client would work with two therapists at the same time? Wasn't this setup inherently rife with psychological land mines such as splitting and triangulation? Of course, these possibilities existed, and the situation wouldn't be appropriate for everyone. It was very important to carefully assess all the possible contraindications of taking on a new client under these circumstances. Although this could be disastrous and absolutely unworkable for some, I discovered that there were some clients, like Mary, for whom such a dynamic would be greatly beneficial. Like any successful therapeutic endeavor, it would take good communication and clear boundaries between all parties involved to make this work.

Looking back now, it was Mary herself and her own description of her process that paved the way for us to work together. Nothing in her presentation raised any red flags for me. She spoke with great admiration about her therapist and had nothing but kind and positive words to describe her relationship with her. She spoke highly of the work they had done and had no hint of using her possible connection with me as a way to hurt or act out toward her therapist. I think if she hadn't been so clear and eloquent about what she wanted and needed, it may not have been such a clear decision for me.

And so, Mary hoped to explore something new with EMDR, in addition to what her current therapist could offer. I was intrigued that Mary's deep therapeutic work over the span of years had not resolved her issues. I was open to considering the idea that I would enter into this work with Mary as an adjunctive therapist using EMDR, while she maintained an ongoing connection with her primary therapist. With Mary's permission, I called her therapist and discussed the possibility of working this way. I also wanted to get her impressions of working with Mary. I was curious about whether her therapist would feel threatened or closed to this type of collegial collaboration.

My talk with Mary's therapist yielded a great deal of valuable information. She described Mary as a motivated client who was enjoyable to work with. I was mostly interested in her assessment of Mary's capacity to tolerate the affect that would be produced with processing traumatic material. Not knowing yet what that traumatic material would be, I intuited, by Mary's descriptions of her somatic symptoms, that traumatic material would invariably emerge once we started our work. Mary's therapist said that, at times, Mary could get overwhelmed and flooded with tears, but she had no concerns about her decompensating or becoming suicidal. She commented that Mary was basically a healthy person with a need to work on the development of internal resources and the ability to contain her affect when triggered. The issues, as she saw them, were around chronic, long-term aloneness, chronic emotional neglect, profound sadness, and being an "unmothered" woman. The therapist seemed open to the possibility that EMDR could offer something that she, herself, could not. She wanted the best for Mary and realized that her own way of working, while valuable and substantive, did not offer Mary an avenue to take the work further than they had already gone.

Both Mary's therapist and I openly discussed that this would be a new way of working, and we were both unsure about how it would evolve. There were some concerns expressed over how our individual styles would intersect, and we had questions about the effect this would have on Mary. I was clear in saying that if, at any time, she felt my work was contradicting the basic principles of her work, we would need to be in direct communication about that. I was acutely aware of wanting to help preserve Mary's positive experiences and feelings toward her therapist. In fact, there were times in the early part of our work where she would use her therapist as a much-needed resource. And so, much to her credit, Mary's therapist was open and willing to support Mary's exploration of EMDR. The therapist and I agreed that I would begin by strengthening Mary's internal resources, and we would reevaluate things based on how that process went.

Taking on the role of adjunctive therapist also worked well for me due to a recent change that was taking place in my practice. I was starting to work as a consultant on military installations overseas and would be spending some time away from my office.

I was up front with Mary from the beginning about the possible disruptions to our work, and she felt this would be all right as long as she had advance notice of my schedule. Normally, for ethical reasons, I wouldn't think about taking on a new client knowing that I would be gone, off and on. However, because she already had her primary therapist in place, I felt open to the idea.

We planned to work intensively when I was in town; when I was gone, she would have her regular sessions with her therapist. Because my anticipated absences were clearly not an ideal way to start off with a new client, I offered to give her names of other EMDR therapists who could give her more consistency. She was clear that she wanted to start the work with me, but would let me know if my absences were too disruptive for her. We both agreed that we would assess this arrangement often and if, at any time, it was causing any undue distress, we would reevaluate and make a new plan, including the possibility of referring her to other practitioners. In my mind, the process of clarifying the treatment structure was a vital part of starting to create a positive alliance with Mary. I genuinely wanted her to have a good experience with EMDR and I think she could feel my care and concern.

HISTORY

Mary was born 2 weeks after her mother's sister had died. The hospital had given her the wrong blood transfusion and it had killed her. Mary told me, "I think I came into this world with energetic grief around me." She reported that her mother told her she couldn't nurse her because of colic. Mary was the older of two children; her sister was 3 years younger. She described her mother as "toxic, very cold, neglectful, critical, and rejecting." She had trouble finding any positive memories of her mother from childhood, although in the years before her mother died, Mary had some positive experiences with her. During that time, her mother was medicated, which finally "softened her." However, during her childhood, she described absolute terror and pain related to being around her mother. Her mother was a medical professional and as Mary put it, "didn't ever want to have children. She couldn't be bothered." Her father was more emotionally available, although often absent due to work. She had more positive memories of him and he would serve as a resource for her during our processing. Mary and her sister were looked after by a series of housekeepers/nannies. Some were nice enough, but one, in particular, was mean and sadistic, playing tricks on Mary and using a switch to punish her.

In gathering more history, it seemed that we were dealing with developmental/ attachment/relational traumas rather than with clearly defined, discernable, discrete traumas. There were no reports of sexual abuse.

Mary had a relatively stable life with good friends and was financially independent. Overall, she appeared functional, even though she reported periods of depression, chronic fatigue, and incapacitation.

COURSE OF TREATMENT: RESOURCING

Starting with the first session, I wanted to get more history about Mary's symptoms and a better sense of how we might work best together. I listened carefully as she shared her story and also tracked her body as she spoke. I watched for any signs that her nervous system was entering an activated state (either hyper- or hypoaroused) as I paid attention to her skin tone, breathing, eye contact, posture, and overall presentation. Was she able to regulate herself or not? Was she able to stay in relationship to me as she was telling her story? I listened for negative, critical beliefs and watched for somatic indications of possible areas for us to target with EMDR.

Her most troubling symptoms revolved around a very dramatic cluster of somatic reactions that emerged when she felt rejected by her boyfriend. Coupled with a tight belly and restricted breathing, she would spiral into negative beliefs such as, "I'm gonna be on my own. I'll be alone forever. I think I'm going to die." Due to these dramatic and painful symptoms, I knew that we would need to do a solid job of resource development before we attempted any reprocessing. We would both need to feel confident that once we started reprocessing work with her symptoms, she would be able to tolerate it.

Toward the end of our initial session, I explained more about the EMDR process and showed her the Tac/AudioScan pulsers that I often use for processing. Over the years, I have found that most people prefer using the tapping function on the pulsers because the tactile sensations seem to be comforting when working with difficult material. In general, if processing doesn't unfold to resolution or starts to loop or get stuck, I might try another form of processing, such as bilateral audio beeps or using eye movements. For Mary, as with the majority of my clients, tapping was the preferred way of processing.

At the end of the first session, I made some notes indicating that Mary appeared to be very well resourced with good ego strength. Based on my visual observations and my own internal experience of how I felt sitting with Mary, I was fairly certain that she was an ideal candidate for EMDR. I liked her and felt an immediate connection to her; she also readily connected with me. Because of all of these factors, I felt we could immediately begin with moving into the development of resources. I wanted to give her some tools for self-soothing so that she could get some relief from these dramatic somatic reactions into which she so easily slipped.

Because we were at the end of our session, I asked her to start thinking of resources during the week. These are the resources I have found to be most helpful: safe place or alternatives such as pleasant or comfortable place, nurturing figure(s), protector figure(s), and spiritual/wise figure(s). I would need to gather much more history in subsequent sessions, but because Mary was so motivated to get going, I assigned her this resourcing task as a way to keep her excitement and motivation moving forward. It was also a very good assessment exercise; determining if she could imagine and connect with resources was a good way to assess her strengths and deficiencies.

Mary arrived at the second session excited and glad to be there. She reported that she had thought a lot about the resources but had had trouble coming up with a safe place and protector figures. I made a mental note that she didn't mention anything about nurturing or spiritual figures. She reported that it made her sad to think that she didn't have those resources in place. Even though she used the word sad, I detected a note of self-judgment in her tone. This would be a running theme in our work; Mary could be very critical of herself and her perceived lack of abilities. She left herself little room for not being perfect, which stemmed from having an overly critical mother. She had internalized many negative beliefs, and we would have to work hard to shift those thought patterns. It became clear that those negative, critical thoughts were what fueled her pattern of becoming immobile and paralyzed.

Mary was also letting me know that she expected herself to be perfect in relationship to me and to the "homework" assignment I had given her. In hindsight, in my enthusiasm to match Mary's eagerness, I probably assigned this task too early. It was clear that Mary needed my help in the development of her resources. This was a good opportunity for us to work together and for me to provide a regulating presence in the process of resource development.

I asked her to think of a place, real or imagined, where she felt comfortable, good, and relaxed. She closed her eyes and quickly came up with a beautiful valley, a real place she had lived years ago. The cottage was close to a creek on a dirt road and she described it by saying, "I felt safer there than anywhere in life." I invited her to fully imagine being in this wonderful place, and her body noticeably relaxed as she took a deep breath. Being in this mindful experience led her to say, "I can be myself here."

I invited her to bring all of her senses into this scene as she immersed herself in the experience of remembering this special place; this invitation deepened the experience and provided more connection to soothing and comforting feelings. She saw the beauty of the green hills, heard the sounds of the babbling creek, felt the cool, fall-like temperatures. Once the whole experience of this safe valley was fully activated, I turned on the tappers and instructed her to "just let whatever happens, happen. Don't try to make anything happen." My hope was that the BLS (>>>>>) would strengthen the safe place and its powerful effect.

THERAPIST: What do you notice now?

MARY: More details. I'm remembering all kinds of things inside, different seasons. It feels good.

THERAPIST: [These comments indicated that the BLS was helping to deepen a positive experience, which was what I was hoping for.] Go with that. >>>>>

MARY: I feel spacious and positive.

THERAPIST: Is there anything else you want to add to this experience to strengthen this resource?

MARY: I'd like to bring in a tribe of Indians as my protectors.

THERAPIST: [I thought it was interesting that Mary organically connected to a protective resource as part of her safe place, even though we had not begun to formally work on developing a protector resource, and she had had trouble thinking of a protector resource on her own the previous week.] Imagine that. >>>>>

MARY: This is nice. They are watching out for me. They are letting me know that there is always somebody there.

THERAPIST: Does the "little girl" part of you like this safe place, or does she want another? [I wanted to assess whether younger, more vulnerable parts of her felt safe in this place. This was important because when processing early traumatic relational wounds, it was the young, childlike aspects that would be accessed, and it was those parts that would need resources that were easily available. Establishing those safe places ahead of time was vital before reprocessing of traumatic material began.]

MARY: She [the little girl part] likes that I'm [the adult self] there; that helps her. That surprises me because I haven't protected her much. She would love this place to explore. She didn't get to explore as a kid.

THERAPIST: Is it ok to let her come into this scene?

MARY: Yes.

THERAPIST: Go with that. >>>>>

MARY: This is such a good place for her. She is running around. We are both safe. We both can do what we want.

THERAPIST: Would she like to add anything else?

MARY: Animals. >>>>> It seems perfect (*begins to cry*). I like that the little girl is there.

THERAPIST: [Her tears were a good indication that Mary was open-hearted toward this vulnerable part of herself.]

Because we were at the end of the session, I wanted to help Mary integrate this piece of work, so I asked how she would like to use this safe place resource in the coming week. She said, "I think I could go there if I start to feel bad."

This became her homework assignment for the upcoming week. I added the thought that she might explore this place whether she was feeling bad or not, so that she could practice giving herself a positive, calming experience. She willingly agreed. I felt very encouraged (and relieved) that Mary was able to find a comforting and safe place so easily.

Mary came into the next session saying that she was excited to see me. She reported that she had practiced going to her safe place and that, for the most part, it felt really good. Then she got news that her primary therapist might be leaving town in a year, and she began to feel abandoned. She tried to use the imagery and found that "it didn't make me feel ok. I wanted it to make me feel ok. I wanted it to be magic." We discussed how this news and her reaction to it provided an opportunity to continue working with her internal states as she became activated around the theme of abandonment.

She agreed to practice going to the safe place again with the tappers. She was able to easily connect with the safety of her beautiful valley and reported that it felt wonderful and strong. She also developed an additional safe place image of a forest with lots of animals, which would become the "go-to" safe place for most of our future processing.

We then moved on to creating protector resources for her. She immediately thought of the Indians (from the previous session) and brought up the image of Indian spirits creating a circle of protection around her. She could sense their fierceness and protective energy. Once this image was fully activated, I turned on the tappers to strengthen it. >>>>>

MARY: I can see them and feel them dancing. They circle around me. The spirits got bigger. They aren't worried. There is no question; it's no big deal to protect me.
THERAPIST: Do you feel a sense of that protection?
MARY: Yes I do. I feel no fear. They have no fear.
THERAPIST: Go with that. >>>>>
MARY: When I first felt it, I felt I was an adult. There was a feeling I could do anything and be safe and then I thought of the little girl.
THERAPIST: Are they protecting the little girl as well?

MARY: Yes, the little girl isn't fearful, and we like them.
THERAPIST: Would you like to strengthen this feeling?
MARY: Yes, I like the feeling a lot. >>>>>

With this feeling strengthened, I asked if she wanted to add any additional protector resources, and she did. She brought up an image of her dog and we installed the strength of that connection. I like to bring in mindful awareness of how the body is processing these resources, and when I asked what she was aware of in her body, she said that her whole body felt "strong, warm and tingly, with a relaxed belly."

THERAPIST: Is there anything else about protection that you or the little girl would like as a resource?
MARY: In some way, the little girl wants me to be a protector. I would like to be, but I don't trust myself.
THERAPIST: Have you ever protected someone?
MARY: Yes.
THERAPIST: Focus on the memory of that and let me know when you've got it. [I didn't feel it was necessary to find out more about this memory since she appeared to connect with it so easily; if she had had more trouble accessing it, I would have fleshed it out more.]
MARY: Got it. >>>>>
THERAPIST: What are you noticing?
MARY: How immediate that mother-bear reaction is in me. There is no question.
THERAPIST: Are you willing to bring in that quality of protection for the little girl?
MARY: I'd like to do that for her.
THERAPIST: [This affirmative response clearly signaled that Mary wanted to help the little girl feel protected.] Get back in touch with that quality and bring it in.
MARY: I can feel that place. It's strong and powerful.
THERAPIST: Go with that. >>>>>
MARY: I have a sense of myself as protector. Separate from being protected. That I, myself, have this mother-bear aspect. It's surprising to me and to the little girl. It feels good. I haven't felt that way toward "her" before, but it seems like I want to do that for her. It feels true.

This was a wonderful new awareness for Mary. She had mostly been in touch with her need for protection, but organically she brought up the idea that she could also be a protector for herself. This was a very important part of the work as we went along, allowing her own internal power and resourcefulness to come to the fore and provide help and protection for her little girl self.

As the therapist, this was a very good sign for me to see. I have worked with clients so traumatized that the idea of lovingly protecting oneself was not even in the equation. In fact, some people have been so traumatized that they actively want to harm that vulnerable, hurt part of the self. Clients who present like this are unable to feel compassion or a sense of empathy for their wounded, younger parts. In those cases, it takes much more psychoeducation, establishment of present safety, and slow and consistent building of resources before they are able to proceed into EMDR reprocessing work. In this case, it was a very positive sign that Mary felt tenderly toward her younger self and wanted to be her own protector, even if she didn't feel entirely confident in her ability to do so. It would take multiple processing sessions (over many months), but in time, she did become a dependable and powerful resource for herself. We would eventually use the adult Mary to come in and help with "little Mary" during our EMDR reprocessing sessions.

With her safe place and protectors established, we moved on to creating a nurturing resource. Mary found this to be a harder resource to imagine because, as she said, "I scan through the universe for people and I don't find anyone." She commented that her primary therapist came to mind as a resource, sort of like a "fairy godmother." She continued to work hard to nail down the exact quality she was looking for. She said, "I want something *big* because this is the biggest hole in me. I get it that I don't know what a mother is. I want it [the resource] to be larger than life. I don't have a . . . it makes me sad, I don't have a person."

I asked if she would like to create an ideal nurturing, mothering figure using her imagination. She really liked this idea. I suggested that she get in touch with the qualities of a nurturing figure and I would turn on the tappers to see what images might come. This has been a useful technique for me. Oftentimes, when there is some kind of exploration that needs to take place, I will pose a question and turn on the tappers. The client will hold the question in mind and allow the BLS to bring to mind possibilities that were otherwise not forthcoming.

THERAPIST: Let yourself be open to whatever comes. Imagining your ideal mother or nurturing figure. >>>>>

MARY: She has dark skin, and she's big and beautiful with long hair and brown eyes. She's a combination of American Indian, Hawaiian, and African American—she is a big, graceful, beautiful woman who is tall and strong.

THERAPIST: What is she wearing? [I'm trying to deepen and expand the image of this woman.]

MARY: A dark-reddish long skirt, big clothes. She is joyful and earthy. She's skilled at being a mother, and she knows all these things about caring for me, cooking for me, and being watchful over me.

THERAPIST: Is it ok to approach her? [I am hoping she can begin to feel attached to this inner figure.]

MARY: Yeah.

THERAPIST: Is it ok to allow her to hold and cradle you? [This was probably too much too soon, I quickly realize.]

MARY: I don't know how. The little girl can jump in.

THERAPIST: [The younger part of herself knew what she wanted.] Go with that. >>>>>

MARY: She's saying, "You are so cute and beautiful." She picks up the girl and says, "We are going to have so much fun." The little girl is excited. I see myself as an adult. I crawl into her arms. She's big. I'm not too big. The little girl is on one side and I am on the other.

THERAPIST: [Mary's adult self needs this nurturing resource just as much as the little girl.] Go ahead and allow yourself to feel her skin against yours. [I hoped to deepen the bonding here.] >>>>>

MARY: She is moving around with us, dancing around. This is going to be fun. We are there in her arms. She has lightness. She is so much bigger than we are. She's muscular, with soft breasts, a soft belly, strong arms and hands.

THERAPIST: Is there anything you or your little girl needs from her right now?

MARY: We need her to be with us at anytime.

THERAPIST: Ask her how that can happen. >>>>>

MARY: She's laughing and she says, "Just call me. I'll appear. Imagine me. I'm here anyway, but I can be here now if you want."

THERAPIST: Go with that. >>>>>

MARY: I told her that we need her to be here now to help us feel safe, to teach us what we need to know, to protect "us." We need you to listen to us, to help us when we need help, to know what we are like; we need a lot. *We need you to see us, to really see us.*

THERAPIST: [This was clearly the missing experience for Mary in her developmental years.] How does she respond? >>>>>

MARY: She says, "This is what I do. I'm right here." I want to feel completely loved, and I don't know if I know what that feels like.

THERAPIST: Let her show you that you are loved completely. >>>>>

MARY: She says, "I'm right here." I can *feel* it in how she holds us both (*begins to cry heavily here*). She will never let go. She doesn't care if I'm crying. She says, " I'm never going to let go." I say "Really?" And she says, "YES!"

This powerful resource became lovingly known as *Big Mama* and she would prove to be one of the most powerful resources I have ever seen. She came to represent her protector, nurturer, and spiritual figure all rolled into one. It's important to note that all of this material came from within her. All of the healing messages and the loving messages from this nurturing resource originated *from her own process*. She knew exactly what she needed, informed by what she had never received as a child.

At the end of this session, I invited Mary to bring all of her resources together, and when that felt complete, she could open her eyes and come back into the space. I gave her the suggestion that she could practice connecting to all of her resources, especially Big Mama, in between sessions.

I like to use resourcing as a barometer of whether someone is ready to move into processing with EMDR. I was encouraged by Mary's ability to develop her resources in a relatively short period of time. If she was not able to tolerate the process of finding and strengthening resources, much more time and work would have been needed before proceeding with the reprocessing of traumatic material.

CHAPTER 11

Creating Targets and Modifying the Protocol

This chapter describes ways to develop EMDR targets that will give you access to the memory networks most directly linked to the client's symptoms or problems. Instructions are provided on the "bridging technique" for target development and the three-part protocol. These are followed by a review of the EMDR standard protocol and instructions and rationale for use of the EMDR modified protocol.

CREATING TARGETS

The selection and creation of targets are crucial to successful EMDR. I wrote about this subject extensively in *A Therapist's Guide to EMDR* (Parnell, 2007). I believe in using a *symptom-focused* approach to target selection—in other words, the target selected is the one that is most directly linked to the symptom or problem. This is the best way to induce a generalization effect that reduces symptoms. Where is your client most distressed? What symptoms or problems does the client present with? These are the focus of the treatment. If the client is triggered by sexual intimacy, then the question is *what in the past is most directly linked to that symptom*? Sometimes clients know, and sometimes they do not. If they know—for example, it might be linked to sexual abuse in childhood—then the question then is, what is the earliest, strongest experience of this anxiety response? The answer then provides the target. You want to process traumas chronologically, beginning with the earliest/ strongest experiences and working your way up the chain. Using a three-part protocol, you process the past linkages first, anything associated with it in the present next, and if possible, imagine a positive future.

Sometimes a client may come in with a set of problems and goals for treatment and knows more or less the incidents that are linked to the problems. In such a case, a target map can be created that guides the work. You can work on one set of symptoms or problems at a time, targeting the associated memories chronologically.

I have had very few clients with complex trauma who are able to work this way, however. Most don't know what associated incidents are linked to their symptoms, either because the memories are dissociated, because they did not register as large traumas, or the links are not obvious. For most of my clients I use the bridging technique (Parnell, 1999, 2007) to bridge back from their symptoms, triggers, transference, problematic behaviors, negative beliefs, emotions, and body sensations to discover the early links.

The Bridging Technique

The bridging technique was adapted from a hypnotherapeutic technique called *affect bridging* (Watkins, 1971, 1990). A similar method for finding targets, called *floatback*, is taught by Francine Shapiro's EMDR Institute. The bridging technique I developed is simpler and more somatically based. I don't want my clients to "float" because I believe that this image encourages dissociation. Instead, I want clients to connect to their bodies and emotional experience as they trace the complex back in time. I also do not ask for a memory. I want to keep them out of their heads and their thinking, and instead make this a right-brain experience. What pops in can be an image or a metaphor that can be loaded with meaning and is associated with their symptom or problem.

The idea with the bridging technique is to activate as many of the components as possible (picture, emotions, body sensations, and immediate thoughts or self beliefs) that are linked to the current symptom or problem, and then trace the whole complex back in time to get an early scene that can be reprocessed.

For example, say that a client is triggered by her boyfriend when he approaches her sexually. She doesn't know why she got so upset. She tells you that she froze, dissociated, and felt like a small child. She couldn't even speak. He is a loving man, and she is puzzled as to why she was so triggered. She does not know what in the past is associated with this trigger. I would tap in her resources (peaceful place, nurturing figures, ideal mother, protectors, wise figures, and resource team) and then ask her to close her eyes and go inside.

THERAPIST: Bring up the moment when you felt most triggered by your boyfriend. Can you find that moment?

CLIENT: Yes, it's when I saw him naked. I freaked out.

THERAPIST: In this moment, what emotions do you feel?

CLIENT: Panic, terror.

THERAPIST: What do you notice in your body?

CLIENT: I'm dizzy. I feel like a small child. My whole body is frozen.

THERAPIST: What thoughts or beliefs go with that?

CLIENT: Something bad is going to happen. I'm not safe.

THERAPIST: Trace it back in time; let whatever comes up for you come up, without censoring it. Go back as far as you can.

CLIENT: (*silent for a while*) I'm 3 years old, and it's the middle of the night. My father has just come in my room. He's naked. I'm terrified, but pretend I'm asleep.

This is our target. I ask for the body sensations and beliefs, then process with BLS. When this target is complete, I return to the scene with the boyfriend. If this has lost its charge, I say, "Go with that," and process this. Finally, I might do a future pace, "Imagine seeing your boyfriend naked in the future," or something like that.

Frequently, clients think that what has arisen is not associated with the symptom from which they have bridged, but I trust that the unconscious mind has its own logic and I nearly always explore the scene or image that has arisen with the client. Then, *I use this image as the target image, even if it seems irrational.* In nearly every case in my experience, the image that arose was a significant target that led to important new insights and information. The following box summarizes the steps involved in bridging from a symptom, issue, or current problem to the source.

STEPS FOR BRIDGING FROM A SYMPTOM, ISSUE, OR CURRENT PROBLEM

1. Ask the client for an example of the problem:
   "Can you think of a time recently when you had this experience? Can you think of a time when this came up for you?"
   You want a time that has emotional charge (e.g., the client describes the situation with her boyfriend).

continued on next page

STEPS FOR BRIDGING FROM A SYMPTOM, ISSUE, OR CURRENT PROBLEM *(continued)*

2. Ask the client for the worst part of the recent situation:
   "Close your eyes and go inside. What picture represents the worst part?"
   The client in our example answered, "Seeing my boyfriend naked."
3. Ask the client for the emotions that go with the picture:
   "As you see that picture, what emotions do you feel?"
   Our client answered, "Panic, terror."
4. Ask for the body sensations.
   "What do you notice in your body?"
   "I'm dizzy. I feel like a small child. My whole body is frozen."
5. Ask for the immediate thoughts or negative cognitions.
   "What do you believe about yourself now?"
   These don't have to be self-referencing beliefs. They can include any words or phrases that pop out of clients' mouths and are associated with the scene from which they are bridging (e.g., "Something bad's going to happen. I'm not safe").
6. When all of the elements are activated, bridge back in time. It is essential that the memory network be well activated. It is important that the client stay in the experience.
   "Trace it back in time. Let whatever comes up come up without censoring it."
   Don't let clients intellectualize or try to figure things out. Stress the importance of not censoring their experience. Whatever scenes come up are probably significant. Encourage clients to go back as far as they can, but remember that whatever they retrieve must have charge. Images that come up may or may not be memories. They can include composite scenes, confabulations, symbolic images, metaphors, and scenes created from stories they heard or images from vicarious traumatization. For that reason I don't ask them to go back to a memory. These images, which are linked to their symptoms, are usually very significant. *You are not using BLS as you bridge back.*
7. Target and reprocess the scene to completion using the modified protocol. In our example, we would reprocess this scene: "I'm 3 years old and it's the middle of the night. My father has just come in my room. He's naked. I'm terrified, but pretend I'm asleep."
8. After the installation of the positive cognition on the early target, return to the recent picture or situation and check for any changes.

continued on next page

<u>STEPS FOR BRIDGING FROM A SYMPTOM, ISSUE,</u>
<u>OR CURRENT PROBLEM</u> *(continued)*

"Let's go back to the scene with your boyfriend. What comes up now?"

9. If cleared and close to positive resolution, add BLS as the client installs the positive cognition "I feel comfortable and safe with him now."
10. Do a future pace.
    Therapist: "Can you imagine being with your boyfriend sexually in the future?"
    Client: "Yes."
    Therapist: "Go with that."
11. If the recent situation is not cleared, explore what else is there. You can bridge back to another scene if time allows, or plan to check in at the next session.

You can bridge back from the *transference as you would from a symptom.* If the client is feeling something about you in the moment that is linked to earlier material, you should first repair anything in the relationship that has triggered the reaction. For example, if your client is feeling like he or she can't trust you because you were late for the session, you can apologize and listen to how your client feels about this. When there has been sufficient repair and your client feels safe again, bridging can be done from the trigger to an earlier memory.

"When you bring up the moment when you noticed that I was late, what emotions do you feel? What do you feel in your body? What do you believe about yourself? Now trace it back in time, let whatever comes up come up without censoring it. Go back as far as you can."

I have also had success working with problematic behaviors such as procrastination, overeating, bingeing, cutting, and drinking. Bridging back and finding the roots of the problem and reprocessing them can help to change the behaviors, sometimes quite quickly. The trick here is to activate the memory network of the moment before they engaged in the behavior. What was their internal state—their emotions, body sensations, and cognitions—right before they acted? For example, loneliness might be a trigger for eating. Light this up and then trace it back. If the early contributors to the behavior can be targeted and reprocessed, the behaviors can shift.

You can bridge back from any negative beliefs, emotions, or body sensations. You will read examples of these in the cases that follow in this book. I explain the procedures in detail in *A Therapist's Guide to EMDR* (Parnell, 2007) and also have several demonstrations of this work in my DVD demonstrations (www.emdrinfo.com).

MODIFYING THE STANDARD EMDR PROTOCOL

When working with clients with relational trauma, it is essential that they feel attuned to, cared for, and *not* objectified. The standard EMDR protocol's assessment phase, when applied without adjustments, will not work well for many of these clients. Some of the steps are not clinically useful, create an empathic break in the therapeutic relationship, activate memory networks other than those that are the focus of treatment (e.g., perfectionism), confuse the client, and *deactivate* the memory network. It is important to remember that the memory network must be activated in order for processing to occur. Therefore, if the standard procedural steps deactivate the memory network, the steps should be modified in order to *activate* the network.

Standard EMDR Protocol

The standard EMDR procedural steps begin with the *assessment phase*, or development of the EMDR target. Targets in EMDR are the entryways to memory networks and EMDR processing. Targets contain the image, emotions, body sensations, and/or erroneous beliefs associated with the traumatic memory.

The target for a trauma is the *most disturbing part of the incident*. I would ask the client who is targeting a rape, "When you think of the rape, what is the worst part of it?" After the target incident or memory has been chosen, the therapist asks the client for a picture that represents the most charged part. "What picture represents the worst part of the incident?" A woman who is working on a memory of being raped might choose the *image* of the rapist's face.

Next the client is asked for a *negative cognition*—an erroneous, self-referencing belief associated with the incident that has carried over to the present. I might ask, "When you bring up the picture, what do you believe about yourself now?" Her belief might be "I'm powerless."

I would then ask the client for a *positive cognition*, a positive self-referencing belief that corresponds, in the opposite, to the negative cognition. What would she like to believe about herself when she brings up the image? In this case such a *positive cognition* might be "I'm powerful."

Now I ask the client to rate the validity of the positive statement on a scale from 1 (completely false) to 7 (completely true): "When you bring up the image of the man's face, how true does 'I'm powerful' *feel* to you now on a scale of 1 to 7, where 1 feels completely false and 7 completely true?" (Shapiro [1995, 2001] originally developed the Validity of Cognition Scale, or VoC, for the purposes of her dissertation research.)

After she rates the validity of her positive cognition, I ask the client what *emotions* she feels: "When you bring up that incident and the words 'I'm powerless,' what emotions do you feel *now*?" In this example, the client might report fear and anxiety.

At this time I would take a SUDS (Subjective Units of Distress Scale) reading, a scale developed by Wolpe (1991) to determine the degree of disturbance. A SUDS reading is taken at different times during the processing to measure progress. "On a scale from 0 to 10, where 0 is no disturbance or neutral and 10 is the highest disturbance that you can imagine, how disturbing does it feel to you *now*?" In this case the client may report that she feels it is a 10.

In response to the client's SUDS rating, I would ask the client for the *location of the body sensations*: "Where do you feel the disturbance in your body?" She may feel tension in her stomach and sensations in her hands and arms. At this point the client is ready to begin *desensitization*. The BLS is used to reprocess the trauma memory. The target memory is checked from time to time, and the SUDS assessed until the client reports a SUDS of 0 or 1. Then a positive cognition is asked for, measured on the VOC scale, and if it is a 6 or 7, installed, with the client pairing the belief and the picture or incident in his or her mind with BLS. If the session is complete (i.e., the SUDS at 0 or 1), then a body scan is done with the client repeating the positive cognition as he or she mentally scans his or her entire body. Finally, the session is closed and debriefed (see "Standard EMDR Procedural Steps" on page 181).

The Modified Protocol

It can be helpful to invoke the safe/peaceful place, nurturing figures, protectors, wise figures, and others your clients have chosen before starting the processing, especially with clients who have severe early trauma and neglect. In later sessions, when clients are ready to identify the issue or memory to be worked on—something they experience as highly charged—it can helpful to reinstall the peaceful place and resource figures developed in prior sessions. They can draw on the support of these

---

<u>STANDARD EMDR PROCEDURAL STEPS</u>

1. Issue or memory
2. Picture
3. Negative cognition (NC)
4. Positive cognition (PC)
5. Validity of Cognition (VOC): 1, *completely untrue*, to 7, *completely true*
6. Emotions
7. Subjective Units of Disturbance Scale (SUDS): 0, *no disturbance or neutral*, to 10, *the highest level of disturbance you can imagine*
8. Body sensations
9. Desensitization to SUDS 0 or 1
10. Check PC and rate on VOC scale
11. Install PC
12. Body scan
13. Closure
14. Debrief

---

figures as they process the trauma memory. After this is done, we activate the trauma memory using the modified protocol and then begin its desensitization.

After we have determined what memory we are going to target (or we have bridged back and found the target) and have installed the resources (if necessary):

I instruct clients to close their eyes and go inside and then I ask for the image that represents the worst part of the incident, thus beginning the activation of the right-brain neural net.

Next I ask for the emotions, body sensations, and any other significant sensory information (e.g., sounds, smells, or tastes) that can be elicited to enhance the activation in response to the image.

At this point I ask for the negative cognition: "What do you believe about yourself?" Or "What negative belief do you have about yourself?" The negative belief will often spring forth spontaneously, arising from the body experience, rather than from left-brain thinking.

The positive cognition and VOC are omitted, but a positive cognition that arises out of the processing is installed at the end. After the negative cognition is located, the BLS can be initiated with the instruction to the client to "let whatever happens, happen without censoring it."

The SUDs is omitted if it is obvious to you that your client is at a high level of distress. If you cannot determine if the neural net is sufficiently activated, then ask for the level of disturbance, from 0 to 10. The client continues to process the experience as in the standard protocol, until the SUDs is a 0 or 1.

After the SUDS, ask the client to scan his or her body. Process any body sensations that arise and are associated with the trauma memory. When the body is clear, ask for the positive cognition: "When you bring up the incident, what do you believe about yourself now?" The positive belief or statement that arises is installed with the picture or incident. Sometimes there are multiple positive statements that arise for the client. Install all of them with the incident or picture. The VoC is not measured.

This procedure goes directly into the memory network and activates all of the components. It feels organic and flows easily. If they are comfortable, clients can keep their eyes closed as the questions are asked and the components are activated. While they name the emotions, body sensations, and the negative cognition, they go deeper into the memory and are primed to begin the desensitization. By asking for the negative cognition after the emotions and body sensations, the belief comes from the body experience and bypasses the thinking mind. In this way it comes quickly and spontaneously without discussion that can divert attention from the processing and deactivate the network.

I do this in a streamlined way that quickly gets the client into the network and processing: "Close your eyes and go inside. Bring up the picture that is most disturbing to you. Now what emotions do you feel? What do you notice in your body? What do you believe about yourself?"

If the client is clearly distressed, I say, "I'm going to turn on the pulsers. Let whatever comes up, come up without censoring it," and I begin the BLS. This whole process of setting up the target can take as little as 5 minutes. There is no going back and forth and discussing the best cognitions. They get immediately into the memory or image and they begin to process it. The resources are set up ahead of time so that safety is well established. If I cannot tell that the client is activated, I will ask for the SUDS. This may or may not interfere with their ability to enter into the trauma network.

Because the modified procedural steps are streamlined and efficient, they take very little time to activate the memory network and ready the client for the desensitization. This is especially helpful when you are limited to 50-minute sessions. I have found this modified procedure to be smooth and easy for clients. They are able to find a negative cognition quickly from the emotions and body sensations and are in the memory network ready to process.

MODIFIED EMDR PROTOCOL

1. Picture
2. Emotions
3. Body sensations
4. Negative cognition
5. SUDS (0–10) is optional if not obviously activated
6. Desensitization (process to a SUDS of 0 or 1)
7. Body scan
8. Installation (install PC[s] that arise spontaneously)
9. Closure
10. Debrief

The Rationale for Modification

The positive cognition and VoC used during the assessment phase are unnecessary steps. According to the AIP (adaptive information processing) model, when the trauma network is activated and BLS added, clients move toward an adaptive resolution of their trauma. They naturally move toward health and wholeness. With this as the foundational theory for EMDR, why then do we need to front-load a positive cognition? In truth, we do not. I have witnessed this natural drive in thousands of sessions with hundreds of clients. According to Shapiro (1995, 2001) the role of the positive cognition is to provide a sense of hope, a light at the end of the tunnel for our clients. But for many it doesn't provide this. Instead, it takes them out of the trauma network and up into their heads, where they get lost in analysis, derailing the process, and deactivating the network that we were seeking to activate. Later, when we try to bring them back into the memory network and we ask for the emotions, they struggle to find them and have difficulty reactivating the memory network in order to process the memory.

Many clients have difficulty coming up with a positive cognition. They often feel so distressed with the traumatic memory activated that trying to think of something positive feels impossible and frustrating and can cause them to feel like a failure. They may also feel that the therapist is insensitive to their present pain. The struggle for many adults with childhood trauma to find a positive cognition can also pull them out of the child self's experience and take them from the right hemisphere to the left, for an adult intellectual response.

Clients (and therapists) with perfectionist tendencies can become stuck with the cognitions, spending too much time trying to find the "correct" ones. Unfortunately, what may happen in this process is that memory networks associated with punitive teachers or parents can get activated, taking clients away from the issue on which they came to work. To ask clients to then rate their positive cognition can also feel like a useless or futile exercise.

I liken the VoC to a math quiz for a traumatized person. As we know, trauma is stored on the right side of the brain. The computation of numbers takes place on the left. The questions we ask to elicit the VoC are complicated and necessitate a left-hemispheric, frontal-lobe response. This shift requires clients to abandon the trauma memory and work to find the right answer to a quiz for which they don't even understand the instructions. This can be so frustrating and impossible that clients quickly come to believe that they cannot do EMDR; they are failures at it.

In addition, the number rating challenges the adult self (left hemisphere) who cannot even imagine a VoC above a 1 for the positive cognition. For instance, it is very difficult for a client who has activated a memory of being sexually abused by her father and threatened with death to rate the positive cognition "I am safe" above a VoC of 1. This whole process can derail the flow of the therapy. Furthermore, *insisting on getting a VoC can harm a fragile therapeutic alliance*. In retrospect, this whole endeavor, however well meaning, has been a waste of precious processing time, given that at the end of the session an entirely new belief has emerged that is a perfect fit for where the client has arrived.

Taking a VoC at the end is also not necessary if clients come up with a positive cognition that they report is true for them. To ask them to rate their belief on a scale is splitting hairs and does not serve the therapy. For some clients it can feel as if you are doubting their response, causing confusion, and taking away the positive statement they have just made. This step can thereby cause an empathic break—the last thing we want as therapists.

As an EMDR trainer and consultant, I have found that therapists have the most difficulty learning and understanding the VoC. If these highly educated professionals have a difficult time understanding it, then it must be even more difficult for clients. The rationale for the VoC, according to Shapiro (2001), is that it helps the therapist and client assess the validity of the positive cognition. It serves to give feedback about the change that has occurred during the session. But, because of its subjectivity, it is not really a valid measurement. And, since the positive cognition that arises at the end of the session is often different from the one chosen in the beginning, the client is measuring the validity of two *different* cognitions. What does this mean?

In my experience clients can express in words the change they have experienced without the use of the VoC. Many well-educated American clients have difficulty understanding the VoC scale, but this problem is amplified 10-fold for clients from different cultures, clients who are not well educated, and clients for whom numbers and scales are unfamiliar and alienating. It can trigger shame in our clients with relational trauma and create therapeutic alienation and a break in the therapeutic container. Some clients who have difficulty with the cognitions and the VoC don't believe that they are competent enough to do EMDR and avoid it altogether. Because of these problems, I have found the VoC to be the least helpful component of the standard protocol and typically omit it. In my opinion, the cost–benefit ratio justifies this.

The standard protocol takes clients from right brain to left brain to right brain, back and forth. For some clients this can be helpful and containing, but for others it feels as if they are being manipulated—which can disrupt the therapeutic relationship and feel like a reenactment of their early trauma. *Many clients with early attachment trauma are highly sensitive to feeling manipulated and are easily triggered.* I believe the establishment of safety through the resource work, as well as some of the distancing techniques we use, can help keep clients safely within the window of tolerance without front-loading the PC and VoC. The dual focus of awareness can also be reinforced through alternate means, such as the use of distancing techniques, metaphors, and the therapist's use of voice and touch, as well as other methods.

For some clients, the SUDS can also be omitted in the beginning. This is the case if the memory is so obviously distressing that asking them for a SUDS reading creates an empathic break that disrupts the therapeutic alliance. If your client is crying, don't take a SUDS reading. Start the BLS and help him or her process through the memory. Later, during the desensitization, it can be helpful to take the SUDs when your client provides feedback that indicates the processing is near completion. The SUDS helps you to determine if the processing is complete, or if there is still something left to process.

Additional Modifications

Though for the most part I recommend using the modified protocol, EMDR-M, the main idea is that we must seek to maintain a connection with our clients, help them to feel safe, and activate the memory network that is most directly linked to their current symptoms or problems.

BENEFITS OF THE MODIFIED PROTOCOL

- It helps maintain the therapeutic connection.
- It facilitates empathic attunement between therapist and client.
- It enables the client to quickly and smoothly access trauma networks.
- It is time efficient.
- It doesn't feel manipulative.
- Clients are less likely to feel objectified.
- It avoids the pitfalls of perfectionism.
- It creates safety *and* enables the client to activate right-brain trauma memory networks.
- It keeps the client from intellectualizing.
- It helps maintain the emotional charge.
- It is not too confusing for clients.
- Clients are better able to contact affect and body sensations.
- The negative cognition that arises from the emotions and body sensations is easier to locate, has affective resonance, and is more directly linked to core schemas.

Targets do not have to contain all of the components in order for EMDR processing to be successful. Modifications can be made in the target by eliminating components that you either cannot find or that are not clinically appropriate or necessary for the client. This is a clinical decision and relies on the therapist's empathic judgment. *The most important elements are the following*:

- An image
- Body sensations and/or emotions
- Some kind of negative cognitive component
- Combined with BLS.

It is possible to begin processing with only body sensations, but the processing is more likely to be diffuse and go into many different channels. *Well-developed targets that include the image, emotions/body sensations, and negative cognition set the stage for more thorough and complete processing and increase the likelihood of successfully resolving the target. The idea is to activate as much of the memory network as possible and then process it with the bilateral stimulation.* Therefore, it is best to have some kind of image, emotion/body sensation, and negative belief to most vividly stimulate the memory network.

It is important to develop the target in a fluid, easy way that is attuned to the client. Do your best to help your clients come up with each of the target components, but move on to the next one if too much difficulty arises. *Do not struggle with the components. If you sense that the client is getting frustrated, move on to the next part.* You don't want the setup to traumatize your clients. You can guide them, offer suggestions, and do your best to come up with the parts.

Changing the Location of the Body Scan Phase

Recently, I came to the conclusion that the location of the body scan phase in the standard protocol is misplaced. In the standard EMDR protocol the body scan comes after the installation of the positive cognition and right before closure. I have found that often body sensations, which are significant and associated with the target memory, are discovered after the installation of the positive cognition. I believe that the reason this occurs is because when we ask for the SUDS ("How disturbing does that feel to you on a scale of 0 to 10?"), clients may say that they are at a 0 or 1; in essence, they are not experiencing the body sensations as "disturbing."

This component becomes problematic when we are near the end of the session, believing that we have a complete process, only to discover that significant unprocessed trauma remains in the body. This can be experienced as sensation in the jaw or throat; tingling in the hands, arms, or legs; or tightness in the head, neck, or stomach. With the body scan near the end of the session, there is often insufficient time to process these remaining sensations, leaving clients with unprocessed trauma that causes symptoms during the time between sessions.

I have found that doing a scan of the body after the SUDs and before the installation of the positive cognition can catch any unprocessed body sensations. A body scan can be taken again after the installation of the positive cognition too. *I believe, however, that it is most important to catch anything remaining in the body before you are out of time.* The important message here is that you want to clear as much trauma out of clients' systems before the end of the session. Doing the body scan after the SUDS and before the installation of the PC is recommended.

MODIFIED PROCEDURAL STEPS OUTLINE

Safe Place and Resources Installed or Evoked for Support (Optional)
Therapist helps the client to recall previously installed resources or taps them in: safe or peaceful place, nurturing figures, protector figures, wise figures, inner support team.

Picture
"What picture represents the worst part?"

Emotions
"What emotions do you feel?"

Body Sensations
"What do you notice in your body?"

Negative Cognition
"What do you believe about yourself?" The BLS can be started at this point if the client is obviously distressed. If you can't tell if the network is activated, ask for the SUDS. If not, begin the BLS.

SUDS
(Optional: Take if it is clinically useful to know; skip if it takes the client out of the process.) "How disturbing does that feel to you now on a scale from 0 to 10, where 0 is no disturbance or neutral and 10 is the most disturbance you can imagine?"

Desensitize
"I'm going to start the bilateral stimulation. Let whatever happens, happen without censoring it." (Continue until SUDS is 0 or 1.)

Body Scan
"Close your eyes and scan your body. Let me know what you notice."

Installation
When the body scan is clear and the SUDS is 0 or 1, ask "What do you believe about yourself now?" Skip the VoC. Install the positive cognition.

Close and Debrief
Be sure to create a thorough experience of closure. Always leave enough time to debrief. You may return to the safe or peaceful place and bring in the resources for extra support.

CLOSING INCOMPLETE SESSIONS AND SUGGESTIONS FOR HELPING CLIENTS MANAGE BETWEEN SESSIONS

Often clients with attachment trauma have incomplete sessions, especially if there are *feeder memories* (i.e., multiple contributors to the issues they are processing) or their symptom/problem is chronic. For clients with multiple childhood traumas, one trauma memory may link into another and then another, making it difficult to reduce the distress down to a level of calm and peace. It is important to take the time necessary to bring your client to a sense of safety and containment even if it means going overtime. You need to know various techniques for lowering the level of distress so that your clients can safely transition back into their lives. It is essential that clients feel safe and emotionally contained before they are allowed to leave your office.

An incomplete session is one in which a client's material is still unresolved; that is, he or she is still obviously upset or the SUDS is above 1. *Be sure to leave sufficient time at the end of the session to close it down— for most people, 10–15 minutes.* Spend the remaining time talking with the client about the session, helping him or her to begin to digest and integrate the material that has arisen during the session. *Make sure the client is grounded and in his or her body before leaving your office.* Clients may need to splash cold water on their faces and walk around before they get in their cars and drive. *If the client is still too upset to leave your office, go overtime until he or she is in a calm state. Set up an appointment for later in the day or the following day if necessary. Do not leave a client in a distressed state for a week. Make sure the client knows that he or she can call you if feeling upset or out of control.* EMDR processing causes many clients to regress. An adult regressed to a child state may feel very distressed and unable to function properly. It is important to help the client contact the adult self and feel that part functioning and in control.

There are a number of ways you can help your client feel more contained when the session is incomplete. You might find the following closure techniques helpful.

Therapist-Suggested Interweave to Help with Closure

Interweaves can be used to help bring some kind of closure to incomplete sessions. You can use a strategic interweave to tie things together for your client in a way that brings rapid closure. During this time you can be more active and directive, helping your client bring in resources and connect disparate memory networks and ego states.

These interweaves can include any of the types described in Chapter 14. Oftentimes interweaves that bring in the adult self or protector/nurturer figures to comfort or protect the child are useful to help calm down the client who is distressed when time is running low.

THERAPIST: What does your child need?
CLIENT: I need to get out of there.
THERAPIST: Who can get you out?
CLIENT: My adult self along with my team of resources.
THERAPIST: Imagine that. >>>>>

For a client who grew up in a chaotic, unstable household of drug addicts, a question eliciting the adult's perspective can be used.

THERAPIST: Do you still live in that house?
CLIENT: No.
THERAPIST: Think about that. (*Add BLS to link memory networks.*)
CLIENT: I feel relieved. I don't live there anymore. I have a nice home where I live now.
THERAPIST: Do you ever have to live there again?
CLIENT: No.
THERAPIST: Go with that. >>>>>

For the sorrowful child self, bringing in the loving adult self, nurturer figures, or spiritual figures can be helpful for closing.

THERAPIST: Would you like to imagine your nurturing figure holding your child self and giving her love? If you like, you can imagine her saying all the things your child self needs to hear.
CLIENT: Yes, I'd like to do that.
THERAPIST: Imagine that. >>>>>

Or:

THERAPIST: Can you imagine your grandmother holding your child self on her lap and telling her that she loves her?
CLIENT: Yes.
THERAPIST: Go with that. >>>>>

For clients who lived in chronic abusive situations, it can be helpful to end sessions by having someone rescue the child self and take him or her out of the situation to a place of safety. This is detailed in Chapter 14. A Socratic interweave can be used for clients who describe hovering outside of their body because they believe it is not safe to be in the body:

THERAPIST: It wasn't safe to be in your body then. Is it safe to be in your body *now*?

CLIENT: Yes.

THERAPIST: Go with that. >>>>>

Installing a Positive Cognition or Image

It is important to *install something positive at the end of a session as a way to bring closure. This can include a positive cognition, statement, or image.* It is my experience that installing something positive at the end of the session helps the client feel contained and grounded. You can ask the client, "When you bring up the original incident, what do you believe about yourself now?" Install what he or she comes up with. The client may have a *process-oriented positive cognition* (Wildwind, 1993) that shows movement in the direction of positive change. For example, "I'm learning to love myself" or "I can heal this in a safe way" are such cognitions.

If the target incident is still unresolved at the end of the session and a positive cognition cannot be found, the therapist can ask the client, "What did you learn from today's session?" When the client reports what he learned, you apply the BLS to install it. You can also ask, "What do you understand now?" In answering this question, the client begins to form a coherent narrative, putting the pieces of his life together in a meaningful way. Some clients may ask you to help them review the session and your notes. The areas of insight or nuggets of wisdom that came from the client can be repeated to him or her along with the BLS for installation.

You may want to guide your client to his or her peaceful place and install images and statements about safety. *It is most important to install something positive so that the client feels like he or she has gotten something from the session.* This installation of something positive or constructive feels very good to clients. It creates a feeling that things have been tied together in a meaningful way, helping them to feel contained, cared for, empowered, and that they are moving in the direction of healing.

Imagery as a Closing Technique

For clients with complex trauma, I spend more time with closure and may use imagery to begin and end sessions. Whether or not the work is complete, I often ask clients to return to their peaceful place, imagine their adult self or other resource figures holding their child self, and feel as strongly as possible the feelings of safety and security. Either I, or their imagined resources, repeat positive cognitions discovered during the EMDR processing along with affirmations that are beneficial to them. Oftentimes the positive statements are related to the issues of safety, responsibility, and choice: "You are safe now," "You were a little girl who was hurt by a mean, angry grownup—it wasn't your fault," "You didn't have a choice then as a little boy, but you do now as an adult," and so on. Positive cognitions that express movement toward health, such as "I'm beginning to heal," "The hurt is beginning to lighten," or "I can change" are also used if appropriate. When clients report feeling calm, peaceful, and safe, I may install the image, cognitions, and feelings with a short set of BLS.

Sometimes I ask the adult self to soothe the child self with caring words. Sometimes it is the nurturer, protector, or spiritual figures that are called upon to do the comforting. It depends upon the client and his or her needs at the time.

There are times when I feel that it is helpful to use *healing imagery* to increase the feeling of healing. After clients have processed a very intensive memory of having been assaulted, their bodies reverberate with the aftermath of the remembered abuse. Clients often feel raw and wounded. The therapist can suggest to such a client:

"Imagine healing light flowing down through the top of your head and down into all of the places of pain . . . the light gently heals these places with warmth and love. . . . Slowly the wounds are beginning to heal. . . . Feel the warmth and healing. . . . The healing light moves to all of the places of pain bringing new life and renewal to all of those places."

Use the words and images that you believe will work best for clients and give them permission to create the imagery that works best for them. It can be helpful to develop imagery with the client that can be used in this visualization. One woman chose to imagine herself under a beautiful waterfall with crystal clear water that cleansed her body of pain from past assaults. We installed the imagery and feeling with knee taps. She was later able to imagine the waterfall when she took showers to continue the feeling of healing and renewal.

Another important use of imagery in closing sessions is for *containing the unfinished material*. Many different imagery techniques can be used for this purpose. It is helpful to work this imagery choice out with the client ahead of time. Some clients like to imagine leaving their unfinished material in a file folder in your office, where it will be stored until they come in for their next session. Other clients like the image of putting the material in a locked vault or safe.

A colleague of mine asks many of her clients to leave whatever feels uncontainable in some place in her office. Many clients choose a basket. She then asks them to "imagine all of the unfinished images, feelings, body sensations, tastes, and smells and put them into the basket." As they imagine this, she asks her clients to do a short set of BLS. After the image and feeling of containment have been installed, she tells her clients that if they choose, they can continue to work on the contained material when they come back the next week.

Another colleague uses the following imagery to close incomplete EMDR sessions. Clients are asked to imagine the traumatic scene as if they were viewing it on a movie screen. The therapist then asks them to imagine the scene becoming miniaturized. Next clients are asked to imagine putting the scene in a chest that is a very strong container. They then imagine dumping the chest out of a boat so it goes out of sight, yet they know they can retrieve it whenever they like. After the visualization clients are asked to go to their inner sanctuary or safe place and bring in whatever guides or resources they might need. The resultant sense of safety can be installed with a short set of eye movements or other form of BLS.

Another method of containment is to have clients imagine that the remaining traumatic material is on a DVD that they can edit, eject, and store until they want to replay it at a later time. This gives them a sense of control over the material, and many people can readily imagine using a DVD.

Art as a Closing Technique

Art can be a useful tool for closing EMDR sessions. The physical act of drawing or sculpting something is grounding, and the product is a concrete representation of the client's inner experience. Clients can *draw the new image, belief, or feeling* that they have gained by the end of the session. The drawing brings into form that which has been privately held inside, and it can be shared with the therapist. If the client began the session with a drawing, the drawing at the end provides a comparison and a sense of movement. The drawings give a concrete sense that change has occurred during the session and also information about what other work is yet to be done.

Clients can also *draw the containment image*. For example, the client who has imagined his distressing material in a chest at the bottom of the ocean might be asked to draw the image. The drawing further reinforces the sense of containment.

One woman, who had been sexually abused as a child by her grandfather, was afraid that the good memories of her grandfather would be contaminated by the bad ones. Just imagining the separation of the memories was not sufficient for her. After exploring various potential solutions with her therapist, she found a large box with a lid and placed physical representations of the distressing images inside it. She left this box containing the disturbing material with the lid firmly closed in her therapist's office, where she felt it would be safe.

Clients can also reinforce the feeling of safety at the end of the session by *drawing the safe or peaceful place with their adult and child selves and nurturer and protector figures*. After drawing the safe place image, clients can take it home if they wish, as a reminder of their safety in the present.

Closing with Love Resources

You can also close sessions by using any of the love resources I described in Chapter 7. These can include recalling those who love or have loved them, those they love, the circle of love, the heart as a place of refuge, and the loving-kindness meditation.

SUGGESTIONS FOR HELPING CLIENTS MANAGE BETWEEN SESSIONS

There are a number of things you can do to help your clients manage between sessions if they are having a difficult time. These include the use of transitional objects, recordings of personalized guided imagery, and homework.

Transitional Objects

Many clients who have been abused as children have a difficult time with object constancy, especially if the abuse was by a parent or someone close to them. Because of that early betrayal, it is hard for them to carry the therapist inside as a positive inner representation for any length of time. They have a hard time remembering that their therapist continues to exist and cares about them between sessions. For this reason it can be helpful for clients to have what Winnicott (1971) called *transitional objects* with them that represent the therapist and the nurturing/healing environment as physical reminders. These transitional objects can take a variety of different forms. Some clients take objects from the office (e.g., a stone they held in their hand for grounding) as a reminder of the therapist and the office as a safe place. Of course, one must be aware of transference issues that can arise and be cautious that the client does not become overly dependent on the therapist.

Making tapes of relaxation exercises and safe place resources can also be helpful between sessions. These guided imageries, recorded by the therapist speaking directly to the client, are designed for each individual client. These tapes can be very comforting to clients. Clients can play the tapes to help them sleep at night or to relax. If they feel disconnected from the therapist, they can play the tapes as a reminder of the relationship. The tapes can be particularly helpful when therapists take vacations and clients need regular reminders of the reality of the therapeutic relationship.

Clients need to know that their therapists also continue to hold them in their hearts between sessions. It is important for some clients to leave objects that represent aspects of themselves with the therapist in the healing space. Artwork, poetry, special rocks or carved figures, and childhood photographs are given to therapists for safekeeping. Sometimes they are gifts, and sometimes they are "lent" to the therapist for a time. I realize that there are various opinions about this issue and different ways of working with it, depending upon one's theoretical orientation. I do not interpret the gifts because I feel that to do so would create an empathic break. Usually, there is an unspoken understanding of their meaning. I feel honored to be trusted enough to be asked to hold these things for my clients, and I do so until they request their return.

Homework

There are many things clients can do between sessions to help with containment or to facilitate the continuation of the processing, depending on what is in their best interest. Journal writing is very useful to help clients continue with the processing and integration of material. Many clients find poetry writing an important outlet for feelings that cannot easily be expressed in prose form.

Clients can also be encouraged to do artwork. Drawing, painting, collage work, and sculpting can all be done to express feelings and images that arise for clients. Artwork is very integrative and empowering. The focus should be on the expression, not the product. Let whatever wants to be expressed come out in whatever form it takes. Creative expression can be spiritual and enlivening, helping clients experience themselves beyond the victim identity.

Clients can be encouraged to take walks in nature, meditate, do yoga or tai chi, or any other activity or form of expression that will help them reduce their stress and connect more with themselves. Attention should be drawn to the need for a healthy diet, regular exercise, and getting enough restful sleep. Some clients may find group work helpful or a course in self-defense or model mugging. As clients experience stress with the EMDR processing of painful memories, they should be reminded not to drink alcohol or take drugs. If it appears that the client is in need of antianxiety or antidepressant medication, a referral to a psychiatrist for a medication evaluation should be made.

STEPS FOR CLOSING INCOMPLETE SESSIONS

1. Ask the client's permission to stop the session and explain the reason.

   "We are almost out of time and we will need to stop soon.
   How comfortable are you about stopping now?"

   If the client is not comfortable stopping, find out how much time he or she needs, and then continue until the client is at a better place to stop. Go overtime if it is in the client's best interest.

2. Do an interweave.

   "What does the child need? Imagine giving her that."

3. Help the client clarify what was gained in the session, or a positive cognition. (Even if the SUDS is not a 0, look for *some* kind of positive self-statement. It can be a process positive cognition, e.g., "I am learning to love myself.")

continued on next page

STEPS FOR CLOSING INCOMPLETE SESSIONS *(continued)*

"What do you want to take away from the hard work you've done today?" or *"What was the most important thing you learned today?"* or *"What do you believe about yourself now?"* or *"What do you understand now?"*

5. Install the response with a short set of BLS.
   "Think about 'I'm learning to love myself.'"
6. The nurturers, protectors, or other resources can be brought in.
   "Would you like to go to your peaceful place and bring in your resource figures?"
   The resources can be installed with a short set of BLS. Don't use BLS if you are concerned the client will resume processing.
7. Containment exercise: Offer the client the opportunity to leave the distressing material/ feelings in an imaginary container until the next time that the two of you meet to do this work. Acknowledge that the client worked hard in the session and the difficult feelings between sessions. The image of the material in the container can also be installed with a *short* set of BLS.
8. Grounding exercises: You can use different exercises to help clients feel more grounded if they have been dissociated or deep in child networks. You can have them stand up, feel their feet on the floor, imagine deep roots, like on a tree, going down into the earth. When they have a sense of this grounding, add BLS. You can also have them think about what they are going to do during the day that has no conflict in it and add BLS. In this way you are connecting them to their ordinary adult life. For example, the client may go shopping for food and prepare dinner for her family. Add BLS as she imagines these activities. It is like changing the channel so that clients are no longer connected to the childhood trauma channel. You can also ask them about their favorite objects, favorite activities, or even favorite meals as a way of changing the channel. Add BLS as they think of these things.
9. Closure/debrief: Allow sufficient time at the end of the session to talk about what they processed and how it was for them to do so. This reflection helps them connect to you and to the present time. This is the time during which you can provide your observations and insights.

CHAPTER 12

Reevaluation and the Pacing of Treatment

In this chapter I review ideas for the reevaluation of the therapy along with some suggestions for the pacing of treatment.

REEVALUATING THE THERAPY: ASSESSING PROGRESS

In my work as an EMDR consultant I often find that many therapists neglect to regularly reevaluate the therapy. Many fret that they are stuck, that the therapy is not progressing, when in fact it is going quite well. When I ask them to go back to the list of symptoms and problems the client sought treatment for, or check the target, they often discover that their clients are indeed changing. This is often a boost for their morale and an indication that they are on the right track and just need to keep going.

I find it helpful to assess the therapy at the beginning of each session. This is Shapiro's (1995, 2001) eighth phase of EMDR. At the beginning of the session, I check in with my clients about their symptoms, any changes in behavior, any dreams they may have had, any insights, new memories, or changes in their relationships. I will also go back and check the target from the previous session. Has the work held? Is there a new element we didn't get to before, or a new related memory? For example, the client may have another memory associated with the one that was cleared that now feels upsetting. All of these things give me feedback about our progress in therapy. Is it working or not? Where do we go next? Clients who keep journals, write poetry, or do artwork as part of their between-session work may bring that in and talk about it. Depending upon what has come up during the week, together you and your client then decide what the next target for EMDR processing will be.

Reevaluation lets you and your clients know how the therapy is progressing. Checking your work from the previous session and checking in, from time to time, about the symptoms the client came in with helps direct the treatment and provide a sense of hope and accomplishment. If you can return to the list of symptoms from your history taking at the beginning of treatment and ask about them, clients can let you know what has changed and what still remains to be targeted. Often clients are not aware of the reduction they have experienced in their symptoms. I think it is very much like the experience for someone who has been in chronic pain. When the pain is gone, they do not continue to think about it or how they used to be in pain. They just live normally. I believe it is the same with EMDR. After there has been a shift, and clients are free from past emotional pain and symptoms, they forget that they used to be in so much pain. They are just living fully.

A common question I am asked by my EMDR consultees is, how do I know if EMDR is working? *The best way to find out is to check the target.* When you return to the original picture or incident, what comes up? If it is changing, losing its charge, then it is working. Check the client's symptoms. If the symptoms are improving, it is likely that the EMDR is helping. How does the client view him- or herself? Has his or her negative beliefs changed? Have his or her behaviors changed? Is there a reduction in anxiety, flashbacks, nightmares, or triggers?

This way of working—focusing on symptoms—is different from what is done in traditional psychodynamic psychotherapy, in which the therapist follows whatever the client brings up during the session. I have found that in doing symptom-focused work, clients feel held and cared for by the therapist. Their needs are being taken into consideration. Therapy doesn't drift along for years without completing anything. When the symptoms are checked, clients have more control over the therapy and can decide when they have accomplished what they came in to do.

For example, a man who came to see me originally for severe social anxiety and fear of public speaking reprocessed memories of childhood abuse and neglect. At the beginning of each session I would review his symptoms and see how he was doing. Did he have any panic attacks? Was he able to speak in any groups? Was he able to make any bids for construction work in his job as a contractor? When we checked his target from the week before, the charge was still at a 0. We then focused on areas that were still troublesome for him and targeted those. Interestingly, with this client, he spontaneously began taking leadership positions in groups, speaking in public, and taking more initiative at work. His anxiety diminished significantly and his self-esteem increased.

From time to time I like to do a review of the therapy. I will review my notes and the client will review her journal or log. We can look at what symptoms and behaviors have changed and which remain to be worked on. This is especially helpful for clients with complex, early childhood traumas. They can sometimes feel as if they are making little progress because of the quantity of symptoms.

It can also be helpful for the therapist, who may feel discouraged by the lack of progress and the debilitating early trauma and neglect. This was true for therapist Holly Prichard, whose remarkable work with a woman who had attachment trauma is described in Chapters 10 and 16. Holly often felt discouraged by the slow pace or seeming lack of progress in her work with this client. She was in a consultation group I supervised, and I and the other group members could see the progress that she had difficulty seeing. I would ask her to restate the original symptoms and then ask what the client was currently experiencing in that area. We could see that she was getting better. This feedback was helpful for Holly and gave her support to keep going.

Reviewing the work you are doing with clients can provide a sense of hope. When a memory is cleared, it usually does not come back unless there are aspects of it that had not been revealed. Clients often don't realize that their symptoms have lessened until they check back. Issues or problems that have multiple contributors can take longer to clear than something that is linked to a single traumatic incident. As you review the work you have done together, it can be beneficial to tap in the successes. Make a list of what has changed, the symptoms that no longer trouble the client, and then add BLS to strengthen and integrate those positive changes. You can do an entire session of reviewing the work and then highlighting and tapping in successes. After this, you can focus on where you want to go next, mapping out future work.

PACING OF TREATMENT

Depending on the needs of the client, EMDR can be used every session or it can be interspersed between integrative talk sessions or with other methods. I have seen clients on many different schedules according to their needs. Some clients do well with 90-minute (or longer) sessions on a weekly basis. They spend the first part of the session talking and checking in, reevaluating the work from the week before, and then are ready to focus and reprocess a new memory. For some clients this pace would be too intense; they need a single 50-minute session to talk and integrate the information from the EMDR processing session. Some clients with good ego strength can tolerate several EMDR sessions in a week, working intensively in a short period of time on an area of difficulty.

The pacing of treatment should be flexible, adapting to the changing needs of the client as much as possible. Some clients cannot tolerate EMDR processing on a weekly basis. They need more time to integrate the information between sessions. Some clients need talk therapy sessions to integrate the information that has come up during the EMDR sessions and also to connect more fully with the therapist. Ensuring this connection is an important part of the attachment-repair work. Some clients with severe neglect and abuse need more resourcing sessions intermixed with the EMDR trauma processing sessions. For example, you may spend a session tapping in an ideal mother, and then going through the client's development with this new mother, using the BLS. This developmental repair and/or other resourcing can be done in single (50-minute) sessions.

Art, sand tray, Somatic Experiencing, guided imagery, and EMDR Resource Tapping can be useful ways to help with the pacing of treatment. Art and sand tray work can facilitate the integration of the information that has come up and gives clients more of a sense of control over their process.

Some clients like to come in every other week for EMDR, whereas others prefer to intersperse talk therapy sessions with their EMDR sessions. I saw one woman, who had an extensive abuse history, twice a week for 2 years—one 90-minute EMDR session, followed 3 days later by a 50-minute integrative session. She later decreased the frequency of her sessions to a weekly 90-minute session and then to one weekly 50-minute session, with only occasional 90-minute EMDR sessions. Finally, she decreased to one 50-minute session every other week until she ended treatment. Some people have chosen 90-minute EMDR sessions for all of their treatment, whereas others do intensive EMDR work for several weeks and then several shorter integrative sessions.

We want to help clients with childhood trauma and neglect process their memories at a pace that they can tolerate so they will not feel overwhelmed and revictimized. You want to check to see how your clients are functioning between sessions. If they are handling their daily life well, then the pace can be continued, but if they are not, you may wish to slow it down by doing more talk therapy, Resource Tapping, or other processing work. Some clients who were sexually abused have difficulty asking for what they want or are not in touch with themselves enough to recognize their needs. You want to help them discover what works best for them. Some clients may even push themselves too much, doing more EMDR than they can tolerate comfortably.

After intensive EMDR processing of a childhood trauma memory, the client may want to spend several sessions talking about and integrating the information that came up during the EMDR work. At the end of an EMDR session it is helpful to discuss with the client what he feels he needs in scheduling the following session. Some clients, even if they think they want to do another 90-minute EMDR session the following week, may change their minds when they return and assess how they feel, with the therapist's guidance. Postponement of EMDR processing should not necessarily be interpreted as a resistance. The work can be so intensive that some clients need to spread out the EMDR sessions more so that they can better integrate the information that came up and feel grounded and stabilized enough before further processing.

Interestingly, clients with attachment wounding don't necessarily need to have consistent sessions with their EMDR therapists to make significant progress and experience healing. Because I teach and travel frequently, I am not able to see my clients on a regular weekly basis. Despite my erratic schedule, my clients with attachment trauma still make considerable progress. This was also the case with Holly Prichard's client, described in Chapter 10. Holly had a travel schedule that created frequent long breaks from treatment, and still her client made significant progress and was ultimately relieved of the symptoms that had brought her into treatment. Though I don't recommend such a schedule with clients with this kind of background, I find it intriguing that the therapy can still be so effective. I attribute this unexpected efficacy in part to the strength of the positive therapeutic relationship and the resources that were installed and integrated into the clients' nervous systems, where they were then available to them independent of the therapists' presence. In other words, clients were able to develop object constancy through the integration of the resources, including the therapist.

CHAPTER 13

Bringing an Attachment Focus to Desensitization

In this chapter I review the desensitization phase with suggestions as to how you might integrate an attachment focus, keeping in mind the basic principles of client safety, the importance of the therapeutic relationship, and a client-centered focus.

Desensitization begins after you have created safety and then activated the client's target memory with the image, emotions, body sensations, and negative beliefs. The goal is to stimulate the memory network in which the memory is stored so that its various components can be reprocessed. It is important to activate the memory network before starting the BLS. Remember, *memories must be activated in order for processing to occur.*

If the client is processing a memory of being abused as a child, I would instruct her in the following way, using the modified protocol:

THERAPIST: When you bring up the image of your father's face as he hits you, what emotions do you feel?

CLIENT: Shock, fear.

THERAPIST: What do you notice in your body?

CLIENT: Tension in my chest, my throat is constricted, and my heart is racing.

THERAPIST: What do you believe about yourself?

CLIENT: I'm going to die (*begins to cry*).

THERAPIST: [I skip the SUDS because she is obviously distressed and asking her to rate that distress would take her out of the memory network.] I'm going to turn on the pulsers, so let whatever happens, happen without censoring it. (*After she signals to me that the memory is activated, I begin the Tac/ AudioScan.*)

THE DANCE OF DESENSITIZATION: FOLLOWING THE CLIENT

Begin the BLS at the speed the client has told you is the most comfortable. After the first set, you might ask how it is going for the client and if he or she would like any adjustments.

Clients may want to maintain eye contact with you throughout the processing as a way of feeling safe and connected to you—and as a way to not get pulled back into the old trauma memory. Eye contact helps facilitate right-brain to right-brain attachment repair. Some clients will close their eyes initially, process, and then open their eyes after a set of BLS and meet your gaze. It is important to be present and connect with clients when they resurface. Try to keep a gentle, compassionate gaze to meet your client's eyes lovingly. As noted previously, clients take us into their neural nets, resonating with our compassion, which in turn changes their internal circuitry. They should feel free to open or close their eyes as they process according to their needs. Eyes open connects them to you and the present; eyes closed takes them into the neural nets from the past.

Some clients will want you to hold their hand as they process or hold it when they get into highly charged material. Some clients may want you to tap on their knees or the sides of their legs for BLS, as it helps them to feel more connected to you and provides a somatic resource.

These same clients may also want you to use your voice more to give them gentle encouragement as they process. One client needed me to repeat positive statements to her because she couldn't say them herself. I would say things like, "It wasn't your fault, you were a good girl. They did bad things to you. You deserve love." Generally, I don't talk when my clients process unless it's to provide support through abreactions and to reinforce the dual focus of awareness. But sometimes they need more than that, so I follow their lead and provide what they ask for, if I can.

Clients can talk or not talk according to what feels best to them. Some people find that they connect more to their experience and to the therapist if they narrate their experience as they go along. Others only talk when they report in after a set of BLS. Sometimes clients are silent, and then they speak aloud as they process. For some clients, however, talking distances them too much from the memory and they are not able to process it and talk at the same time. In general I refrain from directing clients one way or the other—from talking or not talking—in the beginning. I let them do whatever feels best to them. However, if the original picture has not changed when they return to it, I then ask them not to speak and to focus on the body sensations and emotions.

Find out what feels best for your clients, don't assume. Adjust what you do and how according to their needs (type of BLS, short or long sets, whether it feels better to talk or process silently, eyes open or closed, the use of resources, etc.). If a client goes for a long set of BLS and does not speak, I might stop him and ask what is happening. This is especially true in the case of a new client. I want to know if he has dissociated or gone off on a tangent. The desensitization is like a dance where the therapist follows the client and you learn how you dance best together. Trust the process, listen to your inner voice, and listen to the verbal and nonverbal cues of your clients.

I believe the best therapeutic stance for attachment repair is one of *grounded, spacious, attunement*. I try to be *grounded* in the present, creating a feeling of stability. I remind myself that my client survived whatever she experienced, and we are both safe in the present. I can feel myself sitting in my chair, my feet on the ground. If my mind wanders, I gently bring myself back to the sensation of sitting, or to my breath. Our clients can tell when we are present with them or if we are impatient and distracted. It feels comforting to be with someone who is present and well grounded.

I try to be *spacious*, allowing whatever arises in my client and in myself to be there without judgment. I try to just notice the thoughts, feelings, and body sensations that arise in my mind and body. They mean something, but I don't always know what. I let them be, and at times I use this information to guide my work. For example, I might feel a tension in my chest, though the client has reported a SUDS of 0. Because of this, I might ask her to scan her body and see if she notices anything. She might discover tension in her chest, which reveals more sadness to process which she focuses on with BLS. When I create a feeling of spaciousness, or openness, I find that my intuition is clearer and easier to follow. The intuitive process is a right-brain one and is therefore important in attachment repair. This spacious therapeutic state is similar to the vast, open state cultivated by the practice of mindfulness meditation (Goldstein, 1976; Kabat-Zinn, 1990; Kornfield, 1993). Through years of this practice I have learned to be more present and spacious with whatever arises, allowing this information to simply be. In this way I also nonverbally communicate to my client that whatever arises is OK, promoting acceptance and even a welcoming of the content of the body–mind process. Through the interpersonal subjectivity created between us, my client experiences this openness too, and can more comfortably be with what is coming up for her.

I try to *attune* to my client. I'm feeling *with* her, but not in a way that is intrusive. I try to be relaxed and present, paying attention to what I experience in my body, as well as attending to what I perceive going on with my client. My attention goes fluidly back and forth between my body sensing and my observations of the client. As I connect to my client, feeling with her, I am nonverbally communicating to her that she is not alone as she processes the trauma. We communicate so much nonverbally to our clients. When we are confident in the wisdom inherent in clients, they pick this up from us and feel more confident too. When we attune to and resonate with our clients' wholeness—with the part of them that has not been touched by the trauma—they begin to feel that wholeness more themselves. Our wholeness resonates with their wholeness, and it seems to intensify the healing process. The traumas and resulting erroneous self-constructs are seen as false, as not representing who they really are. I believe it is important, therefore, to both hold the view of clients' wholeness and capacity to heal, and, at the same time, to feel with and acknowledge the damage and suffering they have experienced. Both are true simultaneously. It is important to stay attuned throughout the session and not impose your ideas or interpretations on your client.

According to Schore (2000, 2009) it is the right-brain to right-brain connections that helps heal attachment wounds. These include the connections experienced via attunement, intuition, tone of voice, facial expression, and touch (if touch is experienced as safe for the client). All of these can be integrated into desensitization as appropriate for the client.

MULTIDIMENSIONAL ASPECTS OF THE DENSENSITIZATION EXPERIENCE

During desensitization clients go through a multidimensional free association of thoughts, feelings, and body sensations. Some clients have intense emotional releases, whereas others process more cognitively, their emotions more subtly released. Many experience fantasies and imagery that are dream-like. Everyone has their own processing style, and different memories are processed differently.

Some clients process in long sets of continuous waves, one after another. Stopping the BLS too soon derails the processing of these clients, causing them to lose their train of thoughts and associations. Some clients process in discrete waves with a noticeable beginning, middle, and end. Some process extremely rapidly, needing as few as five saccades (right–left passes) to complete a channel. There are clients who process memories like a flipbook, going through them in rapid succession. These clients are like super processors, defying the therapist's beliefs about what is possible. One client processed dozens of abuse memories in one session. I never would have believed it possible, given her trauma history.

You can tell when to stop the BLS by watching for the waves for many clients. In these waves is a buildup of intensity, followed by a decrease. Some clients will take a deep breath, others will swallow, and some will open their eyes to indicate they have completed a wave. Sometimes you can see their eyes moving rapidly under their eyelids, and then they slow down or stop. For some you can see a flushing of their face, tension in their jaw, or other indications that they are actively processing something, and then they relax. It is not always obvious by looking at the client to tell when to stop. It is more difficult to tell where clients are when they have their eyes closed. Sometimes I am unable to read what is going on in the client, so I just guess and stop the BLS after a few minutes to check in. I ask if I stopped too soon, or if the client would like me to go longer.

I can often track clients by attuning to how I feel as they process. When I am attuned to my clients, I can sense when they are in the processing and when it has been released. I can *feel* the release. There is lightening up, a feeling of openness in my body. I follow the energy and listen to my body response. When the client is intensely processing, my attention is riveted, whereas after a wave has passed there is a sense of relaxation. When the therapist and client are attuned in this way, there is synchronicity, even a feeling of oneness, that I believe is "installed" in their nervous systems as a positive resource. It is helpful to have worked on your own issues with EMDR so that you can be more available to your clients in this way.

At the end of the wave, stop the BLS, pause for a few moments allowing a space, then ask an open, nondirective question, such as:

- "What do you get now?"
- "What's happening now?"
- "What's coming up now?"
- "What are you noticing now?"

Don't ask what they are feeling. *You don't want to guide clients. You want to know what their experience is.* I tell my consultees that what we are really asking our clients is (but I would never say it this way to a client), "What is most predominant in your awareness right now?" We want to know if it is body sensations, emotions, a new memory, an insight. What is most present for them right now?

Sometimes clients will feel obligated to give you a report of all that they have just processed. You don't need all that information, unless they really want to convey it to you. Oftentimes a long report will take them out of the process and up into their heads. It can be helpful to gently tell them that you don't need to know all that right now, and to keep going, and if they want, you can talk about it at the end of the session. If you have lost the charge because of all the discussion, you can redirect the client back to the target and pick up the processing again.

It can be helpful to ask your client to let you know when to stop. After the first few sets of BLS, they get the hang of the wave experience and can themselves feel when it is a good time to stop. This isn't "Stop— I'm overwhelmed"; instead, it's "Stop, it's time to check in, reflect, and talk about what just came up." The processing and talking facilitate the integration of the material the client is processing. It also helps clients to stay connected to you and to remember that they are safe in the present as they are processing the past.

FOSTERING DUAL AWARENESS

It is important to help your clients maintain a dual focus of awareness, in which they feel safe in the present as they process the unsafe trauma from the past. Use your voice if it is helpful to clients. Your voice reminds them of your presence and serves to create distance from what they are processing. However, your voice may be a distraction for some clients and therefore not helpful to them. According to the needs of each individual client, you might reassure him or her during a set of BLS: "That's it. Good. That's it." Do not interpret or comment on the content. It is essential that you stay out of the client's way. It is most helpful to use your voice when clients are abreacting to remind them that they are safe in the present as they are processing the past. "That's it. It's old stuff. Just notice it." You might use the metaphor of the river, a movie, or train. "Remember, it's just a movie."

With clients who tend to dissociate, you might ask them to keep their eyes open, even if you are doing tapping or auditory stimulation. Eyes open helps to maintain the present awareness and to provide assurance that they will not go as deeply into the memory. It can also be helpful to have clients talk as they process. Talking aloud helps us maintain the dual focus of awareness (Parnell, 2007). If they are completely overwhelmed and interweaves are not working, you can ask your clients if they would like to return to their peaceful place. However, it is always better to complete the processing than to go to safe/peaceful place.

Clients do not have to show emotions when they process for the processing to be working well. Sometimes the processing is so rapid that the affect flicks by their awareness, barely registering. EMDR does not have to look a certain way for it to be successful. *Don't push for affect.* Don't push for anything. Follow the client's process. Therapists are so conditioned to dig for emotions that they can cause an undemonstrative client to feel that he or she isn't doing it right. Some clients just don't process with much affect, and yet still experience a successful reduction in SUDS and symptoms. Some memories have more emotions associated with them than other memories. Oftentimes clients have many insights and not much happening in their bodies. This is fine. It is *all* fine.

EVALUATING THE PROCESSING

The way to tell if the processing is working is to return to the original picture or incident. "Let's return to the scene with your father. What do you get now?" If it has not changed—the picture, the emotions, body sensations, and negative cognition are the same as when you began desensitization—then focus on the body or emotions. But if it has changed and the client wasn't emoting, don't worry about it. It is my feeling that if we impose our view that it is essential to emote during EMDR, then we are communicating to our clients that they are wrong, that who they are and how they process are wrong. I feel very strongly that it is most important not to add anything that is not needed to the EMDR process. *Stay out of the way as much as possible.* Trust the client and the process. Intervene only if the process is stuck or you are running out of time. By allowing the processing to unfold organically, you support clients' confidence in their own inner wisdom.

Some clients process primarily kinesthetically, with few images or stories, just sensation arising in different areas. Some have no imagery at all. This type of processing can go on for many sessions. You can tell that the processing is progressing by returning to the original picture or incident and checking it. If it has changed, then the processing is progressing. One man I worked with processed in this way. His body would jerk and shake, his arms would move spontaneously, and he would yawn. There was very little content, but the image he began with decreased significantly in disturbance.

As I said earlier, I think of EMDR processing as a dance. The first session with a client is awkward because my client and I have not yet found our style of working. Does he like long sets or short ones? Does he like to talk or remain silent? Does he indicate *stop* by opening his eyes? Together we figure it out and then develop a flow and rhythm to our work together. Don't worry about stepping on your client's toes. *When in doubt, ask your client*: "Did I stop you too soon?" "Did I go too long?" "Would you like me to tap faster?"

After the client reports her experience, say simply, "Go with that" or "Focus on that." Don't repeat the client's words or statements unless the client is confused about what to go with—in short, no reflective listening. The idea is to keep a flow of processing going. Nothing remains the same. Don't let your client talk for too long between sets. You can tell that she has talked too long when there has been a loss of energy or focus in the work. The momentum from the processing has been lost. It can feel too analytical, less of a full body–mind process. You want to keep the processing moving along. Clients and therapists who are used to talk therapy may get caught up in analysis and discussion of content, but doing so can derail the processing and waste time. Yet, you also don't want to cut off your clients if what they are saying feels important to them. There is an art to this delicate part of the dance. If you feel that your client is derailing the processing by talking too long, gently encourage him to "go with that," and begin BLS. Also, *if it feels as if the energy of the processing has been dissipated by talking, return to the original image or incident and check it*: "Let's go back to the scene we started with. What comes up for you now?"

If the client asks you what she should go with, tell her to *go with the most charged part. Follow the charge.* In general, we want to go with whatever is disturbing to the client. Because what is positive and resourceful will increase on its own we don't need to focus on the positive during the desensitization phase. As we focus on the dysfunctional information, it will decrease and the healthy part will grow and strengthen naturally. The exception is clinically depressed clients or clients with histories of neglect. If positive feelings or cognitions arise for these clients, I might focus on them longer for a set or two.

If the client reports two things of equal charge, ask, "Which one feels the most charged to you?" If she can't decide, you can ask her to choose one and focus on it, and return to focus on the other later. I think of this like a fork in the road. Take one road now and then come back, if you wish, to take the other one. Often what happens is that the second one is resolved during the processing of the first, and there is then no reason to return to it.

MANAGING CHANNELS OF ASSOCIATIONS

Clients tend to process down *channels of associations*. These channels radiate from the target and can be imagined like fingers on a hand. Channels can include associated thoughts, images, emotions, body sensations, and memories. Clients can need several sets to process one channel, or only one set may complete it. You can tell clients are at the end of a channel when they report that nothing is happening. Sometimes they will say that they are stuck or blocked. When this happens, ask them to return to the original picture or incident and to tell you what comes up now: "When you bring up the incident with your father when you were 3, what comes up now?" It can be helpful to give clients a few key words so that they know to what incident you are referring.

If the processing becomes too diffuse, they seem to be associating to tangential memories, or they connect to memories they don't have time to process or don't want to go into, bring them back to the original scene or incident. It is important during the processing to keep the client from becoming too dispersed. Some clients can go down many different associated channels that get further and further away from the original issue or memory. In these cases it can be helpful to return to the target image and check in. For example, you might ask, "When you bring up the image of your father's face, what comes up for you now?" This check-in gives you an indication of how much of the processing has been done. If in this case the client responds, "I feel angry now," then you know that things are processing (i.e., because the client began with feelings of fear). The therapist says, "Go with that," and begins the BLS again. If you have a short session, you may return to the target more frequently to help manage the time. *When in doubt, return to the target.*

One of the most common fears for multiply traumatized clients is that they will open up too many memories and become flooded. You can make an agreement with the client at the beginning of the session that you will work on one memory and if another should open up, he or she can signal you to stop. Then return to the original picture or incident. Do bring clients back to the target from time to time. Don't let them drift too far afield. The protocol is containing and comforting. If you let them go too far, it can feel frightening, as if they are unraveling.

Don't let clients spin in their heads analyzing all the details or getting stuck in despair that they never got what they needed and never will, etc. This is unproductive processing that will only leave them stuck in a rut. Gently redirect them to the target, and if they are stuck and looping, do an interweave.

TIPS ON MANAGING SESSIONS

Return to target if . . .

1. The client says that things are blank, stuck, or that nothing is happening.
2. The client is opening up a memory that he or she doesn't want to process.
3. You want to contain the work and keep it more focused.
4. You are running low on time.
5. The processing is too diffuse.
6. You want to check your work and see where you are.
7. When in doubt, return to target.

DON'T

- Talk while the client processes unless it is to say encouraging words.
- Interpret.
- Repeat the client's words—no reflective listening.
- Get into a discussion with the client between sets. Instead, keep the processing moving along.

One additional caveat on this topic: *If the client starts to work on one memory, and during the processing opens up an earlier, more charged memory, make the earlier, stronger memory your new target.* For example, if the client begins with a memory in high school, and after a few minutes of processing links to a memory that is much stronger from age 5, make the earlier memory your target. You don't have to set this up formally. Just tell the client, "Let's check the memory from when you were 5 and your father was yelling at you. What comes up now?" Keep returning to this new target until it is complete, install a positive cognition with it, and then, only if you have time, return to the high school memory and check it. Process that memory to completion if you can. If the client links to an earlier memory *later* in the session, make a note of it, but don't make it the target for the session if you don't have enough time. It is better to process the one you began with as far as you can and tie up any loose ends than to open up a target memory you won't have time to finish, while also leaving the original target memory activated.

TARGET NUANCES

I want to say a few words about what I mean by *target*. The target is the scene or picture with which you began the EMDR processing—the scene on which you focused and used BLS. If you have used the bridging technique to find your target, then the scene to which you return is the scene to which you bridged (the earlier scene, chronologically). For example, if you bridged the client from a recent trigger, such as an argument with her husband, to a childhood memory of abuse by her father, the target that you would begin and end with would be the memory with her father. When this is complete, you would then work on the trigger with her husband.

When you check the target, you do not bring up the emotions, body sensations, negative cognition, or details of the incident again. You simply want to return to the scene and see what still remains. Sometimes the picture becomes a video clip of several scenes that move forward in time. I ask the client to scan the movie of what he has processed, and to tell me what is still there. Sometimes the incident has been changed by the client, who has creatively brought in resources or imagined doing what he couldn't do at the time. When this happens, I do not force the client back into the "original incident" as it happened; rather, I check the "evolved" scene or incident. Sometimes the picture or scene vanishes entirely; in these cases you can ask your client to "think of the incident" and see what comes up for them.

When you check the target, if clients describe new material or any disturbance, continue with BLS. If they report no disturbance, take a SUDS reading: "When you bring up the incident, on a scale of 0–10, where 0 is no disturbance or neutral, and 10 is the highest disturbance you can imagine, how disturbing does it feel to you now?" If the SUDS is 0, do a body scan and process any remaining body sensations that are linked to the target.

When the scan is clear, proceed to the *installation of the positive cognition*. If the SUDS is greater than 0, ask, "What keeps it from being a 0?" or "What makes it a 2?" When the client tells you, say, "Go with that," then do more BLS. Don't take the SUDS if the client is still in the middle of processing. Remember that every time you take the SUDS, you take the client out of his or her experience, possibly derailing the processing. If clients are reporting a disturbance, you don't need to scale it—just keep processing. It is most helpful to take the SUDS if you suspect that the processing is stuck, or if you think the client has completed reprocessing of the target.

Some clients will never give you a 0 SUDS because they don't believe in 0's. Others will give you a 0 because they feel sorry for you and they want to please you. If that is the case, encourage the client to go a little longer. I have had many experiences of clients thinking they had gone as far as they could, but with my encouragement continued on for another set, only to find a very important piece remained to be processed.

When the client returns to the picture or incident and reports that it doesn't disturb her anymore, gives a SUDS of 0 or 1, and has a clear body scan, you can install the positive cognition that arises from the processing itself. I simply ask, "When you bring up that scene with your father, what do you believe about yourself now?" As I explained in Chapter 11, you can install whatever arises for them organically as a result of their processing. If the session is incomplete, you can still install, using BLS, something positive they gained during the time, such as what they now understand or what they learned along with any positive cognitions.

DESENSITIZATION SEQUENCE

1. Activate the memory network (image, emotion, body sensation, and negative cognition).
2. Add BLS and process.
3. At the end of a wave or channel, stop BLS.

The therapist asks:

- "What do you get now?"
- "What is happening now?"
- "What are you experiencing now?"

The client answers. The therapist listens and does not comment or interpret what the client says. The therapist says, "Go with that" and begins BLS.

The client processes, and the therapist checks in, saying "Go with that." They continue processing back and forth until the client reaches the end of a channel.

The therapist stops BLS and asks, "What do you get now?"

The client responds with "Not much is happening," or "I'm stuck," or "It's blank," etc.

The therapist asks the client to go back to the original picture or incident: "What comes up for you now?"

The therapist waits to hear what the client says.

If the client reports something that has charge, the therapist says, "Go with that," and resumes BLS.

If the client says, "It doesn't feel very disturbing" or that it feels flat or neutral, the therapist takes a SUDS reading. (*Do not take SUDS if the processing is moving along. It takes the client out of the flow of processing.*)

If the SUDS is above a 0, the therapist asks the client, "What keeps it from being a 0?"

The therapist listens to the client's response and then says, "Go with that," and resumes BLS.

If the client reports the disturbance to be a 0 or 1, then the therapist is ready to install the positive cognition.

CHAPTER 14

Using Interweaves to Unblock Processing

Clients who have early childhood abuse and neglect or other childhood traumas often loop in the child memory networks and need help getting the processing back on track. I have found that they tend to benefit particularly from resource and imagination interweaves, which enable them to create healing scenarios that repair past hurts and unblock places of blocked impulses. *Inquiry interweaves* can also be helpful in linking networks together and in sorting out "threads" that don't belong. What follows is a review of information on working with blocked processing, interweaves and how and when to use them, and case examples of attachment repair.

There are several different ways that clients may be blocked in their processing. One of the most common is what is called *looping*. Clients are looping when they are cycling through the same emotions, sensations, images, or thoughts in successive sets without a change. Typically the client is very distressed, but the BLS is not able to link up the different memory networks to keep the processing moving along. Looping seems like a broken record repeating over and over the same thoughts, feelings, and emotions without change.

When the client is looping with the same affect, she might be crying and repeating "I'm going to die" over and over. A client who is looping with the same cognition may not exhibit high affect, which can be confusing, as you may not realize for a while that the processing is not progressing. I have seen clients move from one memory to another with a similar theme, such as times when they felt powerless, without an evolution or resolution emerging. When they return to the original scene, the SUDS and cognitions remain unchanged. Clients looping with body sensations might repeat that the sensation is not changing after subsequent sets of BLS; for example, a client who continues to report a feeling of tension in his chest.

Sometimes there is a resistance to, or blocking of, processing that is different from looping. This may take the form of clients saying that nothing is happening after several sets of BLS. They simply do not seem to be processing. This may be an indication that they are at the end of a channel, in which case it is best to return to the target and check it. They may need to reactivate the network again if they got distracted or had difficulty getting into the processing.

At times the processing is continuing, but there is little time left in the session, and the SUDS is 2 or above. In this case you might need to become more proactive in helping your client weave networks together. Adults abused as children frequently are not able to complete sessions, especially if there were several abuse incidents. In these cases, therapist-supplied interweaves are very useful for closing the sessions. It is very important that you not leave your severely traumatized clients at SUDS levels above a 3. I rarely leave clients at a SUDS above 1 or 2. I have found that becoming more active in the use of interweaves is essential to helping clients close sessions in the safest and most effective way.

In my experience as an EMDR consultant, I have found that EMDR therapists are weak in this area. Many do not understand that it is important to actively use interweaves to close sessions. It is far more effective than the use of the safe or peaceful place and containment imagery alone in closing sessions with SUDS above 2.

There are several approaches you can take if you suspect that your client is looping or stuck. The most common approaches include (1) checking for blocking beliefs, (2) asking the child self what he or she needs, (3) checking for blocking body sensations, and/or (4) checking for feeder memories or blocking ego states.

CHECKING FOR BLOCKING BELIEFS

If the client seems to be looping, I commonly look for blocking beliefs— that is, beliefs that the client experiences as true on an unconscious level that impede the processing. You can find the blocking belief by simply asking the client, "What do you believe about yourself?" If he answers, "If I cry, then they win," you might say, "Go with that," or do an interweave. Sometimes by just saying aloud the belief that has been blocking the processing and then adding BLS, the processing gets back on track.

Oftentimes, the client is reluctant to express the blocking belief if it evokes feelings of shame, a broken agreement (prohibition against telling, threats of harm), issues of trusting the therapist, or taboo subjects. You can offer suggestions or hypotheses to the client, who then accepts or rejects them. For example, if I suspect that the client is experiencing feelings of sexual stimulation in the genitals, as a body memory associated with the abuse memory she is processing, I might say something about this being an experience common to people who have been abused, thereby normalizing it without asking her directly if she is experiencing this.

Sometimes clients may appear to be stuck in a sensation, but it actually is a *belief* that is causing the sensation to be blocked. For example, if the client feels a blockage in the throat, the unconscious belief might be "It's not safe to tell."

There are four main issues with corresponding beliefs that frequently cause clients to loop or become stuck: *safety, responsibility, choice/control* (Parnell, 1997, 1999, 2007; Shapiro, 1995), and *shame* (Parnell, 1999, 2007). Though there are other concerns that can block the processing as well, these four come up most frequently when working with adults who have been traumatized as children. It is important to listen for these issues when they arise and intervene appropriately. These issues arise throughout the course of treatment, affect the transference and therapeutic relationship, and are important themes in the EMDR processing sessions. Keep these issues in mind as you explore with the client what belief might be impeding the processing.

When using interweaves to address blocking beliefs in these key areas, it is important to know what belief is blocking the processing. You can ask your client what he believes about himself, or deduce the belief from what he tells you. *You want to match the interweave with the belief.* For example, if your client is looping in "I'm not safe," then you could use a Socratic interweave and ask, "Are you safe now?" When the client says, "Yes," you say, "Go with that," and add BLS. You could also do an imagination interweave and ask the child self, "What do you need to be safe?" The client might say, "I need the police to come and put him in jail." You then say, "Imagine that," and add BLS.

Safety

Safety, as I explained earlier, is very important to establish in the therapeutic relationship and in AF-EMDR because it is the foundation upon which the therapy takes place, and it creates a corrective emotional experience for the client, thereby creating new neural nets. Clients who were abused or neglected did not feel safe as children and continue to believe that they are unsafe as adults. They bring this belief into the transference with us, as well as into other relationships. An adult client abused in childhood may unconsciously believe that the perpetrator can still harm her, even if she knows the perpetrator is old, disabled, or even dead. This belief can continue to come up repeatedly in EMDR sessions, even with successful processing of target memories, especially if the client experienced multiple traumas or grew up in a home that was unsafe physically or emotionally.

For example, one client was not physically abused as a child, but she witnessed her father abusing her brothers, and she herself was verbally tormented by those brothers. No one in the family felt safe, as they were all subjected to ridicule and humiliation by the parents. The general atmosphere of her home environment was one of fear and unease. It wasn't safe to express oneself freely, to be oneself. As a result, in order to survive, she developed a façade, a false self. EMDR targets were not easy to find, as specific traumas were hard to locate. It was the general feeling of *unsafety*, the very air that they all breathed growing up, that caused the problems. In our EMDR work, the belief "I'm unsafe" came up in nearly every session, and we would use interweaves to get her out of the loop. Over time the belief began to lose its power. She did not feel as fearful, as her nervous system calmed down.

Responsibility

Children tend to believe that they are responsible for the behavior of the adults in their lives. Almost all children blame themselves for the abuse they received. "It's my fault—I made him mad. If only I were a better son, my father wouldn't have beaten me." I found this assumption of responsibility to be present even in a case where the client had been abducted and abused by a stranger. The client continued to believe unconsciously, throughout his life, that he must have deserved this terrifying experience; he must have done something wrong. Many adult children of alcoholics believe that they are responsible for taking care of their families. They take on an inordinate amount of responsibility for themselves, their siblings, and their parents. This is also true in families where a parent suffers from a mental or physical illness.

I have found that many clients confuse compassion and responsibility. For example, a client might feel compassion for his mentally ill mother who, in the throes of a manic episode, beats him and his siblings. He believes it is his job to take care of her because no one else is. Socratic interweaves can be helpful to sort this out, but the client may need resource and imagination interweaves as well.

For example, say that the client is looping in a memory of one of his mother's violent manic episodes. He feels unsafe and terrified. The therapist asks, "What does the child need?" The client responds, "I need to get out of here." The therapist asks, "Would you like to imagine being rescued?" The client then says, "I can't leave her, I have to take care of her! I can't leave my siblings with her!" This state can feel like such a stuck place. The client feels responsible for his mother and siblings, yet in the memory he is just a 6-year-old child. You can ask, "Would you like to imagine bringing in help for your mother, and for your brother and sisters too?" When the client answers affirmatively, ask, "Who would you like to bring in?" Then allow your client to create a scenario in which the mother and siblings are taken care of. After the client imagines this, ask, "What do you need now?" The client answers, "I need to get out of there." Then you say, "Imagine that," and add the BLS for the imagination interweave. (I provide more examples of these interweaves later in this chapter.)

Choice/Control

For many traumatized people, the moment of loss of power or control gets locked in their nervous system along with the belief "I'm powerless" or "I have no control over anything." This can be true for clients who experienced traumas in childhood or adulthood. The child who was small and defenseless when she was traumatized or abused often develops a sense of being perpetually helpless, a victim forever. This victimization may get repeated throughout her life. The perpetrator took away her power and she continued to feel disempowered in her current life. Our clients didn't have a *choice* about what happened to them *then*, and they continue unconsciously to believe that they have no choice in their adult life *now*. Client empowerment is very important in this work, and attention should be paid to this issue throughout the therapy by helping clients draw from their own inner wisdom, connect with their bodies in the present, and learn healthy assertiveness.

Clients who were neglected also feel powerless. No one took care of them when they were children, and often the system failed them too.

Despite coming to school dirty and disheveled, no adults came to their rescue. Or, if they did, it wasn't helpful. Maybe they were left with their drug-addicted parents, or they were placed in overcrowded foster homes. These children grow up to be adults who may be depressed, anxious, and have difficulty in social situations. They don't believe they can make an impact on their lives, as they couldn't as children.

Clients with histories of repeated medical or dental procedures in childhood can also present with similar beliefs. As a helpless child in a hospital receiving repeated intrusive examinations and injections, the child develops the belief that he has no choice or control over his body. He cannot say no. He feels powerless in much the same way as a victim of abuse does.

Shame

The feeling of shame, with the beliefs associated with it such as "I'm bad, I'm disgusting, there's something wrong with me," will often stop the processing. Shame is a deeply felt emotion that many survivors believe defines their core self. "I am this shameful piece of shit. . . . If he's mad, it is because I am bad," one woman said. This feeling of badness becomes a self-defining belief that affects their self-esteem and forms the foundation for their self-concept.

Seductive perpetrators often convince children that they wanted the abuse they received. These children are often lonely and vulnerable, craving the attention these predators provide them. When their bodies respond with pleasure, the perpetrators tell the children, "See, you like it!" thereby persuading them that they are complicit in the act. When the child returns, lured by the attention he is receiving, the perpetrator further convinces him of his guilt. Because of this guilt and shame, the client processing these memories will frequently loop in the feelings that can be so strong and upsetting; he cannot tell the therapist what he is feeling. In these cases it can be helpful for the therapist to guess the issue and address it with the client. I have found that naming and normalizing shame feelings can help to diffuse them, making it possible to use an intervention to help the processing to resume.

TALKING TO THE CHILD SELF

If the processing is blocked and the client is in a child state, you can talk to the child self in order to find out what might be blocking the

222 Attachment-Focused EMDR

processing: "What does the child need?" or "What does the child want?" or "What does the child feel?" or "What does the child self long for?" It is helpful to use simple language and a gentle tone. If the child self is frightened, what is scaring him or her? What is she or he seeing that is distressing? What is happening in the scene? What does the child self need in order to feel safe? This open exploration can lead to a blocking belief or image. The therapist and client can then design an interweave.

I use this intervention frequently when working with clients who have childhood trauma. They will frequently loop in the child state. No one was there to help them, no one paid attention to their needs or asked them how they were doing. I believe the inquiry we use, "What does the child need?" is healing for our clients. No one ever asked them that question. *We ask them the question, then wait for their response. Don't assume what they will tell you, and don't assume that what they need is a resource.* Often I will think I know what a client is going to tell me, and I'm wrong! Listen and wait for the child self to answer.

If clients have difficulty coming up with an answer, offer suggestions and wait to see what fits for them. *Ask, don't tell.* They may come up with something you never would have thought of. Encourage your clients to be creative. They can ask for anything their heart desires. Even if it was impossible then, they can have it in their imagination now. In AF-EMDR we use a lot of resource and imagination interweaves to link in, through imagination, to experiences the client did not have. These interweaves are powerful and reparative. Clients link in, through their imagination, to the experiences they needed to have as a child. A client might answer the question "What does your little girl need?" with "I need a new mommy." You can then say, "Would you like to imagine having a new mommy?" If she says, "Yes," say, "Imagine that," and add BLS.

For example, the client who is processing a memory of seeing his father beat his mother is looping in helplessness. The therapist asks, "What does the child need?" The client responds, "I need someone to stop my dad!" The therapist responds, "Who can do that?" The client says, "My grandfather." The therapist says, "Imagine that," and adds BLS.

I provide more information and case examples for resource and imagination interweaves later in this chapter, and also in the cases in Part IV of this book.

CHECKING FOR BLOCKING BODY SENSATIONS

Sometimes it is a body sensation that is blocking the processing. This might manifest as tightness in the throat or jaw, constriction in the chest, tingling in the hands, or any number of other signs. For clients who have difficulty attending to their bodies, you can direct them to "press the area of the sensation" to amplify it and make it easier to bring the attention there. Clients can focus on the most pronounced sensation if there are many of them and they can't decide where to focus. Sometimes clients avoid focusing on their bodies because they feel sexual arousal—body memories that are being activated by the processing of the old memories. If this is the case, you might need to talk about any blocking beliefs (e.g., "I'm bad for feeling this") and possibly do an education interweave.

Clients can also use movement to emphasize something they are feeling in order to amplify it. They can move their hands or arms or stand up to increase the feeling and to unblock any blocked energy they might be feeling. Consider a client who is processing a memory of being abused and is very angry, but also frustrated because she cannot express it. The therapist can suggest that she stand up and move around, as she feels compelled to do in the present, confronting her abuser with her imagination. Clients can act out punching, hitting, or even protecting themselves from blows. Movement can effectively activate the somatic memory component, which, with the BLS, can increase the effective processing of the traumatic memory.

Inviting clients to imagine saying or doing something they couldn't do at the time of the trauma allows the body to get out of the stuck somatic loop. If they wanted to run away but couldn't because they were a helpless child with abusive parents, giving them permission to imagine running completes the process their body wanted to do and takes them out of the loop. They can move their legs or just imagine the movement. Either way activates the motor neurons and allows for the completion of the frozen act. There are many places in the body where actions become frozen in trauma. When clients report these, give them permission to say or do what they couldn't say or do at the time. It can be helpful to explain that you know they couldn't have done it at the time, but that they can do it in their imagination now. When they imagine it, add the BLS.

Oftentimes, clients feel a constriction in the jaw or throat. Something may want to be expressed; it may not even be words, but simply sound. I'll ask, "Is there something you want to say, or a sound you want to make?" Again, don't assume what it is. If they say, "Yes," respond with "You can imagine saying it, or actually say it out loud—whichever feels best for you." You can encourage clients to speak words or make sounds aloud during processing with BLS. Clients can yell at the perpetrator or scream their terror into a pillow with the BLS. Expressing themselves in conjunction with the BLS helps to remove the blockage. I have had clients stand up and punch, scream, growl, and so forth, through an abreaction.

Many therapists are trained to look for somatic processing and emotional releases. However, these are not necessary for EMDR to work. Different people process memories in different ways. Don't push for any particular way of processing. As I noted earlier, to push for something you have in mind gives clients the message that what they are doing isn't good enough. I only emphasize somatic or emotional experience when the processing is stuck or looping. Again, go back to the original picture and check it. If it is changed—the SUDS is down, the cognitions have changed—then the processing is working. It may have moved so fast that they (and you) were not aware of the somatic component. It is not necessarily a blockage. If their symptoms are improving, it is working, whether or not they reported body sensations. However, at the end of the session, if there is something left in the body, then focus on that with BLS. The processing is not complete until the body is clear.

CHECKING FOR FEEDER MEMORIES

A *feeder memory* (Shapiro, 1995, 2001) is an unprocessed earlier memory that is contributing to the current problem and blocking the processing of the targeted memory. Sometimes clients are able to report that there is another memory coming up that is blocking the processing, but often it is necessary to stop and explore with the client if there is an earlier memory. In some cases it is necessary to shift from processing the target memory to reprocessing the feeder memory before the target memory can be processed.

For example, you may have used the bridging or float-back technique to find a target memory from the client's fear of public speaking. It linked back to an upsetting and humiliating experience in grade school. When processing the memory, the distress would only go down to a SUDS of 3 or 4. What is going on that blocks further reduction? Upon exploring this area with the client, you discover, by bridging back further, that it links to an earlier memory with her father when he humiliated her in front of the entire family, accusing her of being bad and stupid. If you have enough time left in the session, you shift to this new target (you don't have to do a whole new setup) and process this as far as you can. Sometimes it may be necessary to spend an entire session on the feeder memories, returning to the original target memory at another session.

CHECKING FOR BLOCKING EGO STATES

Sometimes there are ego states that are blocking the processing. These are often "protector" ego states that function to keep the person safe from feelings or information "they" deem unsafe for the "host" to know about or to process. While processing, the client might go blank, report no feelings, or feel as if a door has been closed. You want to stop the BLS and explore what is going on.

I might ask, "Is there a part of you that is stopping the processing? Is there a part of you that is protecting you from something?" If the client says yes, I'll begin to ask questions of this part that has surfaced. I might ask if it has a name, what it looks like, how old it is, when it came into being, what its function or purpose is. As I gather information, I learn more about this part. It is important to be respectful and curious about it. Usually the function is to protect and keep the client safe. Sometimes, however, these ego states are very critical and punitive to "protect" the client from making a mistake and getting in trouble. I might ask the part what it needs in order for the client to be able to process the trauma memory. I listen for the response. We may need to bring in imagination resources, or the part may need more time to trust the therapist. I believe it is important to explore this possibility of blocking ego states and come up with solutions that work for all parts. See Carol Forgash's (2008) book *Healing the Heart of Dissociation with EMDR and Ego State Therapy* for more information on working with ego states using EMDR.

ADDRESSING CLIENTS' FEARS

Sometimes fears arise during EMDR processing that cause the client to stop processing. There are many reasons clients become fearful during EMDR sessions. In the beginning many clients are concerned that they are not doing it "right." They stop processing because they are assessing their progress and cannot allow themselves to let go and trust the flow of associations. When this happens, I tell them, "I'll let you know if it's working or not." I also assure them, "There are no right or wrong ways of doing it, it's different for everyone." I find that I reassure my clients a lot. "You're doing fine," I tell them when they have doubts about how it's going. Some clients come in with an expectation that they will have strong emotional releases, and when that doesn't happen, they believe that the treatment is not working. In those cases I tell them, "You don't have to have strong feelings in order to process. You're doing fine."

Some clients are afraid of going crazy with the perceived loss of control, the intensity of the images and emotions that are coming up with EMDR processing, and the fantastical, dream-like imagery that may be emerging. Address these fears and reassure the client, if necessary. Again, I will ask, "What do you need to be safe?" If the client answers, "I need to bring in a protector figure," I will do an imagination interweave bringing in a protector. If the client says, "I need you to hold my hand," I will hold her hand. If she says, "I need to stop," I can guide her to her safe or peaceful place and bring in nurturing and protector figures, if necessary. In some cases I might use distancing techniques, such as imagining the scene like a movie, projecting it outward, or putting a glass wall between the client and the upsetting memory.

Sometimes the fear that comes up has to do with the therapeutic relationship. Perhaps your client does not feel safe with you for some reason. In that case, do whatever you can to repair the relationship. Spend time talking with your client, exploring what came up that made him feel unsafe. What can you do to help him feel safer with you? You might need to apologize for an error you made. After exploring and repairing, you might, if appropriate, bridge back from the transference to find the early link and then target it with EMDR. In any event, do not proceed with EMDR if the relationship is not secure. Furthermore, because some clients may require help with medication to enable them to better cope with the emotions and anxiety that arise between sessions, having adjunctive psychiatric backup and support can be very helpful.

Some clients may block the processing because they are afraid of getting better. Secondary gain issues may be blocking the processing: for example, "If I get through these old memories, who will I be? Who will my friends be? What will my life look like?" The current symptoms, though debilitating, are familiar. If identified, these resistances should be discussed with the client. Perhaps the therapy is proceeding too quickly and the client needs more time to integrate the changes in self-perception and relating to others. You might explore this area by saying, "Imagine what your life would be like if you didn't have these problems." Then use BLS when the client begins to imagine such a future. Imaging and using BLS in this way can help break through some of the old fears and change the old pattern of self-identification. Clients play it out first in the imaginative realm, and then they discover that they can let go of their symptoms and be OK.

Sometimes new images or scenes may arise during EMDR processing that may shock the client. I have had several clients stop processing because images arose that were sexual and involved parents or caretakers. In these cases the clients demanded to know if they were true. They were frightened and overwhelmed by the implications. "Does this mean my father abused me?" When this happens, I tell clients that I don't know if it is true or not; I urge them to suspend judgment, allowing the processing to continue without drawing conclusions. Sometimes fragments of memories, scenes, and things children were told, or images from movies, books, or dreams get confabulated. The mind struggles to make sense of the information. I have found that if clients are able to suspend judgment, the information gets sorted out and eventually makes sense.

Sometimes if the processing is too much, clients can focus on only the part of the memory that they feel they can process during the session. The other parts they can imagine putting in a container. In this way they can focus on what they can handle and put the rest away to work on later.

It is essential to address your clients' fears when they arise. Do not push clients to continue if they don't feel safe. Remember to ask them, "What do you need to be safe?" and address their fears the best way that you can.

ADDRESSING THE IDEALIZED PARENT

It is most difficult for our clients to process the failure of their parents to provide the nurturing and protection that they needed as children. Because of loyalty to the parents, and also survival, children can't fully take in or integrate the fact of their parents' failure. Many create an idealized version of their parents that does not match up with the reality. These children live on the hope that someday their parents will fit the idealized version they created. Because of the threat to their survival, they don't integrate this information and therefore enter into relationships in their adult life that mimic the one they had with their parents. By targeting and reprocessing childhood traumas that include the terrible truth of their parents' failure to nurture and protect them, they are able to grieve the loss of the idealized version of their parents, and then come to a place where they are open to new relationships that are healthy and fit their needs.

These sessions when this information becomes clear to the client can be very intense emotionally. *It is important that we don't circumvent this process for our clients by intervening too quickly with interweaves.* Our clients need to feel their feelings and come to understand the limitations of their parents or caregivers. We use interweaves if our clients become stuck, or loop, or are overwhelmed with too much emotion. I might offer a resource figure for support to help them process their feelings, but I want to keep them processing through their distress as much as possible.

There seem to be three stages that clients who had abusive and/or neglectful parents go through in their processing in order to heal childhood attachment wounds. I heard Colin Ross speak about these at a conference many years ago, and recognized them as stages I had witnessed while doing EMDR with clients who had experienced complex trauma. Instead of taking perhaps years to pass through these stages in talk therapy, clients can go through all of them in a session, though they may need to revisit the stages repeatedly as they process different traumas. As they move through these stages and integrate the often very painful information, clients are better able to make healthy choices in their present-day relationships.

In the first stage, clients *realize* the limitations of their parents. They see the terrible truth. They see what they did not get as a child, that basic needs were not met. They process this information as a kind of awful truth. For example, a client during an EMDR session might realize that her mother was not there for her. Her mother did not love or protect her. She sees this as the truth and processes through her feelings about this. It is important for the therapist to provide the mirroring and validation, allowing the client to see and integrate this new realization without censoring or rejecting it. This can be difficult for the therapist who wants to shield the client from this deep pain.

In the second stage clients *grieve* the loss of the idealized version of their mother/caregiver or the potential to have their needs met by her. For example, after realizing during her processing that her mother did not love her or take care of her, the client processes in the next set a big wave of sadness as she grieves the loss of hope. If I sense that this might be too much for the client to take in, I might ask if she would like to imagine her nurturing figure holding her as she processes this piece. I might also offer to hold her hand. In this way she does not have to experience processing this pain by herself. It makes it more manageable and adds in healing networks of support.

In the third stage, after clients have processed the loss of the idealized version of their mother/caregiver, and if they feel bereft, the therapist can ask if they would like to imagine a new mother. They can imagine a mother who would be able to meet their needs and add BLS as a resource interweave. The sequence might go something like this:

THERAPIST: What's happening now?
CLIENT: I feel completely lost and alone. Now I have nobody.
THERAPIST: What does the child need?
CLIENT: I need a mother who can be there for me. I need a mother who loves me.
THERAPIST: Would you like to imagine a new mother?
CLIENT: Yes. >>>>>

Therapist and client together can create this mother. Use what you know about attachment repair and this client's particular needs. When the client has a good sense of this nurturing mother, add BLS to process.

If a client is having trouble doing this he doesn't want to lose the good he received from his mother, or he feels disloyal, you can create a "co-mother," a mother who can help the client's mother and fill in what she couldn't provide.

Some clients resist creating a new mother because they feel it glosses over the truth of what they didn't get. They feel like it invalidates their experience. A way to work with this is to validate both experiences: the truth of what they didn't get as a child, as well as the creation in their imagination of what they want and need. "Can you hold the truth of what was—that you didn't have a mother—along with the feelings you have about that, at the same time create what you wish you had, what you longed for, your ideal mother?" If clients can hold both perspectives, use BLS to link in the experience. This interweave validates the loss *and* provides the repair through imagination. You might also provide a neurobiological explanation for the use of imagination. For example:

> *"You won't forget what really happened, but when you create in your imagination what you needed, you are activating the parts of your brain where this information is stored and creating new neural pathways. This can help you feel and act differently in your present life."*

One woman was processing a childhood memory that exemplifies these steps. In the target scene, her father was abusing her mother downstairs as she and her siblings were upstairs hearing the screaming and crashing of furniture. (This client processed aloud as I tapped on her knees.) Her mother came up the stairs and said, "Children, get your things, I'm leaving your father." They all hurried to grab a few things and then jumped in the station wagon to go their aunt's house. An hour later, while at their aunt's house, they heard pounding on the door, then more arguing. Then the sound of footsteps, stomping up the stairs to where the children were gathered. Her father burst in the room and said, "Your mother and I are getting a divorce—which one of you is coming with me?" My client, who was a young girl, looked around the room and saw that none of her siblings was volunteering to go with her scary father. Because she felt sorry for him, and didn't want him to feel rejected, she said, "Daddy, I'll go with you." This is when she had a big realization, and she began to sob. It was the realization that her mother had said nothing. She had let her go with her violent father. She told me, "My mother never protected me. She never looked after me. I didn't have a mother who cared for me." She sobbed and sobbed as she reported this. I wanted to stop and do an interweave, but she told me, "I need to see this. I need to feel this. I'm OK." So I continued tapping on her knees. After several minutes of crying, she opened her eyes and reported to me calmly, "That's why my older sister was so important to me. She has always been like a mother to me." I then said, "Go with that," and began to tap again. She had a series of realizations that her sister had always been there for her all her life. She had been looking to her mother for care, and it wasn't there, but her sister was. We continued with the BLS as she took in this new information. I didn't need to bring in a nurturing figure or ideal mother, because one came to her spontaneously. If she hadn't, I would have asked her what the child needed, or asked if she would like to imagine that.

INTERWEAVES

There are times when we need to use interweaves in order to jump-start blocked processing and link in information, rather than depend solely on what arises from our clients. The statements or images we offer serve to weave together memory networks and associations our clients were not able to connect. Interweaves introduce a new perspective and new information, or information that the client "knows" but does not have access to in the state of mind that is activated. Interweaves can be used to link networks together that are not linking on their own, such as information held by the adult self with information that clients are looping in from their childhood. Interweaves can also be used to *sort out* or *delink* information that has become linked and associated, such as confusing the client's husband with her perpetrator. Interweaves can also be used to create a coherent narrative that provides a broader perspective and to solidify what the client knows to be true. There are many interweave methods, and the selection of the appropriate method is mandated by the specific situation. After the interweave is introduced, the processing usually begins to flow again, moving toward an adaptive resolution, a sense of integration and wholeness, and a diminishment of emotional charge.

Traumatic experiences often seem to be stored in one part of the body–mind without being affected by more current information. Interweaves create a bridge between the parts of the client's mind that have been separated. Interweaves facilitate the processing, provide developmental repair, increase ego strength, and move the client toward greater stability.

We can also use interweaves to help close sessions when time is running out. Shapiro (1995, 2001) uses the term *cognitive interweave*, but I prefer simply *interweave* (Parnell, 1999, 2007) because many of the strategies include imagery as well as cognitions.

Creating Interweaves

When creating interweaves in AF-EMDR, it is important that we keep in mind what is salient to attachment repair. We want to listen to our clients and be present with them. We want to be mindful not to impose our theories or beliefs, but rather to discover with them what they need and what works best for them. We want to be sensitive to when they need interweaves so that we do not leave our clients too long in high affective states. Yet we don't want to intervene too quickly either, because of our anxiety and lack of affect tolerance. We want to use our intuition and attune to our clients as they process. Our joining with them helps them to feel that they are not alone in the trauma memory and that together we will come up with a solution. We want to be open to our clients' creativity and to our own. It is important to listen to what comes up for us and to connect with our body wisdom. Keeping eye contact if clients need it; using our voices with a calm, reassuring tone; staying present and grounded through the difficulties—all important to the repair of attachment traumas.

Designing interweaves is often a collaborative effort between you and your client, in which you work together to find the right key that will unlock the door to the processing journey. Many therapists think they must have the "right" interweave before they can offer it to the client. Using what you know about the client and the issues being worked on, you can simply ask a question or offer a suggestion. If it works, great; if it doesn't, think of something else! Keep trying different keys until you find the one that can unlock the door to the processing journey. Our clients don't fault us for trying; they just don't want us to give up on them. Together, you try to come up with something that fits the current problem. You can ask your client, "What fits better for you?" or "What do we need to add that would make this work?" When the client comes up with a solution from his or her imagination, say, "Imagine that," and add BLS. Remember, *the interweave that is offered does not solve the client's problem. Rather, it simply gets the processing going again until the next stop.*

Use interweaves sparingly. As much as possible allow the processing to proceed without intervening. It is best to time interweaves in such a way that they don't feel intrusive or disruptive. *Suggest an interweave in such a way that your clients are invited to reject them if they don't fit. It is best to ask a question, rather than directing or telling them what to do.*

As noted previously, the primary concerns that come up for clients with complex trauma involve issues around *safety, responsibility, choice/control,* and *shame. Listen for these issues and develop the most appropriate interweaves to address them.* These issues come up over and over again in different forms throughout EMDR therapy because they are associated with different memories or incidents. Don't be discouraged if

---

INTERWEAVE STEPS

1. Client is looping or stuck.
2. Stop the BLS and ask the client what is happening.
3. The client responds.
4. You can do one or more of the following with the client's response: Look for blocking beliefs, talk to the child self (e.g., "What does the child need?"), check for feeder memories or blocking ego states, check for client fears, or check for blocking body sensations. For example, if the client said she was afraid of her uncle, the blocking belief is "I'm not safe."
5. The therapist constructs an interweave. In the above example the therapist might ask the client, "Where is your uncle now?" (The therapist knows that her uncle is deceased.)
6. The client responds to the therapist's inquiry. For example, "He's dead."
7. The therapist says, "Go with that," and adds BLS.

it seems like the same issue keeps recurring. It is not an indication that the EMDR is not working. Many different incidents create the same beliefs. With persistent EMDR work, it is my experience that clients eventually shift at a deeper level. Current life betrayals or traumas may activate the old beliefs, but they don't seem as completely true to the client anymore.

Interweaves mimic spontaneous EMDR processing. Therefore, one of the guidelines for deciding what is needed to craft your interweave is to think about what EMDR does naturally, where the processing is stuck, and what you might do to get it going again. Interweaves can be used to link memory networks, separate or sort, educate, bring in resources, aid in the expression of forbidden impulses, and creatively solve problems. They can also be used to help the client see the bigger picture and to assemble the pieces of a coherent self-narrative.

Interweave Pitfalls

There are several common pitfalls that EMDR therapists fall into when working with clients who have histories of abuse and neglect. I wrote about these in *A Therapist's Guide to EMDR* (Parnell, 2007), and I want to go over them in more detail here because they relate specifically to what I have observed working with these clients and providing consultation to therapists.

Intervening Too Quickly

Many therapists jump in too quickly with interweaves before they have allowed the processing to go where it can. This is a problem with therapists' affect tolerance levels. I have made this error myself and have been corrected by my clients, who have told me, "I need to feel this, and it is important for me that you witness this with me." Clients need to feel their feelings and experience moving through them. Many of our clients are seeing and feeling these things for the first time. They never had their experiences validated by anyone. They shut their feelings down long ago and are just beginning to feel them. It is healing for them to see what happened to them and then to feel the associated emotions within the context of a caring therapeutic relationship. They are not alone, and your presence as a witness and caring person validates their experience. One of my clients told me that my presence with her through her processing of the pain of the abuse memory was very healing for her. What she valued most was my presence with her, witnessing and mirroring her experience through my empathy.

If I think that my client may be looping but I'm not sure, I'll ask, "Are you stuck, or is the processing moving?" Almost always, clients are able to tell me, "No, it's moving, keep going," or "Yes, it's stuck." I have found that I often think they are stuck when they are actually moving well, with strong emotion that seems to go on for a long time. Checking with your client when you don't know what to do is always a good idea.

Talking Too Much

Many therapists fall into old patterns of talking too much when they do interweaves. You want to offer the interweave, and then allow the processing to move along again. Even if your client tries to engage you in discussion, try to avoid it, unless it pertains to repair of the therapeutic relationship or to creating more safety. Therapists often do one interweave, then end up derailing the process by resorting to talk therapy, or do more interweaves than the client really needs. It is better to get the client back on track and moving along. When you *tell* your clients something, instead of *asking* them, you take the power away from them. You become the authority, instead of nurturing and supporting the authority and wisdom within your clients. You can connect with your clients during the debriefing. That is the best time to do it. If you feel the urge to interpret, pose a question instead; that way the question draws from the client.

Bringing in a Resource Too Quickly

When clients are abreacting, don't assume that they need to bring in a resource. If they are stuck, do an interweave, but a resource interweave may not be the best choice. You can ask, "What does the child need?" and find out what might be best for them. Often it is not a resource, but something you haven't thought of. Therapists are often anxious to bring in resources when the client really needs something else. It could be information, or to imagine something, or even simple Socratic interweaves such as, "Did you survive?" or "Can he still hurt you?"

Not Using Interweaves When They Are Needed

Some therapists forget that they can intervene with interweaves, and clients are left to loop in abreactions for too long. This looping can be retraumatizing for clients. Some of our clients do not have good affect tolerance. They have been so severely abused and neglected that they can't process the horrors of the past for very long without help getting out of the trauma network. This may seem like a contradiction to the pitfalls above, but we must remember to adjust what we do for each of our clients. For example, one woman with whom I worked had been severely abused and neglected by her mother and other caregivers. This abuse had spanned her entire childhood, and she had traumas in her adult life too. She was fragile in many ways, yet had good basic ego strength and was functioning well at work and had friends, but no intimate partner. We had a strong therapeutic alliance, and she had many good and reliable internal resources, but she couldn't tolerate abreacting for very long and always got stuck in looping. When I thought that maybe she was stuck, I would ask her, "Do you feel stuck?" When she would answer, "Yes," I would ask, "What does your child need?" She would then relate to me what she needed, which was inevitably one or all of her resource figures providing nurturing or protection, or wise and compassionate advice, and we would do interweaves.

I cannot provide a rule for how long to go before doing an interweave, such as number of sets of BLS, and so forth. *But I can suggest that if you are concerned, ask your client.* I often can't tell if clients are stuck and looping, or if their processing is progressing. "Do you feel stuck?" or "Does it feel like it is progressing?" are perfectly valid questions, and frankly, comforting to the client. You are paying attention to their needs and addressing them as you go along.

Another matter to take into consideration is that you have only so much time and so much energy in your session. The goal is to complete the target memory the best that you can in the time that you have, hopefully getting the SUDS down to a 0 or 1, and then have time for session closure. With this framework in mind, you may need to get more proactive with interweaves in order to tie things together so that your client ends in a good place, feeling grounded, integrated, and ready to leave your office intact in his or her adult self.

Neglecting to Use Interweaves to Close Sessions

If you are running out of time or cannot get the SUDS down below a 2, begin to use interweaves proactively to link networks together. This is where you do use more interweaves, sometimes several in a row, to tie the loose ends together so that the client can leave the session feeling more intact. You might use interweaves such as the following:

THERAPIST: Do you still live in that house with your parents?
CLIENT: No.
THERAPIST: Go with that. >>>>>
THERAPIST: What does the child need?

CLIENT: I need to get out of there.
THERAPIST: Who can do it?
CLIENT: My adult self, my friend Angela, and my husband John.
THERAPIST: Where would you like them to take you?
CLIENT: I'd like to go to where I live now.
THERAPIST: Imagine that. >>>>>

Rescue interweaves can be very helpful to many clients who had years of neglect and abuse. Clients will do much better between sessions if you close each session using interweaves.

INTERWEAVE CATEGORIES

I have organized interweaves into different categories. Some of these are from Shapiro's texts (1995, 2001) and some from my books (Parnell, 1999, 2007). What follows are several interweave strategies that you might consider when your client is looping or stuck.

Inquiry Interweaves

Inquiry interweaves link or sort two or more memory networks together. The client has all of the needed information in his or her mind but may need help in merging the two memory files. In many cases, the adult memory network has information that is not connecting with the child self's network. Questions can also serve to separate associative strands that don't go together. Issues of safety, responsibility, choice/control, and shame commonly arise. Several interweave subcategories fall under this inquiry category:

- Socratic method
- "I'm confused . . ."
- "If this were your child . . ."
- "If this were your best friend, client, sponsee, etc. . . ."
- Open-ended question (e.g., "Why *did* you do that?" or "Is that true?")
- "What happened next?"

These cognitive interweaves involve asking clients short questions that are intended to elicit information from other networks, which is then connected using BLS.

Socratic Method

In this method, which can take the form of a single question or a dialogue, you ask the client a simply worded question that elicits an answer from the memory network that he or she is desiring to link to the one that is currently active (Shapiro, 1995, 2001). The questions you ask lead the client to a logical conclusion. This method is quite powerful, as it enables clients to integrate what they already know in one memory network but somehow don't know in another. It can be likened to merging two computer files.

A client who is processing a memory of being abused by her stepfather is looping and stuck. She believes she is bad. The therapist stops the BLS and asks her what is happening. She tells the therapist that she is bad.

THERAPIST: Who did the bad thing?
CLIENT: He did.
THERAPIST: Go with that. >>>>>
THERAPIST: Who should have known better?
CLIENT: My stepfather.
THERAPIST: Go with that. >>>>>

"I'm Confused . . ."

This technique (see Shapiro, 1995, 2001) is used to link information that the client knows but does not have access to at that point in the processing. For example, many children feel responsible and blame themselves for not being able to stop the behavior of the adults in their lives. Consider the client who, during a session, is looping in a childhood memory in which he is 6 years old and frozen as he watches his father beat his mother. He is angry at himself, believing that he should have stopped his father somehow and protected his mother. In this case the therapist might say the following: "I'm confused. How big were you? And how big was your father? How could you have stopped him?" If the client says, "No, that's not possible," the therapist then says, "Think about that," and does a set of BLS to link the information.

"If This Were Your Child . . ."

With this technique you try to elicit empathy for the child self that the client is blaming (see Shapiro, 1995, 2001). If you know your client has a daughter, son, niece, nephew, or other loved child, you seek to stimulate your client's thoughts about this beloved child with sympathy, and then transfer the sympathy and understanding to his or her own child self. For example, if you know that your client has a 4-year-old daughter and the stuck part is blaming her own 4-year-old child self for the abuse, you could ask, "If this were your daughter Kerry, would you see it as her fault?" If your client says no and means it, then you follow with a set of BLS.

You can use variations on this theme by asking, "If this were your friend, what would you say?" For example, with a client who was in a battering relationship and is looping around guilt over leaving her husband, you could ask, "If this were your friend, what would you tell her? What advice would you give her?" When she answers, use BLS to link it in. "If this were one of your patients, what would you tell him?" I find this interweave helpful when I feel the impulse to give my clients advice. It is much better to help them draw from their own inner knowing.

Open-Ended Question

Sometimes it is helpful when clients are looping or stuck to inquire as to the reasons for their behavior or actions. I always assume that there was a good reason for what they did; they are just not in contact with that reason. I might ask, "So why *did* you do_____?" The question is posed with curiosity and respect. It's an open-ended question, different from the typical Socratic method, which usually guides the client to an answer that is obvious to the therapist. In the case of the open-ended question, the therapist does not necessarily know what the client will come up with, but trusts that the information revealed will enable the processing to get back on track. I pose the question, and then use the BLS as clients explore what comes up for them.

This interweave helps open up the processing and gets it moving. Sometimes clients will loop in the question about other people, or why things happened the way they did, often with the implication that they were somehow to blame. I will turn it around and make it an inquiry with the open question and exploration. For example, the client is looping in the question "Why did my mother hate me so much?" I might say, "Go with the question, and see what comes up for you." And add BLS. This often leads to an opening up of networks and a broadening of perspective.

Another variant on this can be implemented when clients get stuck in negative statements about themselves and their lives. I might ask, "Is this really true?" and add BLS. This again opens up the processing so that clients can discover what really is true for them.

If clients are stuck struggling to make a decision about something, I might ask them to explore each scenario with their imaginations. For example, if they are conflicted about staying in or leaving a relationship, I might say, "Let's explore each scenario. First, imagine staying with your partner." BLS. After that, I would say, "Now imagine leaving your partner." BLS. This interweave allows them to explore and discover what feels truest for them.

CASE EXAMPLE OF SORTING USING AN OPEN-ENDED QUESTION
The client was a young woman working on a memory of being sexually abused by her grandfather, who molested her from ages 4–8 during times he babysat for her. He was someone to whom she felt connected, yet he also hurt her. During a session in which she was processing an abuse incident, she looped in fear. Interweaves of her being rescued from the situation or leaving were elicited. Yet whenever she thought about the incident, she saw herself returning to her grandfather. Despite what she knew about him, her child self wanted to be with him. Full of self-hate and condemnation, she was furious with her child self's behavior. She was stuck. In order to help sort out these tangled threads, I asked her child self an open-ended question:

THERAPIST: Why *do* you return to your grandfather?
CLIENT: Because he pays attention to me.
THERAPIST: Go with that. >>>>>
CLIENT: No one else pays attention to me.
THERAPIST: Did you want the touching?
CLIENT: No.
THERAPIST: Go with that. >>>>> Who can give you the right kind of attention? [I'm bringing in an appropriate resource figure.]
CLIENT: My husband.
THERAPIST: Imagine that. >>>>>

With these interweaves I was attempting to tease out the threads of association, of complicity, that had become entangled. It was important to separate out what she wanted. Often perpetrators choose needy children and get them to believe that they are complicit in the abuse. "You wanted it" is a message repeated often—when what the child really wanted was love and attention, not sex.

"What Happened Next?": Focusing on the Outcome
It can be helpful for some clients who are looping or stuck to focus on the outcome of the traumatic experience—the fact that they *did* survive.

Sometimes when a traumatic event has been quite shocking, the person becomes stuck in the "I'm going to die" moment. It can appear in the processing like a broken record, repeating over and over, stuck in the same place. In these cases I have found it helpful to *remind the client of the next thing that happened after the moment of terror*. It is like picking up the arm of the record player and placing it on the next groove of the record.

Truth Interweaves

Truth interweaves are employed to help clients integrate and establish what is true for them. These interweaves are typically used when clients are confused about what they experienced and about their perceptions of the truth, and when they lack a coherent narrative or understanding. These clients are typically fragmented and dissociated because of abuse, or they are clients whose parents had mental illnesses such as DID or bipolar disorder or were alcoholic or drug addicted. In all of these cases the parents behaved radically differently at different times, often not recalling their aberrant behavior. Children of such parents have no way of understanding what they are experiencing or how to make sense of it. They may fragment and dissociate along with their parents. One client, whose mother tortured her as a small child, described from her child's perspective how "Mommy's face changes. There's my real mommy, then blank-face mommy, then scary mommy." The real mommy didn't seem to recall putting the baby's feet in boiling water. She told everyone that the child was "our little ballerina" because she walked on tiptoes.

Three interweaves fall into this category:

- Validating personal reality: "What do you understand now?" or "What do you know to be true?"
- Facilitating a broader perspective: "Look at the scene. What do you see?"
- Holding the complexity with a nondual interweave

Validating Personal Reality: "What Do You Understand Now?" or "What Do You Know Now to Be True?"

Sometimes clients will loop with "I'm confused." They are confused because in the childhood memory they are processing, they are experiencing intense affect and body sensations while, at the same time, remembering being told by adults that nothing had happened to them. I have found that what helps clients get out of this kind of loop is to ask them to explain what they understand or know to be true. I add BLS as the client states what he or she knows. Sometimes clients give a long narrative, with the BLS going continuously. Many insights can arise about what was going on in the family. This interweave helps clients sort out what is true from what is not and create a coherent narrative. It helps link the pieces together that heretofore have been fragmented.

In one case my client was looping in confusion. I stopped the BLS and asked her what was happening. She had been processing an abuse incident from childhood, with strong body sensations. Then she said, "My mother said that it didn't happen to me. She told everyone I was a liar. I don't know what was true." She was essentially looping in the belief, "I can't trust myself, I can't trust my reality." This can be a very destabilizing belief. When you don't know what is true—when you don't believe you can trust yourself—you lose your ground. You begin to float. It is another reason our clients dissociate. They have been cut off from their ground of knowing. Some of our clients are told all their lives that they are liars. Because children trust the adults they depend on, they partly believe them and so don't trust themselves, and partly know that something *did* happen to them and that they are telling the truth.

I have found that when clients are able to get some of the truth pieces in place, others begin to assemble themselves, and the anxiety and distress diminish. It is inherently destabilizing to not know what is true. When even simple truths are integrated, our clients feel more whole, more solid, more embodied.

One client told me she felt "solid" at the end of a session in which we had integrated what was true for her. I asked her to focus on how *solid* felt in her body, and we kept eye contact as the BLS continued. She saw me seeing her becoming solid and whole. For part of the session, as she told me what was true, we kept eye contact so that she could take in my seeing and validating her reality. Instead of scorn and doubt in my eyes, she could see care and confidence. This interpersonal connection was very healing for her. Not only was she reprocessing the trauma of not being believed, but she was able to integrate a new experience with a live person into her nervous system, a corrective emotional experience of attunement and validation. This mirroring helped her to feel real. My client told me at the end of the session, "When you are not believed or validated, you feel like you are invisible and that you don't exist. Without mirroring, you don't feel alive."

CASE EXAMPLE: "WHAT DO YOU KNOW TO BE TRUE?"

This client was severely sexually and physically abused as a child by a close relative. As an adult she had a good observing ego, was functioning well in her life, had insight into her problems, and had done considerable work on herself. Yet despite all of these strengths, many of her abuse memories remained fragmented and dissociated, causing her to become easily dysregulated and triggered.

As she was abused throughout her childhood, she was told that what she was experiencing had never happened, and her family acted as if nothing had occurred. This gross denial created a feeling of unreality in her. She couldn't trust her own perceptions of what was true, and the denial made her feel "crazy." In the session she targeted an incident in which she was brutally raped as a 4-year-old, then cleaned up, dressed in a party dress, and fed a lunch—during which her family acted as if nothing horrifying had just happened to her. This was a scene she had processed in previous sessions. At this point in our work she needed to process the part of this trauma in which no one acknowledged what had happened to her. It made her feel crazy and invisible.

During this session she took control and told her therapist exactly what she needed from her. She needed, more than anything, for her therapist to reflect back her words, her reality, as she narrated what had happened to her, and to tell her "I believe you" while tapping on her knees, maintaining eye contact, and attuning to her. The therapist's eyes filled with tears, feeling with the client. It was so important, so validating, for this client to see her therapist moved by her experience. The therapist tapped through this dialogue:

CLIENT: I was raped, cleaned up, and told that nothing had happened to me. I need you to say that back to me.
THERAPIST: You were raped, cleaned up, and told that nothing had happened to you.
CLIENT: I was raped, and I was told it didn't happen.
THERAPIST: You were raped, and you were told it didn't happen.
CLIENT: I know this happened. I can trust my own mind.
THERAPIST: You know this happened and can trust your own mind.
CLIENT: I have a good mind, and I can trust my reality.
THERAPIST: You have a good mind and can trust your reality. (*pause*) How does that feel to you, to have me see and feel with you?
CLIENT: It feels good. I can see and feel you with me.

She said she felt less anxious, more grounded, and good after doing this. The lack of validation and connection at the time of the trauma was very destabilizing. She could trust her reality. What she experienced, *did* happen.

Facilitating a Broader Perspective: "Look at the Scene—What Do You See?"

This interweave can shift the client's attention, bringing in information from a broader perspective. Often clients will spontaneously do this, but when they don't, this interweave can be helpful to get the processing back on track. For example: "Look at your mother—what do you see . . . what do you notice?" The client responds, "She's so young. She is all alone taking care of all these kids. She needs help. It's not that I'm a bad kid, she just can't handle all of us by herself." You then can say, either, "Go with that" or "Would you like to bring in a resource for your mother?" If she says yes, say, "Imagine that" and add BLS.

Holding the Complexity with a Nondual Interweave

I developed this interweave to help clients integrate two things that don't seem to go together. Often the need for this interweave shows up when the client loops in "I'm confused." For example, this type of interweave could be used for the client who cannot reconcile how her grandfather could be loving *and* abuse her at the same time. She ends up splitting inside: He becomes two different people she cannot integrate. Often clients will loop in confusion because they cannot integrate these two seemingly opposite parts. This can include disparate parts of themselves, as well as conflicting emotions. We tend to think, if *this* is true, then *that* can't be true too. If he abused me, then he can't also be loving. What if they *are* both true, but not understandable? With the nondual interweave I say something like the following:

> *"Imagine a vast space within which all of these things exist at the same time. It is large enough to hold your grandfather as kind and nurturing, as well as the part of him that is cruel and hurtful. Can you imagine this, and allow all of these things to be there at the same time?"*

If the client says yes, I add the BLS. What typically ensues is an integration of the parts that clients had not been able to reconcile before. Even if they don't understand how this can be true, they are able to experience that it is true. They shift out of the limitations of what their minds can understand to identification with the space that holds it all. Clients often experience a release of the struggle in their mind to make sense of the conflict. This release, in turn, creates a decrease in anxiety as the exertion to understand and to keep the parts separate disappears. Even if they can't make sense out of why someone acted as he or she did, they accept that it was as it was and can sense the space that holds both truths. They often feel hugely relieved.

Clients can experience this vast space also holding their conflicting emotions and contradictory aspects of themselves too. "Can you imagine a vast space large enough to hold these different parts of yourself? A space large enough to hold all the different feelings you have?" If they answer affirmatively, say, "Imagine that" and add BLS.

Resource Interweaves

During the preparation phase of treatment, you and your client have identified and tapped in a team of resources: safe/peaceful place, nurturing figures, protector figures, wise figures, and others. These resources can be brought in when the client is looping and unable to naturally connect with these resources. These resources can be called upon to nurture, protect, rescue, or explain.

When the client is looping or stuck, I will often ask, "What do you need?" or "What does the child need?" When the client responds, I will ask, "Who can do that?" When clients tell me who, for example, their protector figure is, I say, "Imagine that" and add BLS to link it in. If clients respond with "I don't know," I begin to offer suggestions. I might ask if they need someone to protect them, nurture them, or explain something to them. Then I will ask, "Who can do that for you?" If clients cannot come up with a response, I offer suggestions, some of which will come from the resources that we installed earlier or that I remember from the history taking. *I believe it is always best to first ask the client before offering suggestions.* In this way you are pulling the information from his or her memory network. This is experienced as empowering. If the client cannot answer easily, then I offer suggestions. *Do not assume what the client needs.* I have often been mistaken in my assumptions.

Also don't assume which resources the client needs. Just because clients installed certain resources in the beginning of the session or treatment doesn't mean that these are the resources they will need in their interweaves. Often, when asked, clients come up with resources they had never thought of before. If they can't think of any resources to bring in because they are blocked in some way, too caught in the helplessness of the childhood memory network, you can offer the resources the client installed. "Can your protector figure come in to help you?" At this point it can feel like throwing ropes out to a drowning person. You hope that they will find one that will work, grab hold of it, and get pulled to safety.

When working with clients who have childhood neglect or relational trauma, you can have them imagine resource figures giving birth to them, caring for them as an infant and toddler, and up through the developmental stages. They can create imaginal mothers or fathers, as we saw in Chapter 5, and use them as resources to repair attachment traumas.

RESOURCE INTERWEAVE SEQUENCING

1. The client is looping and stuck. For example, the client is processing a childhood abuse memory of being left all alone. She is looping at a high level of affect.
2. The therapist asks the client what is happening.
3. The client responds, for example, "I'm sad and lonely. No one loves me."
4. The therapist asks, "What does the child need?"
5. The client responds, "I need someone to take care of me, someone to love me."
6. The therapist asks, "Who can do that?"
7. The client responds with the needed information. "I need a new mother."
8. "Would you like to imagine a new mother? You can create the mother you would like to have—one who loves you and takes good care of you."
9. The client responds, "Yes, I can do it."
10. The therapist says, "Imagine that" and adds BLS to process and link in this information.

Bringing in Resources for Family Members

There are clients for whom it can be useful to bring in resources to help family members. For example:

- Clients who feel responsible for family members
- Clients who were enmeshed with their mothers
- Clients who took care of their family because there wasn't anyone else doing it
- Clients who were codependent

Clients who as children felt responsible for taking care of family members will sometimes get stuck and loop. They need to get out of the family, but they can't because of their feeling of loyalty or responsibility. Very young children can feel that it is their job to take care of their mother and/or siblings. They love their family, but it is more than they can do to care for their needs. These clients are tangled up with their parents or siblings and feeling responsible for their well-being, yet they also need to take care of themselves. They can't imagine getting their needs met because others' needs are more important, or they can't imagine abandoning their parents or siblings to escape for their own survival. I have found that it is not possible to process out compassion. Therefore, if a child believes that taking care of his own needs will cause harm to someone whom he loves, he will often sacrifice himself.

In other cases, the client knows it wasn't her job to take care of her mother (so the Socratic interweave "Who is responsible?" won't work), but her mother had no one else. She was overwhelmed with too many children and needed help.

Some mothers depend on their child to fulfill their own unmet developmental needs. Such a mother "sucks" on the child's energy. And the child believes it's her job to take care of her mother for both her own and her mother's survival. This child also feels compassion for her mother and wants to help her. When the child fails at this "job," however, her mother may punish her by abusing her or withdrawing her love. Because the child believes it is her responsibility to take care of her mother, and fails at it, she believes she is bad and defective in some way. She may then develop a lifelong pattern of taking care of unstable or unhealthy people, often sacrificing her own needs in the process.

To remedy this looping problem, you can ask the client if she would like to bring in resource figures for the others, as well as for herself:

THERAPIST: Who would you like to bring in for your mother?
CLIENT: I'd like to bring in a kind mother who can give her love and teach her how to be a mother.
THERAPIST: Great, imagine that. >>>>>

CASE EXAMPLE OF ENMESHED MOTHER

The client, "Patty," was processing a scene she bridged to of her mother crying while holding her as an infant. Patty's mother was abused as a child and was not loved or nurtured by her own parents. She was emotionally unstable, unloving, and abusive toward Patty. As long as Patty could remember, she felt that her mother depended on her to meet her unmet emotional needs. As she processed the infant memory, she felt angry at her mother, but then felt protective of her. She realized that she felt responsible for taking care of her—that she has felt this burden all her life.

In the scene Patty was 3 months old and her father had recently left her mother. She was seeing her mother crying and believed in that moment that it was her responsibility to take care of her. "I left myself in that moment and began to take care of her." She realized that she took in all of her mother's pain, trauma, and sorrow. She believed that her *mother* believed it was her (Patty's) responsibility to take care of her (the mother). As she processed this, Patty cried and began to feel overwhelmed. I did an interweave to bring resources to the mother and child, who both needed resources and also to help the child separate from taking care of her mother.

THERAPIST: Would you like to bring in someone to take care of your mother, and someone who can take care of you?

CLIENT: Yes.

THERAPIST: Who would you like to bring in for each of you?

CLIENT: I'd like to bring in Carolyn, who is a good therapist, for my mother, and Harriet for myself.

THERAPIST: Imagine that. >>>>>

CLIENT: (*crying, and then begins to calm down*) I'm feeling relieved. I'm feeling more separate from her. She is being taken care of, and so am I. I can let go of taking care of her. >>>>>

THERAPIST: What's happening now?

CLIENT: I feel calmer. I feel better.

THERAPIST: Can a baby really take care of a mother?

CLIENT: No (*chuckles at the absurdity*).

THERAPIST: Go with that. >>>>>

CLIENT: I'm feeling her energy go with her (mother) and mine with me. I feel myself more fully. I feel it leaving my body.

Imagination Interweaves

There are three types of imagination interweaves. In all of them, you and your client work together, using imagery, to come up with a solution to a problem that is causing the looping or stuck processing:

- Creating an imaginary scenario or solution to a problem
- Rewriting the scene: "Knowing what you know now, what would you do differently?" or, "If you could redo this scene, what would you do?"
- Expressing forbidden impulses

Creating an Imaginary Scenario or Solution to a Problem

When the client is looping and stuck, you stop the BLS and ask what's happening. If it is a dilemma for which the client sees no solution within the memory itself, you can give him or her permission to do or say whatever is needed in his or her imagination. Imagination interweaves can be used to link as well as sort networks. Sometimes clients will say, "I wish I could have done _____." When I hear this, I ask, "Would you like to imagine doing _____?" If the client answers affirmatively, I say, "Imagine that" and add BLS. For example, the client might say, "I wish I could tell my father what a jerk he is and take my child self out of there and never come back." I would say, "Would you like to imagine that?" and add BLS.

Often you see the looping in an action that clients were not able to complete. It might be a desire to flee, fight, scream, or express certain thoughts and feelings. These frozen places are locked in time and "want" to be released. Giving clients permission to do or say whatever was incomplete in their imaginations frees up the energy that has been stuck in their systems, making them feel powerless or creating a myriad of symptoms. They can imagine running away, calling in a protector to beat up the bad guy, punching someone, or expressing rage at a perpetrator. They can imagine telling the secret they have been made to keep. Whatever is stuck and keeps them from living fully can be expressed within imagination and accompanied by BLS.

Sometimes clients will resist using imagination interweaves. They'll say "I can't do that" or "It's not real, so it has no validity." I agree with them: "We cannot change the past, but we can change how the past is stored in our nervous system. You don't have to live with this old story." I encourage them to explore with their imagination. "Let yourself imagine it the way you'd like to." Sometimes it can be helpful to be playful and use humor. "What would you like to do to that mean teacher? Let's come up with some creative things we can do."

Rewriting the Scene: "Knowing What You Know Now, What Would You Do Differently?" or "If You Could Redo This Scene, What Would You Do?"

This imagination interweave comes up during processing when clients say they feel stuck in regret that they didn't do or say something. Oftentimes it is something that they could not have done at the time because they didn't have the information or the perspective they now have. When this issue comes up, I ask the client, "Knowing what you know now, what would you do differently?" When they tell me what it is, I say, "Imagine that" and add BLS. "If you could go back in time, what would you like to do?" For example, a rape victim was looping in regret because she got into a stranger's car.

THERAPIST: Knowing what you know now, what would you do differently?
CLIENT: I'd trust my gut. I wouldn't get into a stranger's car.
THERAPIST: Go with that. >>>>>

Expressing Forbidden Impulses

Many clients who were abused as children lock their strong emotions deep inside because at the time of the abuse, it was not safe to express these feelings. The inhibited expression of emotion can manifest as tightness in the throat or jaw and can block the processing. With EMDR, we can encourage our clients to express the angry thoughts and feelings in whatever way arises for them in their imaginations. The full expression of anger frees up energy that has been blocked and that has reinforced the feeling of being powerless. With the BLS going on, clients who have been horribly hurt and shamed tell their perpetrators how they feel about what they have done to them. When clients fully express anger and rage at the perpetrator in the safety of the therapist's office, they feel a sense of empowerment and freedom from fear. *The anger is then cleared from the system, in many cases eliminating the desire for revenge or need for actual confrontation.* Sometimes the expression of violent feelings can be alarming to the therapist. I have never found clients to act out on these feelings; I'm not working with anyone who has or would actually harm someone. Typically when clients fully express their emotions with the BLS, these emotions dissipate. Too often therapists become frightened and shut down their clients' full expression. Keep them moving through the feelings and fantasies, allowing them to complete.

Sorting Interweaves

There are two types of interweaves that fall into this category: the split-screen interweave and the two-handed interweave. These interweaves are used for sorting out networks that have become tangled in the client's system. For example, a client may be confusing herself as a child with her daughter, or a man may project his difficulties onto his son. These interweaves can be used to sort out the past from the present, or anything that you want to help the client disentangle, and they can also be used to help clients make decisions. I typically use them when clients are looping in confusion, or I can see that they can't differentiate something.

The Split-Screen Interweave

The split-screen interweave is a method for sorting networks that are causing the client to loop. The notion of using the split screen as an interweave was first introduced by Martinez (1991). With the split screen clients can either imagine both parts on either side of an imaginary screen, or they can draw the two sides using art materials. Drawing enables clients to take the confusion and externalize it, allowing them to see it more objectively. I have found drawing very useful in helping clients to sort networks that have become entangled.

CASE EXAMPLES OF THE SPLIT-SCREEN INTERWEAVE

Adults sexually abused as children often confuse their partners with their perpetrators. The use of the split screen can help clients differentiate between the two. Clients who were abused by a man may fear all men, having difficulty distinguishing between men who are safe from men who are unsafe. In one case the client, a medical student married to an artist who was sensitive and gentle, was processing the memory of making love with her husband when she began to loop, her father's face superimposed over his. When I stopped the BLS, she told me what was causing the looping. I asked her if she could imagine a split screen and on one side see her father's face, on the other her husband's. I then asked her to notice as we did the BLS, "What is the same and what is different between the two?"

At the end of the set she looked at me calmly and said, "At first they looked the same: They both were men, they both had passion in their eyes, but my husband looked loving and kind, and my father scary. They are not the same." We did more BLS and the processing continued. After that session she reported being more comfortable making love with her husband, her father's face no longer superimposed over his.

Another client, who'd had a very engulfing mother, was looping, unable to distinguish what feelings belonged to her mother, and what feelings were hers.

THERAPIST: Imagine a split screen. On one side is you and your feelings, on the other is your mother and her feelings. Notice what is yours and what is hers. >>>>>

CLIENT: I can feel my feelings separate from hers. I feel my own feelings. The yuck is off of me. I feel cleaner.

The Two-Hand Interweave

The two-hand interweave, developed by Robin Shapiro (2005), is much like the split-screen interweave. It can be used to sort or to integrate networks. She recommends using it to differentiate events, feelings, cognitions, and ego states from the past from those in the present. The following is the protocol:

1. Client anchors one conflicting feeling, thought, choice, belief, or ego state in one hand.
2. Client anchors another feeling, thought, choice, belief, or ego state in the other hand.
3. The therapist begins BLS, or the client can alternate opening and closing hands.
4. If there is distress in one or both of the choices, it is cleared with the standard protocol. After the clearing is complete, both hands are rechecked.
5. After the BLS the therapist asks the client, "What difference do you notice?"

For example the client from the case mentioned above could be asked to hold her husband in one hand and her father in the other and then "go with that" as she receives BLS. Next the therapist would ask, "What do you get now?" If she says, "My husband loves me and my father wants to hurt me," the therapist would say, "Go with that," and add more BLS continuing on with the processing.

For case examples and more information on the use of this interweave, read the chapter "Two-Hand Interweave" in *EMDR Solutions* (Shapiro, 2005).

Education Interweaves

With the education interweave you introduce new information to the client that is not in the system. Many people with childhood neglect and abuse need information about healthy parent–child relationships and normal child development. Sometimes when doing the attachment-repair work, I provide the information that clients lack and then ask them to imagine receiving that from an imaginal parent figure. You can teach clients in detail about healthy parent–infant bonding, including the eye contact, tone of voice, touch—anything you can think of that would help them integrate that information into their system. Then they can imagine receiving this nurturing. In some cases the therapist may offer information about the way in which healthy family members interact with one another. In other cases the therapist may provide more technical information that can be used in an interweave.

Clients who were sexually abused as children typically believe that *they are bad if their bodies experienced pleasure during the abuse.* When this came up with a client and she could not shift the negative cognition because neither the child nor the adult had any information to the contrary, I did an education interweave. I told her:

> *"It is normal for the body to experience pleasure when it is touched a certain way . . . just like if you stub your toe or bump your knee, the body responds with pain. Certain kinds of touch make you feel pleasure. What he did was wrong, bad. You are not bad for your body's natural response."*

Both the child and the adult needed this information because it was not in the system. Her SUDS went down and her positive cognition became "My body responded in a normal way. He was bad for doing what he did to me." She felt great relief from the guilt and shame associated with the abuse memories and her body's responses to the stimulation. The perpetrator had told her repeatedly that she was bad because of her sexual stimulation. The interweave helped to deprogram this negative and harmful message.

Using Interweaves to Close Sessions

It is important to become more active with interweaves toward the end of sessions in order to achieve a more complete closure. I have found that EMDR therapists are often too cautious and don't use interweaves for closure as they could. I rarely leave clients above a SUDS of 2 or 3. Instead I begin to ask questions and link networks more actively when we are running low on time. For example, I might ask a client still stuck in a house where she was being abused, "What does the child need?" She might respond, "She needs to get out of there." I would then ask, "Who can get her out of there?" When she responds, "My adult self can do it," I would say, "Go with that" and add the BLS. Adults who were traumatized as children often need interweaves to help close them. These can include interweaves of rescue, nurturing, or linking networks.

Using Imagination Interweaves of Rescue for Clients with Multiple Abuse Memories or Extensive Childhood Neglect

Clients who have had multiple abuse incidents throughout childhood may need to experience an imagination interweave of rescue to end each session. I have found that it is important for these clients to feel that the memory they processed is over, and they are no longer in the situation. Bringing the child to the present, in a safe place—the therapist's office or the client's present home—can be very helpful in closing sessions. These clients will often say, "I know there is more to come. This will never be over." But if, with each memory you take the child out of the house where the abuse took place, the adult will have a greater sense of safety in the present. That scene they processed is over. There may be more to come, but *that one* is done. A generalization effect will begin to permeate the network. The client will become more stable, more present, and increasingly embodied.

For example, a man with whom I worked came to me with severe social anxiety. He was so anxious he could barely leave his house. Growing up, his mother was a severe alcoholic who neglected him and beat him and his siblings. His father worked all the time and was unaware of just how bad things were at home. As a child he'd had to fend for himself at school, where he was bullied on the playground, and he was not fed or taken care of at home by his mother, whom he feared. Because of the neglect and abuse, he never felt safe. This affected his self-esteem and his ability to focus and be successful at school. In our EMDR work he processed the childhood traumas well and made good use of resources in interweaves. But because his entire childhood was unsafe, we always ended our sessions with his adult self coming in and rescuing his child self from that home environment. He would imagine taking his child self out of there and bringing him to where he lived now. He would go into a very long and elaborate imagination with the BLS going. He would imagine himself as father to his child self, his wife as his mother, and his children as siblings to his little boy. During this imagination his children taught his child self how to be a free, happy child playing together, riding bikes and climbing trees. Because he had the model of his own children, he could easily imagine what normal, healthy children do. He would spend several minutes at the end of sessions imagining this new life for his child self. At the end of the sessions he felt much better, his confidence high, his anxiety greatly diminished. Over time, he reported significant decreases in his symptoms, so much so that he found himself taking leadership positions in groups. This all happened spontaneously. He was also able to function better at work as the symptoms stemming from his traumatic childhood were resolved.

SUMMARY OF INTERWEAVE CATEGORIES AND SUBCATEGORIES

Inquiry Interweaves
> Socratic method
> "I'm confused"
> "If this were your child . . . best friend, client, sponsee . . ."
> Open-ended question ("Why did you do that?" "Is that true?")
> "What happened next?"

Truth Interweaves
> Validating personal reality: "What Do You Understand Now?" Or "What Do You Know Now to Be True?"
> Facilitating a broader perspective: "Look at the scene. What do you see?"
> Holding the opposites with a nondual interweave

Resource Interweaves
> Nurturing figures, protector figures, wise figures, and others can be called upon to nurture, protect, rescue, explain, and help in some way. These resources can be for the client and/ or for significant others, such as mother, father, and siblings.

continued on next page

SUMMARY OF INTERWEAVE CATEGORIES AND SUBCATEGORIES
(continued)

Imagination Interweaves

Creating an imaginary scenario or solution to a problem

Rewriting the scene: "Knowing what you know now, what would you do differently?" or "If you could redo this scene, what would you do?"

Expressing forbidden impulses

Sorting Interweaves

Split-screen interweave

Two-hand interweave

Education Interweaves

Providing information the client lacks (e.g., "It is normal for the body to experience pleasure when it is touched a certain way")

Using Interweaves to Close Sessions

"What does the child need? Go with that."

Using imagination interweaves of rescue

CHAPTER 15

Five EMDR Sessions Demonstrating the Use of Interweaves to Repair Attachment Trauma

The sessions in this chapter demonstrate AF-EMDR with clients who have relational trauma, and all of them show the use of many types of interweaves. Three of the sessions were with participants from my EMDR trainings who volunteered to participate in live demonstrations. Two of these sessions were videotaped and are available for review (www. emdrinfo.com). The last two sessions are provided by psychologist Dr. Nancy Ewing, who presents a case of a woman utilizing animal resource figures to repair attachment trauma. I believe that these sessions are good examples of many of the important subjects I described in previous chapters, including resource installation, using bridging for target development, and using interweaves.

CASE EXAMPLE OF SOCIAL ANXIETY

"Mirium," whom you met in Chapter 4, was an orthodox Jewish woman in her 50s who presented with a lifelong problem of social anxiety that was affecting her current functioning and self-esteem. Mirium reported feeling unwelcome or unwanted in any group. She had felt ostracized at different times throughout her life. Through the use of the bridging technique, we discovered that the roots of the client's current symptoms connected to damaging relationships with her mother and father. We began EMDR with a childhood dream, which then linked to a scene from childhood. We reprocessed each of these targets, then the present situation, and finally did a future pace. Transference arose repeatedly during the session, and we worked with it. The client discovered a loving spiritual resource that she used in her interweaves to heal her. Throughout the session, resource and imagination interweaves were used successfully. Finally, the session ended with the client feeling alive and optimistic about her future.

In this session the client chose to use auditory stimulation. In the beginning of the session I gave her the headphones as I held the controls and adjusted the tempo of the sounds that she heard as well as the volume. We set it up so that it felt most comfortable to her. Throughout the session I followed her lead and turned off the machine when she opened her eyes and began to report her experience. (The full case can be seen on the DVD, *Attachment-Focused EMDR for Social Anxiety*, at www. emdrinfo.com)

During the installation of her resources, Mirium was self-conscious and nervous, often laughing anxiously, needing a lot of reassurance from me that she was doing it right. (See Chapter 4 for the transcript of this part of the session.)

In order to find a target for our session, I asked her to give me an example of when she had felt anxiety recently. She told me about an experience at work where people were talking in the hallway and she felt left out. I used the bridging technique to find the target for the session. The most distressing image was seeing her colleagues talking in the hallway; the emotions were fear and anxiety; the body sensations included tingling in her hands and arms and a tight stomach; and the beliefs were "I'm hated, I'm unlovable, unlikable, and I don't belong." I asked her to then trace this back in time and she linked back to a memory of a childhood nightmare: "I used to have a lot of nightmares. I dreamt that my mother had a convertible, a cool 1950s convertible, and I dreamt that the top was down and we were going down the southern state parkway and I blew out of the car and I landed on the island between the two sides. I wasn't hurt, but they didn't notice and they just kept on driving." She told me that she was 4 or 5 years old in the dream, felt anxious and angry, and had tingling in her hands and running down her thighs. She couldn't find a belief before going up into her head, becoming insecure and distracted. I directed her into the dream, with the feelings, and began the BLS.

MIRIUM: I'm just picturing myself at 4 or 5 years old, standing in the living room. Nowhere to go, nothing to do, nowhere to turn.

I'm really associating. I realize you look like a neighbor, like another mother that was in the neighborhood that was very close to my mother, and I liked her but she also had this dark side like my mother did, and the truth is that I couldn't trust any woman. There was no woman I could trust, and then I had my father talking so contemptuously and impatiently. Not always, sometimes he was really lovable. What's wrong with me? I've nowhere to go, nothing to do, there's no protection. I just felt so exposed and naked, is what comes up. I often have dreams still of being undressed, or in this case now that I'm religious, no wig on, you know.

LAUREL: [I'm trying to reorient her and find out where she is in the imagery.] OK, so are you still in the living room or where are you?

MIRIUM: I'm in the living room, yeah, just standing in the living room, and I don't remember actually doing this, but that's where I am, I'm standing in the living room with nothing to do, nowhere to go, and I'm so afraid that you're sorry that you decided to work with me. That's really what's coming up right now.

LAUREL: [The transference is coming up. She's afraid I will reject or criticize her. I decide to follow that thread and see where it goes.] OK, so go with that. >>>>>

MIRIUM: I'm really getting hot in my body, really hot. It's so good to have God in my life, you know (*begins to sob*). There's nowhere to go. As a teenager my drug of choice was fantasy, it's the only place (*sob*) I had to go. I was too straight to do drugs or alcohol, and most people weren't doing that yet in my high school, so I used to play music really loud and just make up stories or pretend I was loved and wanted (*sobbing*), and when I felt good, even I didn't know what to do with myself when I felt good, so I would do this fantasy thing, but I didn't know how to turn it into anything constructive, you know.

LAUREL: So, what I want you to do now is to go back into the scene in the living room and tell me what comes up.

MIRIUM: Well, I just sat on the floor at least, kind of plopped down on the floor. [She is looping and stuck in the same scene for a few sets. We need to do an interweave.]

LAUREL: OK, so what does this little girl need?

MIRIUM: I need a mommy (*sobbing*)!

LAUREL: OK, so who would you like as a mommy?

MIRIUM: I don't know, I've been looking for a mommy for my whole life (*laughs nervously*) . . . I don't know.

LAUREL: You can create any kind of mommy you like, any mommy you want, you can create. [This is an imagination interweave.]

MIRIUM: (*crying*) I just made one up, I just pictured like a very heavy woman with very big breasts—actually, my grandmother. My grandmother was sort of a mother figure for me, a benign mother sometimes. I imagine just resting my head on her bosom.

LAUREL: So you have a sense of this mother . . .

MIRIUM: Yeah.

LAUREL: Ok, so let's just go with that. >>>>>

MIRIUM: (*laughing*) It's funny. I just pictured a Spanish woman, talking to me in Spanish. She's too big, like she's too big, I can't get close enough in a way. Like her breasts are almost pushing me away.

LAUREL: OK. Do you want to make smaller breasts on her? [She can make her mother figure any way she wants.]

MIRIUM: (laughing) I don't know, you know, it's so funny that you're guiding me to create a mother. I want to say: "I don't have one, there is no one," and leave it at that and we'll go with that, you know. Like there's no mother for me.

LAUREL: I don't know. We can create another mother you want that fits you.

MIRIUM: OK. OK. OK! I have a figure. I used to imagine a female angel, a very beautiful angel. Your coloring, actually. I guess because it was my coloring, you know? I was the only blond, blue-eyed person in my family. We all have blue eyes but I was the only blond, and, just wise and strong and confident and powerful and calm and she doesn't have to talk . . . my mother talked a lot.

LAUREL: OK, wonderful, so bring in this angel with these qualities that fit for you.

MIRIUM: Yeah, yeah!!

LAUREL: And just feel yourself being taken care of and loved and nurtured by her. >>>>>

MIRIUM: She's saying, "I've always been there, I never left," and she's not an emotional woman, she's an angel. She's deeply, deeply,

deeply compassionate . . . yeah. I really am making connections. There were two main reasons that made me come to therapy and they're both equal. One is my own growth and my own recovery, and the other is I feel I have so much to give to people (*deep sobbing*). I've got so much to give, like it's been in me all my life and somehow this angel is sort of a figure of what's inside me (*deep sobbing*).

LAUREL: OK, go with that. >>>>>

MIRIUM: (*sobbing deeply*) Yeah, that's great! (*sobbing*) And I want to let her out! I want to let her out so badly. There's so much fear (*deep release*) like I'm going to be killed. No one wants me, like I just feel I'm going to be killed if I let her out (*sobbing*).

LAUREL: OK, what's coming up?

MIRIUM: I don't know. I just had this thought where she said: "But I'm eternal, so don't worry about it" (*chuckles*). It's like she's part of my soul, you know, it is my soul. Right now I'll tell you what's happening. My body just feels so sensitive, like I don't know, like I can't even explain it, like jumpy.

LAUREL: OK, I want you to go to the last thing that I heard her say to you.

MIRIUM: Yeah.

LAUREL: And take that in more fully, let your body really take that in! >>>>>

MIRIUM: OK, I'm eternal. They can't do anything to us, you know—what can they do? (*deep breaths*) She's gotten really tall, like really big, really tall. And my father looks tiny, like I wasn't even thinking of my mother, she's not even in the picture, but my father, like, got very tiny. (*At this point she got distracted with philosophical thoughts and I directed her back to the target.*)

LAUREL: Let's go back to the little girl in the living room.

MIRIUM: OK.

LAUREL: Let's just check that now. Tell me what comes up.

MIRIUM: Yeah, this angel just came into the living room, took my hand, and just walked me out of the home. That's just what happened.

LAUREL: OK, so let's go with that. >>>>>

MIRIUM: *Oy*, this is wild. So we walked out of the house, but the main thing wasn't where we're going but just holding her hand in my hand, snug and warm and just going with her. I don't care where we're going, she's just holding my hand and she's not letting go and it's permanent, you know, and then I pictured my husband, how I feel when we hold hands. It's a nice, firm, comfortable, strong, connected feeling, and then I picture taking other people's hands, you know, being able to take their hand and then that self-conscious part of me that's always judging myself saying: "Oh it's so corny, you're making this up," but I'm not, you know. These images are coming up.

LAUREL: Yeah! So now when you think of the 4-year-old, are you still in that house or are you out with the angel, or where are you now?

MIRIUM: Yeah, well I feel like maybe there's a part of me that's still in the living room, undressed and alone.

LAUREL: Check it out and see.

MIRIUM: Yeah, she's there, she's still there. [This is stuck; it hasn't moved.]

LAUREL: OK, so what does she need?

MIRIUM: I think she needs to be held right where she is, you know, like someone needs to get on the floor with her and like just hold her right there.

LAUREL: OK, and who could do that?

MIRIUM: *Oy*, this is so hard for me! Maybe I'll pick my husband.

LAUREL: OK, let's try and see if it'll work. Just imagine that. >>>>> (*long set of BLS*)

MIRIUM: OK, actually he morphed into someone else. I used to have a very intense fantasy around a boy my age that looked just like me and he grew up with me. I forgot all about this. He was my age, like a twin, and then I found out about the twin theory, that maybe, because my mother had a miscarriage, that maybe I had a twin, but anyway the point is that, he was also like an angel, very nice, very wise, very calm, very knowing, understanding me completely. He has a good sense of humor and he actually got on the floor with me. He was laughing with me and it's OK, it's OK, you're going to be fine. The figure like that I had was Peter Pan, when I was 7 years old. I saw Peter Pan, and it was Mary Martin but at the time I thought it was Peter. He definitely was my nurturer and protector. He was throughout my childhood.

LAUREL: So now with the scene, what comes up?

MIRIUM: I think we're OK. We're sitting together on the floor, we're like leaning on each other. We're fine, that's what's coming up.

LAUREL: Is there any distress? On a scale from 0 to 10, with 0 being the least and 10 the most?

MIRIUM: I want to get out of the house. I hate that house! I'm sick and tired of trying to make the house OK. The house is not OK!

LAUREL: OK, so how do you want to do that?

MIRIUM: I'd like to get up and just get out. That's what I tried to do with the angel but you know . . .

LAUREL: Do you want to go out with you and the boy and the angel altogether?

MIRIUM: Yeah!

LAUREL: OK, so imagine that [imagination interweave]. >>>>>

MIRIUM: All right! I'm good, I feel like I really do have a team. They're really watching my back 'cause the angel took me out the front, he followed from the rear. He slammed the door behind him, locked the thing, threw the key away like, OK, now we're a team. I'm in a group, I'm in a group, and it feels very good!

LAUREL: Do you want to go with that? Does that feel complete to you?

MIRIUM: That feels complete!

LAUREL: And 0–10, any disturbance there?

MIRIUM: No, 0.

LAUREL: What do you believe about yourself in that picture?

MIRIUM: I believe I'm connected, I'm lovable, and I'm powerful!!!

LAUREL: Great! So put all those beliefs with the picture you have now!

MIRIUM: Wait, what picture is that?

LAUREL: The one you have now, with the team [the evolved picture].

MIRIUM: OK. >>>>>

LAUREL: (*After installing these positive beliefs with the picture from the living room, we checked the dream.*) OK, let's check the dream out now, the dream with the convertible. Tell me what comes up when you go to the dream?

MIRIUM: (*chuckling*) So now I'm my age and I get up and say, "Thank God I wasn't hurt," and I flag down a car going the other way. So I can just go back and away from the other car. So I hitch a ride! (*laughs*)

LAUREL: (*laughing*) OK, so imagine that. >>>>>

MIRIUM: OK. We started actually a bit of a new line, though we don't need to go there. First of all I feel great. I feel like I can go anywhere now. I have all of these choices ahead of me. I remembered as a young adult, 18 or 19, I started doing these trips across country, which terrified my mother but was absolutely what I needed to do. That's why I picked the train [for her metaphor] because the whole idea of traveling for me is very liberating. You know, I got out of the house and I'm ok.

LAUREL: (*trying to wrap up the session*) And what belief goes with the dream now, with this new evolved dream picture?

MIRIUM: The belief is that I'm enough. In myself, I'm enough.

LAUREL: OK, so put that belief in the picture. >>>>>

MIRIUM: OK, it's great, like I feel like we could do this forever, like, I'm making all these connections. Like growing up looking at all the cowboy movies, like the Lone Ranger. There's always the lone masculine guy who comes and saves everybody and then he disappears. Who was that masked man? And there's this part of me that's that person. The quiet person, savior. But I don't want to be a savior either, but it is another part of me.

LAUREL: OK, so now, let's check out the scene where you're at work and people are talking in the hallway and you're looking out. What comes up now when you bring that up? [This is the original scene from which we bridged.]

MIRIUM: Well, I do picture myself getting up and walking into the hallway to say: "Hey, guys, how're you doing? What's up?" I'm picturing myself doing it, although part of me is saying, "No, no, don't do it!" (*laughs*).

LAUREL: OK, so let's just go with doing it.

MIRIUM: Just doing it. OK. >>>>> (*smiling*) Wow, it's interesting 'cause first of all, I really have been doing this. I belong here. I have room here, and I'm allowed to claim my space and I deserve to be wanted and be in a place that's comfortable. So yesterday I led a group. I've been put to work with adolescents and now I'm leading two groups from our GED [General Educational Development] programs, mostly boys.

LAUREL: So with your coworkers now, that feels better, you can imagine yourself going out and talking to them? [I'm checking our work.]

MIRIUM: Yeah!

LAUREL: OK, so now, let's do one more. Imagine yourself really taking this out into the future, doing more of this. You can start in a work setting. Can you imagine doing that?

MIRIUM: Yeah. >>>>> This is about being able to set up a private practice, 'cause I knew coming in here, there was some trauma stuff stopping me from that. I don't know. I have all these actions I could do to set up my private practice, but I haven't been doing it.

LAUREL: OK, so imagine doing those things. >>>>>

MIRIUM: Yeah, the key thing is give talks for free, and I did that once this year and I got a client that way. (*She began to find other areas that needed work around writing and preparing talks or papers. I needed to move toward closure.*)

LAUREL: OK, How does your body feel?

MIRIUM: Ooooh, ohhhh, good! Like energy is just flowing through my body! It's unbelievable. Like my arms, my legs, my stomach, not so much but a little, yeah, like I feel tingly, tingly all over.

LAUREL: Fantastic. So you feel in a good place to stop?

MIRIUM: Yeah!

LAUREL: So the processing may continue. You might, you know, have more insights, more dreams, more things come up. Just notice them and see where you are. Test this work out. See how you feel in group situations, see if there's anything else there, so whatever else, if you notice something, it may be another way to find other targets.

MIRIUM: Right! Let me give you a hug. Thank you so much! I was so right to ask you to do this!

LAUREL: Yes, it was perfect!

CASE EXAMPLE OF AN ALCOHOLIC CLIENT WITH CHILDHOOD TRAUMA FROM PARENTAL ALCOHOLISM

This is a session with a woman from my EMDR Advanced Clinical Workshop and Refresher Course who volunteered for a demonstration to work on repairing the damage done to her from childhood trauma related to her parents' alcoholism and the resulting chaos in the home.

Presenting Problem

"Leah" was an attractive woman in her 50s who wanted to work on her abuse of alcohol. Married for many years to a man she loved, she was concerned that her drinking was affecting her marriage, her health, and her self-esteem. "I'm a high-functioning alcoholic," she said. When I asked her to be specific about her drinking, she said that she drank chardonnay, one to two glasses daily in the evenings, but when she was alone she would drink a half to three quarters of a bottle. When she drank, she would get nauseous and uncomfortable; she felt miserable physically. "I will drink until it hurts." She told me that she had been anorexic as a teen and bulimic in her 20s, bingeing and purging up to five times a day. As a result, she developed "stomach issues." She told me, "I don't digest very well and I have irritable bowel."

I asked her for more information about what happens when she is alone and drinking. I was trying to see if there was a trigger, and also how she might be feeling when she was drinking. She told me that when her husband went out of town, "I have a party with myself. I put on music, drink wine, and dance with 'Teddy,' our golden retriever. I feel quite euphoric. I'm all alone and no one will get hurt by me. The next day I'm miserable and in physical pain. Being alone is a trigger to drink. My drinking is worse when I'm alone. I get a signal to stop because it's hurting me. Then I cook a meal." I asked her about the evenings with her husband when she drank wine. How was that affecting her and her relationship? It seemed like a small amount of alcohol to me. She told me that she had a low tolerance for alcohol; even in small quantities it affected her. "After two glasses I'm not there anymore. I get feedback from my husband. I have a history of dissociating and I don't remember," she said.

Resourcing

We installed resources, which she was able to do easily. We used tactile stimulation in the form of pulsers, which vibrated alternatively as she held them in her hands or placed them under her knees. Her peaceful place was a bathtub shrine. She had several nurturing figures: Teddy her golden retriever and friends "Penny," "Maggie," "Michele," "Francine," and "Ying." Her protector figures were her husband "Tom" and her dog Teddy. Her wise figure was a woman named "Dorothy." After she tapped each of them in separately, I asked her if she'd like to imagine them all together as a team. She liked the idea, so we tapped in her inner support team. Despite her distressing childhood and her current symptoms, she could readily find and tap in resources. We also had a good rapport, all of which gave me confidence to proceed with EMDR.

History and Background

Leah grew up in a middle-class neighborhood. Her father, a professional, worked in San Francisco, and her mother was a homemaker.

She described both of her parents as "drunks." Her father would begin drinking on the train on the way home and was sometimes so intoxicated that he forgot to get off the train and the family would drive an hour all the way to the end of the line to pick him up. Both parents would drink to the point of passing out. Her brother was a severe alcoholic by the time he was 15 and her younger sister abused marijuana. "I would put my mom and dad to bed. I was the only sober one in the house."

Then Leah asked me, "Do you want to hear what a typical day in my life was like, Laurel?" When I said, "yes," she began to relate to me a terrible story that represented the worst of the alcohol abuse in her family and its affect on her. As she described the scene, strong feelings arose in her, so I felt that it would make a good target for our EMDR work. I used the modified protocol to go right into the memory network and process.

EMDR Session

LEAH: I was 15 and Mom got drunk. She was lying on the couch in the living room, chain-smoking. She hated her marriage. Dad was passed out in the hallway. My sister was in her room, smoking marijuana. I put my dad to bed. My brother was drunk and going to drive. I was frantic trying to keep him from driving. I took the keys from him. I went to talk to my sister in her room, but I could smell the marijuana wafting up from under her door. My parents were useless. Then my brother tricked me and took the keys. He got in the car, locked it, and drove away. I was completely helpless to stop him. It was really lonely.

LAUREL: Do you want to process this memory?

LEAH: Yes. OK.

LAUREL: What picture represents the worst part of this for you?

LEAH: My brother driving away. I can't stop him.

LAUREL: What emotions go with that?

LEAH: Rage, sadness.

LAUREL: What do you notice in your body?

LEAH: I feel a hole in my heart; my chest hurts.

LAUREL: What do you believe about yourself?

LEAH: I'm all alone.

LAUREL: I'm going to start the BLS. Just let whatever comes up, come up without censoring it, OK? (*She has the pulsers under her legs, and I turn on the machine.*) >>>>>

LEAH: Sometimes I prefer to be alone.

LAUREL: Go with that. >>>>>

LEAH: I don't want to be around them or like them.

LAUREL: Go with that. >>>>>

LEAH: I'm afraid I'm like them, and I'm running away from being close.

LAUREL: Go with that. >>>>>

LEAH: (*begins to cry*) I'm realizing, I'm doing to Tom what my family did to me. When I drink, I'm not there. I feel so ashamed. I'm hurting the one I love the most, just like my parents did to me. I swore I'd never be like them, but I have been. This is hard to look at.

LAUREL: Go with that. >>>>>

LEAH: I don't want to do that anymore.

LAUREL: [This is an important insight. She has been defending against this by compartmentalization. She indeed has been hurting him, but she couldn't take this in. Now she has processed the feelings and the shame, with a new determination not to repeat the behavior. She now has access to her empathy.] Go with that. >>>>>

LEAH: I get so anxious, like I'm on alert around people and I have to take care of everything. I'm tired of taking care of everything. I think of the times I can sneak away and don't have to do anything. Now those times are not safe for me anymore. They never were safe.

LAUREL: Because?

LEAH: I didn't learn how to express myself and ask for what I needed. I have a memory of childhood. I painted everything blue. I sat on a blue pillow and that's when I overate.

LAUREL: [I'm concerned that she is going too far afield and want to check her progress, so I direct her to go back to target.] Let's go back to the scene where your brother drove away. What comes up for you?

LEAH: I don't have attachment to them, and I feel slimed by them.

LAUREL: Go with that. >>>>>

LEAH: They are falling into a rabbit hole; if I follow, I fall, too. I just don't have a family. It's an empty feeling.

LAUREL: [I don't want to leave her with no family. I want to do an attachment repair for her, so I offer an interweave.] Would you like a new family? You can create one, be safe, and feel loved and taken care of.

LEAH: I've done that with my friends.

LAUREL: You can do this as a little girl, not as an adult. Would you like to imagine a family adopting you, taking you out of the house and you go elsewhere?

LEAH: Yes, that feels good. >>>>> I still feel like the odd one out—like I did with my family. I want to believe they could love me.

LAUREL: [This interweave isn't working. It needs some adjustment so it fits her and does work.] Pretend this *is* your real family. They'd be like you—responsible, loving, happy, attentive. You were born to her—to this loving, responsible mother.

LEAH: And I have siblings that like me.

LAUREL: [Now this imagination interweave is working; it fits her needs.] Imagine that. >>>>>

LEAH: That's good.

LAUREL: (*I can see that she feels much better. The tension has left her face, she is relaxing, and there is a smile on her face.*) Imagine going through adolescence with parents like this. Your parents are paying attention to you. There are limits and boundaries. [I am attempting to help her repair the damage from the lack of parents in her adolescence by helping her to imagine good parents to heal the wounds from the lack of parenting.] >>>>>

LEAH: A bad memory came: I imagine protecting my parents. They let my brother emotionally incest me. He couldn't get girls, so they encouraged him to take me to dances so he felt better. It's hard.

LAUREL: [This is a whole new trauma memory opening up here. I'm concerned about veering off into it.] Do you want to move into that and then do your new family?

LEAH: I want to bring my new family to talk to my parents.

LAUREL: OK, imagine them doing that. >>>>>

LEAH: They don't get it, but it's OK because someone is protecting me and my needs. When my mom got sick, there was no one there to explain anything to me.

LAUREL: Is there someone who can explain it to you? [another imagination/resource interweave]

LEAH: Yes, Dorothy.

LAUREL: Imagine her doing that for you. >>>>>

LEAH: That felt good.

LAUREL: [I wanted to check the progress of the work, so I asked her to check the target scene.] Can you go back and check the scene we started with, the scene with your brother driving away? What comes up?

LEAH: I see light around me.

LAUREL: Go with that. >>>>>

LEAH: I feel better.

LAUREL: Scan the scene. Look at your mother, father, brother, sister. Is there any charge anywhere?

LEAH: They are not my responsibility. The charge is gone. I feel relief.

LAUREL: On a scale from 0 to 10, where 0 is no disturbance or neutral, and 10 the highest you can imagine, how disturbing does it feel to you now?

LEAH: It's a 0.

LAUREL: What do you believe about yourself now?

LEAH: I have a lot of resources inside; I'm courageous. I can reach out to others.

LAUREL: Put that all in—that understanding with the picture you have now [installing the positive cognitions]. >>>>>

LEAH: I am able to love. Any family would be lucky to have me (*looking elated, luminous, joyful*).

LAUREL: Take that in too. >>>>>

LEAH: That feels great.

LAUREL: [I want to check the symptoms and triggers for drinking to evaluate our progress.] Go to drinking in the evening. Where are you with your desire to drink? Do you want alcohol?

LEAH: I don't want it now.

LAUREL: Go with that. >>>>> What comes up?

LEAH: Other triggers. It's the end of the day, I'm depleted, and I can get triggered.

LAUREL: [I want to quickly address this trigger by bringing in a resource.] Can you imagine giving yourself something other than alcohol?

LEAH: I can imagine giving myself my husband.

LAUREL: Good, imagine that. >>>>>

LEAH: He's still there, even if he's mad at me.

LAUREL: [I want to see if we can address the other trigger for her drink-

ing—being alone when her husband goes away.] Imagine that
Tom isn't home and you are alone. What comes up for you?

LEAH: I'm scared—I can be slippery.

LAUREL: Feel this. >>>>> [This is the first time she has been able to
feel the feelings that are triggered when her husband leaves. I
believe she can tolerate them now, so I ask her to go with that,
with the BLS.]

LEAH: It's about soothing myself again; I'm hungry for something
warm—it's almost desperate.

LAUREL: [She has insight about what is going on with her. This is new.
If we had time, I would bridge her back to get an early target memory, but we are at the end of the session, so I bring
in resources to help her address these needs.] What resource
could you bring in to help with that feeling?

LEAH: I need air; maybe I can get just a breath.

LAUREL: Just start there—BREATHE. >>>>>

LEAH: It's calming.

LAUREL: Do you want to imagine bringing love to that place? [I had
the feeling that she needed love to counter the shame and
aloneness she was feeling.]

LEAH: Yes, that feels right. >>>>>

LEAH: That feels good (*tears in her eyes*).

LAUREL: [I want to try a future pace to see if she could imagine doing
something different in the future instead of drinking.] Can you
imagine being home alone and giving yourself love instead of
alcohol? You are alone, and instead of wine, you are giving
yourself love.

LEAH: (*nods and smiles*) >>>>> Everything is opening up. (*She is
radiant. Both of us are in tears. The room is full of love. She is
very expanded, almost ecstatic.*)

We spend some time debriefing the session. I ask Leah to pay attention to how she feels by keeping a log or journal; the processing may
continue in her dreams, and more memories may come up. We hug, tears
in both of our eyes. I feel elated, mirroring her. During the week I hear
from her: She had not had any wine. She reported that the desire to drink
had gone. Even being around others drinking wine had not caused her to
want to drink. Her husband was happy and grateful.

The next week she told me: "I want to let you know that this week has
been amazing. I have been absent any craving for alcohol—even after a

full day of work! I remain cautiously optimistic about this turn around for me. I need more time to make it real, but I am truly amazed! Thank you again from the bottom of my heart."

CASE EXAMPLE OF A WOMAN TRAUMATIZED BY A MOTHER WITH MENTAL ILLNESS

This is a session I did as a class demonstration at the New York Open Center in January 2012. (The full case can be seen on the DVD, *Attachment-Focused EMDR with a Woman with Complex PTSD, Traumatized by a Mother with Mental Illness*, at www.emdrinfo.com). "Carla," a Jewish woman in her 50s, was born in Baghdad, Iraq, where she lived until she was 11 and her family had to flee for their lives to the United States. She experienced traumas throughout her childhood. She was persecuted as a Jew in a Muslim country, which created an overall climate of fear. She described her mother as "crazy" and "histrionic," as well as severely depressed. Carla was also physically and sexually abused in childhood.

In the session that follows, Carla wished to focus on the trauma she experienced by her mother. She told me that after her brother was born when she was 11, her mother became severely depressed and underwent electroconvulsive therapy (ECT). "When she came home from the hospital, she looked dead and was bedridden for 10 months with a newborn." She added that when her mother came to the United States, she was "crazy" and attempted suicide.

Her mother was diagnosed as paranoid, with agitated depression, and borderline. Part of what was most distressing for Carla was that she was enmeshed with her mother. She had a hard time feeling her own feelings, separate from what her mother was feeling. She both hated her mother *and* felt responsible for her. She felt very traumatized by having had such a mother.

Carla was very upset when she told me that 2 months ago she was hospitalized and no one in the family came to visit her because her mother had had a stroke and they were all attending to her. "They couldn't bother to come to see me," she said. This recent experience seemed to represent what had happened throughout her life—her needs were not taken care of because her mother's needs were so much greater and more important. I summed it up for her, "Your own needs didn't get taken care of." To which she responded, "My mother's needs always came first."

In this session, her resources were very important to install because they provided a stable base that calmed and grounded her, and were readily available to use as interweaves. She spoke aloud as she processed and would often go off on tangents. I would gently refocus her to keep her in the childhood network and keep her contained and from flooding. My calm, gentle presence as she processed helped to regulate her in a way her mother never could. I had the feeling that I was working with a fragile child who had never been soothed by a stable, loving caregiver. Her nervous system was easily triggered and dysregulated. During the session, I kept her focused and helped her to separate out what was hers from what belonged to her mother, so that she could feel her own feelings and let her mother have her own experience. We addressed her need to take care of her sick mother by bringing in resources for her mother, which helped her to separate from her mother in a healthy way.

At the beginning of the session I had a great deal of difficulty getting a coherent narrative from Carla. She bounced from one thing to the next, the past, the present, mixing up time periods, making it difficult for me to follow her. She was also emotionally labile, crying easily, and needing reassurance. I could tell from how disorganized she was in her ability to tell her story and by her emotional lability that she had severe attachment trauma. She was dissociative, internally disorganized, and easily dysregulated.

After taking a brief history, we installed resources, which she was able to do rather easily and which immediately calmed her. This was quite encouraging for me. She had the resources; they just were not integrated and available to her. She told me that she'd had EMDR therapy before, but the therapist had not installed any resources other than the safe place one. Because her ill mother was hysterical and engulfing, she needed to connect with secure figures to regulate her nervous system.

She chose a Caribbean beach as her peaceful place, and her former therapist "Ann," her aunt "Maria," and two friends "Jamie" and "Andrea" as nurturing figures. We also installed her nurturing adult self, the part of her that nurtured her own children. I felt that because she'd had no nurturing as a child from a stable mother, I wanted to create an ideal mother that we might use in our EMDR work.

LAUREL: I'm wondering, would you like to create the mother you wished you'd had—loving, nurturing, attuned to you, and providing you with everything you need emotionally?

CARLA: Yes. I'd love to do that.

LAUREL: Do you have a picture of her in your mind?

CARLA: Yes, I can imagine her.

LAUREL: Good, imagine her. >>>>>

After installing the ideal mother, I could see an immediate effect on her nervous system. She seemed even more grounded, present, and calm. We then installed the protector figures she chose: God, Superman, and her friend "Rita" and therapist "Ann," as well as her protective adult self. Finally, she installed all of her resource figures as a team. It was difficult focusing Carla to find a target to work on, but because she had become so distressed around the idea that she lacked a mother, we decided to focus on that issue for the session.

LAUREL: When you think of not having had a mother, is there a memory that goes with that?

CARLA: When she had the baby and had electric shock for 10 months. She didn't get out of bed for 10 months.

LAUREL: Go inside yourself and bring up the image of your mother in bed, and her unresponsiveness. What emotions do you feel?

CARLA: Terrible sadness.

LAUREL: What do you notice in your body?

CARLA: My hands are clammy.

LAUREL: What belief goes with this?

CARLA: She's going to die. I'll be all alone.

LAUREL: Let's go with that. >>>>> [I wanted to get her into the network and process her quickly before she jumped out again and became distracted. The network was well activated, so I began the BLS.]

CARLA: What's wrong with you? You're a big girl—you are overreacting. [She is criticizing herself. I don't know if it is her voice or her mother's. She is saying these things as the BLS goes. I decide to take her back to the target to see where she is.]

LAUREL: Let's go back and check the scene with your mother in bed depressed. What comes up for you?

CARLA: I dissociated. I cut out.

LAUREL: [I decide to do an interweave to help her with the dissociation.] What does this little girl need?

CARLA: She needs to flee.

LAUREL: Let's have someone get her out of there. >>>>>

CARLA: I feel angry.

LAUREL: Let yourself feel the anger. >>>>>

CARLA: (*I keep the BLS going as she narrates her experience.*) My mother did nothing to help herself. She was so passive. It was always someone else's fault. She took no responsibility. It was all my fault. I was evil. I remember when I left my husband. She said, "Who could tolerate living with you?" I hated her. It scares me 'cause she is so unstable.

LAUREL: [At this point I stopped the BLS because she was going too far afield. I wanted to keep her focused on the childhood memory. She also seemed to be looping. I decided to do an interweave in which I linked her adult perspective to the child memory. The child did not have the perspective that her mother had a mental illness.] Can you go back and look at it as an adult?

CARLA: Yes. >>>>> (*She is speaking with the BLS going.*) I see my mother, who was mentally ill and should not have been raising a child. She was terrified and didn't know how to take care of children and shouldn't be taking care of children. [This insight elicited compassion for her mother. Then she had a positive memory about her mother.] She was generous and creative as a chef. She entertained beautifully.

LAUREL: What's happening now?

CARLA: I feel sad.

LAUREL: Go with the sadness. >>>>>

CARLA: (*Again, she narrates with the BLS.*) I don't have to join her crazy world. I can be with you without jumping into your skin. I'm seeing her as separate, I'm empowered. I see her as fragile, sad. I worked hard at not fleeing, escaping the depression, inner stuff. No one could help her, not even the psychiatrist, no one.

LAUREL: [It seemed to be the end of a channel, so I directed her back to the target.] Let's go back to the scene you started with—the scene with your mother depressed and in bed. What comes up now?

CARLA: She's in bed. She doesn't look as threatening. I feel I'm watching her.

LAUREL: How are you feeling?

CARLA: Removed. Detached. I'm not feeling I'm in her body and that this is my future. I'm not feeling, "When will I lose my mind and this trauma will catch up with me?" There was a wish to join her . . . if we are one, then I have a mother.

LAUREL: [This was a new insight, a new realization.] OK, let's go with that. >>>>>

CARLA: (*Narrates as the BLS continued.*) I feel scared, anxious, lonely. I desperately want her to jump out of bed or I could jump into the bed. (Silence for a bit while she processed internally.) I'm standing away—I bring my adult self and my resource team in and they support me. "We're with you and can help you grow up." I didn't have to be dependent or a victim to get attention. She got negative attention. I feel so sad.

LAUREL: [I felt the need to do an interweave as she was still feeling sad.] Can you imagine nurturing figures holding the child?

CARLA: Yes. >>>>> I'll put in Robin and Jamie, and God is with me. They are creating a circle around me and her. I love that replacement of what was and what is. [She loved the use of creativity to change the scene.] I survived it. A lot changed. Positive stuff exists. I never take in anything positive about myself.

LAUREL: Do you want to imagine taking in the positive?

CARLA: Yes. >>>>> She feels bad. I'm leaving behind the mother (*cries*). I never wanted to. I feel all clammy. I was enmeshed . . . that's why I stayed.

LAUREL: [I wanted to help her separate from her mother. She was having difficulty doing this. In order to help her separate, I asked her if she wanted to bring in resources for her mother so that she could let go of having to do that job.] Do you want to bring in resource figures for your mother?

CARLA: Other than me? I love that idea to help my mother. I'd bring in my Aunt "Rita," and another chef. >>>>> (*As BLS is going on, she speaks.*) Aunt "Rachel" can help her . . . my dad, whom she trusted, can too. He stabilized her. I was in the middle. Let him support her. I love having Dad around to help. [She seemed to be at the end of that channel, so I directed her back to the target again.] It is even hard to imagine her in the bed.

LAUREL: What do you experience now?

CARLA: I feel good.

LAUREL: Is there any charge there now?

CARLA: I feel much less—it's a 3 [on the SUDS scale].

LAUREL: Are we at a place to stop now? [We were nearly out of time and I wanted to begin to close the session and wrap up.]

CARLA: Yes.

LAUREL: What do you believe about yourself now?

CARLA: I can create my own reality and have choices. I'm not my mother.
LAUREL: Put all of that together as you think of the scene with your
          mother [installing the positive cognitions]. >>>>>
CARLA: I want to close with my resource figures.
LAUREL: Do you want to do it with or without the BLS?
CARLA: With. >>>>> I feel I'm enough . . . just came up.
LAUREL: Great, go with that. >>>>>

Carla ended the session feeling greatly relieved. She was especially happy
about feeling separate from her mother. She felt integrated, with a new
sense of wholeness and stability. She was excited to continue with EMDR
to repair the childhood wounds.

TWO SESSIONS DEMONSTRATING THE USE OF ANIMALS IN INTERWEAVES TO REPAIR DISRUPTION IN EARLY MATERNAL ATTACHMENT
Nancy Ewing

These two session are provided by Nancy Ewing, a San Francisco Bay
Area psychologist who was trained by me in AF-EMDR. Nancy has
become quite proficient in adapting EMDR to clients with unmet developmental needs, and she is able to seamlessly integrate it into her work.
She provided me with background, notes, and comments from EMDR
sessions in which her client drew upon her loving attachment to pet animals to repair early disruption in her maternal attachment. The client
uses the pulsers from the Tac/AudioScan for BLS.

Background, Presenting Problem, and Treatment Summary

"Tina" is a 47-year-old bright, clever, and artistic woman who sought
treatment because she felt stymied in her ability to utilize her tremendous creative potential. Her husband encouraged her to pursue her creative talents, and she was a loving mother of a school-age daughter.

Tina had a pattern of volunteering for community projects that distracted her from working on her personal passion—writing and illustrat-
ing children's books. She was unable to focus and work steadily on her
stories. Eight years earlier, before her daughter was born, she submit-
ted a partially finished book to a prestigious publishing house that was
seriously considering it for publication. She didn't persist in making the
changes they suggested and failed to resubmit it at that time.

The root of her inability to utilize her potential in a focused manner lies in the trauma of being the brunt of her mother's emotional abuse from infancy onward. Tina felt that her mother never forgave her for "ruining her life" when she became pregnant with Tina and dropped out of college. In contrast, her younger brother was wanted and favored by her mother. Her father, an academic, was quietly more supportive of Tina, but didn't protect her from her mother's attacks and the alcoholic rages directed at her. Tina felt like a "crumpled piece of paper"—that her mother psychologically crushed her as her father stood by. Sometimes her mother's abuse was private—she would take Tina aside and say horrible things to her.

Previous to EMDR treatment Tina had held the belief that she was impaired—that there was something wrong with her. She had a pervasive feeling that she was "broken," "shattered," "crumpled," and "crushed" by her mother. However, she had not explicitly processed the maternal abuse that had given rise to these painful, disabling feelings. In a series of EMDR sessions specific incidents of maternal neglect and abuse she had endured from infancy onward became palpable. She processed the more subtle attacks of her mother upon her as a child, and her mother's verbally vicious attacks on her as an adolescent.

The overall therapeutic approach with Tina consisted of a series of EMDR sessions woven in with regular talk therapy sessions, in conjunction with setting weekly and daily goals for working on her manuscript. She utilized pet animals in some of her sessions as powerful reparative attachment figures, as presented below.

The EMDR sessions presented here exemplify how drawing on the love of pet animals can provide a powerful source of healing in cases of failed maternal attachment. As Tina stated, "Animals are unconditionally loving, and I didn't get that from my mother." These sessions are reminders that loving relationships with animals can serve as saviors to children and adults who have experienced early parental neglect and abuse. In the course of EMDR sessions Tina also drew on the love of her family members and friends to detoxify the maternal abuse she had experienced.

First EMDR Session Utilizing a Dog

The first EMDR session reveals the type of abuse and blame that Tina's mother inflicted on her. Tina utilized her attachment to a dog to heal from her mother's attack and to gain a sense of the goodness, innocence, and joy of being a child. The session begins with her telling the story of the traumatic incident that occurred when she was 6 years old.

TINA: My dad was on sabbatical for a year in Ireland, where we lived on a farm and rented a house from the Wards on their farm. They had a labrador retriever named Lily who was good with kids. Mrs. Ward, the owner, taught me how to knit and garden. The property was beautiful with green rolling fields. One day we kids—my younger brother and two girl cousins—walked through the pasture to a sweet shop in town. We were back on the property eating sweets. All of a sudden there was a commotion. Mom came out and told us there was an accident—that a motorcycle had come around a curve in the road and hit Lily and killed her. We were all crying and so upset that Lily had died. Then Mom came over and took me aside and said, "You left the gate open, didn't you? You shouldn't have let Lily follow you. Now look what you've done! Lily is dead and it's your fault and the Wards are going to blame us."

THERAPIST: What is your child self feeling?

TINA: I have a feeling of my stomach dropping out from under me. She singled me out to blame me. I am shocked.

THERAPIST: What does your child self believe about herself?

TINA: I'm trying to believe that it's not my fault. But I was a child, so I just thought that she was right, that it was my fault and that I'm bad. She turned my innocent upset that Lily was killed into shame.

THERAPIST: [At this point enough elements of the target have been identified and activated that the client is ready to reprocess this memory. Her mother blaming her for Lily's death is the target.] >>>>> What's happening with your child self?

TINA: She ran away and hid in the woods. She's afraid that her mother is right—that it was her fault that Lily was killed. She has an upset, desolate feeling because she can't turn back the clock and make Lily not be dead. There's no chance to do it over again.

THERAPIST: What does she need?

TINA: She needs to go to a place where a benevolent being forgives her.

THERAPIST: Who could do that?

TINA: Lily could do that.

THERAPIST: Can you imagine that?

TINA: (*nods*) Yes. >>>>>> (*silent tears streaming down cheeks*)

THERAPIST: What's happening?

TINA: She's the only one who could tell me.

THERAPIST: Imagine that. >>>>>

TINA: (*BLS is on as she's speaking.*) The 6-year-old me is down in the woods looking into a pond. I'm crying and my tears are falling, making ripples in the water. I stir the water around and then I see Lily's face appear. Her appearance feels magical. I say to her, "I'm so sorry." She talks to me and says, "You don't need to be sorry." Then she's smiling. "I am all right and you didn't do anything wrong." Then I say, "But I'm going to do things wrong in the future." Then she's still smiling and says, "Yes, you are. The most important thing is just to be real in every moment and stay connected to your heart and to life. If you are really connected with what you know is right and being true to yourself, then you're doing the right thing. And forgive yourself. I am happy. I can run faster than I could ever before and I have three companions to run with."

THERAPIST: [I think that Tina identifies with Lily and the three dogs are representative of her brother and two cousins.] What's happening?

TINA: I run back to the house and bring back my two cousins to see Lily and the three dogs running in the fields. We see them, and they are free and happy.

THERAPIST: How does your child self feel?

TINA: I feel strong, happy, and proud that Lily is all right and that I could show my cousins . . . my adult me is there too.

THERAPIST: What is your adult self doing?

TINA: My adult me is watching us and comes over to me and walks over to a very special rock where we sit down. (*Therapist turns on the BLS.*) She says to me "Everything's all right, you see." Then she tells me, "Don't bring Mom to this rock because she won't be able to see it or Lily and the dogs." (*Her child self spontaneously says*) "I can see the rock and, the cousins can see it too."

THERAPIST: How does your child self feel?

TINA: I feel good. I run down the hill and run with the dogs and pet Lily, and she licks me. I feel worthy, warm, and equal with the rest of the world. I run back to the rock sweaty, happy, and laughing. I feel calm and happy.

THERAPIST: On a scale from 0 to 10, how would you rate it now?

TINA: 2—I feel a tiny bit of sadness because my little brother is still at the house with Mom and Dad. I go get him and bring him to the rock, and he sees Lily and the dogs running. >>>>>

THERAPIST: How does your child self feel now?

TINA: I feel good and the last bit of my sadness has gone away.

THERAPIST: 0–10?

TINA: 0.

THERAPIST: What does your child believe about herself?

TINA: I'm fine and I haven't done anything wrong, and life is fun and joyful.

THERAPIST: Can you put a picture with the belief?

TINA: Yes. >>>>> All of us—me, my brother, and two cousins—are running with the dogs.

THERAPIST: (*BLS off*) Go back to your mother blaming your child self for Lily's death. What comes up now?

TINA: Then I could see how she made it my fault, but I was only 6 years old. Looking back on it now, I can see that a mother shouldn't let her 6-year-old child go out on the road by herself. My adult me is telling my child me that it's not my fault. A young child isn't responsible for a dog's death. It's a parent's responsibility, and it was an accident.

THERAPIST: How does your child self feel?

TINA: Calm and peaceful.

THERAPIST: On a scale from 0 to 10?

TINA: It's a 0.

Tina had these spontaneous reflections right after the session:

"This is why I'm so angry at my mom. She was probably feeling like Lily's death was her fault. She couldn't stand the feeling of guilt. She used me, her own child, for a repository for her guilt that she couldn't tolerate. She was willing to do that to me. I don't do that to anybody. I don't do that to my daughter. My mom won't accept fault for anything, and she never did. She blames others and she blamed me as a child for everything. She took me aside and did it privately so no one knew.

*She inflicted the blame on me and made me suffer and to feel that I
was bad. I think she's suffering from tons of unconscious guilt, and she
pushed it onto me."*

Second EMDR Session Utilizing a Cat to Repair Disruption in the Early Maternal Attachment

In this EMDR session Tina wanted to explore the trauma of her mother stopping breastfeeding her and leaving her alone in her crib as an infant. I kept the bilateral stimulation on for the entire session because she started processing immediately, intensely, and continuously. In this session she brings in her cat Katz, with whom she has a deep, loving bond, to nurture her and help her repair her early faulty maternal attachment.

TINA: Mom stopped breastfeeding me. I'm in my crib crying. (*I turn the BLS on and leave it on the entire session.*) She turned on the music box with Brahms's lullaby and left me there. I'm so young. I'm a baby and I don't have words yet. I know I'm going to cry (*sobbing, tears rolling down, gasping*). . . . I'm really confused because she's not coming. There's nobody coming. She's not there and it's confusing being in the room with the same sounds, smells and colors, but she's not there. It feels wrong.

THERAPIST: What is your infant self feeling?

TINA: Unloved.

THERAPIST: Where in her body?

TINA: I'm small—in my whole body.

THERAPIST: What is her belief about herself?

TINA: That there's something I don't know that could maybe explain this. I guess I'm tired from crying. I can feel the wetness of the lambskin pad under my face where I'm crying. It doesn't taste the same as my mother's breast. I'm feeling that I'm not enough. I need something else to be all right. I can taste myself—my tears and my saliva—and it's not good enough. I guess I think I'm being left because I don't matter. I'm not good enough.

THERAPIST: What does your infant self need?

TINA: I want my mom. (*Tears quietly fall down her face.*) But I think I'm also angry at her. I want someone to pick me up and hold me. I want someone to take me out of the crib and take me out of this place because I've been staring at it for too long. [She needs a resource or imagination interweave here.]

THERAPIST: Who can do that?

TINA: (*deep sigh, silence*) Hmmm . . . my cat, Katz . . . but she's not big enough, but I guess I could make her be big.

THERAPIST: Imagine that.

TINA: I'm imagining big Katz coming in (*laughs*). OK. I'm doing that. (*Tears roll down her face as she sobs, sighs, gulps. Eyes fluttering closed, then more relaxed breathing, deep breathing, quiet, deep breathing, more relaxed, calm.*) She's been communicating with me . . . hmmm . . . in her own cat voice, and I've been understanding and responding in her language, as it's just as natural to me. She's taking me out of the crib just like a kitten with her mouth on the back of my neck (*tears coming down*). . . . So she's lifted me out and over the crib bar and walking out of the house with me. She's carrying me to a tree that's hollow in the base, and she's curling up there and we're going to sleep. I think I know I could nurse from her if I wanted to, but I'm just happy in her fur curled up next to her in her stomach. It's really soft (*deep relaxed breathing, intermittent deep breaths, relaxed eyes closed . . . eyes fluttering*). She's licking me and licking her paws and her tongue is really warm and she's cleaning my face and tears and cleaning me up. It's really rhythmic and soothing. I remember I used to feel soothed when I watched her clean herself. I'm asking her if later, if I hurt her and neglect her and maybe contribute to her dying too young, if all that guilt is going to flood back and keep this soothing and adoption of me from working out. She says it won't because this is happening right now, after her death, and she's not mad at me and she never was. I ask her how she can forgive me and she says just like you forgave your mom. But I don't think I have forgiven my mom for hurting me. She's nonchalant, licking her paws and she says, "You haven't, are you sure?" I can't tell if I've forgiven my mom, but I feel really warm with Katz, and she's acknowledging how safe and warm I am and that I have her. "Your mom didn't have this. Doesn't it make it easier to forgive her? Do you have to forgive your mom to accept my forgiveness?" I say, no I don't. I'm exploring how safe I feel and I'm thinking about how deep this safety feeling goes right now and how my mom doesn't have that.

THERAPIST: Can you accept Katz's forgiveness?

TINA: I can when she's so big and strong like this. I can totally. But she was small and fragile.

THERAPIST: But isn't she big in spirit?

TINA: (*sobbing*) Yeah. (*deep sigh*)

THERAPIST: Isn't she an all-loving, nurturing, and forgiving being?

TINA: Yeah she is . . . (*silent tears down cheeks*) I'm starting to get mad at myself. When she was small and fragile, I was renovating my house—and my cat, dog, and daughter got lost in the shuffle. I can accept her forgiveness, but I can't accept my own forgiveness. She's saying just to feel safe right now, right here, being here with me. She said that you're not going to forgive yourself until your child gets what she needs and that she's giving me love and in turn I'm giving my daughter love. Katz is saying, "I'm always giving you love right here, in this tree, in my body and in your body, and you can come here whenever you need to, until you can forgive yourself and beyond. I'm not going to get old. I'm not going to die." She's like a redwood tree. It's really deep. It's really safe. The love's right here.

THERAPIST: What do you feel?

TINA: She feels way, way better.

THERAPIST: What do you believe?

TINA: She feels worthy, safe, and loved.

THERAPIST: Can you put that belief with the picture?

TINA: Yes, uh-huh . . . no, not really . . . (*breathing heavy with deep sighs*)

THERAPIST: Does she know that Katz is always there?

TINA: Yeah . . . but I'm bothered by thinking about all the times I treated her bad before she died. She's putting each of those times in clear glass jars, like candy jars, behind her. She's saying, "If you want to look at these things and torture yourself, you can, but I'm not thinking about them. There is and always has been so much love between us—it weathers through hard times and storms—the wind and rain and cold—it's unfaltering. I'm past it, and I think you should be past it too." She's putting the jars inside of the tree, and that looks like a shelf in a candy store, and then she turns her back to them and turns to me licking her paws then nestles up with me. I feel good. I know she loves me and I know I'm allowed to relax. I feel good about myself right now. I can go back to Katz any time I want to. She is always there. I am worthy, safe, and loved.

THERAPIST: Can you put the belief with the picture?

TINA: Yes, now I can. I'm enveloped by Katz's warmth. She's licking me (*almost purring with a Mona Lisa smile, as she's imagining being held by Katz and the belief that she is good and worthy of love*).

As a result of the EMDR sessions such as the ones presented here, woven in with regular talk therapy sessions in conjunction with setting weekly and daily goals for working on her manuscript, Tina has been able to make headway toward submitting children's books to publishers, and she has developed a more loving attitude toward herself. The EMDR sessions validated the horrible psychological abuse she had suffered from her mother and its crushing impact on her child self. She saw that her mother's treatment of her was not right, that she deserved to be loved and nurtured. As a result of several EMDR sessions, she integrated a good and lovable child into her adult self and was able to overcome the belief held by her child self that she was impaired, bad, and to blame. Her self-esteem has improved considerably, and she is better able to nurture and mother her own daughter.

Part IV
CASE EXAMPLES

CHAPTER 16

Using AF-EMDR as an Adjunctive Therapist to Treat Lifelong Depression, Developmental Neglect, and Attachment Wounding

Holly Prichard

THERAPIST BIOGRAPHY AND BACKGROUND

I am a marriage and family therapist practicing in Sonoma County, California, and specializing in the treatment of trauma. I have worked in multiple treatment settings, including a residential crisis center, a low-fee counseling clinic, the mental health unit of the county jail, and private practice.

My therapeutic orientation has followed an eclectic path ranging from psychodynamic, transpersonal, pre- and perinatal psychology, and attachment theory to mind–body, somatically oriented psychotherapy. I have studied ego-state therapy, dissociative processes, complex PTSD, Sensorimotor Psychotherapy, and Hakomi psychotherapy.

About 10 years ago, I took the EMDR Level I and Level II trainings, and in 2004, Laurel Parnell's Advanced Clinical Workshop and Refresher Course. I joined Laurel's monthly consultation group for further learning. Over the years, I have found that EMDR has allowed me to synthesize all of my training to provide a comprehensive treatment approach.

In the case of working with "Mary," I enjoyed finding creative ways of incorporating body-oriented techniques with EMDR to help bring healing to her developmental, attachment/relational trauma.

THE CLIENT

Mary was a 60-year-old woman who'd had significant early attachment trauma that was causing her debilitating symptoms as an adult. The first part of the treatment with Mary is described in Chapter 10. When Mary felt rejected or not important/valued by her boyfriend, she would go to a very dark place. Rejection for her could mean not getting a phone call from her boyfriend when expected or perceiving a disapproving look. She described "spiraling down" into an endless pit and would become immobilized with fear. She described times when she stayed in her house, in this place of immobilization, for long periods of time. In the past, it may have taken her several months to come out of her dark funk. The beliefs that accompanied these somatic reactions were, "I'll be alone forever. I think I'm going to die." Her fear of loss and abandonment made her feel as if she were dying. Her biggest fear was a sense of "falling and there is nobody there." She said that, "When I'm in that place, all I want is someone to be there." She had experienced numerous depressive episodes and had taken medication off and on for years.

COURSE OF TREATMENT: EMDR REPROCESSING

As you may recall from Chapter 10, we spent several sessions installing resources, which Mary responded to well, including an ideal mother that she called "Big Mama." By the fifth session, Mary's resources were firmly established. In between sessions, she had practiced connecting to Big Mama and tapped on herself as she imagined her. We were ready to move on to processing the problematic somatic responses that had brought her into therapy.

We first accessed all of her resources: safe place, protectors (Indians), and Big Mama. She described the feeling that she wanted to work on: a feeling of "falling, black, infinite, no support, nowhere to reach out." I was sure, based on her history and description of her mother, that we would need to go back to her childhood to process the root of this problem. Because her somatic reactions were so strong around this theme and she had no specific early memory that tied directly to her symptoms, I felt that activating her body around a current experience of abandonment would lead us back in time to where this started. I decided to use the bridging technique to find targets that were connected to the deeper material fueling these reactions. It really didn't matter what experience, past or present, we used to activate this channel to get there.

THERAPIST: Go to a time when you felt this way.

MARY: It's hard. The most recent is with my current boyfriend when he said to me that he "couldn't do this now" [be in a relationship with her]. It's like I'm gonna faint.

THERAPIST: Is there an image or picture that goes with this?

MARY: I'm thinking of a time when I was in this feeling a lot. [I assumed that she would go to a recent time with her current boyfriend, since she had started to talk about him. But she went to an earlier memory of when a previous boyfriend had left her. Since it obviously related to the theme of abandonment, it felt totally appropriate to use this as our way into the channels relating to rejection/abandonment.]

THERAPIST: What is the picture?

MARY: Getting left. Being in that apartment. I'm sitting there doubled over.

THERAPIST: What emotions are you feeling?

MARY: Panic in my upper chest.

THERAPIST: What sensations are you aware of?

MARY: Constriction in my throat, clenched belly (*grabbing her throat as if she can't breathe, difficulty swallowing*).

THERAPIST: What are you believing about yourself in this moment?

MARY: I can't handle this. I don't know what I'm gonna do. *I'm powerless.*

THERAPIST: Allow all of this to be here and trace it all back in time, as far back as you can go, without editing it. Let me know when you are aware of something.

MARY: In a crib, screaming and crying. Afraid, black, no one is there, falling, terror, crying, throat tight, I'm small and powerless. Something bad about me. *I'm BAD (voice escalating in panic, chest collapsing, body doubling over, and crying).*

THERAPIST: [I didn't need to ask the formal setup questions because she was already in the full experience. I invited her to go with the whole composite of her experience, knowing that subsequent sets would flesh out the most important aspects.] Go with all of that (*turning on the tappers*). >>>>>

MARY: It feels like this isn't bearable (*crying very heavily here, heaving and sobbing*).

THERAPIST: Go with that. >>>>> [I wanted to see where her system would take her before intervening, but I was prepared to do an interweave quickly if she started to loop in this unbearable place.]

MARY: (*stops crying*) I'm not in that place. I'm back here, relieved not to be there. [I wondered if she had dissociated and come out of it because the intensity was too much.]

THERAPIST: Go with that. >>>>>

MARY: At the end, I started to have a moment of going back to another bad feeling. Now I'm more relaxed. Not having throat or chest clenching. Glad to be here and not there. When I was going to the bad place, the tappers helped relax me.

THERAPIST: Go back and check the original image in the crib. What do you notice?

MARY: It looks the same. I'm not crying. I feel neutral, removed from the drama. I believe I'm not very worthy because there would be someone there if I were. It's more factual than emotional.

THERAPIST: Go with that. >>>>> [I am confused with her report, as she seems to give mixed messages; she says the image is the same, and yet she is not crying or screaming. I'm not really sure what is happening now—if she is dissociated or if something has really moved—but I am curious to see what another set will bring up.]

MARY: I switched back to being an adult. It is what it is. Then, back to the crib. I feel it's still what it is, but a little *curious*, wondering why that is. [I have no idea what she was referring to here, but I picked up on her curiosity, which felt like a shift.]

THERAPIST: Go with that. >>>>>

MARY: In the crib, what I did just now was start to look around a little with interest and a smile. I thought, "Wow, I can look at and play with my toes." I didn't have anything before except screaming, crying, fear. All I did was move my head, looking around the room. A little lighter, slight color. I feel like I'm the observer and my body feels relaxed and open, and I don't have clenching, crying, fear. Breathing is OK.

THERAPIST: Go with that. >>>>>

MARY: Another thing is happening now. I want someone to come. [Here is the attachment piece.] I'm frustrated, mad. I want to get up and do something. I'm standing up in the crib.

THERAPIST: Who would you like to come?

MARY: I don't want my mom. Maybe I should have Big Mama. My dad could come; he would pick me up.

THERAPIST: [Her father, although often absent due to work, was basically a loving presence in her life.] Check in with the little girl. She can have anyone.

MARY: I think she wants my dad.

THERAPIST: Go ahead and let that happen. >>>>> (*Looks peaceful and her breathing is regular.*)

MARY: Dad came and got me and picked me up and moved me around like an airplane, smiling, jiggling me, smiling. I feel really good; that's exactly what I wanted—to have someone hear me and pick me up and play with me and hold me and be delighted to do that.

THERAPIST: [She is describing attuned attachment, something she didn't get from her mother.] Go with that. >>>>>

MARY: When I come back to being an adult, I feel good and relaxed. The picture is so sweet. I have a photograph of my dad holding me up, and I have a smile and I had that feeling when he came and got me—excitement, playing, and laughing.

THERAPIST: When you go back to the original picture, what are you aware of?

MARY: The crib is different. I'm different. I'm standing up. I don't want to be lying down. I'm standing up looking out. I feel content.

THERAPIST: What do you believe about yourself now?

MARY: I'm cuddly. I'm lovable (*smiles*). It makes me want to cry because it's a good feeling.

THERAPIST: Go with that. >>>>>

MARY: I'm fine being by myself, jumping up and down. If I want to call somebody, they'll come and they will want to come. It will be my dad, not my mom. He'll be excited to do that. I'm OK by myself. I'm curious. There are a lot of things to do. I'll be happy right here.

THERAPIST: Go with that. >>>>> [This feels like such a good place for her; I wanted to solidify it with another set.]

MARY: I was walking around the crib. I saw a mobile and decided to lie down. I picture myself as adult and as baby. As adult I'm on grass looking up thinking it's wonderful. As the

| | little girl, I curl up in a blanket and sleep. I feel completely fine even though I'm by myself. I'm wrapped up, peaceful. I feel pretty peaceful right here in adult "me." I have a sense of lying in the grass with my hands behind my head looking at the trees. It's a good thing. |

THERAPIST: [She is alternating between her adult self and her child self. This felt like some kind of integration.] Go with that. >>>>>

MARY: That's a really peaceful feeling, and it's a good thing to be able to do that.

THERAPIST: When you think of the original image, what do you get? [I am trying to assess if the charge is completely processed and if the good feeling would hold.]

MARY: I'm feeling snuggly, comfortable, sleeping and waking up. I'm fine with going to sleep.

THERAPIST: What do you believe about yourself?

MARY: I'm a sweet, cheerful, lovable little baby.

THERAPIST: Are you worthy of love?

MARY: Yeah. [Her SUDs level was a 0.]

THERAPIST: Bring the picture of the baby together with those positive thoughts. >>>>>

MARY: I sensed my dad saying that I'm the perfect baby. I'm lovable. I sense about myself that I'm creative and can find things to do. I'm lovable and loving. It felt really good.

Because this experience felt processed and the level of distress was down, I wanted to see what would happen if I asked Mary to move forward to the original scene in the apartment after being left by her boyfriend. I thought that this scene might also reflect a lowering in distress level. However, as soon as she thought of the original scene in the apartment, she was reactivated, almost as if the previous processing had not taken place, and she was right back to where she had started: highly activated and distressed. She had cleared the past incident in the crib, but couldn't totally shift the symptoms yet because there were too many links to it that were yet unprocessed. This was a good learning for me. In the case of complex developmental wounding, far from being a linear process, it would take perseverance and repetition over a period of time before the links from the past could be fully cleared and her current symptoms could be neutralized.

EMDR REPROCESSING: MOTHER AS TARGET

Over the next seven sessions, we targeted the activation in Mary's body (throat constriction, panic in the chest, tightness in her belly) to trace back in time to discover more memories that fueled her issues around abandonment and rejection. These sessions all focused on Mary's relationship with her mother. The following transcripts are the highlights of these sessions. Mary thought of her boyfriend not calling, and we used the bridging technique to trace back in time to an earlier event where she experienced abandonment by her parents.

THERAPIST: Where are you?

MARY: Outside of school. Waiting for my parents to come pick me up. I'm panicked.

THERAPIST: How old are you?

MARY: Eight or nine.

THERAPIST: What are you wearing?

MARY: A dress. I'm alone. I'm hearing cars go back and forth, no one is around; the doors of the school are locked. There is nobody to call.

THERAPIST: What is the worst part of this picture?

MARY: There is nobody around. I feel rising panic in my chest. I don't know what to do. There is impending horror.

THERAPIST: What are you feeling in your body?

MARY: Panic; I don't feel my legs or arms, just my chest and throat.

THERAPIST: What do you believe about yourself right now?

MARY: I'm not worth being picked up.

THERAPIST: What is your level of distress?

MARY: 7–8. It will be a 15 any minute; it's on the way and I'm anticipating it will be horrible.

THERAPIST: Go with all of that [image, feeling, belief]. >>>>>

MARY: I'm completely helpless, claustrophobic, I can't stand it. There is nothing I can do. I'm trapped. I want to be cradled and there is nobody there. I feel panic.

THERAPIST: Go with that. >>>>>

MARY: I seem to be retreating from it someway.

THERAPIST: [I am wondering if she is dissociating.] What are you noticing?

MARY: I'm reminded of real claustrophobia: free falling, black space; too big, claustrophobia, too small, crib, alone, crying so hard. There is something claustrophobic about that; I can't stand it, I'll go crazy. I'll explode or something.

THERAPIST: [I am wondering, if this is perhaps related to her birth, but I put my own thoughts aside and allow Mary's process to inform us.] Go with that. >>>>>

MARY: I can't do it. When I go back to the crib place, I went to the good crib place. I can't handle being in a bad crib place.

THERAPIST: [I am wondering if the processing from the previous session that cleared the crib space is why she can't "handle being in a bad crib place."] What happens when you think about the image at school? [I am trying to keep the session focused on one event so we can see that through to completion; otherwise, it may become too diffuse, with multiple events/memories, which could muddle the processing.]

MARY: Same, still scared. I see more of it. Stairs, pacing around to do something to make time pass. Panicky. I'm wondering what I can do; can't think of anything to do. No way to reach anybody. How could they do this? I must be bad. How could they leave me here like I'm not so important (*crying*)?

THERAPIST: Go with that. >>>>>

MARY: I'm thinking of me in the house and Mom doesn't want me there; she doesn't like me. She wishes I would disappear (*heavy tears*).

THERAPIST: What are you aware of? [I want to keep the processing focused.]

MARY: How horrible that makes me feel.

THERAPIST: What do you need?

MARY: I need to feel important and wanted. I need to feel that I'm OK in any way. I feel like I could be some place else besides that house.

THERAPIST: Go with that. >>>>>

MARY: I was just trying to find something good about Mom, but I couldn't.

THERAPIST: What do you get when you think of the image at school? [I want to refocus the processing.]

MARY: It's like I just expect not to get picked up.

THERAPIST: What would help you now? [It feels stuck. She seems to be looping.]

MARY: Somebody else coming to take me someplace else.

THERAPIST: Who would you like?

MARY: Big Mama.

THERAPIST: Go with that. >>>>>

MARY: I can feel that and picture Big Mama. She wants to say that it's not about me. Other things make people late. "It's not because you are bad." She says that she will wait with me; she says that they are coming to pick me up. Being with her, I feel OK.

THERAPIST: Did somebody come to pick you up? [I want to link in the fact that she was picked up eventually—another interweave.]

MARY: Yeah.

THERAPIST: Go with that. >>>>>>

MARY: They come. I'm glad to see my dad, not my mom. Thought maybe at first I made this into a big deal, but there were no other kids around and it wasn't OK; I don't want my mom there.

THERAPIST: Go with that. >>>>>

MARY: I feel sad for that little girl (*tears*) to have to be in that environment where she isn't ever good enough. Always trying to behave and be perfect and how hard that is. I feel bad for her (*tears*).

THERAPIST: Go with that. >>>>>

MARY: What my sister and I really needed was to have another mother.

THERAPIST: Can you go ahead and imagine what kind of mother you needed? [This is a resource interweave.]

MARY: I'm imagining someone who is fun and likes to do stuff outside. Likes getting dirty and doesn't mind if we do; likes to joke, cuddle us, and play games.

THERAPIST: What messages would she be giving you?

MARY: We are great kids. We are smart. She would never leave us. She'd ask what we want. She'd pay attention to us and watch us; not make us afraid of everything. She'd be more concerned with how we feel than how it looked.

THERAPIST: [This comment speaks to her narcissistic wounding.] Would you feel worthy?

MARY: Yes.

THERAPIST: Go with that. >>>>>

MARY: A good feeling. I thought about school and if she were picking us up, I wouldn't be worried because she wouldn't NOT pick us up. It would be possible there was something wrong to make her late. Like the crib, I'd be more filled out rather than tight and worried. I'd have looser muscles, a softer belly.

THERAPIST: Check back with the image of the school. What do you get now?

MARY: I'm not so worried. I'd turn my attention to going down the block and looking at what is there. I'm not so collapsed in the chest. I'm looking around at the trees. I'm walking, feeling curious to look around.

THERAPIST: What is your level of distress now?

MARY: 0.

THERAPIST: What do you believe?

MARY: I believe I'm loved enough and that my parents will come. I'm not so scared. I don't feel so weak and vulnerable. I'm OK waiting for them. I'm OK till they come.

THERAPIST: Hold the picture and the thought "I'm OK" together and go with that. >>>>>

MARY: That was good. I wonder if I could do some mischief around the corner; it's a fun feeling, a cool feeling. I like having that feeling; maybe I'll go across the street, mainly because it is forbidden.

THERAPIST: Go with that. >>>>>

MARY: I climbed a tree across the street. I'll wait until they come and then scare them.

THERAPIST: Go with that. >>>>>

MARY: When they came and saw me, they were playing with me. I feel myself coming down and we laugh and get in the car. It's great.

THERAPIST: Scan your body from head to toe with the image and belief, "I'm OK." What do you get?

MARY: It feels good.

During this reprocessing session, Mary connected with the desire to have parents who would never forget to pick her up. She used her imagination to create what she wished she'd had.

I taught Mary the container exercise, which was a way to create distance from emotionally charged material. Using her imagination, she was asked to come up with a strong container that she could use as a place to store negative and distressing material between sessions. She could then practice putting troubling material "away," should she need to do so during the week.

The next session we checked in to see how the week had gone. Mary reported periods of feeling good. She thought a lot about the mother that she imagined in the last session and realized how negative her "real" mom was. We rechecked the schoolyard and the crib scenes to see what level of activation she felt. They were both neutral; when she thought of the school, she didn't feel scared; she saw the little girl looking around and knew that her "new" parents were coming to get her. When she thought of the crib, she saw herself as a child standing up and looking around the room, rather than crying and screaming inconsolably. I interpreted this stable image as a positive sign that the treatment effects were "holding" from week to week.

We decided to work more directly with her mother, since she was the most troubling person for Mary. Since Mary couldn't think of one event that stood out in her mind, we chose to target an image of her mother that would encapsulate all the negativity and rejection that Mary felt from her.

THERAPIST: What is the image of your mother that brings up the troubling sensations?

MARY: My mother's face with a disapproving look and walking around the house, not paying attention to my sister and me. She didn't want us there.

THERAPIST: What is the worst part of this image?

MARY: She is walking away from us. She doesn't want anything to do with us. Her head is turned away and she is not looking at us.

THERAPIST: What emotions are you feeling?

MARY: Panicked.

THERAPIST: What sensations are you aware of?

MARY: My throat and chest are tight.

THERAPIST: What do you believe about yourself?

MARY: I'm bad. I'm horrible (*body collapsing, clutching throat, fearful voice, crying*).

THERAPIST: [Mary is fully immersed in this experience, so I go straight into the processing.] Go with all of that. >>>>>

MARY: (*tears*) I feel like I am going to be left, but I also don't really want to be around her—but I'm afraid I'll be left.

THERAPIST: [This is the attachment wound and dilemma that symbolizes her relationship with her mother; it's also the exact dilemma in her current life as it relates to her boyfriend. There were times when she didn't want him around her, but at the same time, she didn't want to feel that he was rejecting her.] Go with that. >>>>>

MARY: Same crib feeling (*tears*). Feels like I'm afraid I'm not gonna survive. I don't know what to do to make this feel different; feels trapped, can't move, don't go after her. I don't want to be in this place. Life is unbearable this way (*heavy tears*).

THERAPIST: Go with that. >>>>>

MARY: I feel like I hate her. I need her, but I hate her. She hates me; I'm in the way. It makes her life bad that I exist.

THERAPIST: Go with that. >>>>>

MARY: (*heavy tears*) It makes me want to shrivel up and be tiny and go away and have her not look at me like that. I want to be about the size of a pea. I don't want to be in the way or see her react that way. It would be better if there were nobody there than to have her there.

THERAPIST: Recheck Mom's image. What do you notice?

MARY: Now all of a sudden she turned to look at us. She doesn't have the scowl; she doesn't know what to do.

THERAPIST: Go with that. >>>>> [There is a shift in Mom's image, and I am curious what will happen next.]

MARY: She doesn't know what to do with us. I have a sense that she is afraid of us. I'm afraid of her. She's different. I'm paralyzed. I don't want to do the wrong thing. She's looking at us. She doesn't know what to do. We are strange beings to her.

THERAPIST: Is there anything you want to say to her? [I think she needs to take action and find her voice after noting that she felt paralyzed. Taking action can often move someone out of feeling helpless and paralyzed.]

MARY: I'm too afraid to speak to her. If I say something, it will be wrong and she'll turn away.

THERAPIST: Go with that. >>>>> [I probably should have used an interweave here to help her.]

MARY: There is a standoff. Mother might be feeling the same thing.

THERAPIST: Who can help her? [I am thinking that her mother needs help here too in this scene. This is an interweave, bringing in a resource for her mother.]

MARY: Big Mama could help—could tell her how to be and what to do. Maybe she can be more like Big Mama.

THERAPIST: Go ahead and let that happen. >>>>>

MARY: My mom is resistant. She doesn't feel like she can pick us up or be encouraging. I feel like she'd like to. The options of Mom and Big Mama: I'd much rather be with Big Mama than my mom. I think that makes her sad. It feels like she'd like to be different.

THERAPIST: What would she like to be able to do?

MARY: It feels like she'd like to be able to be warm, pick us up, play with us. She can't bring herself to do that, but she is walking closer to us. I feel like she is asking us, "What should I do?" I'm still too afraid to talk.

THERAPIST: Can you show her what you'd like?

MARY: My sister is going up into her lap. I can't do that; I'm paralyzed, too afraid. If I do anything, it will scare her away and she won't like it.

THERAPIST: What do you need to help you? [an interweave]

MARY: I need Big Mama to pick me up and remind me it's OK to be held. My dad, too. He would say it's OK to be playful. I think I'll do something wrong or get dirty; Dad says, "It's OK, she won't mind."

THERAPIST: Let that happen. >>>>>

MARY: I'm so scared. I say, "I don't believe you." Both are being so supportive, Big Mama and Dad. I'm like a stick; I'm too scared (*tears*).

THERAPIST: What are you afraid of?

MARY: She'll yell at me, hate me, and think I'm horrible and be upset. I'll make her sick. She'll have to go off and have a headache.

THERAPIST: Do you have the power to make her sick? [I am trying to do a reality check here and link up to her adult knowledge.]

MARY: I have the power to make her have a headache. Dad will be torn between taking care of her and explaining to us, and then I'll feel really bad that I caused this and I'll want to disappear more.

THERAPIST: Who is responsible here? [I am attempting another inter-weave because the first one didn't work.]

MARY: It's my fault.

THERAPIST: You really believe that you have the power to make her feel bad?

MARY: She's miserable because of me.

THERAPIST: [This belief is so deeply ingrained, I'll need to keep at it to find an interweave that will work.] What would Big Mama say about that?

MARY: She would say, "That is ridiculous! You are just a little kid." She wants to say to my mom, "Get over it!" She wants to say to me, "You are supposed to be a kid, noisy, don't pay attention to that. It's not your fault." I believe her. When Big Mama says this, it makes me listen to her.

THERAPIST: [Finally, Big Mama is the necessary resource; Mary believes this message.] Could Big Mama explain how things like this work in the world, because the little girl may not know? >>>>>

MARY: She picked me up and said that this doesn't have anything to do with you. I told her I wanted to know what it has to do with. She said, "Your Momma is just like this. She would be like this even if you weren't around. It wouldn't matter what you do; this is how she is."

MARY: So I would say, "So, I can just run around and be noisy?" Big Mama would say, "We can go do this away from your mother—we can go to the park."

THERAPIST: Go with that. >>>>>

MARY: A "new" mom comes and says, "Let's play."

THERAPIST: Go with that. >>>>>

MARY: I'm confused. Mom is in the bedroom, and the new mom says for me not to worry. I am sitting in the backyard. My new mom is there with Big Mama; my mom is in the bed-room. I don't know what the right thing to do is. Panic in my throat and chest. I can't get it right.

THERAPIST: Who can help you now?

MARY: I want Big Mama to come and take me away from here.

THERAPIST: Where would you like to go?

MARY: I want to go to the forest with the animals; also to the secret valley. I'm sad; I feel like I don't belong anywhere.

THERAPIST: What would Big Mama say to that?

MARY: She says, "You can just be in my arms." I just want to crawl in her arms and not see anything outside of her.

THERAPIST: Go with that. >>>>>

MARY: Big Mama says I can be here as long as I want. She is holding me tightly. I want to feel this. I want to feel enclosed.

THERAPIST: [This was the missing attachment experience for Mary.] Go ahead and feel that. >>>>>

MARY: I feel like an infant. She has me against her chest, in burping position; she walks around with me. It feels good.

THERAPIST: When you think of your mom, what do you get now? [I am returning to the target to check our progress.]

MARY: She is looking at me now. She is confused; she doesn't know what to do.

THERAPIST: She's uninformed?

MARY: Yes.

THERAPIST: What do you believe about yourself now?

MARY: I don't feel as bad. I feel like she doesn't understand me. I don't feel as bad, but I don't feel like I could say or do anything.

THERAPIST: What is your level of distress?

MARY: 8. I'm still really worried that I'll do something to make her angry or make her hate me. I'll get a cold, disapproving look. I have to stand tight, like a little soldier.

THERAPIST: In closing, would you like to get out of there and be with Big Mama?

MARY: Yeah.

THERAPIST: Go with that. >>>>>

MARY: Big Mama says that I don't have to go back there. I feel safe and good with her.

THERAPIST: What do you believe about yourself when you are with Big Mama?

MARY: I am a good baby and lovable. She seems to love me.

THERAPIST: Go with that. >>>>>

MARY: I feel sad for that little child. I'm afraid of how I'll be when I leave here [my office]. I'm afraid of going to that empty place.

THERAPIST: What do you know you can do to avoid going there?

MARY: Use the container.

THERAPIST: That's right. Gather up all the feelings, images, shapes, sounds, and colors that are disturbing and when I count from 5 to 1, you can let them go into your container. 5, 4, 3, 2, 1 . . .

MARY: I can feel that happening.

We ended by going over self-soothing behaviors that she could practice after the session and during the week. She chose to practice walking, meditating, reading, and praying.

EMDR REPROCESSING OF THE NEGATIVE MOTHER AND INSTALLING POSITIVE RESOURCES THROUGHOUT DEVELOPMENTAL STAGES

The fear/anxiety in Mary's body (mostly in her chest and throat) never went away completely during the week in between our session. By focusing on doing some of the soothing things we came up with in the last session, she was able to stop the fear from moving deeper and becoming a panicked place. She expressed a desire to have this sensation be totally gone. When she thought of her mother, sadness and anger came up.

The original feeling that brought her into therapy was shifting some. Originally, she felt a frantic, spiraling, free-fall feeling; now she described the feeling as deeper and denser. Now it felt heavier, more core, like a lead weight in her. There was still some constriction in her breath. We acknowledged that the quality of the feelings in her body were shifting.

THERAPIST: Revisit the image of your mother. What do you get?
MARY: She is looking away again.
THERAPIST: What are you feeling?
MARY: This feels normal.
THERAPIST: [Even though this is a thought, I let this comment go and don't push her to find a feeling.] What sensations are you aware of?
MARY: My neck is stiff; I'm worried, tense. I feel like I should be doing something else: push–pull.
THERAPIST: What do you believe about yourself?
MARY: There is something wrong with me.
THERAPIST: Bring all of that up and trace it back in time, without editing it, and let me know when you are aware of something.
MARY: Mom comes home from the hospital with me. I'm a baby in the crib.
THERAPIST: What is the picture?

MARY: I'm in the crib and my mom is not wanting anything to do with me. I can't stand it. My father is trying to get my mother involved, and she's just angrier and angrier at him. She wants to get away from me (*tears*). She doesn't want to be with me.

THERAPIST: What are you feeling?

MARY: It's my fault (*tears*). My dad is torn; he doesn't know what to do. It's horrible. I'm the cause and it doesn't feel good (*heavy tears*).

THERAPIST: What do you believe about yourself?

MARY: I'm bad. I'm hated.

THERAPIST: What is the worst part of this picture?

MARY: I'm not going to get picked up. That aloneness is the feeling. I can't stand it. I'm gonna die. Everyone will leave and I'll be alone in this room.

THERAPIST: (*Mary is sobbing, and writhing, so I turn on the tappers.*) Go with that. >>>>>

MARY: When they go away, I don't know what to do. Crying isn't good; I curl up in a ball . . . to not exist.

THERAPIST: Go with that. >>>>>

MARY: I just want to not feel alive, not exist.

THERAPIST: [This processing was not progressing and was starting to loop; I don't want to leave her in this negative place for long without a shift.] What do you need right now?

MARY: I need someone to pick me up and make me know that life can be different.

THERAPIST: Who do you want?

MARY: Something soft. I don't even imagine a human being. I don't want to exist. I don't feel like there is anything good (*heavy tears*).

THERAPIST: [These comments indicate that Mary has lost hope of a person helping her; I need to help her get attached to a resource.] Who do you want?

MARY: Big Mama, New Mommy, all the spirits, everybody.

THERAPIST: (*I move closer and hold her hand and tell her that I am right there with her too.*) [It feels important to bring the current attachment between us into this experience, creating a dual awareness for her that there is someone there for her.] Let that happen. >>>>>

MARY: Big Mama picked me up. The Indian spirits are there too;

they tell me I'm wonderful. I'm laughing and they are all passing me around.

THERAPIST: Go with that. >>>>>

MARY: It's like I'm the best present. They all want me. (*Crying has stopped and she is smiling.*) I'm in Big Mama's lap.

THERAPIST: What do you believe about yourself?

MARY: I believe I'm special to them; they really want to be around me. I am protected.

THERAPIST: Go with that. >>>>> [I want to further install this feeling.]

MARY: They say they will always be there. They are part of my body.

THERAPIST: Can you imagine all of these resources being with you from the crib all the way up to this present moment? [I want to help create an alternative experience for her and have her imagine this support throughout her lifespan.]

MARY: Yes.

THERAPIST: Go ahead and do that. Starting in the crib, moving forward every year, toddler years, preschool years, school years, having them with you. >>>>> (*I offered intermittent suggestions during this set: school years, college, young-adult years, midlife, up until the present.*) What do you notice now?

MARY: I feel like I have a force field of beings around me. We've been together forever. They make me feel not alone. I'm happy to be with them. They are happy to be with me. It's a good feeling. My body feels warm and tingly.

THERAPIST: When you think of your mother and the crib, what do you get now?

MARY: I can see her with her head turned away. She's supposed to pick me up and be different, but it's not the way it's going to be. I'm aware of it. I'm watching her but not expecting that she'll do anything.

THERAPIST: How disturbing does it feel?

MARY: 2 or 3.

THERAPIST: What keeps it from being a 0?

MARY: She's supposed to be different, do something different. Something is out of place. It's more disturbing than a 2 or a 3; it's a 4 or a 5. She's not right (*becoming more upset at the thought that her mother is supposed to be different than she is*).

THERAPIST: What needs to happen?
MARY: She needs to go away. She needs to go away to Mom school!
THERAPIST: Go with that. >>>>>
MARY: She's gone and everyone is in the crib with me—Big Mama, Indian spirits, my dog. I feel much better.
THERAPIST: Go with that. >>>>>

Mary had sent her mother to "Mom school" in order to get some training at being a good mother. This option felt right to her. We explored the idea of her mother receiving her own healing so that she could be a better mother to Mary. Mary wanted to leave her mother in "Mom school" while she enjoyed time in the crib with the resources she wanted.

THERAPIST: If you think of the crib now, what do you notice?
MARY: We are all in there now; it's filled with beings and family. It's safe. I feel good being with them.
THERAPIST: What do you believe about yourself now?
MARY: They love me and I am lovable. I am special to them and they are happy to be around me.
THERAPIST: Do you believe that you are lovable?
MARY: Yeah.
THERAPIST: Do you believe that you are worthy?
MARY: Yeah.
THERAPIST: Do you believe that you are good?
MARY: Yeah.
THERAPIST: Go with all of that. >>>>>
MARY: They all seem delighted to be with me.
THERAPIST: What are you believing about yourself?
MARY: I'm lovable. I'm loved. I'm a good person. I'm worth loving.
THERAPIST: Put the image of the crib together with those thoughts and scan your body. What do you notice?
MARY: I feel good, relaxed.
THERAPIST: Do you need anything else now?
MARY: I'd like to take this feeling with me.
THERAPIST: [This comment speaks to her desire to integrate the positive treatment effects with her life outside of my office.] Imagine taking this feeling with you out of my office and into your day and as far into the future as you would like. >>>>>

Some fear started to emerge, so I invited Mary to check in with the "little girl" inside to see if she needed some soothing. Mary practiced tapping on herself to reinforce her sense of the resources there, within her; she felt good about this, saying that the fear dissipated when she tapped on herself. She was glad to have a tool that she could use to help give her a sense of control when she felt scared.

At the next session, when I invited Mary to recheck the image of her mother, the image was basically the same: Her mother was looking away from her. I thought that perhaps our targets of her mother were not necessarily getting the whole picture, and I was curious if there might be a scene that would present itself and hold some important information. I asked her to imagine that she was playing a DVD and to tell me what was happening on the television screen. I also asked her to describe what she was seeing like a free association to see if there was a charge that we could target.

THERAPIST: Scan the movie of Mom. Tell me, what you are seeing?

MARY: I'm standing up, saying "Momma"; I want her to look at me. She's wearing a red robe with gold things on it. She is all perfect looking, and her hair is curled. She is purposely ignoring me. She is walking away from me. I want to go toward her, but I don't move [expressing the ambivalent attachment that she felt toward her mother]. I'm in a position that feels like a human can't be in—leaning forward, feet together, and I can't move.

THERAPIST: Keep scanning the movie and see what happens next.

MARY: She turns around, and I am saying "Mom," and she has a horrible look on her face, in her eyes. She says, "Get away from me—leave me alone!" I am seeing the infant, but I am not the infant. [There is a dual awareness here; Mary has developed a witnessing self.] I am starting to go to "that place." Not knowing what to do, I can't move.

THERAPIST: Keep the movie playing and tell me what you see next.

MARY: I'm screaming but I'm not an infant. I'm older, like 6, 7, or 8. Or maybe younger, like 4 or 5, but not an infant or toddler. I'm beyond that. [I interpreted this as a positive sign that Mary was psychologically getting "bigger" over these multiple sessions, and was developing more internal resources to deal with her feelings about her scary mother.] She turns around toward me and is looking at me. Now I am crying less. When I cry less, she looks at me curiously. She doesn't know what to do. She's taking little steps toward me; I straighten up. I need to be quiet, so that I don't scare her away. She's tiptoeing toward me. I think she's scared of me. Scared I'll cry or make a sound. She comes toward me, putting hands out now. Her body is leaning away. She puts her hands out. I'm still—feet together, arms clinched. She is coming toward me; I'm quiet. She is looking at me. I'm older now and I'm saying something like, "I won't hurt you. I'll be good." [What a dilemma for a child!] Her hands are on my shoulders, and she should hug me but she can't. I don't think she likes me. I'm trying to be good. I'm saying, "What's wrong with me?" She says, "I don't know." I want her to be nice to me. She's not nice to me. She doesn't really like me (*starts crying*). I crumble down on the ground. She doesn't know what to do. She wants me not to cry, so it's easier for her. Then I stand up again and I try to act OK. She says, "That's more like it." I'm older and I'm more her size. We both turn away. I take her hand. She's walking next to me. Now I think I'm an adult. She doesn't like me.

THERAPIST: Is that the end of the movie?

MARY: I'm not feeling great. I don't like her much either. I feel like I should hold hand, but I don't get anything from her. I don't get anything from her. That's the way it is. Her hand is a stick. I'm partly accepting and partly angry, but not very sad.

THERAPIST: [This was a big shift from her usual collapsed and fearful/sad place.] Run through the movie in your mind, from beginning to end, and stop when you notice a charge.

MARY: She turns away from me. I'm watching her turn away from me. My feet are rooted to the floor. I don't want her to say anything. She turns away, and then she looks at me and says, "I hate you."

THERAPIST: [This felt like a place to target, so I asked her the basic set-up questions.] What is the image?

MARY: Her whole body is aggressive, leaning forward, scowling, eyes slit like knives. She would like to kill me.

THERAPIST: What are you noticing in your body?

MARY: Shaking in my neck, across my shoulders. I used to have this feeling a lot; it feels like my body is diffusing into space, almost like death. All my atoms are spreading out. [I am interpreting this as dissociation, but she appears able to go on.] I'm panicky (*tears*).

THERAPIST: What do you believe about yourself?

MARY: I should be dead.

THERAPIST: Go with that. >>>>>

MARY: She wants me dead. I can feel it into my legs. She is coming toward me, and I'm scared. I think she'll kill me. I need to disappear. My atoms are spreading out so I'm invisible so she can't see me or get to me. I want to run away but my feet are stuck there. My atoms are spreading out. I really want to be dead. I feel like disappearing. I want to go away but I can't. I feel like she wants to choke me and wants me dead. Her hand is around my throat. She doesn't want me there; she wants me dead (*heavy tears*).

THERAPIST: [I consider intervening here, but don't.] What are you noticing now?

MARY: She backed away and I'm alive. She's moving away.

THERAPIST: Go with that. >>>>>

MARY: She is moving away. She has no emotions. She should be appalled at what she did; she isn't human. She is bigger than I am now. I'm getting smaller. I'm trying to disappear. I'm watching her; she is walking away. She doesn't like what she did, but she has no feelings about it at all. I'm stunned that I'm alive. I'm just numb/stunned.

THERAPIST: What do you notice now?

MARY: I feel quiet and I'm feeling myself here; I'm not that child. I'm not scared right now. I can feel my feet and I still can't move.

THERAPIST: Go with that. >>>>> [I probably should have offered her a suggestion to notice what parts of her body would like to move; this potentially would have helped her to begin to unfreeze her body. I didn't do this here, however.]

I ask Mary if she needs someone to come in and help her, and she asks for Big Mama. Big Mama stands up to her mother and speaks for her to let her mother know that what she did was unacceptable. Mary spent the rest of the session being comforted by Big Mama. She wanted her mother to be different, but knew that she could never give her what she needed. Even in her imagination, it would prove too implausible to have her mother give her some of what she needed. It became obvious that her mother was too toxic of a person to whom to attach.

In the following session, Mary reported that she felt good. She described feeling shocked but validated by the information that had come up in the previous session. She commented, "No wonder I've felt such fear with my mother." She also reported that, in that moment, it was hard to bring up the image of the mother who tried to kill her.

It's important to note here that I was not concerned with the historical facts of whether this event had happened or not; I was only concerned with helping Mary process her relationship to the material that emerged. We would have many more sessions of processing additional links connected to her fear of her mother.

The common theme in processing the feelings related to her mother was her collapsed, immobilized, dead-like state. Her helpless, powerless, dysregulated state in the crib seemed to illustrate Stephen Porges's polyvagal theory (2011). If there is no way to move into fight–flight when someone is being traumatized, the body may dissolve into immobilization and paralysis, wanting to disappear and feeling dead. This response isn't a conscious choice, but rather one that the body's nervous system goes to in order to survive the situation. Whenever Mary senses a trigger in the environment, her nervous system would take her to this hardwired circuitry from an earlier time—which, although maladaptive in later years, was a state that had helped her survive the toxic environment in which she had lived as a child. However, it was not so helpful when she would become immobilized for days as an adult.

My challenge was to help her create a new, more adaptive experience for her nervous system so that she could gradually build new neural circuitry that would offer her a greater range of options from which to respond when she got triggered. My sensorimotor trauma training helped me conceptualize the remedy: to help Mary identify what her body had wanted to do, but had never gotten a chance to do. If Mary could be encouraged and invited to get in touch with her impulses, now that she was in a safe place, and allow those impulses to come forward, she would be able to reconnect with her own life energy and not continue to feel so paralyzed (Ogden et al., 2006). This focus would become part of our work in the later months as she got in touch with her desire to run away from her mother.

As we processed her terror and ambivalence toward her mother, I expected that Mary's perspective of her mother would shift. I also expected that her bodily activations would lessen over time. And, because we were working on the theme of rejection, I had hoped that this lessening would generalize to the channels of her neural nets to alleviate the panic in her current life when her boyfriend didn't call.

It felt like there *were* shifts in each session, but when Mary would come for the next session and we rechecked the target of her mother, it seemed that the activations were still there. She could talk herself back into feeling the same feelings. I began to question whether the processing was fully working. I brought this up with my consultation group, hoping to get some perspective. The group members gave me the feedback that perhaps Mary's mother was too toxic to attach to and would never be a safe person for her. Even though her mother was dead, Mary's imagination could not extend to transforming her "real" mother into someone to whom she could attach. It wasn't an ecologically valid option for Mary. This view felt intuitively right, given that we had spent multiple sessions trying to reprocess traumatic events that didn't seem to change her overall feelings about her mother. The group pointed out that the processing was working, as evidenced by shifts in Mary's day-to-day life; however, the processing wasn't done yet. It was really helpful for me to hold this larger perspective, and I was able to make this same point to Mary when she would occasionally get discouraged.

In subsequent sessions, we continued to process the activation around her mother. She moved from fear as the prevailing feeling to more and more anger toward her mother. I viewed this shift as a positive sign that Mary was connecting more and more to her own power. She was also understanding that she wasn't responsible for making her mother treat her so poorly.

TAPPING IN THE CREATION OF AN IDEAL MOTHER AND REBIRTHING WITH HER

It became obvious that trying to process events with her "real" mother was not moving her toward more resolution; the mother was too toxic of a figure to whom to attach. Mary was looping, not moving toward resolution. She got to the point in her processing where she realized "what I really need is another mother."

Mary had organically developed a "new" mommy in several previous sessions, but I felt she could use a session focused solely on creating the kind of mother she wished had given birth to her. I felt that it would serve her well to have an established mother figure, in addition to Big Mama, to whom she could attach.

I shared with Mary that we could work to create an ideal mother that she could use to connect with, rather than keep trying to attach to a toxic mother. She really liked this idea. As Laurel Parnell has said to me in our consultations, "Sometimes we have to install what people need if they never got it to begin with."

Because Mary had no internalized experience of a secure attachment to a loving mother, we needed to install this image into the neural circuits—to create those new pathways. She needed the experience of being born to a mother who wanted her and who loved her. This new, revised history could become the new default setting for Mary. We extended this idea to the creation of the ideal mother and father for her. Because she'd had a good-enough relationship with her "real" father, we focused solely on finding the ideal mother.

THERAPIST: What kind of mother did you want?

MARY: A mom who would be excited to have me. (*I asked Mary to keep her eyes open and to allow herself to imagine the mother she wanted as she remained in eye contact with me. I invited Mary's unconscious mind to get in touch with the qualities of this ideal mother, and then I turned on the tappers.*) >>>>> She is an "Annie Oakley" mom. She has light brown hair, athletic, tan, natural. She is pretty, but not glamorous. She is excited by life and happy (*tears*).

We used BLS as she imagined being in the womb of this ideal mother (moving through each trimester), and then being born to her. Mary had an active imagination that allowed her to embellish and develop the imagery and feelings. We strengthened her connection to this new mother by tapping in developmental essentials: eye gazing, being seen and mirrored, being encouraged and supported, being attuned to.

Because Mary could veer into negative directions when she closed her eyes, I invited her to keep her eyes open and maintain contact with me. I wanted her to stay grounded and use the connection with me to take in the positive experience of installing her ideal mother and father and the experience of being born to parents who wanted her.

THERAPIST: When you have a sense of the mother and father you want to be born to, let me know.

MARY: OK.

THERAPIST: Your mother and father are excited to think of your being born. They make love, and your mother finds out that she is pregnant with you. She tells everyone how happy she is. >>>>> (continues throughout the session).

MARY: They tell me, "Welcome. We are going to do this together. This is the start of our life with you."

THERAPIST: (I speak these words back to her, using eye contact, saying how happy they are to have her as their child, even though she isn't born yet.)

MARY: I'm safe, happy, excited.

THERAPIST: You are safe, happy, and excited.

MARY: She likes being pregnant. She makes clothes with my name on it. We are together. I'm in her. I'm part of her all the time. Dad is excited and talking to me. He says, "Welcome. We are going to have so much fun." It feels so good in the womb. She gets bigger and bigger. I'm moving inside. She talks to me and says, "I can feel you. What are you doing in there?" She loves everything.

THERAPIST: (*I repeat these messages back to Mary as she maintains eye contact with me.*)

THERAPIST: What will it be like to see them, to be held by them, and to touch them? Move forward to being born. Your mother is excited to give birth to you.

MARY: They are talking to each other, and they see it as a blessing. My mother is born to be a mom. She's got good humor. I'm liking this. I'm excited because I know it will be a wonderful life with them. I come out and she is beaming. "Welcome. You are beautiful." They are both holding me. Now they are quiet, in awe. She isn't gonna let me go. It feels so safe. It's the best feeling there could be.

THERAPIST: And you sleep, and dream of each other, and wake up and see them looking at you. And you nurse and feel the warmth of your mother.

MARY: I have everything. I want to embody that there is enough.

THERAPIST: Look into her eyes. Can you see her? Feel it? Skin to skin.

MARY: She will pay attention to what I like. She wants to know me. I need her to know I'm sensitive. She looks at me with her gaze that says, "I see you and I will pay attention to you and I will get what you need. It will be fun. There is nothing I don't adore."

THERAPIST: (*I repeat all of these messages back to her while maintaining eye contact with her.*)

MARY: I'm relaxing. I'm relieved; I can be real. She wants to know all about me.

THERAPIST: (*The session was coming to an end. I asked Mary how she wanted to bring this to a close.*)

MARY: I want to see her understand. I feel relief and safety. And I feel her willingness. I feel completely safe. It's everything.

As the session was coming to a close, we discussed having her practice this experience over and over in her mind, imagining having Annie Oakley as her mom from birth all the way up to the present day. I offered her a glass red heart as a symbol and anchor. Whenever she held it and looked at it, it could remind her of her ideal mother's loving gaze and all the love that was there. It could also serve as an anchor to the connection to me.

Annie Oakley would come to represent the positive mother Mary had needed throughout all of her developmental years, and she would come to think of her whenever she needed solace, both in session and in her life.

THERAPEUTIC SHIFTS

Mary reported a profound shift after this session, calling it "life changing." The creation of an ideal mother and a new birth experience helped to shift her sense of being unlovable. She said that when times got hard, she would go to Annie Oakley in her mind and talk to her. Mary internalized this loving presence: "Annie Oakley would say that she is always here. She helps me calm down; I feel like she's always been there; I get it in my cells what it's like to have a mom." Over time, this internal experience began to shift her sense of lovability. She was beginning to believe she was worthy of love.

Mary also began to realize that she wanted to be treated better in her relationship with her boyfriend. She began feeling and saying things that indicated she was shifting her beliefs about herself. She reported that she felt more and more that she deserved to be valued, cared for, and made to feel important. She became less and less willing to tolerate being ignored and unattended. She attributed this shift to the work with EMDR. We explored what she desired and how she wanted to be treated. She said, "I want to be loved for who I am." This is how she described what she wanted in future relationships: "I want my partner to be interested in me, to want to know what I am feeling. I want to figure in the other person's plans. I want the other person to smile when he sees me and to want to do things with me. I want so badly to be important to someone. I want someone to want me to love him."

Mary reported that since she had started EMDR, she had not gone into that full spiral and immobilized place when she felt triggered. She described going to the "edges" of it without going into the full-blown experience of it. She had learned to witness her own process and utilize her self-soothing skills (distraction, self-tapping, talking with Big Mama and Annie Oakley, reaching out to friends for support) to keep from falling into the depths of the old despair. Despite the fact that she had more work to do, she could sense that her life was changing.

Over time, as we worked with her somatic symptoms and traced the activation back in time, she "grew up" developmentally. Rather than being the helpless infant, she "grew older" in years, and we would process other events in her life that corresponded to these older ages. School events and other hurts and disappointments in her relationships with men were processed.

Mary gradually began feeling better about herself. She eventually regained her energy and was able to begin working more. Her physical health improved. She reported that, in the past, she was only able to do one thing a day; now she was able to be busy all day, for up to 12 hours at a time. She started doing things that she loved again, like dancing and drumming. The internalized hatred had shifted to more self-compassion and self-love.

EMDR PROCESSING: TAPPING IN THE POSITIVE TRANSFERENCE

From the very beginning of my time with Mary, it was clear that she had a positive transference with me. She listened intently to my thoughts and often expressed positive thoughts about the work we were doing together.

During some of my consultations with Laurel Parnell and the EMDR group, it was suggested that I start making the relationship with me and its healing repair more explicit in our process (Fosha, personal communication, November 27, 2007). I began to actively bring myself into our processing to help mend her attachment wound. Over and over during the reprocessing of early traumatic feelings, I would encourage her toward the end of each session to open her eyes and connect with me. As the pulsers were still going, I would ask her how it felt to have me there with her. She would invariably say that it felt really good to have me with her, supporting her, listening to her and "seeing" her. This was helping to solidify a corrective emotional experience that had been missing for Mary. She was able to receive and take in the experience of having a supportive, loving person with her in the moment of experiencing such painful memories. I was helping make the repair explicit by connecting directly with her.

Installing Positive Statements from the Therapist

I also found it helpful to say some of the things that she had needed to hear as a child, but never got to hear from her mother. Using a technique from Hakomi psychotherapy, I experimented with combining "probes," which are statements often relating to missing experiences in childhood, with BLS. Probing statements are designed to evoke some kind of experience that can then be studied in a state of mindfulness (Kurtz, 1990). While the tappers were still going, I would say some of the things that she longed to hear. For example: "You are loveable just the way you are. You don't have to do anything to deserve love. You are enough just the way you are. You have done nothing wrong. You are precious. You are a good person." Of course, I wholeheartedly agreed with all of these statements, and my words wouldn't have been effective if I was anything less than genuine. This piece of making the therapeutic relationship a conscious part of the work allowed Mary to internalize and experience attachment in a healthy way. She began to use her attachment to me in her daily life by thinking of me, by actually seeing my face and hearing my voice, during times when she needed it. She told me, "I feel your presence all the time. We are connected."

Examples of Tapping in the Therapist's Attachment Repair

At the end of one of our sessions when we were targeting her mother, Mary's "little girl" was still feeling scared and rejected by her mother. Mary was reporting that she wanted to disappear and curl up in a ball. Big Mama had come into the scene and she was saying to Mary, "There is nothing wrong with you. Anyone would be pleased to have you as their little girl." At this point, I asked Mary to open her eyes and connect with me. With the tappers going, I repeated this resourceful message from Big Mama back to her.

THERAPIST: There is nothing wrong with you. Anyone would be happy to have you as their child. (*I repeated this slowly, over and over*).

MARY: Then it's not me who caused my mom to be like this!

THERAPIST: It's not you who caused your mom to be like this. (*I repeated this over and over, slowly, as the tappers were still going.*)

MARY: I can feel my little girl listening to you.

THERAPIST: Can your mother hurt you anymore?

MARY: No.

THERAPIST: Is your mother dead?

MARY: Yes. Then my sister and I can be free!

THERAPIST: Go with that. >>>>>

At the end of this session, Mary commented that she had been sad her whole life and didn't want to be that way anymore. She said, "I want to be oriented toward joy."

By repeating back these positive messages while Mary was looking at me, she started to shift her old belief that there was something wrong with her. She began to feel that this wasn't true, which started to lead her into more joyful living. At the end of many reprocessing sessions, I often invited Mary to engage with me in real time.

THERAPIST: Open your eyes so that we can connect (*the tappers are on*).

MARY: A part of me is unsure of how to connect; it's off to the right.

THERAPIST: I welcome this part of you. I am grateful to this part of you that is so diligent in its intent to protect you. I think this part is trying to help you stay safe by making you believe you don't know how to connect. But, in fact, you do, as we are connecting right now.

MARY: So, I'm not bad for having this part?

THERAPIST: No. I'd be more concerned if you didn't have a part that was trying to protect you. You can have this part that is vigilant at trying to protect you, and still be open to receiving.

At this point, I offered to say some things that she had missed hearing when she was young, things that she would have liked to hear. I wanted to offer Mary the experience of being able to receive something positive from me in an explicit way while tapping in the experience in the moment.

THERAPIST: I'd like you to stay connected to me as I say some things to you. Just notice what happens inside as I say these things to you. (*These statements were said slowly, with pauses in between. The tappers are still on.*)

"*You don't have to do anything to have me here with you.*"
"*I think you are wonderful.*"
"*I'm happy to be here with you.*"
"*I see you.*"

Mary said that she felt she could receive and take in all of what I said. She felt it was true in the moment. She spoke of wanting to remember it, and she repeated the statements that were especially important to her. She felt energized and excited by this experience. I invited her to take those feelings out into her day. She said that she wanted to add me to her daily meditation by imagining me saying these things to her.

The following session she reported the following: "You were in my mind all the time this week. I want you to say more. I started filling in what I wanted you to say; I used your voice and face all week. I was energized for 3 days after our last session. *The whole week, I thought it was possible and probable that I can change my hardwiring, that my life can be different.*" She reported that she had had a stressful week, but that she moved through it without getting "down." She attributed this shift to bringing up my face during the week, saying that it "energized" her.

CONCLUSION

It is challenging to encapsulate my 3 years of working with Mary into a synopsis. So much more happened than can be reported here.

There were sessions that focused on activating her internal impulses (mostly her flight impulse) to run away from her mother. Paired with BLS, she would imagine running away and feel the muscles in her legs contracting. It wasn't possible to run away from her mother back then, but she could now offer her body a chance to free up this impulse and live it out in the safety of our sessions. Doing so helped unfreeze her paralyzed state and activated more of her own powerful impulses. She began to feel more empowered.

Once she didn't have to defend her survival anymore, she was free to develop and explore more of who she really was. And, she was finally feeling that she was deserving of good things. There were sessions devoted to allowing her repressed creativity to come alive by going back in time to high school and reprocessing those years doing the things that she wanted to do, rather than what her parents had wanted her to do. This got her in touch with her own creative desires, which motivated her to begin pursuing areas that she wanted to explore in her current life.

There were homework assignments where she posted all of her negative internal messages on poster board (to externalize her internal thoughts) around her house and came up with alternative, healthy responses posted right alongside them. Over time, she became drawn to the positive messages more than to the negative. She began to replace her negative self-talk with gentler and more compassionate messages.

There was a homework assignment during a long period of time when I was away in which she was invited to look at herself in the mirror and say positive messages to herself, shifting from hearing those messages from me to internalizing them for herself.

There were sessions where she would act as her own rescuer as the adult by coming into a traumatic scene and rescuing her own "little girl" by taking her out of the traumatic situation and comforting her, thus becoming her own best protector.

We did boundary exercises to help her establish a sense of herself as a separate person. We explored moving toward and away from each other so that she could study what felt right to her in any given moment as it related to being in relationship to another person. She was free to study her own impulses and desires without fear of judgment or criticism.

There were sessions devoted to Mary's relationship with her boyfriend and whether she should continue being with him or not. We used a combination of talk therapy and EMDR to process emotions to gain greater clarity about what was right for her.

There was the time that Mary, toward the end of our work together, had been sidelined with unexplainable back pain that lasted for the entire 2 months I was away during one of my overseas work assignments. Once I returned and we talked about the timing of her pain, it became apparent that she had somaticized her pain around the ending of her relationship with her boyfriend. Even though she had finally had the courage to break things off, she was left feeling incomplete with him because he had left their last conversation saying that he would call her to continue the discussion. He never called back. Her physical pain had begun around this time and had lasted the entire time I was away. She had connected with her primary therapist during this time, but the pain had not subsided.

We did EMDR around this last meeting with him, and she realized that she needed to follow up with him and have a talk. We used BLS to have her go into the future to imagine what she needed to say; we came up with an action plan about how she would contact him and what she was going to say. She reported at the next session that she had been able to have that talk and that the pain in her back was reduced drastically. She had been stopping herself from taking action on her own behalf, which was literally making her sick, and once she carried through with her action plan and acted on her own behalf, she felt better instantly. This was a powerful learning for both of us. The way to mediate collapse was to take action.

Throughout our time together, the constant variable was our strong therapeutic attachment. Working with Mary taught me a great deal about perseverance. No matter how many times we needed to process the theme of abandonment, in its many forms, it was important to stick with it and continue processing for however long it would take to shift how she felt. I learned to hang in there and never give up. I learned to trust in the power of the client's process, even when it sometimes appeared to go off course. Being part of the EMDR consultation group was an invaluable resource during times when I needed support and encouragement.

Working with Mary gave me the opportunity to stretch myself and learn new ways of working as a therapist. I was surprised that my long, periodic absences did not interrupt the process; rather, Mary described needing those breaks in order to integrate the material more fully. I think the breaks served to help pace the work, so that she could assimilate the shifts without the pressure of weekly processing.

I learned that attachment repair doesn't necessarily require week-to-week consistency; there can be healing even with interruptions in the connection. The key factors to sustaining the positive benefits were that she always had a way to connect with me, even during my absences, and we always preplanned our next session date so that we knew when we would be reconnecting.

I learned that being an adjunctive therapist using EMDR is a viable option for some clients, and in fact, can promote a deep and profound transformative experience.

And, my experience with Mary reaffirmed that the most important ingredient of healing is the therapeutic relationship. Through all the tears and pain, she knew that I was right there with her, offering her consistent, loving, trustworthy support and unconditional positive regard.

Undoubtedly, Mary will continue to encounter times when she gets triggered. However, her ability to handle these times from a new, more adaptive place has replaced the older, more primitive responses. She doesn't go to that dark, immobile place anymore. She doesn't berate herself anymore. She doesn't express the same critical voice of her mother anymore. She has learned how to tolerate her feelings and knows that they won't kill her. She knows how to soothe and comfort herself. When she does feel triggered, the amount of time and energy she spends there is much less. She knows how to come out of it now, but more important, she doesn't have the predisposition to be vulnerable to that dark place in the same way anymore. She now has the ability to witness her process and make a choice about what to do in those times, rather than be a helpless victim of it. She has a much deeper understanding of the dynamics that underlie this place and holds it with more compassion. She has shifted her relationship to her past. She has developed more of her authentic self and is now enjoying creative outlets she was never allowed to enjoy. She is connected to friends and community and celebrates herself for who she is. She doesn't need to come to therapy anymore. She carries me with her. She is living her life.

FOLLOW-UP

It's been 8 months since my last session with Mary. Recently, she sent me this update via e-mail:

> *"I'm doing so well. Everyday I realize that I'm just happy . . . a feeling that's SO different and something I never thought I'd experience. Even with some setbacks, primarily financial in nature, I seem to just be enjoying the days no matter what occurs in them. Overall, life is now so gentle and joyful most of the time that I feel like a kid with a giant new toy all the time. I attribute this mainly to you and your work. I still don't understand how such a major change could happen, but know it did. I bring Annie Oakley Mom to mind fairly often, just to check in and partly because I just love the energy around her presence/image/whatever it is. I saw my therapist this week for the first time in many, many months just to check in and tell her how wonderfully I'm doing. We talked about what/how this all happened . . . but really, it almost seems like a miracle, or grace or something. I am more grateful than I could ever express."*

CHAPTER 17

AF-EMDR With a Young Woman With Eating Disorders, PTSD, Anxiety, and Early Attachment Trauma

Elena Felder

THERAPIST BIOGRAPHY AND BACKGROUND

I am a marriage and family therapist specializing in working with abuse and trauma. I was trained psychodynamically and relationally. I have a private practice in Berkeley, California, and run a training program for interns at the Iris Center in San Francisco, an outpatient recovery clinic for women struggling with addiction and trauma.

I trained and then consulted with Laurel Parnell and over the years found ways to incorporate the EMDR and resource development into the frame of the therapy I provide. There have been the one- to three-session miracles, but much of the work is slower and longer. I came to rely more and more on developing and tapping in the internal resources and to explore ways to use them with addiction and with eating disorders, while doing EMDR using the modified protocol with the underlying traumas.

THE CLIENT

The case presented in this chapter is a composite of three clients with whom I have worked, whom I call "Aliyah." This young woman initially contacted me by e-mail and left no phone number. I responded and then did not hear back from her for a couple of months. When she wrote back, I offered to talk to her by phone, but she preferred to just set a first meeting.

Before the first session Aliyah stood on my porch smoking and seemed reluctant to put out the cigarette and come into the office. In the session I noticed that she had difficulty making eye contact with me and spoke so softly that I had to lean forward to hear her. She was in her 20s and was beautiful but carried herself in a way to hide her body and kept her face down, so when I noticed her beauty it surprised me. When I asked for her phone number, she gave me her work number and seemed visibly reluctant to give me her cell phone. I noticed a pull in me to take care of her and fantasized about wrapping her in the blanket. We spent the first few sessions setting goals and taking a history.

PRESENTING PROBLEM

Aliyah had a history of childhood physical and sexual abuse symptoms consistent with PTSD. She had intrusive memories of her abuse, but there were also gaps in her memory where whole periods of her life seemed blank to her. She had difficulty going to sleep, nightmares, periods when she could not concentrate, and periods when she described feeling far away from herself, almost unreal. She was frequently triggered and extremely anxious about being triggered. Previously she had used self-injury to try and manage her symptoms, and she currently had a prescription for Klonopin, which she used (without abusing it) to manage symptoms of anxiety.

In addition to her PTSD, Aliyah also had a history of anorexia and bulimia. She had been in residential treatment for her eating disorder a few years back. She had also been in a dialectical behavior therapy (DBT) group, which she found very helpful. Since being in treatment, she had maintained a healthy weight but continued to struggle with thoughts of restricting her eating and episodes of binge eating. She wanted help managing her PTSD symptoms and the symptoms from the eating disorder. She had also come for therapy because she said her partner was struggling with her shutting down, and she really valued this relationship.

I was struck that she had reported two previous treatments as being very helpful: both her residential treatment and the DBT. As I took her history, I also became aware of her integrity, strength, and creativity. She wrote richly layered descriptions in her journal, and created beautiful if sometimes chilling sculptures and exquisite jewelry. She was also in a long-term and generally supportive relationship with a woman. She had put herself through school and worked as a vet tech. Her connection with animals had been a saving grace for her. I have a policy that clients can bring dogs into session, and the presence of her dog quickly became an important part of her therapy. She had a gentle and loyal large dog, "Bianca," whom she had gotten from an animal rescue.

CLIENT HISTORY

Aliyah's parents split up when she was 2 and her father left, maintaining only sporadic contact with her thereafter. Her mother was obsessed with both her daughter and her daughter's appearance and entered her in child beauty contests. By fifth grade her mother was putting them on mother–daughter diets and taking both their measurements weekly. By eighth grade Aliyah was purging a few times a week. Throughout her childhood Aliyah's mother had a series of abusive boyfriends and husbands. As the situation at home got worse, Aliyah was dropped off with different family members and friends, one of whom sexually abused her. She was physically abused by her mother and watched her mother being abused. At 13 she got into a sexual relationship with a 17-year-old boy, who physically and sexually abused her.

When Aliyah was 16 she ran away from home, lived with friends for a while, then moved in with her father for a short period. Around this time her restricting got worse. When she would see her mother, her mother would immediately comment on her weight. By 18 Aliyah had become so thin that she collapsed and was rushed to the hospital. She entered a residential treatment setting, her weight stabilized, and shortly thereafter she cut off contact with her mother.

TREATMENT OVERVIEW

Initially we worked to develop and tap in resources for Aliyah. When I talk to my clients about resource installation, I explain that we react not to the events we experienced exactly as they happened but to what we perceive, the memories we play, and the stories we tell ourselves again and again. With complex PTSD resulting from long-term developmental trauma, the stories that we replay again and again reinforce our fear, negative beliefs, and distrust in relationships. We then look around us and see evidence that confirms these ingrained beliefs. When we install new resources, the mind and body have an opportunity to react to the new stories, the new patterns these stories open up—stories of being protected, cared for, resilient. These stories not only shift the way we respond but also open us up to evidence and memories of evidence that reinforce these beliefs.

Aliyah chose tactile stimulation as the form of BLS she wanted to use, holding the pulsers in her hands and occasionally slipping them beneath her legs. Aliyah vividly described a redwood grove, using her art supplies. For her protective figure she chose Bianca, her dog. She could not come up with a nurturing figure. There was no person, animal, or spirit she felt she could trust to nurture her. Finally she decided she could use one of the trees from the grove. We spent a session developing and tapping in these resources. The following session she reported being able to tap these resources in herself by imagining them and tapping on her knees or crossing her arms and tapping her shoulders. She reported that she noticed a decrease in her anxiety when she used her resources.

When I asked her what she wanted to focus on first, Aliyah told me that she wanted to work on her eating disorder. I had referred her to a nutritionist and when I checked her diet, it seemed generally well balanced and reasonable. But Aliyah was occasionally bingeing, and thoughts about restricting or bingeing were occupying a larger and larger portion of her mind. I was aware that her eating disorder was likely linked to the trauma from her childhood, but Aliyah was clear that she did not want to process her memories at this time. She said the thought of coming into session was so scary sometimes that she felt nauseous the whole day before the session.

I hoped that installing internal resources would not only help with her present symptoms but also increase her trust in the therapy and her willingness to process childhood trauma. We began looking for triggers for the urge to restrict or to binge. I would ask her for a memory or incident of when she was triggered to restrict or binge. For example, when she ran into a friend with whom she used to share "dieting tips," Aliyah began to fantasize about going to pro-anorexia websites and starting to restrict again. I asked her to notice how she felt emotionally and in her body, bringing a mindfulness and somatic awareness to her urges. Aliyah was aware that she felt empty and wanted to be in control. I had her bring her attention to these feelings and body sensations. She became aware of a desire to be safe enough that she didn't need to be in control. I asked who could help her feel that safe, and she was able to imagine Katie, a nurse from her residential treatment, holding her. We used the pulsers to install Katie. She noticed an increasing sense of relaxation in her body, and the urge to restrict dissipated. Aliyah was able to practice this technique outside of session and install resources when she felt an urge to restrict or to binge. *So instead of turning to food for comfort or to restricting food for a sense of control, she was able to turn to her internal resources for nurturing or safety, and she noticed a significant reduction in symptoms.* Through this process Aliyah was able to come up with several animate nurturing resources, including Katie, her own goddess, and her Aunt Carol. She drew and sculpted some of these resources and put them around her house. This resource work on her eating disorder has continued throughout our work together.

After about 3 months, Aliyah said she was ready to process some memories connected to her eating disorder, but she still did not want to process the early physical and sexual abuse. In these initial EMDR sessions, we generally worked by starting with a trigger to restrict or purge and using the bridging technique to trace it back in time to an earlier, linked memory. I use the modified EMDR protocol: picture, emotion, body sensation, and negative cognition. I've found that if I take clients in and out of different scales of measuring, the charge is often diminished as they begin to think it through, and when I try to bridge back, they go back where they think they should go (or where they think I want them to go) rather than following the charge back through the memory network.

EMDR SESSION ON A TRIGGER

THERAPIST: Can you give me an example of when you felt triggered this week to either binge or restrict?

ALIYAH: Yeah. My mom sent me a picture of myself from when I was 18 and at the height of my eating disorder. She sent the picture with a note about how beautiful I looked.

THERAPIST: Close your eyes and go inside. What picture do you see?

ALIYAH: The picture my mom sent me.

THERAPIST: What emotions do you feel?

ALIYAH: Rage, desperation, and sadness.

THERAPIST: What do you feel in your body?

ALIYAH: Hungry. I'm feeling high and dizzy.

THERAPIST: What do you believe about yourself?

ALIYAH: I'm worthless.

THERAPIST: Trace this all back in time. Go back as far as you can without censoring it and tell me where you land.

ALIYAH: I'm watching my mom push her food around her plate without eating. I'm maybe 9.

THERAPIST: What picture do you see?

ALIYAH: My skinny mom.

THERAPIST: What do you feel?

ALIYAH: I'm scared.

THERAPIST: What do you feel in your body?

ALIYAH: My chest is tight; my heart's beating too fast.

THERAPIST: What do you believe about yourself?

ALIYAH: I'm not loved.

THERAPIST: [I could have tried to get her to the underlying negative belief "I'm not lovable," but she was activated, her body shaking slightly and a look on her face that she gets when she is trying to hold back tears. I didn't want to pull her out of the flow of the narrative or have her feel I was correcting her.] How charged is it?

ALIYAH: 7. (*We began the BLS using the Tac/AudioScan pulsers.*) >>>>> OK.

THERAPIST: What's happening?

ALIYAH: I don't know what to do. My mom's not eating. I have to eat less.

THERAPIST: I'm confused. How will eating less help you? [I was feeling a genuine confusion and trying to understand what belief was guiding her behavior.]

ALIYAH: So my body will stay the same, stay skinny so she'll like me.

THERAPIST: [Here she connected with her belief that to stay connected with her mother and to be loved, she had to restrict her food.] Go with that. >>>>>

ALIYAH: We are at the dinner table. My mom keeps saying she's not hungry. She barely eats. I'm hungry. Sometimes I eat, sometimes I don't. I threw my lunch away. (*Her voice sounds child-like and I feel she is lost in the child's world and perspective.*)

THERAPIST: Aliyah, why isn't your mother eating?

ALIYAH: I keep asking her why she isn't eating, and she says she's not hungry. She's telling me we're not supposed to eat.

THERAPIST: Is that true? [There is a part of her that does not believe this, and I'm hoping to give her access to this part.]

ALIYAH: No, everyone is supposed to eat.

THERAPIST: Go with that. >>>>>

ALIYAH: She just keeps saying she's not hungry.

THERAPIST: [She seems to be having a difficult time separating from her mother's perspective.] What do you know about your mom now that you didn't know then? [I'm trying another interweave, linking in her current understanding with the past, while creating a separation between her perspective and her mother's.]

ALIYAH: My mother has an eating disorder.

THERAPIST: Go with that. >>>>>

ALIYAH: She says she doesn't.

THERAPIST: Who can explain to you about eating disorders? [The prior interweave didn't quite work because she couldn't hold out against her mother's perspective, so I'm trying to call in someone with more authority.]

ALIYAH: Katie [her favorite nurse at the residential eating disorder clinic].

THERAPIST: OK, go with that. >>>>>

ALIYAH: She said that my mom had an eating disorder, that her life's out of control and she's trying to control it, but the way she looks at the world is distorted. She asked if I wanted to end up like that. I said no. She said that I needed to eat to be strong and to function. She asked if I wanted to be strong, and I said yes.

THERAPIST: Go back to the picture and tell me what's there. [I feel she is at the end of a channel and want to check the work.]

ALIYAH: I feel scared for my mom.

THERAPIST: [This is a new channel.] Yeah, go with that. >>>>>

ALIYAH: I told my mom that she has an eating disorder and that if she doesn't eat, she's going to die and I won't have anyone to take care of me.

THERAPIST: Did your mom die?

ALIYAH: No.

THERAPIST: Go with that. >>>>>

ALIYAH: I asked Katie why my mom's not dead. She said that some women will get along on as little food as possible and not die. My mom says I don't understand, but I do understand.

THERAPIST: [She has gleaned the difference in their perspectives now and is able to hold it.] What do you understand? [I want to more fully link in the client's understanding.]

ALIYAH: I understand her hair could fall out and that she could have a heart attack.

THERAPIST: Can you save her?

ALIYAH: No, she'd never let me.

THERAPIST: Go with that. >>>>> What happened?

ALIYAH: I asked my mom to eat more. Katie put her hands on my shoulders and said I couldn't do it. My mom had problems I couldn't solve.

THERAPIST: [She is integrating Katie as a nurturing attachment figure to whom she is turning for advice and support. By imagining Katie putting her hands on her shoulders, Aliyah is linking in right-brain attachment healing via imagined touch.] Do you believe her?

ALIYAH: (*nods*) >>>>>

THERAPIST: Go back to the picture and tell me what's there.

ALIYAH: I'm at the table looking at my food.

THERAPIST: What's the charge for you now?

ALIYAH: About a 6.

THERAPIST: What keeps it at a 6?

ALIYAH: I'm still scared.

THERAPIST: What do you need to help you feel safe?

ALIYAH: I can't help my mom.

THERAPIST: I know. Would you like someone else to help your mom? [I'm using a resource interweave so that Aliyah can let someone else take care of her mother.]

ALIYAH: (*nods*) >>>>>

THERAPIST: Can we hand her over to her therapist, who will help her?

ALIYAH: (*nods*) >>>>>

THERAPIST: Do you need anything else to feel safe?

ALIYAH: I need to break up with my mom's eating disorder.

THERAPIST: [Now that her mother has been safely handed into the care of a trained profession, it becomes safer for Aliyah to separate.] Go with that. >>>>>>>>

ALIYAH: (*nods*)

THERAPIST: Is there anything else you need?

ALIYAH: I need to eat. I'm going to die if I don't eat. Maybe Katie can stay with me when I eat.

THERAPIST: Ask her to do that. [Aliyah is using a resource interweave to heal her eating disorder and to heal the attachment wound.]

ALIYAH: She says she'll stay with me and I'll see her again when I go to treatment, and that in my life there will be people to eat with me and comfort me. (*She looks at me.*)

THERAPIST: [In this moment I could feel her taking in Katie and me as resources and taking in the knowledge that things got and will get better.] Go to the picture and tell me what's there. [Returning to the target to check the work.]

ALIYAH: I'm eating and Katie is sitting with me.

THERAPIST: What's the charge?

ALIYAH: 0.

THERAPIST: Scan your body and see what's there.

ALIYAH: I feel tired but OK.

THERAPIST: What do you believe about yourself?

ALIYAH: I deserve to eat.

THERAPIST: Great, hold the picture and the belief together in your mind. >>>>>

At this point I asked Aliyah if she wanted to go to her safe place. She imagined going to a garden inside the treatment center where Katie and her adult self held her and told her that she deserved to eat. Then we went back to the picture we began with, the one her mother sent her that had triggered her. When I asked her what came up for her, she said that she saw a hungry, scared girl who needed help and would get it. She said it had no charge.

After about 6 months of work Aliyah reported no desire to purge and almost no desire to restrict. Binges had become more infrequent and were more a matter of eating past comfort. But Aliyah was still struggling with nightmares and extreme anxiety and would close down and withdraw from relationships when she was emotionally upset. At several points I had urged her to begin processing the abuse and abandonment memories, but she maintained that she was not ready and that she was happy with how therapy was going.

Soon after this point, Aliyah said that she wanted a "break" from therapy. I believe she was not ready to work more directly on the childhood abuse and abandonment. She said that she was happier than she had ever been about her relationship with food and that she regularly used Resource Tapping. She was able to recognize when she was triggered, sit with what resources she needed, and tap them in. I knew Aliyah had a lot more work to do, but I didn't know if I would see her again. I worried that I had pushed her too hard to do the trauma processing and that by letting her go, I was abandoning her. But I also felt that she needed to be in control—for now, anyway.

Almost a year later I was walking down the street in San Francisco (my office is in Berkeley) and I saw Aliyah. She looked at me and started crying, held onto me and cried. "I'll call you," she said. It was almost 2 weeks before I got a call from her. She made an appointment. We started again by strengthening her resources. She talked about wishing she had had different parents and I suggested we give them to her.

In the past I have had clients use EMDR to process their grief around the limitations of what their parents could give them. After this work some clients have chosen to install imagined parents (resource figures) who could have nurtured them and met their needs. They begin by imagining being born to these parents and then having the parents raise them through the different developmental stages, witnessing them, holding them, protecting them, challenging them as they grow. This exercise can allow clients to take into their system a deep sense of being seen and cared for and can open them up to new attachment templates. With Aliyah I was well aware we had not yet processed her grief around her actual mother. But I was hoping that by installing the imagined parents, she might feel the strength and security to begin processing that grief. I felt her fear of going back into her abuse so acutely and I was afraid that if we moved into it and her resources were not strong enough, she would leave again.

First Aliyah chose her parents. As with any resource figure, the imagined parents could be real people in her current life or historical or fictional people. Aliyah chose her Aunt "Carol" and Uncle "Sam." Her Aunt Carol had been a warm and loving presence when she was a child. Her Uncle Sam, while more in the background, had been a gentle and steady figure. After she had chosen her parents, I handed her the pulsers.

THERAPIST: OK. Imagine that you are being born to Carol and Sam. How do they feel about having you? >>>>>
ALIYAH: Carol is excited to be having a little girl. Sam talks to me and sings to me.
THERAPIST: Go with that. >>>>> Can you tell me what's happening?
ALIYAH: They're joyous to have me. I'm warm. >>>>>
THERAPIST: [When she said that, I thought of my first urge to wrap her in a blanket.] What's happening now?
ALIYAH: I can't imagine my parents ever being that happy.
THERAPIST: [I knew that she was beginning to go into the unprocessed grief, and I wondered if I should say, go with that. But I

was also concerned about her falling into overwhelming grief around her parents that was not attached to any specific memory, so I decided to bring her back to Aunt Carol and Uncle Sam.] They're [Carol and Sam] happy?

ALIYAH: Yeah.

THERAPIST: What can you imagine Aunt Carol doing when you start crying? [I'm trying to help her take into her nervous system the day-to-day aspects of being taken care of.]

ALIYAH: She would pick me up and hold me.

THERAPIST: Go with that. >>>>> What's happening now?

ALIYAH: I've had to hold myself. Imagining her doing it is so comforting.

THERAPIST: [She's taking it in.] Yeah. If you want to be held, you would let her know and she would pay attention.

ALIYAH: OK. >>>>> (*Her face starts closing down, her brow wrinkles and her body tightens.*)

THERAPIST: What's there?

ALIYAH: I'm angry. I don't understand why people bring kids into this world they don't want. Abortion's legal, there's birth control. I don't understand it, and I'll always have that question.

THERAPIST: [There was still so much grief about who her parents were. I was also feeling, I'm glad you are here, glad you were born, and maybe I should have said that. Instead I did an interweave.] Can you ask your wisdom figure?

ALIYAH: People like the idea but not the reality.

THERAPIST: [We are losing the emotion and getting caught in the ideas.] What did you need? [I'm trying to bring her back to her resources.]

ALIYAH: A stable figure, someone to love me. >>>>> (*looking at me and I look at her*)

THERAPIST: [This is a powerful attachment repair moment through the therapeutic relationship. Normally Aliyah keeps her eyes closed or looks at Bianca, but this time she looks at me and sees me seeing her. In this moment she feels real, valid, seen, understood. This is a moment of intimacy in which she is also taking me into her neural nets as a resource figure.] You deserve that. You've always deserved that. That's your birthright. You've wanted this a long time, and I want you to have it. >>>>>

ALIYAH: (*Starts crying; I could feel her taking in what I was saying. Her dog stands up and puts her chin on Aliyah's lap.*)

THERAPIST: [Her dog is a resource figure also who is real and responding to her—another means of healing her attachment wounds.] Can you tell me what's there?

ALIYAH: It's so amazing to tell myself it's not my fault and actually believe it. I've told myself that my whole life, but I've never believed it. >>>>>

THERAPIST: Just hold your little girl and tell her that.

ALIYAH: I need someone else to hold me too.

THERAPIST: [Aliyah is aware that she has other needs and is able to ask for them. Here is a person who had only a tree as a nurturing figure at the start of treatment, and now she can draw on many others and know they are there for her.] Who?

ALIYAH: Aunt Carol.

THERAPIST: Aunt Carol is holding you with that acceptance and love. You can see it in her eyes [adding in the attachment-repair, implicit right-brain information]. >>>>>

We ended the processing this session with this image of Aunt Carol holding her, looking at her with acceptance and love. Aliyah said that she felt comforted and reported later that she carried that feeling with her as she left my office and could call on it throughout the week.

Shortly after this session, Aliyah left a message about a scheduling question. I got my 7-year-old son settled in his room with a book and the usual admonishment to let me make a private phone call and then called her back. While I was talking to her, my son came into the room and I had to let him know I needed a few more minutes. The next session she brought up the phone call. She said that she had heard how I spoke to him—how I had made him wait but didn't yell at him—and that she had tapped it in. She had essentially tapped me in as an example of a mother having a healthy interaction with her son. In other words, she tapped in the positive transference relationship. Since coming back into treatment and doing the resource attachment-repair work, and hearing me as a mother and tapping that in, I could feel something shift between us. She said she was ready to begin processing her feelings of abandonment around her mother. She trusted me and felt safe enough now to do this work.

The next session we started with a memory from when she was 8. She and her mother had gone East to visit her Aunt Carol and Uncle

Sam. She woke up in the morning and looked out her window and saw snow for the first time. She ran to her mother's room to tell her, only to discover that her mother and all of her belongings were gone. As usual, we used the modified EMDR protocol.

EMDR SESSION PROCESSING ABANDONMENT

THERAPIST: What picture represents the worst part?

ALIYAH: The tire tracks in the snow.

THERAPIST: What do you feel?

ALIYAH: Lost, hurt, scared.

THERAPIST: What do you feel in your body?

ALIYAH: My chest is tense. I feel empty.

THERAPIST: What do you believe about yourself?

ALIYAH: There's something wrong with me. She left because there's something wrong with me.

THERAPIST: How charged is it?

ALIYAH: 9 (*crying*). >>>>>

THERAPIST: (*beginning the BLS*) What's there?

ALIYAH: It's so raw. Anger, angry.

THERAPIST: Go with the anger. >>>>> (*long, silent processing*) Can you tell me what's there?

ALIYAH: Just the perfect snow.

THERAPIST: [It felt too soon for resolution.] What's the charge?

ALIYAH: A 4.

THERAPIST: What keeps it at a 4?

ALIYAH: I guess, confusion.

THERAPIST: Can you go with the confusion? >>>>>

ALIYAH: (*trembling, shaking*)

THERAPIST: It's OK, it's OK. [I'm using my voice to provide comfort, connection, and a dual focus of attention. The client is not alone in her sadness.]

ALIYAH: (*Starts to weep.*)

THERAPIST: What's there now?

ALIYAH: It wasn't my fault.

THERAPIST: It wasn't your fault, that's right. Just go with that. >>>>> (*She's crying in earnest now.*) That's good, just let it out, you're OK now, let it go. (*Her face becomes stronger, more set.*) What's there now?

ALIYAH: I just feel still.

THERAPIST: [This channel feels clear, and I want to check the work.] Can you go back to the picture and tell me what's there?

ALIYAH: Just the clean snow.

THERAPIST: OK, what's the charge?

ALIYAH: I think about a 1.

THERAPIST: [With some clients a 1 is OK, but Aliyah can almost always process to 0.] What keeps it at 1?

ALIYAH: It wasn't my fault, but it was horrible. It doesn't have to feel horrible.

THERAPIST: Go with that. >>>>> What's there?

ALIYAH: My resolve for it not to feel horrible.

THERAPIST: [At this point I was concerned that she was trying to push the feelings away, a child who had to tell herself "I'm not going to let myself feel bad" because there was no comfort. So I did a resource interweave.] What do you need, as a little girl, what did you need?

THERAPIST: I need my mom. I needed a mom. My mom couldn't do it, couldn't offer me comfort and security.

THERAPIST: Who could?

ALIYAH: My Aunt Carol. She was amazing, they were great with me. The 3 months there—I didn't want to leave afterward.

THERAPIST: So your Aunt Carol is there to comfort you. >>>>>

ALIYAH: I was remembering how she would come home from work and make me food and help me with my homework. >>>>>

THERAPIST: Can you go back to the picture and tell me what's there?

ALIYAH: Just the snow.

THERAPIST: What's the charge?

ALIYAH: No charge.

THERAPIST: Can you scan your body and tell me what's there?

ALIYAH: I feel OK, tired, OK.

THERAPIST: What do you believe about yourself?

ALIYAH: I didn't deserve to be left.

THERAPIST: What did you deserve?

ALIYAH: I deserved to be raised by Aunt Carol.

THERAPIST: What did she give you that you deserved?

ALIYAH: Love, security, food, comfort.

THERAPIST: Can you hold your little girl and say that you deserve love, security, food, comfort? [I'm adding in an attachment component to the installation of the positive cognitions, asking her to hold her little girl as her adult self says the positive things to her.]

After this work we went to her safe place, where she had her dog Bianca, her adult self, and her Aunt Carol surround her little girl self. This is another way I am trying to add in the attachment repair, by emphasizing the attachment figures who can love and support her.

Shortly after this session, Aliyah remembered looking around at the skeletal young women at her residential treatment center and making a conscious choice to eat, to live. In that moment she connected to the part of her that had always believed that she deserved to live and to take up space. We were able to tap in that part of her, as well as the realization, "I deserve to live and to take up space," along with the people she has, and has had, who reflect that worthiness to her.

Since that session we have processed other memories of abandonment, as well as memories of physical abuse. Sometimes Aliyah comes in with a memory she is ready to work on; sometimes she is triggered in her day-to-day life and we trace back the charge from that trigger and target the memory that comes up. An example is when her house was broken into. Aliyah sent me an e-mail letting me know about the break-in and telling me that she felt particularly violated because the last safe place we used was in her house. I e-mailed her back, reminding her that she carries her safe place inside her and that it can't be broken into, and letting her know we would reclaim the space in our next session. Her next e-mail (an excerpt of which is below) was powerful. She was not only able to use her resources and was less reactive than previously, but she was also now able to reach out to a friend, to let people nurture her. With the attachment repair and strengthening of her internal resources came a corresponding ability to trust the people in her life.

"Last night [a friend] came and spent the night. I felt pretty good this morning, until about the time I discovered my house for the first time yesterday. I had a rough 2 hours dealing with wanting to go check my house, being terrified to do so. . . . I tapped and did my visualizations. I cried a lot. I phoned a friend. . . . I'm really proud of how I've held it together through this experience. [Work went] without mishap yesterday and today, something I wouldn't have been able to do, especially being alone the way I am right now, before I started working with you. I actually moved out of a place because my downstairs neighbor was

broken into and pretty much stopped sleeping until I did (not even my own home). I'm really proud of the work we've done."

After our e-mail exchange we did a processing session just around the break-in, and although we got the charge all the way down when we checked the work the next session, she reported still feeling intense anxiety. So we went back in. At this point in the work, Aliyah was willing to process whatever memories came up.

EMDR SESSION PROCESSING THE BREAK-IN

THERAPIST: What picture represents the worst part?

ALIYAH: The window. [When she had come home, the window was ajar.]

THERAPIST: What do you feel?

ALIYAH: Fear.

THERAPIST: What do you feel in your body?

ALIYAH: My heart is beating too fast, tense in my shoulders and chest.

THERAPIST: What do you believe about yourself?

ALIYAH: I'm not safe.

THERAPIST: Close your eyes and go inside, hold the picture of the window, the fear, feel your heart beating, the tension in your shoulders and chest, and the thought that you're not safe and trace them back in time without censoring and tell me where you land.

ALIYAH: (*She starts crying and tells me that she is about 8 years old and her mom is in a violent relationship, trying to leave the guy and moving them every month, while he is looking for them.*)

THERAPIST: What do you see? [She was clearly in a memory, and so rather than ask what picture represented the worst, I wanted to know where she was.]

ALIYAH: I'm in a motel room. I'm alone and I hear noises (*sobbing and shaking*).

THERAPIST: [She's activated and very much in a specific memory. I did not ask for her emotion, body sensations, or negative cognition at this point because it seemed to me that she was right where she needed to be and that she needed to start processing.] OK, OK, just go with it, but let me know if it becomes too much. >>>>> [I was trying to help her by activating a dual focus of awareness as she went through this memory aware of her connection to me.]

ALIYAH: (*Continues to sob, trembling with her head down, her breath coming in ragged gasps.*)

THERAPIST: [I tried to use my own steady deeper breathing to calm her, and within a minute her breathing pattern matched mine.] What's there?

ALIYAH: I'm so terrified of what's outside. I'm trapped, I'm stuck.

THERAPIST: [At this point she seemed overwhelmed by the memory and I thought that she needed a resource to move her through it.] What do you need?

ALIYAH: To feel stronger than what's outside.

THERAPIST: [She is saying that she wants to feel stronger, but I'm concerned that in her terror, she is going back to thinking that she must be invincible, so I shift her phrasing to try and allow someone to support her.] Who can help you feel stronger?

ALIYAH: Bianca [her dog and her most reliable protector figure].

THERAPIST: OK, bring Bianca into the picture. You can open your eyes and look at her, and when you've taken her in, you can close them again. >>>>> [I hoped that seeing Bianca right there with her would help her maintain a dual focus of awareness, ground her in the room, and really allow her to bring that love and protection into this terrified part of her.]

ALIYAH: OK (*closes eyes, face looks calm, breathing slow and steady*). >>>>>

THERAPIST: What's there?

ALIYAH: I don't have anyone that's out to get me anymore.

THERAPIST: OK, just go with that, just take that in. >>>>> [She separated the past from the present, and I wanted to strengthen that differentiation in her system.]

ALIYAH: (*Face stays very calm.*)

THERAPIST: What's there now?

ALIYAH: I was thinking how amazing that something today can bring up all these feelings I lived with then.

THERAPIST: [At this point I think one channel was complete, and I probably should have gone back and checked the picture.

	But while she may have been out of that motel room, part of me was still there picturing her at 8, trapped and terrified in this motel room, and so I wanted the end of the story where she got out. As so often happens with processing sessions, the client ends up taking us where we need to go, even when I misstep.] What ended up happening there?
ALIYAH:	My mom went back and forth. I got left with friends and relatives. The last time I thought [the abusive boyfriend] would kill my mom. He had a gun. I wouldn't stop screaming. He said he'd shoot me if I didn't stop. My mom grabbed the gun and we left. I never saw him again. It took that [degree of threat] to get her to leave. She chose him over me again and again.
THERAPIST:	[As she talked, I became concerned that I had opened a whole new memory and I also felt waves of rage riding through me, so it was hard for me to think. But I also knew that this was the attachment wound and was, in many ways, deeper than the terror.] Go with that. >>>>>
ALIYAH:	(*sobbing*)
THERAPIST:	It's OK, OK. [I'm trying to use my voice to soothe her and to bring her back.] Tell me what's there.
ALIYAH:	Just that there was a time when my life actually wasn't safe, but it is now.
THERAPIST:	[Again she is able to separate past and present, and I feel like it's time to check the work.] Can you go back to the second picture and tell me what's there now?
ALIYAH:	Hmmm, I'm there with Bianca and we open the door and walk through it.
THERAPIST:	[I'm relieved that she is out of the room, but I feel like she needs something or someone more.] What's the charge?
ALIYAH:	Probably a 2.
THERAPIST:	What keeps it at 2?
ALIYAH:	(*crying*) It's just sad, that part of my life.
THERAPIST:	[It is more than sad, and it seems to me that while she has taken the charge out of the terror, the attachment wounding is what she feels pulling on her now, and I'm hoping we are moving in that direction.] Just go with that sadness. >>>>>
ALIYAH:	(*Crying and petting Bianca, she is taking that touch into her nervous system.*)

THERAPIST: What's there?

ALIYAH: It's OK to be sad. It doesn't have to be overwhelming.

THERAPIST: [Laurel Parnell had suggested here that I could have asked if she would like someone to hold her while she cried. Looking back, I think of a baby overwhelmed by her feelings when she is left alone with them, able to tolerate them when she is held and comforted.] That's true. Where do you and Bianca go when you leave the room?

ALIYAH: The beach.

THERAPIST: And who would you like to be with you? [I want her to have another attachment resource.]

ALIYAH: Just Bianca.

THERAPIST: Your adult self, your child self, and Bianca are on the beach. Can you ask your child self if she would like anyone else? [I'm suspecting that because of the memory, she is scared to trust a person but that her young self wants to have that comfort and that she can allow herself to have that now.]

ALIYAH: She would like Katie.

THERAPIST: [I feel a relief in my body when she says this.] OK, Katie is there with her too. >>>>>

ALIYAH: (*calm and relaxed*)

THERAPIST: Can you go back to the picture and tell me what's there?

ALIYAH: Just an open door.

THERAPIST: What's the charge?

ALIYAH: 0.

THERAPIST: Can you check your body and tell me what's there?

ALIYAH: Just tired.

THERAPIST: Anything else?

ALIYAH: (*Shakes her head.*)

THERAPIST: What do you believe about yourself?

ALIYAH: I'm safe now. I can keep myself safe.

THERAPIST: [Here I was a little concerned because I didn't know if she had gone back to believing that she had to do it all herself. But we were near the end of the session, she was in a good place, and I knew that the attachment piece takes long-term work.] OK, hold your child self and tell her "You're safe now, I can keep you safe." [I installed the positive cognition, while letting her take in the *feeling* of being held.]

ALIYAH: OK.

THERAPIST: [We've installed the positive cognition in this memory, and so I want to go back to the trigger memory and see if it's cleared.] I want you to go back to the first picture and tell me what's there.

ALIYAH: Just a window, it's just a window.

THERAPIST: What the charge?

ALIYAH: 0.

THERAPIST: What do you feel in your body?

ALIYAH: Nothing. Hmmm, just tired.

THERAPIST: What do you believe about yourself?

ALIYAH: I'm OK now.

THERAPIST: Can you hold the image of the window with the belief that you're OK?

ALIYAH: OK. >>>>>

After we had processed this last piece, she chose to end with the image of Katie and Bianca and her on the beach.

FOLLOW-UP

Aliyah continues to use her resources and has not restricted her food intake in over a year. Often now during EMDR processing she will look at me and even more often she will look at her dog Bianca, who is still with her in the session. I see this eye contact as a way in which she integrates us into her nervous system as resources that care for her. She has developed a strong community of friends and has begun showing her art publicly and put her jewelry into stores. Our work is ongoing. Despite successes, there is a lot left: memories and reactions. As the work continues the memories she brings up are often more graphic and traumatic. At times I am in awe of her bravery. She still has a prescription for Klonopin and is still a smoker. But as she experiences life as it happens now or remembers what happened, she is able to move into the sensations, feelings, and thoughts and does not feel alone. As she put it near the end of a processing session: "I wasn't safe, I'm safer now. And I don't have to completely lock down when something hard happens. . . . People will be there if I let them. They're not all my mom. . . . People have a lot to offer me, if I can let them in. I have a lot inside me too."

CHAPTER 18

Brief AF-EMDR With a Client Experiencing Panic Attacks, Depression, and Stalking Behavior

Rachel Howard

THERAPIST BIOGRAPHY AND BACKGROUND

I am a licensed clinical psychologist in private practice in Southern California. I have an extensive background in object relations, attachment, family systems, and psychoanalytic psychotherapy. I received my doctoral degree in psychology in 1998 from California School of Professional Psychology–Los Angeles. I was trained in EMDR by Dr. Laurel Parnell in 2004, from whom I have also received consultation and advanced EMDR training. I am an EMDRIA-approved consultant and a facilitator for Dr. Parnell's EMDR trainings. Additionally, I am trained in somatic therapy and hypnosis, as well as in mindfulness. These skills, in combination, are extremely useful and effective.

THE REFERRAL

At the beginning of January 2007, I received an evening phone call from Michele, a respected colleague who asked me to call her immediately about a possible referral. She wanted to refer a client of hers, "Ken," a 27-year-old law school graduate student who had been referred to her for stalking his ex-girlfriend. Ken was in great distress. If he were caught stalking, it could be the end of his legal career. Michele told me that she was anxious about taking on a stalking case where she might eventually become the client's target, as she had had just such a frightening experience in the past. I told Michele that I needed to hear more about Ken before I accepted the referral, as I too was concerned about my personal safety. I agreed to speak with him on the phone to try and assess his dangerousness and appropriateness for outpatient treatment.

INITIAL PHONE CONTACT

When I spoke with Ken, I asked him how I could help him. He told me that he was upset, anxious, and panic-stricken. He felt so panicked that he was unable to study, eat, sleep, or go to work. He felt outside of his body and was experiencing crushing chest pains—symptoms of a panic attack. He repeated what I had already heard from Michele. He told me that he realized he had a pattern of stalking women after they broke up with him. He didn't want to cause harm to anyone. He felt so completely bereft and abandoned. He simply wanted to see them so that he could feel less heartbroken. He needed to convince himself that the relationship had been "real." I asked him what he meant by that. He said that when he didn't have contact with the women, it felt to him like they didn't exist anymore. It felt completely invalidating to him. In turn, he felt as though he didn't exist either. I had learned from Michele that Ken had been given up for adoption as a baby. At this point, I was thinking that this client had some serious attachment wounds and had difficulty with feeling object permanence as well as object constancy.

Ken kept asking me if he was making any sense. He said that he knew that his behavior was wrong, irrational, and dangerous. He simply felt compelled to pursue this improper behavior. He felt possessed and not in control of his actions.

As part of assessing whether it was safe to see this client in my office, I asked him if he had ever been violent or involved in any physical altercations of any sort with past girlfriends or male peers. He told me that he never had been involved in such violence and that his friendships with his college buddies were extremely close. He also reported that he had close female friends who were very supportive of him. He had also had many years of therapy, had insight into his problems (even though he couldn't seem to control himself), and was highly motivated to change his behaviors. At this point, I made the decision that it would be safe to see this client in my office.

At the time, Ken was sharing an apartment with a good friend from college. His friends, including his roommate, had suggested that he immediately see someone for this problem. They were concerned that he was putting his future in jeopardy, given that he was entering his ex-girl-friend's home with an old key without her knowledge or consent, while she and her daughter were sleeping or away from home. This behavior constituted breaking and entering: a felony.

When he told his friends that he didn't have enough money to see a therapist, they offered to give or loan it to him. They told him that they loved him and wanted to help him. I thought that this client had an excellent network and support system that would be able to help him during the trauma work that needed to be done. Additionally, this was a person who appeared to engender genuine love and friendship from those who knew him well. It seemed that Ken was someone who was going through a hard time, but was generally functioning in his life. I took this as a good sign for treatment, given that there was evidence of a generally integrated, healthy ego structure. Further, he had something at stake: his career and his life. He was motivated to work hard in the therapy.

Ken asked me, "Do you think I am crazy? I feel crazy." I responded, "I know that this may sound like a nonsequitur, but do you know anything about your birth?" He said, "Yes, I was adopted as an infant."

"Then no," I said. "I don't think that you're crazy."

"Then what's wrong with me?"

"I know that it feels like something is wrong with you and that you're feeling crazy. But we all have parts of us, sometimes very primitive young parts, that didn't get our needs met. When we aren't aware of these parts and they aren't integrated into our adult self, the unmet needs they represent can cause problems. We do what we can to get those needs met, even when these actions aren't helpful to us in our adult relationships or in our own best self-interest."

I continued: "You've told me that you are functioning well in your friendships, are a successful student, have functioned well enough in your clerkship to be offered full-time future employment in a prominent law firm. So there's a part of you that is a 27-year-old functioning adult who handles life pretty well [I am pointing out his ability to function in a healthy way for future resourcing]. But I think it's possible that the part of you that's making these emotional and irrational relationship decisions to stalk your girlfriend is that young infant part of you who wants to see his mommy and couldn't because he was taken away from her way too soon and doesn't know that he survived that separation. He continues to want to revisit that part of your life within the context of an adult relationship, without being able to see the consequences of these actions. Who would expect a newborn to understand consequences? All a newborn wants to do is be with, see, and smell his mommy."

[I was attempting to educate his adult self and planting the seeds for his acceptance of this possibility, setting the stage for ego-state integration in our work together.]

There was a long pause, then he said, "Are you kidding?"

I said, "No." There was another long silence. I could hear him crying and could sense him internally making the connection between what I said and how he was feeling.

"Can you fix me?" he asked.

I could feel his relief. I heard his assumption that he was broken and the possible negative cognition, "I am damaged" or "There's something wrong with me." "I can't make any promises," I said, "but I can sure try and help you. I think I know what needs to be done, and I think I know how to do it. That the part of you that is stalking is the part that doesn't realize that he doesn't need his mommy anymore to survive in the same way that he did when he was a newborn. I think that we need to integrate that part of you that needed his mommy to survive into your adult self so that it isn't in charge of your emotional life. I think we need to integrate that part of you that needs help." [I was educating him as to what was happening to him so that he could feel more normal and less crazy. I was providing hope for a good solution to his present difficulties, rather than adding to his self-pathology.]

Ken was no longer crying. "I don't really fully understand what you're saying, but something about what you're saying makes sense to me and it feels right. How soon can you see me?"

MORE HISTORICAL RELATIONSHIP HISTORY

Ken told me that he'd had a pattern of becoming sexually involved with women very soon after meeting them. If women wanted to have a relationship with him and were truly available, he would then become distant, aloof, and not very interested. The relationships were mostly about confusing sex with intimacy and being left feeling empty. His goal was to move onto the next potential source of nurturing, which seemed illusive and impossible to hold onto for any length of time.

He talked about what his female friends called his "urge to merge" with women who turned out to be emotionally unavailable to him. Knowing that this was more of a female quality, it felt humiliating to him. His "romantic relationships," in which he was interested in the women, generally lasted only about 2 months. It took another month for his anxiety and fear of abandonment, along with his perceived neediness, to drive the women away and for the relationship to end. These relationships would all begin in an idyllic manner. Ken and the woman would spend all their time together, enjoy the same interests, have amazing sex, and would constantly text and talk.

When the women wanted to have more autonomy and "return to a more balanced life," he would feel completely abandoned and alone and become clingy and needy. The women would react to his incessant need for togetherness by becoming increasingly unavailable to him and would eventually break up with him. That part of the relationship generally took another month. The inevitable distance would cause him to become more and more anxious, panicky, obsessive, and compulsive. He would feel abandoned, alone, and sad. He described a hollow feeling in his stomach and chest, after which the stalking behavior would commence. He would end up breaking into his ex-girlfriend's place so that he could look at her while she was sleeping in order "to see if she was real." Sometimes, he would enter the house when she wasn't there and take items, the most recent item being a disposable camera.

Ken would also have sex with another woman that he said was "meaningless," while experiencing intrusive thoughts about the ex-girlfriend. He would then become aloof, avoidant, and distant, essentially treating these "stand-in" women as his exes had treated him.

BIRTH AND ADOPTION HISTORY

Ken stated that he was adopted. His adoptive mother had a lot of information about his adoption, which she freely shared with him. She told him that his mother had a long labor and that he weighed 10 pounds at birth. His biological mother, a white female in her teens, became pregnant outside of marriage, and felt that adoption would provide the best family situation for her baby. Ken knew very little about his biological father other than the fact that he was African-American. Ken's birth mother asked to hold him when he was born. He was then taken and given to a foster mother for 2 months. Ken was told that he was very happy while with his foster mother (a possible reenactment of the 2-month honeymoon period in his romantic relationships?). This all came to an end when an upper middle-class white couple who had been unable to conceive adopted him. He reported that although his adopted mother could be nurturing and sweet, he was never able to bond with her and described feeling "neutral" toward her. He said that she seemed like any other woman (at this point I was considering a possible avoidant attachment style). It was not a good fit for him. He described her as cold, aloof, and seemingly depressed.

Ken had a similar reaction to his adopted father, the difference being that Ken didn't like his adoptive father and did not like having physical contact with him. Further, when the adoptive father became angry, which was often, the father would throw tantrums, which made Ken feel even more distant from him. Adding to the difficulties, Ken's mother did not protect him from his father's rage. When Ken was 18 months old, the family adopted another infant, a white baby. He stated that he felt no familial closeness to his adopted brother either.

Ken remembered that when he was just 5 years old, he would get up in the middle of the night and walk around outside. He felt like he didn't belong anywhere in the world and found that he felt better being outside of the house. Growing up, Ken was well liked and had many friends, but he also spent a lot of time by himself and kept his feelings of loneliness and sadness to himself. During the period from elementary school through college, Ken lacked confidence, feeling that he was unattractive and unappealing to girls. As an adult, he hasn't been able to support himself; he has procrastinated and sabotaged opportunities and cannot see himself being in a long-term relationship, married, or having children.

TREATMENT OVERVIEW

While working with a client who demonstrated self-destructive, stalking, and procrastination behavior, I discovered that these behaviors were rooted in feelings of abandonment by his biological mother when she gave him up for adoption and an emotionally unattuned relationship with an adoptive mother and father. Since this was to be a short-term 10-session therapy, I decided to utilize the following approaches: (1) stabilization, resourcing, and imaginal interweaves to develop and enhance feelings of safety, belonging, and early infant attachment repair with the birth mother; (2) constructing an internalized good-enough mother;

and (3) constructing an ideal mother and childhood from conception to adulthood. This approach is demonstrated in the following sessions.

Sessions 1–5: Resourcing and Creating a New Mother: Pregnancy, Rebirthing, Early Childhood, and Repair with Birth Mother

This first session was really like a second one since we had spent so much time on the phone and I had gathered history and assessed his appropriateness for EMDR in an outpatient setting. I already knew his history and background—that he had many friends and a strong, support system, was employed, had insight into his problem—and I knew that his distress and what was happening to him were both unusual to his typical experience and that he was highly motivated. I began to do Resource Tapping with BLS that turned into more elaborate and extensive processing. I had never done the work in this way before. I was really tracking him and being with him in the present perhaps in part because we had only 10 sessions in which to work.

Since I had a cancellation, we made an appointment for the following day. When it was time for the session, I came out to the waiting room exactly at the appointed time. I had expected to see a young-looking male, as he sounded so young on the phone. Instead, I was surprised to encounter a tall, handsome man pacing back and forth right in front of my office door. Yet, after I introduced myself and he interacted with me, his body language was that of a young awkward boy. He sat down on the couch directly across from my chair, the closest seating to me in my office. When I asked him "What was it like to come in?" he told me that he had arrived an hour early for the appointment because he was afraid that he might be late. He told me that he was feeling quite anxious and panicky; that he felt embarrassed because when he arrived at my waiting room, he kept looking up to see whether I was coming out of my office, even though it was clearly way too early for me to come and get him. He wondered whether I had forgotten him or whether there was a misunderstanding about the time.

[The seemingly unfounded young reaction of feeling anxious that I might forget him was a validation of the hypothesis that the issues being dealt with stemmed from early infancy and being abandoned by a primary attachment figure, such as his birth mother, or perhaps he was waiting for his foster mom or adoptive parents to come get him.]

At this point in the session, due to his high level of anxiety, I made the decision to resource and ground him. My intention was to calm him so that we could proceed with the session. I also wanted to inspire Ken's confidence and to create a rapport between us. Further, I thought that with EMDR therapy, I could help empower him to see that these tools were tools that he could take with him and use at home when he needed to calm himself.

After briefly explaining BLS, I asked him to notice his body seated on the sofa and his feet on the ground. I asked him to notice what he was feeling and to locate the sensations in his body. I then directed him to follow my fingers and let me know when something changed. I noticed that Ken quickly began to relax and his breathing became deeper and more regulated. I also introduced him to the light stream technique, to which he also had an immediate positive response. He expressed surprise that his body sensations and anxiety had dissipated so quickly.

I then asked him to tell me a bit about what had happened with regard to his last girlfriend. He spilled out the information (most of which I already knew from our telephone interview). He told me that he felt so compelled to see her that he illegally entered her home on two occasions using an old key—once, when she wasn't home, and the second time when she was home and she and her young daughter were both asleep. He said that he felt driven to see her face. At that time he took a disposable camera (was this a transitional object, I wondered?). After this incident, he gave his car keys to his roommate at night, so that he wouldn't be able to engage in this illegal compulsive behavior.

I looked at him and smiled. "I thought you said that you couldn't control your actions?" Ken looked at me with a puzzled look. "What I am seeing is your ability to set boundaries, ask for help, and recognize that this behavior is wrong and self-destructive. What's a positive statement you can say about yourself as a result of your being able to do that?"

KEN: But I had to give my keys to my roommate to prevent me from leaving!
RACHEL: Who gave him the keys to your car?
KEN: (*smiling at me*) I did.
Rachel: And who asked for help and got the help he needed?
KEN: I guess I did (*smiling sheepishly*).
RACHEL: What's a positive statement you can say about yourself? [I wanted to install a positive statement to help strengthen him.]
KEN: I guess I can get help when I ask for it (*looking sad*). >>>>>
RACHEL: What are you thinking about?

KEN: Why do I feel like I have to do that (*starts to cry*)? It's like it's not me.

RACHEL: [Is this an ego state that wants to make itself known?] I don't know. Let's see what we can find out. Close your eyes for a moment. When you think of doing that stalking, and it's not you, what image comes up? [At this point, I can see that he has resources and is activated so I make the decision to find a target for EMDR.]

KEN: (*closes eyes*) This is really weird. I have an image of myself as an adult, and there's a baby in a sphere that's attached to me with an umbilical chord. The sphere is in front of me, leading us. (*We begin a combination of EMDR and resourcing, using the BLS.*) >>>>>

RACHEL: What's happening now?

KEN: Diane is there [the ex-girlfriend he stalked]. She's turning into this huge piece of plastic wrap and wrapping the baby with the plastic wrap. The baby is really happy being wrapped in the plastic wrap. Without her, the baby is sad and in pain (*crying*).

RACHEL: [I sense a need for an interweave to help the baby.] What does the baby need?

KEN: He needs another plastic wrap provider. >>>>>>

RACHEL: What's happening now?

KEN: All I have ever done is look for plastic wrap, and it hasn't helped.

RACHEL: What does the baby need?

KEN: I need to pick up the baby, but will it feel as good if I do that myself? >>>>> I can't hold the baby.

RACHEL: What's happening?

KEN: Something's preventing me from holding the baby. The baby's in water inside the sphere and I can't get my hands inside the sphere. I can't touch the baby.

RACHEL: What's preventing it?

KEN: It's [the sphere] too fragile. I'm afraid I will hurt it [the baby].

RACHEL: What's needed?

KEN: A gentle hand.

RACHEL: Who can provide that?

KEN: An angel.

RACHEL: Go with that. (*With his eyes closed, Ken gestures with his hand as though entering an imaginary sphere and trying to reach his inner baby. His eyes start to tear up and I see tears running down his face.*)

RACHEL: What's happening now?

KEN: (*eyes open*) My hand is reaching the baby and I am holding him (*crying*). . . . I can feel the baby. I can't believe it (*starts laughing*). It's a pretty cute baby, but very slippery!

RACHEL: (*laughing with Ken*) What does the baby need?

KEN: To be dried off and held.

RACHEL: Who can do that?

KEN: (*laughing*) I can do that. >>>>>

RACHEL: What's happening now?

KEN: The baby is happy and warm. I can't believe it. >>>>>

RACHEL: [Ken is finished with this resource image.] What's happening now?

KEN: I feel better.

RACHEL: What do you believe about yourself now?

KEN: I feel better. I can feel the baby. I can change the image. I have some power. I have some control over my experience.

RACHEL: How are you doing?

KEN: I can't believe how different I feel from when I first entered this office. (*He hands me an envelope with full payment for ten sessions.*)

RACHEL: (*looking inside the envelope*) Thank you. What do you think it means that you are paying me in full up front?

KEN: It's possible to trust someone and think they can help me.

RACHEL: Anything else? [Is he paying me up front to ensure that I won't abandon him?]

KEN: (*smiling*) I am making sure that I come back and go through with it to the end.

RACHEL: So this is your way to support yourself in doing that?

KEN: I suppose it is.

RACHEL: What's a positive statement you can say about yourself?

KEN: I can do what's right for me. >>>>>

[I am a believer in the power of positive resource development and installation. In my opinion, both processes enhance ego strength, provide clients with a more realistic view of themselves, and help them to connect with their essential goodness and authentic self. I install resources and positive affect tolerance any chance I get.]

RACHEL: I want us to construct a container for all the unresolved emotional stuff that we might have stirred up during the session and not had an opportunity to resolve. (*We came up with a container and installed it so as to help contain unresolved issues.*) Imagine putting any disturbing material that we may have uncovered into that container so that you don't have to carry it around with you. You know that it's in a safe place. And if we need it for next time, we'll use it, and if not, we won't. >>>>>

[Next I did a future template.] Now, when you notice you or the baby feeling lonely, sad, empty, or hollow, imagine holding the baby. >>>>> [I am attempting to create containment and empower Ken, so that he can take action within himself to feel better. Additionally, I want him to begin to differentiate between his adult self and the baby who is the one who needs the comfort and nurturing that heretofore women have provided for him. I am attempting to resource him internally, intending to lay the groundwork for him to experience that the feeling of connection he is seeking and yearning for cannot be found externally. My goal is to help him understand that these connections are inside of him and are *always* with him.]

KEN: That feels good.

RACHEL: When you are feeling the need for comfort and nurturing, or if you feel lonely or sad between sessions, I invite you to see and feel yourself holding the baby, imagine holding the baby and comforting him and helping him to feel better.

I suggested the homework as an invitation so that if there's a part of him that's resistant, it is less likely to be activated. Also, if he isn't able to do the between-session resourcing, he will not feel like he failed at the task. I am gathering information, seeing what he is able to do for himself when he isn't in session.

In order to generate hope and excitement for the work and to enhance rapport, I told Ken that in the next session we would construct resources for processing and perhaps create an ideal mommy. We would start to create the features and characteristics and behaviors of a new mommy so that we could construct a new attachment experience. Ken seemed intrigued, stating that he was looking forward to the next session.

In this first session I used eye movements, using my hand, but in subsequent sessions I used the tappers from the Tac/AudioScan. Ken's high level of emotional expressiveness and crying made the tappers the BLS of choice. Additionally, the tappers had an umbilical cord quality. When I was holding the apparatus, he was holding the tappers and there was a connection, the electrical cord, between us.

Session 2: Using a Metaphor as a Resource

I asked Ken how his week had gone since the last time I saw him. Ken reported that he was feeling a little better, less anxious. He was having less intense, vivid, or specific thoughts about his ex-girlfriend, "Diane," during the day. However, his obsessional thinking was still present at night and worsened right before he went to sleep, making it difficult to get a good night's sleep. His compulsion to go over to Diane's home and to see her was occurring less frequently, but was still occurring. I asked him what helped him to feel less anxious. He said that when he was feeling anxious and empty, he imagined holding the baby and being in the hammock. That seemed to help him calm himself. I asked him what his ability to do that said about him, to which he replied, "I can make a difference within myself. I can change how I am feeling."

He told me that he had noticed he was talking to women he referred to as "big-breasted." I wondered aloud whether he was looking for a new breast, which made him laugh. He said he realized he was attempting to distract himself and "get a new fix." I asked him if he had ever gone a period of time without having some kind of relationship, albeit casual. He thought for a moment and said he did not remember a time when he wasn't having sex with someone and had always cheated on girlfriends, even if it was only a kiss. I asked him why he always cheated. He said that he was critical of the women he was in relationship with and always found something wrong with them. I wondered if this behavior was possibly a reenactment of the relationship with his adoptive mother and a way to avoid the feeling that there was something wrong with him. He wondered how he could ever love someone if he was so critical of the person he was with. He felt "doomed." I asked him if there was something about his behavior that worked for him. He said it kept him searching, dissatisfied, and hurting.

RACHEL: Is that something that feels familiar? [I am attempting to draw parallels to his relationship with his adoptive mother so that he can begin to see that this isn't simply who he is and that he isn't beyond repair.] Maybe when you were young, it helped motivate you to go out and find a new mommy who would be the right mommy and who would provide the connection and contact that you need. That was a great coping strategy then. It helped preserve hope that you would one day be able to fill those needs with someone else. Maybe it's not so helpful now and it's actually ensuring that you won't get your intimacy needs met.

KEN: (*pause*) I guess I need the additional contact. I guess I'm scared. I don't want to give up the insurance of a "backup mommy," I don't want to put all my eggs in one basket. What if I never find the right one?

RACHEL: [I hear his anxiety and possible resistance to change. I need to acknowledge these feelings or the work could be ineffective.] Ken, I know this is scary stuff.

KEN: (*nodding*)

RACHEL: The thing I really like about what we're doing is that we aren't going to take anything away from you. You'll still be able to find and have backup mommies if you want them. What we're going to do is give you some additional "menu options" you can choose from when and if you want them. It will be your choice. It will be like going into a restaurant that has an extensive menu and being able to choose anything on the menu to eat, as opposed to going to a restaurant that has only one item on the menu: cheeseburgers. [I am attempting to reduce resistance to laying down the new template resource of an ideal mother, setting it up as a choice he will have without getting rid of any other backup options.] Perhaps after we develop a narrative of a new mom, you won't need to have backup moms or to criticize your partners to create distance from them. But if you want to, you still can (*smiling*).

KEN: (*smiling back*) I hope I won't want to.

RACHEL: What thoughts come up when you think of your relationship with Diane? [I am attempting to surface his negative cognitions and to show him how his negative beliefs have nothing to do with Diane but with his attachment history.]

KEN: How can relationships be all good and then end all bad and wiped away?

RACHEL: Is there anything else?

KEN: This might sound crazy, but why do you hate me so much? I didn't do anything wrong. I'm not bad. Why are you cutting me off?

RACHEL: (*nodding*)

KEN: There's no one out there for me. My life isn't supposed to be good. (*pause*) I keep trying but things don't work out for me. I am meant to suffer and I have to endure it.

RACHEL: Is that really true? [I gaze at him, attempting to be the best container I can be. There is a heavy energy in the room. I am filled with feelings of pain, sadness, and hopelessness that were not there before Ken started talking about his negative cognitions. Therefore, I am thinking these feelings are what Ken might be feeling.] You're looking sad. (*silence*) What's happening?

KEN: (*looking down*) This is really hard to say. (*silence*) I'm afraid that it will not work out. That in eight [remaining] sessions I will walk out of here and it will be a failure. I have to believe that there's a bigger power. I don't know. Maybe the meaning of life is to suffer. And if I have to suffer, I'll suffer, but promise me I'll go to heaven. I just need to make sense of my life (*starts to cry*).

RACHEL: [Uh-oh, going down a wrong path here. I wanted to work on ideal mom and dad. What should I do now?] Is there an image that comes to mind?

KEN: Yes, I feel like I am out on the ocean, and it will push me around until I can't swim anymore and it will push me where it does. It feels hopeless.

RACHEL: [Whew. Thank goodness. An image I can work with to create a resource. I realize that without attachment roots, this is how Ken might be feeling all of the time, which creates the panic and the need to connect to anyone or anything that passes by in the water.] Ken, I'd like to try something. Is it OK with you if we work with that image? [I had not previously used a client's own metaphor as an image to work with. But, as the client said, we have eight sessions left and I want to do as much resourcing as I can. Also, I use the word *we* to create agreement and partnership with my client and (please pardon the pun) to get them *on board.*]

KEN: Sure.

RACHEL: Can you imagine being out there in the water? Can you describe what's happening?

KEN: Uh, I don't know. (*silence as he closes his eyes*) I'm in the water hanging onto a piece of wood.

RACHEL: What are you needing?

KEN: Not to be in the water. It's wet, cold, and scary.

RACHEL: Do you think it would help if you were in a raft?

KEN: Yes, I think so. I would be able to relax my arms and not be afraid of the sharks.

RACHEL: Imagine that. >>>>> (*We are using the Tac/AudioScan pulsers.*)

RACHEL: What's happening now?

KEN: It feels better, but the raft isn't stable enough for the ocean. I'm getting bounced around out here.

RACHEL: What do you need?

KEN: I need a large boat, maybe one that sleeps six.

RACHEL: Okay, imagine that. >>>>>

RACHEL: What's happening now?

KEN: Better, but not big enough. I need a platform to stand on.

RACHEL: Go with that. >>>>>

KEN: Not good enough. I think that I need a huge ship, a really huge one. That's what I need. Maybe even an army ship (*excited*).

RACHEL: (*smiling*) Imagine that. Make it exactly how you want it to be. >>>>>

KEN: I am on the ship (*closes his eyes . . . pause*). I feel safe (*starts laughing*). Wow. (*Tears are beginning to run down his face. He opens his eyes.*)

RACHEL: [Ken seems to be really taking in his imagined experience.] What's happening now?

KEN: (*silence*) I never feel safe. (*pause*) I feel safe, like something inside is different. Not bottomless. Like I have something I am standing on. I guess I didn't realize that I never felt like I had a place to stand (*trying to find the words*).

RACHEL: What do you mean? Do you mean you feel *grounded*?

KEN: YES! That's what I feel. I am not in free fall, being pushed around by the ocean about to drown. I am on firm, dry land. But it's this huge ship.

RACHEL: That's great! (*He simply looks at me and seems incredulous.*) What do you believe about yourself now?

KEN: I am safe. I'm not in free fall. And on that ship, I'm not stuck. I can go anywhere I want!

RACHEL: Imagine yourself on that huge ship and say "I am safe, I'm not in free fall. I'm not stuck. I can go anywhere I want." >>>>>

RACHEL: [Using BLS, I paired the resource and the positive cognition.] What did you learn about yourself today? [I routinely ask this question post sessions to draw attention to the positive.]

KEN: Maybe I can change things. I can feel safe. What's happening inside me has little to do with Diane and more to do with me. Diane is only the trigger. It's my stuff.

I felt relief after the session because there was more movement. I could sense that Ken felt that way as well. It appeared that something structural and foundational seemed to be shifting. I looked forward to the next session.

Session 3: Constructing a Resource for Peaceful Place and for an Ideal Mom and Dad

Ken arrived for the session on time. I asked him how he'd been since the last session and what he'd noticed. He reported feeling better, less anxious, like there was a support beneath his anxiety, but he wasn't feeling good. He was still not able to concentrate well enough to study. He felt he was obsessing about Diane because he kept imagining her in bed with other men. He noticed that the main content of the good memories he had of Diane were of a sexual nature. Further, he was still feeling the emptiness and hollowness he described in the first session, but the urge to go and see his ex wasn't as pressing and the compulsion to stalk her was reduced. I wondered aloud if the feelings of emptiness and hollowness might be similar to how it might have felt to him as an infant being separated from his mommy, and then again being separated from his foster mother. He said that my statements regarding separation resonated for him. (My intention was to make the unconscious, conscious so that these feelings no longer controlled him.) He said that he was able to imagine holding the baby when he felt these painful feelings and that image was helpful to him.

RACHEL: That's great.

KEN: (*looking at me and nodding his head*) Well, I am still in pain, but I think knowing that, I could comfort the baby, which helped me.

RACHEL: You were your own plastic wrap.

KEN: (*smiling*) Yes, I guess so.

RACHEL: What positive statement can you make about yourself as a result of your being able to do all that?

KEN: I can be my own plastic wrap. It's possible to comfort the baby. Also, I'm not as anxious. I didn't stalk my ex. I am better.

But despite these positive statements of progress, Ken looked sad. I asked him what was happening. He told me about a fear he had. If he was successful and had a healthy relationship, maybe the baby wouldn't end up getting his needs met. I asked him if the baby was currently getting his needs met. He laughed and said no. I told him that the baby was more likely to get his needs met when he (the adult) was in a successful and healthy relationship.

At this point I began to set the stage for the rest of the treatment. My hypothesis was that most of Ken's issues—stalking, emptiness, anxiety, procrastination—were due to attachment ruptures that required repair. Since I had only seven more sessions to work with him, I felt pressured to begin doing the attachment repair via reparenting with an imaginary ideal mother. I chose this approach, as opposed to using the present stalking situation as a springboard event and bridging to the past, because the past injury appeared to be the initial separation and abandonment from his biological mother. Additionally, he never felt bonded to a mother. My goal was to create this relationship resource in his imagination, utilizing BLS, so that he could develop an internal structure of the early infant attachment he would have developed if he had bonded to a mother. I chose the Tac/AudioScan pulsers instead of eye movements so that I would be better able to continue the BLS when he became very emotional during the processing. I used the tappers versus the audio so that I could track whether he was dissociating. I began with an explanation:

"We can't undo the facts of the past—the fact that you were adopted or had the mother and father you had. However, we can create an additional menu option of your choosing, one you would have wished you had, so that we have a competing template . . . almost like laying down an additional musical track. It changes the sound of the single-track music. You can still hear it, but it's much more difficult to focus

on the one track. All things are possible in our imagination. That part of the brain doesn't distinguish between reality and fantasy. What we're talking about is the part of the brain that gets scared at the movies or laughs and cries . . . the part that gets so attached to a character in a film or novel, although we don't know the character 'in reality.'

"We need to establish EMDR resources for processing. You need to choose a mom and a dad with whom you feel a connection and begin to imbue them with the characteristics and traits you would have wanted in a mommy and daddy for your baby."

I then asked Ken if he could think of a calm, soothing, or peaceful place. Not surprisingly, he found it challenging to access such a place. He remembered that when he was young and would go out at night, he would sit on his neighbor's wall, with his legs dangling off the side, and that felt calming to him. [Since he associated that memory with sadness, however, we couldn't use it as a resource.] He stated that there were no places in which he felt comfortable for any length of time. Not surprisingly, he didn't feel at home anywhere. After some exploring, he remembered taking the most comfortable, relaxing nap he'd ever had in a hammock under an oak tree while listening to the rustling leaves. We used that memory as his calm, soothing, peaceful place.

I next asked Ken about parental nurturing figures. I told him that they could be real or imagined, living or deceased. He could not come up with anyone. We began to explore, looking for possibilities. When I inquired about parents of friends, he recalled one friend's parents, "Ann" and "Irv," who were always very kind to him. He remembered that Irv had mentored him and would take him to the movies. He was able to talk to Irv about feeling so badly that he sometimes felt like killing himself. Ann was nurturing and really liked him. Ken liked being with both of them, just sitting in their living room. It felt good. He said that he wanted to choose them as his imagined parents. I felt heartened that he was able to come up with these two people. Then we began to develop and tap in an ideal mother, using his friend's mother, Ann.

RACHEL: Imagine all the qualities that you would want to have in an ideal mom.

KEN: She would be kind, beautiful, fun, happy, playful, patient, spending time with me, teaching me, playing with me, reading to me, taking me places, helping me with homework, smart, educated, warm, loving, affectionate, demonstrative, good, loving relationship with my dad, likes boys.

RACHEL: Can you imagine Ann as your mother having all those wonderful qualities?

KEN: Yes. >>>>>

RACHEL: How was that?

KEN: It felt really good!

RACHEL: Now imagine all the qualities you would want to have in an ideal dad.

KEN: He would be wise, patient, smart, affectionate, happy, kind, playful, fun, plays with me, wrestles with me, teaches me things, takes me places, makes time for me, teaches me about girls, is nice to my mom. Is a success and teaches me to be a success.

RACHEL: Imagine Irv as your father having all these wonderful qualities.

KEN: OK. >>>>>

RACHEL: How was that?

KEN: That felt really good, too.

RACHEL: Let's construct a narrative together of your conception, birth, and childhood with these new parents. Imagine where they live, how much they love each other, how much they want to have this little baby boy together, and how excited they are about being parents and raising this planned, loved, wanted baby together. Imagine them finding out that they're pregnant. Imagine all the wonderful things they would do for the baby and say to the baby while you're in the womb. Imagine all of this. Be as detailed as you want. This is your experience and it is only for you.

KEN: OK, I will (*closes his eyes and talks as he processes*). >>>>>

Ken constructed a narrative filled with love. He imagined his ideal parents singing lullabies to the baby, saying loving things to the baby, telling him that he is wanted and that they can't wait to meet him and know and love him his entire life. He imagined Ann and Irv being loving and in love, wanting to get pregnant, and wishing for a son who was like him. He said that part of him felt sad, though, because they weren't his real parents. "It's not real," he protested. But part of him felt good enough to imagine that he was wanted.

RACHEL: Ken, it doesn't make a difference if what you imagine is real or not. The part of your brain that imagines doesn't necessarily distinguish between fantasy and reality. The good news is that you don't have to believe it's real for the imagery to have a profound internal impact. It's like watching a movie and rooting for the good guys. You know they're not real people, yet your mind and body can imagine their being real, and you can feel for them as if they were real people. [Ken appears to take this in. Yet he seems afraid to have hope that this will work. I was wondering at this point if I should have separated out and placed his sadness in a container or should have simply processed the sadness by having him go with the sadness. I chose a straightforward question:] How did it feel to imagine Ann and Irv as parents and her being pregnant with you?

KEN: It felt good. I liked being inside of her. It feels like I am starting to feel connected to her. I could feel their love.

RACHEL: What positive statement can you make about yourself?

KEN: I am looking forward to my being born and imagining Ann and Irv being my parents. It might be possible to feel OK. >>>>>

Ken wondered what he would do if he wasn't spending so much time thinking about his ex-girlfriend, Diane. I asked what he meant by that statement. He said, "I guess it's my way to feel connected to her, to feel less sad and not alone." I asked him if he thought that might have been how he reacted to the loss of his mothers. I referred to "Marie," the name of his birth mother, and to his foster mother, whose name we did not know. He nodded. I told him that when we finished imagining his new mom and processed the rest of the issues, perhaps he would feel differently. Since it was at the end of the session, I asked him what he could do to feel more connected and less sad. I was attempting to help him take steps to develop resources that would enable him to better self-soothe. He told me that going to the movies and golfing with his friends made him feel better. I asked him what prevented him from planning and doing some of these activities.

KEN: Not a thing.

RACHEL: Would you like to imagine calling your friends and making plans to be with them to do some fun things together this weekend so you feel more connected? [I am creating a future template with him.]

KEN: Yes.

RACHEL: Imagine that. >>>>>

RACHEL: Would it be helpful to imagine being with Ann?

KEN: Yes, I think so.

RACHEL: Imagine that. >>>>>

RACHEL: What about holding the baby when you feel sad?

KEN: Yes. >>>>>

RACHEL: What do you believe about yourself now?

KEN: I can make things different for myself. >>>>>

Session Four: Finishing the Birth

When Ken came in, I noticed that he was holding his body differently. He appeared a bit older, more mature. I looked at Ken and smiled. He smiled in return and sat down.

KEN: I bet you want to know how I've been (*starting off the session playfully*).

RACHEL: Yes I do (*smiling more broadly*).

KEN: (*silence*)

RACHEL: [I realized that he was waiting for me to actually ask him. We both laughed. He was playing with mommy. I played along.] So Ken, how have you been since I saw you last?

KEN: I'm feeling better. I don't want to go over to Diane's. I think of her, but not obsessively. It feels more normal. I feel more normal. I'm feeling better and was able to go to my hammock, hold the baby, and be on my ship to feel safe. I was also able to be with Ann and Irv. I felt less anxious and much calmer.

RACHEL: Wow, that's great! I am so glad. [I am still surprised about how quick and effective this work is.]

KEN: I realized something else. (*pause*) What happened with Diane wasn't my fault. I didn't do anything wrong.

In this statement, Ken wasn't shirking his adult culpability for engaging in stalking behavior. He was referring to the fact that the baby ego state had been updated to the present time frame. That ego state realized that the breakup with Diane wasn't due to his original negative cognitions (i.e., "I'm bad; it's my fault; there's something wrong with me; I am damaged").

RACHEL: [Internally, my jaw drops. The treatment seems to be progressing quickly.] That's a lot of good stuff happening. What positive statement can you make about yourself?

KEN: I'm getting better. It's possible to take care of myself. I feel hopeful. I can feel safe.

RACHEL: Let's get you born.

KEN: Yeah! Can you help me with this?

RACHEL: Of course. I will provide you with a narrative. If I say something that doesn't feel right or you want to add something, please feel free to stop me or to add to what I am saying either out loud or in your imagination. (*I begin the BLS.*) Imagine Ann is whatever you need her to be to have a calm, healthy baby, born in to the environment that would be best for you. Imagine Irv there as well, supporting you both, being a part of it all. Imagine that they tell you what's happening during the birthing process and how excited they are to see you. Imagine a space that is warm with soft lighting. Imagine being born in the hospital or at home into water—it's what you and your baby want and need. Imagine that the water breaks and the labor begins and Ann saying whatever you want to be hearing. Now you are coming out and being placed on her skin and imagine that initial vision of your mommy and how she looks at you with such adoring eyes. Imagine suckling at her breast and her holding you and being swaddled, with Irv there, contributing all his love. Feeling safe, secure, warm, well fed, wanted. Imagine all that and more. (*BLS is going throughout.*)

KEN: (*Tears run down his face.*) What else?

RACHEL: Imagine that all your protectors and guides and nurturers and wise people come out and surround you and bless you (*BLS continuously*). May you be healthy, may you be happy, may you be successful, may you find love, be loved, and may you have good friends. Whatever blessings you would wish to have and wish this baby to have. "May I be fortunate and wise, patient and kind, have good judgment."

KEN: (*picking up the narrative as the BLS continues*) >>>>> They take me home and they love me and all my needs are taken care of. My life is wonderful. I feel full, filled, complete, and whole within myself. I want to be with others because I enjoy it. I don't have to be. I can enjoy my life. I am whole. (*pause, then opens his eyes*)

RACHEL: (*stopping BLS*) If you want to, you can go through your childhood and bring it forward as far as you would like. This is for you and for you alone.

KEN: (*Smiles at me and resumes the narrative with BLS.*) >>>>> I am growing and I am loved. My parents love me and read stories to me and teach me about life. I have friends I play with, and I never feel empty or alone, even when I am by myself. It feels good. My dad teaches me how to play sports and we play together. He shows me by his example how to be a man. My teachers love me and I am popular. I don't use drugs when I grow up. I have intimate relationships with women who are meaningful to me. I am good at anything I set my mind to. I have a serious girlfriend. We have a great relationship. We are deeply in love. I am happy beyond my wildest dreams. I accomplish my goals. I am close to my family and love them very much and feel equally loved. I imagine I get married, have my own children, and do for them what these parents did for me. I help them to feel unique and loved. I take them to play sports, support their interests. I give them everything that they need to feel good and whole. I feel I have everything I need. I feel good, I feel whole. (*Stops and looks at me. I stop the BLS.*)

RACHEL: (*I look back at him. His face is wet from tears of joy and happiness. He takes a very full breath. I wait for him to speak.*)

KEN: I am without words. (*silence as I look at him*) I can't believe what happened and how I feel inside. (*pause*) I feel more whole (*touching his chest*). There's nothing hollow. Nothing empty. Nothing cracked. (*His eyes well up with tears.*) Thank you.

RACHEL: (*My eyes are teary. I cannot speak. He is looking deeply into my eyes and holding my gaze. He was unable to do that in previous sessions. There is a guileless adult man looking back at me. I gesture to him from my chest with my hand and clasp my palms together and slightly bow my head. I am so moved by the power of the work and the courage of the human spirit and the healing ability that is innate in us all.*) I am so deeply moved by you and who you really are. I feel privileged to be here with you. (*I feel him being fully present. He is smiling at me. He looks as if years of angst and pressure have been lifted off his face.*) Ken, I feel uncomfortable asking this in light of how profound and moving this has all been today. Would you like to tap in what you learned about yourself today?

KEN: (*thinks for a moment*) I am whole.

RACHEL: Where do you feel that in your body?

KEN: (*gestures to his chest and heart*)

RACHEL: Let's tap that in. >>>>> I think that's an excellent place to stop.

Session 5: Attachment Wound Regarding Birth Mother Giving Up Ken for Adoption

Ken arrived on time looking more grown up and more present in his body. He was smiling as he sat down. He told me that he was doing much better.

KEN: I never would have believed it would take this short a time to feel this good. Last session was amazing!

RACHEL: What have you noticed?

KEN: I am feeling much less anxiety, and the feeling of hollowness and emptiness seems to be gone. And best of all, I have no desire to stalk Diane. It doesn't seem real. It's hard to believe I ever did that.

The power of EMDR and AF-EMDR is that, as a result of the attachment imagery, his foundation appears to have shifted and has made stalking something that he can no longer imagine doing, or that he has ever done.

RACHEL: That's great! What does that say about you?

KEN: I feel more normal. It's possible to know how to feel safe. I feel full. I am me. >>>>>

RACHEL: Anything else? [I sense that he's not done.]

KEN: I feel more connected within myself and with my friends. I don't feel lonely when I am alone. I decided to stop having sex with one of the women I was having a casual relationship with at work. I was kind to her and didn't simply disappear.

RACHEL: That sounds great.

KEN: But something is still there. I still feel like somehow something is my fault, and I don't know what it is. Diane e-mailed me and acknowledged her responsibility in the relationship. She said some nice things about me and that felt good (*pause . . . looks sad*).

RACHEL: You look sad.

KEN: I don't know, I feel sad (*eyes moisten*). I keep feeling I did something wrong. But a part of me knows that I didn't do anything wrong, but somehow in here (*hand to chest*), I still feel like I did. (*pause*)

RACHEL: (*waiting, sensing something weightier coming*)

KEN: (*looking down*) I keep hearing the words "Why are you hurting me, why are you leaving me?"

RACHEL: [I realize that he has come up with our next target. I am attempting to clarify the target and make it more specific.] Do you know who is saying these words?

KEN: The baby.

RACHEL: Who is the baby telling these words to?

KEN: My [birth] mommy, Mary.

RACHEL: Where are you?

KEN: I don't know.

RACHEL: Close your eyes and go inside. Where are you? [I want him to locate a specific picture of the scene, and part of that scene is to locate himself in a specific place.]

KEN: I have an image of my Mary. We're in the hospital—I was just born. She's holding me. I'm so happy to be with her. I feel something wet on my face. She's crying. (*pause*) But she's not happy, she's sad. She keeps crying. Someone is waiting to take me. She hands me over to this other woman. I don't want to go. I don't want to leave my mommy. I start crying and then I start screaming.

RACHEL: [I have the image, I see the emotions. Ken is collapsed on the couch, touching his chest, so I know where he is feeling the grief and sadness in his body. I don't need to ask him more because the trauma is alive and I do not want to pull him out of his feelings. However, I do want to get the negative cognition associated with this scene.] In that moment, what do you believe about yourself?

KEN: (*speaking to his mom*) I didn't do anything wrong—why are you hurting me? Why are you leaving me? (*crying softly*) I'm not bad. >>>>> I need her to tell me that it's OK, it's not my fault. "I'm a mess and I'm unhealthy and that's why it's better for you not to be with me."

RACHEL: Imagine that. >>>>> What's happening now?

KEN: I'm feeling angry.

RACHEL: Go with that. >>>>>

KEN: The baby is feeling confused and angry, but he's scared to feel angry at his mommy (*crying*). Maybe his mommy is leaving because he's angry. So instead, he thinks it's his fault that his mommy is leaving him. (*pause*) He must be bad.

RACHEL: [It is time for an interweave. The client is going into a loop and appears to be stuck in the negative cognitions "It's my fault" and "I'm bad."] If you heard someone else talking about this circumstance, would you think that the baby was bad and that it was his fault?

KEN: No!

RACHEL: Go with that. >>>>>

KEN: I'm imagining my mommy coming to the foster home everyday while I'm in the foster home (*from birth through 2 months of age*) and telling me that it's not my fault, I'm not bad, and that she didn't give me up because I was bad, it's because of her. It's all her fault.

RACHEL: Go with that. >>>>>

KEN: I need someone to share the pain. My birth mother got what she wanted: to avoid a burden. They all get to go off and be fine [Mom and the ex-girlfriends], and I'm left hurting. Everyone else gets to move on and they are fine. They are deserving and I'm not. I don't deserve it.

RACHEL: What would be helpful right now?

KEN: I need for my mom to tell me that I am not a burden.

RACHEL: Go with that. >>>>>

KEN: (*continuous BLS*) I need for her to tell me that she has never forgotten me or forgiven herself for giving me up, and that she always thinks about me and wishes she could be with me. She regrets giving me up and she wishes she could have been my real mom. She did things wrong and she's sorry. She's telling me there's nothing wrong with me. There was something wrong with her.

RACHEL: Go with that. >>>>> [Ken is creating a healing narrative with his birth mother. We are creating another template for him to draw upon. I'm utilizing BLS the entire time.]

KEN: The reason she gave me up is because she was young and scared. [He is developing some perspective and compassion for his birth mother. Now she speaks to him, through him:] "It's not you—you're OK. I did everything wrong. I am so sorry. I am so sorry I hurt you. You didn't deserve it, you were a beautiful baby. It was all me." (*Ken cries deeply.*)

RACHEL: (*I keep up the BLS. He stops crying and looks at me. He is finished with this piece; it is the end of a channel. I stop the BLS.*) What's happening now?

KEN: I need for her to sit there for a little bit and not leave me yet. I need for her to be there till I'm done. I need to have her there till it sinks in that she didn't leave because of me, because there's something wrong with me. (*crying*)

RACHEL: Imagine that. >>>>>

KEN: (*Again begins to cry, seemingly from the depths of his soul. It is the sound of a deeply hurt child. It feels heartbreaking.*) I needed more time with my mom. I didn't have that and I was left alone. Then I was told "what's wrong with you" when I was sad.

RACHEL: Go with that. >>>>>

KEN: (*starts to wonder aloud*) How long will I need her [his birth mother] to stay before I am ready to go? (*I stop the BLS while Ken is wondering.*) I'm hurting all the time. When will it stop? I'm afraid it's a never-ending bottomless pit.

RACHEL: [I'm sensing Ken's despair—things seem to be getting worse. I decide to do an interweave.] What is it that you need now?

KEN: She's right there and she's not going anywhere till I'm ready to go.

RACHEL: Imagine that. >>>>>

KEN: We're now on the beach. She is there sitting with me. She's looking at me and smiling. She's glad to be with me. She's holding me, rocking me. I'm a baby. It feels calm and peaceful.

RACHEL: Go with that (*listening to Ken's narrative, nodding and tracking him, all the while, doing BLS*).

KEN: (*pause*)

RACHEL: What's happening now?

KEN: I'm getting older. We're playing in the sand, with piles of sand and water. She's helping me build something. She admires what I'm doing. She's telling me I'm a good boy and that I'm doing a good job. We laugh. I get up and move toward her. I'm old enough to walk. She scoops me up. She hugs me, kisses me, and tells me how much she loves me. I squirm out of her arms. I'm ready to separate. She puts me down. I begin to walk away from her. I walk toward the water. I turn around and look back. She's still there (*crying*). I'm playing in the ocean. And she's still there (*crying deeply*). I walk further down the beach and I turn around. She'll be there no matter what. I move toward her; she smiles encouragingly and waves at me. She's not leaving. She's there. I turn and walk away even farther. I can still see her, but she's more distant. She's still there and not moving. She's still smiling and waiting for me. I walk toward her and she smiles even more. She is happy to see me. I walk to a place where I can still see her, but out of her sight. I know she's still waiting for me.

RACHEL: [I am amazed to realize that Ken is intuitively acting out the developmental stages of object constancy, object permanence, as well as the developmental stage of rapprochement. Stopping BLS.] What's happening now?

KEN: I'm going far away. I'm getting older and bigger. I'm meeting other people. I can go and do other things, knowing that the person is there [generalizing these new internalized experienced stages of development]. I don't see her, but I know that she's there.

RACHEL: (*nodding*) Go with that. >>>>>

KEN: I go back to her and she is still there [on the beach] saying "No matter how long it takes, I am there for you" (*opens his eyes*).

RACHEL: (*stopping BLS*) What's happening now?

KEN: I want to hold onto that image of her still being there. She's mine. She's not there for anyone else.

RACHEL: Go with that. >>>>>

KEN: (*opens his eyes, then closes them again*) I'm in kindergarten, grade school, in high school, I'm dating. I'm in college. I'm in law school. I do well. I'm successful. I have friends. I meet a woman I love. We have a family. I'm a good, loving father. I feel loved. (*opens his eyes, smiling, face damp with tears*)

RACHEL: [Stopping BLS] What's happening now?

KEN: Nothing. (*pause*) I'm feeling afraid that this won't last; that I won't be able to hold on to the picture of Mary being there.

RACHEL: [Ken is doubting his ability to maintain an internal sense of object constancy and object permanence.] Would it help if we placed the fear in a container till next time?

KEN: It might.

RACHEL: Imagine that. >>>>>

RACHEL: [I want to provide Ken with a resource option he can do on his own. I give him a future template of being able to resource himself with the soothing and comforting image of Mary being there for him, no matter what, so that he doesn't feel so alone.] What if you were to imagine Mary being there and waiting for you when you wake up and feel anxious, or before you go to sleep, to help you fall asleep, and whenever else you feel you need her to be there?

KEN: That would be great.

RACHEL: Imagine that. >>>>>

RACHEL: Anything you want to add?

KEN: No. It feels done.

RACHEL: What do you believe about yourself now?

KEN: (*thinking for a few seconds*) I'm happy. I'm loved. I'm lovable. It wasn't my fault. There's nothing wrong with me. I'm OK. I can feel connected.

RACHEL: Pair those beliefs with the picture of you as a baby right after your birth. >>>>>

KEN: (*silence*)

RACHEL: How are you doing?

KEN: Wow. (*pause . . . shaking his head*) There are no words. That was unbelievable.

RACHEL: Yeah. It's like you redid your childhood with your birth mom and got to separate from her and leave her when you were ready. Not the other way around. How are you doing?

KEN: I feel different inside (*searching for words*). More whole. Calmer. I don't feel as alone (*touches chest*). It feels like that hole [in the chest] and that emptiness are gone.

RACHEL: That's great. [I have no idea how to end this session. It occurs to me to do a future template.] Imagine yourself this week living your life and feeling that way.

KEN: (*Nods and closes his eyes.*) >>>>>

RACHEL: I'm really looking forward to hearing how things are for you when I see you next time.

Sessions Six to Ten: Attachment Figure Consolidation and Permission to Stop Procrastinating and Succeed

In the next session Ken reported feeling markedly less anxious and stated that his obsessional thinking and compulsive behavior with regard to Diane were gone. He no longer experienced body sensations while going past her house during the course of his daily life. He thought about her, but it seemed more normal. He had ended his casual relationship with his fellow intern, as he felt it was unfair to string her along, and he did not feel that he needed her to be his "mommy replacement." He had begun dating someone he knew and liked, but was taking it very slowly, without any unrealistic expectations. "I'm not going down that road anymore." When the woman didn't return his phone call immediately, he didn't become anxious and obsessive. He could be more objective and see his fear of abandonment, but he didn't let it overtake him and paralyze him as he had done before. He had the tools to take control of his feelings. He was able to see that these were old feelings triggered in the present, but had no connection to what was in fact happening within the current relationship.

Instead of the unhealthy behaviors, he was able to soothe himself with self-talk that everyone has a busy life and she would get back to him when she had the time. When he felt bad, he would bring up the resources of the baby, Ann, and Mary to help comfort him. He stated that he was able to fall asleep and remain asleep all night long, and his ability to concentrate was much improved.

Ken spoke about the helpfulness and power of visualizing the image of Mary on the beach, being there as long as he needed her and whenever he needed her. He felt that internalizing the state expressed by his words "I need her to be there till I'm ready to go" was one of the key factors to his ability to repair his feelings of abandonment by her.

For all the remaining sessions, we continued to check on the work done on the abandonment and stalking behavior, which had brought him into treatment. He reported how he was feeling in his current relationships and about Diane, noting that his original symptoms had completely disappeared and that he felt like a different person. He was in disbelief that he had ever behaved in that way. This shift in perspective is consistent with the ego-syntonic foundational shifts resulting from the use of EMDR and from AF-EMDR therapy. Additionally we reinforced his nurturing and self-soothing resources for feeling secure, relaxed, and loved and his ability to track his emotions and body sensations.

During sessions seven, eight, and part of nine, we worked on Ken's self-destructive procrastination behavior that was preventing him from studying and passing his bar exam. Bridging back from the image of the most recent time he procrastinated when attempting to study for the exam, we uncovered two early incidents with his father and the accompanying negative cognitions. These were processed in our last three sessions. Ken reported an increased ability to focus and concentrate on his studying, a decrease in procrastination behavior, and stated he was looking forward to taking the exam, passing it, and moving forward with his life.

In part of session nine we reviewed what we had accomplished. Surprisingly, we had accomplished most of what we set out to do: Reduce or eliminate stalking behavior; reduce or eliminate depression and anxiety; and reduce or eliminate procrastination in studying for the bar exam. We reinforced all these accomplishments with positive cognitions and future templates. Parts of sessions nine and ten were used for termination and further consolidation of the work that was done. We agreed that he would let me know periodically what was happening so that we could evaluate and monitor the effectiveness of the treatment.

FOLLOW-UP

Ken kept his promise—he has checked in with me periodically over the past 5 years. He was able to study for and to pass the bar exam on his first try. He has worked for the same prestigious law firm for the past 5 years. He was recently offered a partnership position within the law firm, which he accepted. Ken stated that he felt confident, successful, connected within himself and within his intimate relationships. His friendships continue to be strong. He still felt that he had little in common with his adoptive family, but in a way that seemed more accepting of them both. He did not think this lack of connection was due to the belief that "there is something wrong with me." He has been able to appreciate his adoptive parents' positive qualities and the ways they have helped him become the man he is today.

He reported having been in a loving, committed, live-in relationship for 3 years, which had ended 6 months prior to our sessions. When she broke up with him, his heart was broken. However, he did not feel the need to stalk her. He reported feeling the typical grief any normal person would have felt, which resolved itself in good time. It turned out that she was cheating on him. He felt devastated when he found out. However, he stated that he had the internal resources and support needed to weather this pain and was able to bounce back within a normal time frame. He had tremendous insight about the relationship and was able to take responsibility for his part in what had occurred.

He reported that the part of the treatment that appeared to have made the most difference in his healing and recovery, and has stayed with him, was the construction of the ideal mother, as well as imagining being loved by his birth mother, going through all the developmental stages, and being the one to leave her on his timeline, not hers. I felt honored and blessed to witness and learn from Ken's healing and integration. I would not have believed that 10 sessions would have been a sufficient amount of time to implement the repair that was needed in this case.

References

Abdulbaghi, A., & Sundelin-Wahlsten, V. (2008). Applying EMDR on children with PTSD. *European Child and Adolescent Psychiatry, 17*(3), 127–132.

Alexander, F. (1961). *The scope of psychoanalysis.* New York, NY: Basic Books.

Alexander, F., & French, T. M. (1946). *Psychoanalytic therapy: Principles and application.* New York, NY: Ronald Press.

American Psychological Association Presidential Task Force on Evidence-Based Practice. (2006). Evidence-based practice in psychology. *American Psychologist, 61,* 271–285.

Amini, F., Lewis, T., Lannon, R., Louie, A., Baumbacher, G., McGuinness, T., et al. (1996). Affect, attachment, memory: Contributions toward psychobiologic integration. *Psychiatry, 59,* 213–239.

Andrade, J., Kavanagh, D., & Baddeley, A. (1997). Eye-movements and visual imagery: A working memory approach to the treatment of post-traumatic stress disorder. *British Journal of Clinical Psychology, 36,* 209–223.

Bowlby, J. (1969). *Attachment and loss, Vol. 1: Attachment.* New York, NY: Basic Books.

Castonguay, L. G., Goldfried, M. R., Wiser, S., Raue, P. J., & Hayes, A. M. (1996). Predicting the effect of cognitive therapy for depression: A study of unique and common factors. *Journal of Consulting and Clinical Psychology, 64,* 497–504.

Chartrand, T. L., & Bargh, J. A. (1999). The chameleon effect: The perception–behavior link and social interaction. *Journal of Personality and Social Psychology, 76*(6), 893–910.

Esch, T., & Stefano, G. (2005). The neurobiology of love. *Neuroendocrinology Letters, 26*(3), 175–192.

Field, T., Morrow, C., Valdeon, C., Larson, S., Kuhn, C., & Schanberg, S. (1992). Massage reduces depression and anxiety in child and adolescent psychiatric patients. *Journal of the American Academy of Child and Adolescent Psychiatry, 31,* 125–131.

Field, T., Figueiredo, B., Hernandez-Reif, M., Diego, M., Deeds, O., & Ascencio, A. (2008). Massage therapy reduces pain in pregnant women, alleviates prenatal depression in both parents and improves their relationships. *Journal of Bodywork Movement Therapy, 12*(2), 146–150.

Forgash, C. (Ed.). (2008). *Healing the heart of dissociation with EMDR.* New York, NY: Springer.

Fosha, D. (2000). *The transforming power of affect.* New York, NY: Basic Books.

Fosha, D., Siegel, D., & Solomon, M. (2009). *The healing power of emotion.* New York, NY: Norton.

Freud, S. (1913). *The interpretation of dreams.* New York, NY: Macmillan.

Goldstein, J. (1976). *The experience of insight.* Boulder, CO: Shambhala.

Hammer, E. (1990). *Reaching the affect: Style in the psychodynamic therapies.* Northvale, NJ: Jason Aronson.

Harner, M. (1980). *The way of the shaman.* New York, NY: Bantam.

Havens, L. (1979). Explorations in the uses of language in psychotherapy: Complex empathic statements. *Psychiatry, 42*, 40–44.

Hayes, S. C., Barlow, D. H., & Nelson-Gray, R. O. (1999). *The scientist practitioner: Research and accountability in the age of managed care* (2nd ed.). Boston, MA: Allyn & Bacon.

Henry, W. P., Schacht, T. E., Strupp, H. H., Butler, S. F., & Binder, J. L. (1993). Effects of training in time-limited dynamic psychotherapy: Changes in therapist behavior. *Journal of Consulting and Clinical Psychology, 61*, 434–440.

Herman, J. L. (1992). *Trauma and recovery.* New York, NY: Basic Books.

Hertenstein, M. J. (2011). The communicative functions of touch in adulthood. In M. Hertenstein & S. Weiss, (Eds.), *The handbook of touch: Neuroscience, behavioral, and applied perspectives.* New York, NY: Springer.

Hertenstein, M. J., & Weiss, S. J. (Eds.). (2011). *The handbook of touch: Neuroscience, behavioral, and applied perspectives.* New York: Springer Publications.

Huppert, J. D., Bufka, L. F., Barlow, D. H., Gorman, J. M., Shear, M. K., & Woods, S.W. (2001). Therapists, therapist variables, and cognitive–behavioral therapy outcome in a multicenter trial for panic disorder. *Journal of Consulting and Clinical Psychology, 69*, 747–755.

Hughes, D. (2005). Psychological treatment within relationships: Attachment and intersubjectivity. *British Journal of Play Therapy, 1*, 4–9.

Hughes, D. (2007). *Attachment-focused family therapy.* New York, NY: Norton.

Jarero, I., Artigas, L., & Hartung, J. (2006). EMDR integrative group treatment protocol: A post-disaster trauma intervention for children and adults. *Traumatology, 12*(2), 121–129.

Jarero, I., Artigas, L., López Cano, T., Mauer, M., & Alcalá, N. (1999, November). *Children's post traumatic stress after natural disasters: Integrative treatment protocol.* Poster presented at the annual meeting of the International Society for Traumatic Stress Studies, Miami, FL.

Jung, C. (1961). *Memories, dreams, reflections*. New York, NY: Random House.

Kabat-Zinn, J. (1990). *Full catastrophe living: Using the wisdom of your body and mind to face stress, pain, and illness*. New York, NY: Dell.

Kavanagh, D. J., Freese, S., Andrade, J., & May, J. (2001). Effects of visuo-spatial tasks on desensitization to emotive memories. *British Journal of Clinical Psychology, 40*, 267–280.

Korn, D. (2009). EMDR and the treatment of complex PTSD: A review. *Journal of EMDR Practice and Research, 3*(4), 264–278.

Kornfield, J. (1993). *A path with heart: A guide through the perils and promises of spiritual life*. New York, NY: Bantam.

Kurtz, R. (1990). *Body-centered psychotherapy: The Hakomi method—the integrated use of mindfulness, nonviolence, and the body*. Mendocino, CA: LifeRhythm.

Lambert, M. J., & Barley, D. E. (2001). Research summary on the therapeutic relationship and psychotherapy outcome. *Psychotherapy, 38*(4), 357–361.

Lambert, M. J., Harmon, C., Slade, K., Whipple, J. L., & Hawkins, E. J. (2005). Providing feedback to psychotherapists on their patients' progress: Clinical results and practice suggestions. *Journal of Clinical Psychology, 61*, 165–174.

Leeds, A., & Korn, D. (1998, July). *Clinical applications of EMDR in the treatment of adult survivors of childhood abuse and neglect*. Workshop presented at EMDRIA conference, Baltimore, MD.

Leeds, A., & Shapiro, F. (2000). EMDR and resource installation: Principles and procedures for enhancing current functioning and resolving traumatic experiences. In J. Carlson & L. Sperry (Eds.), *Brief therapy strategies with individuals and couples*. Phoenix, AZ: Zeig/Tucker.

Levine, P. (1997). *Waking the tiger*. Berkeley, CA: North Atlantic Books.

Lewis, T., Amini, F., & Lannon, R. (2000). *A general theory of love*. New York, NY: Random House.

Maiberger, B. (2009). *EMDR essentials*. New York, NY: Norton.

Main, M. (1992). Attachment: Overview with implications for clinical work. In S. Goldberg, R. Muir, & J. Kerr (Eds.), *Attachment theory: Social, developmental and clinical perspectives* (pp. 407–474). Hillsdale, NJ: Erlbaum.

Main, M., & Solomon, J. (1986). Discovery of an insecure disorganized/disoriented attachment pattern: Procedures, findings and implications for the classification of behavior. In T. Brazelton & M. Yogman (Eds.), *Affective development in infancy* (pp. 95–124). Norwood, NJ: Ablex.

Main, M., & Solomon, J. (1990). Procedures for identifying infants as disorganized/disoriented during the Ainsworth Strange Situation. In M. Greenberg, D. Cicchetti, & E. Cummings (Eds.), *Attachment in the preschool years: Theory, research and intervention* (pp. 161–182). Chicago, IL: University of Chicago Press.

Manfield, P. (2010). *Dyadic resourcing*. On Demand Publishing: Amazon.com.

Marich, J. (2011). *EMDR made simple*. Eau Claire, WI: Premier Publishing & Media.

Martinez, R.A. (1991). Innovative uses. *EMDR Network Newsletter, 1*, 5–6.

McFarlane, A. C. (1992). Avoidance and intrusion in posttraumatic stress disorder. *Journal of Nervous and Mental Disease, 180*, 439–445.

Miller, A. (1981). *The drama of the gifted child*. New York, NY: Basic Books.

Miller, S. D., Duncan, B. L., & Hubble, M. A. (2005). Outcome-informed clinical work. In J. C. Norcross & M. R. Goldfried (Eds.), *Handbook of psychotherapy integration* (2nd ed., pp. 84–102). London: Oxford University Press.

Monk Kidd, S. (2002). *The secret life of bees*. New York, NY: Penguin/Putnam.

Ogden, P., Minton, K., & Pain, C. (2006). *Trauma and the body: A sensorimotor approach to psychotherapy*. New York: Norton.

Omaha, J. (2004). *Psychotherapeutic interventions for emotion regulation*. New York, NY: Norton.

Orlinski, D. E., Grave, K., & Parks, B. K. (1994). Process and outcome in psychotherapy. In A. E. Bergin & S. L. Garfield (Eds.), *Handbook of psychotherapy* (pp. 257–310). New York, NY: Wiley.

O'Shea, K. (2009). The EMDR early trauma protocol. In R. Shapiro (Ed.), *EMDR Solutions II* (pp. 313–335). New York, NY: Norton.

Pace, P. (2012). *Lifespan integration: Ego states through time* (5th ed.). Roslyn, WA: Lifespan Integration (http://www.lifespanintegration.com/p).

Parnell, L. (1996). Eye movement desensitization and reprocessing (EMDR) and spiritual unfolding. *Journal of Transpersonal Psychology, 28*, 129–153.

Parnell, L. (1998). Postpartum depression: Helping a new mother to bond. In P. Manfield (Ed.), *Extending EMDR: A casebook of innovative applications* (pp. 37–64). New York, NY: Norton.

Parnell, L. (1999). *EMDR in the treatment of adults abused as children*. New York, NY: Norton.

Parnell, L. (2007). *A therapist's guide to EMDR: Tools and techniques for successful treatment*. New York, NY: Norton.

Parnell, L. (2008). *Tapping in: A step-by-step guide to activating your healing resources with bilateral stimulation*. Boulder, CO: Sounds True.

Parnell, L. (2010). *Attachment-focused EMDR*. San Francisco, CA: R. Cassidy Seminars.

Parnell, L., & Phillips, M. (2012). *Attachment-focused EMDR* [teleseminar].

Phillips, M. (1997a, July). *The importance of ego strengthening with EMDR*. Paper presented at the EMDRIA Conference, San Francisco, CA.

Phillips, M. (1997b, November). *The importance of ego strengthening with dissociative disorder patients*. Paper presented at the 14th international fall conference of the International Society for the Study of Dissociation, Montreal, Canada.

Porges, S. W. (2011). *The polyvagal theory: Neurophysiological foundations of emotions, attachment, communications, and self-regulation*. New York, NY: Norton.

Rolls, E. T., O'Doherty, J. O., Kringelbach, M. L., Francis, S., Bowtell, R., & McGlone, F. (2003). Representations of pleasant and painful touch in the human orbitofrontal and cingulate cortices. *Cerebral Cortex, 13*, 308–317.

Rossman, M. L. (1987). *Healing yourself: A step-by-step program for better health through imagery*. New York, NY: Walker.

Russell, M. C. (2008). War-related medically unexplained symptoms, prevalence, and treatment: Utilizing EMDR within the armed services. *Journal of EMDR Practice and Research, 2*(3), 212–225.

Schmidt, S. J. (2002). *Developmental needs meeting strategy for EMDR therapists*. San Antonio, TX: DNMS Institute.

Schmidt, S. J. (2009). *Developmental needs meeting strategy*. San Antonio, TX: DNMS Institute.

Schore, A. (2000, September). *The neurobiology of attachment and the origin of self: Implications for theory and clinical practice*. Paper presented at the annual meeting of the EMDRIA, Toronto, Ontario, Canada.

Schore, A. (2001). The effects of early relational trauma on right brain development, affect regulation, and infant mental health. *Infant Mental Health Journal, 22*(1/2), 201–269.

Schore, A. (2003). Early relational trauma, disorganized attachment, and the development of a predispositon to violence. In M. Solomon & D. J. Siegel (Eds.), *Healing trauma* (pp. 107–167). New York, NY: Norton.

Schore, A. (2005). Attachment, affect regulation, and the developing right brain: Linking developmental neuroscience to pediatrics. *Pediatrics in Review, 26*, 204–211.

Schore, A. (2009, August). *Part I: Right brain affect regulation—an essential mechanism of development, trauma, dissociation and psychotherapy*. Plenary at the annual meeting of the EMDRIA, Atlanta, GA.

Schore, A. (2011). *The science of the art of psychotherapy*. New York, NY: Norton.

Schore, A., & Schore, J. (2008). Modern attachment theory: The central role of affect regulation in development and treatment. *Clinical Social Work Journal, 36*, 9–20.

Selhub, E. M. (2009). *The love response*. New York, NY: Ballantine Books.

Shapiro, F. (1995). *Eye movement desensitization and reprocessing*. New York, NY: Guilford Press.

Shapiro, F. (2001). *Eye movement desensitization and reprocessing* (2nd ed.). New York, NY: Guilford Press.

Shapiro, F., & Silk-Forrest, M. (1997). *EMDR: The breakthrough "eye movement" therapy for overcoming anxiety, stress, and trauma*. New York, NY: Basic Books.

Shapiro, R. (Ed.). (2005). *EMDR solutions: Pathways to healing*. New York, NY: Norton.

Sharpley, C. F., Montgomery, I. M., & Scalzo, L. A. (1996). Comparative efficacy of EMDR and alternative procedures in reducing the vividness of mental images. *Scandinavian Journal of Behaviour Therapy, 25*, 37–42.

Siegel, D. J. (2007, September). *The mindful brain: Reflection and attunement in the cultivation of well-being*. Paper presented at the annual meeting of the EMDRIA, Dallas, TX.

Steele, A. (2007). *Developing a secure self*. Gabriola, BC, Canada: Author.

Stern, D. N. (2005). Intersubjectivity. In E. S. Persomn, A. M. Cooper, & G. O. Gabbard (Eds.), *Textbook of psychoanalysis* (pp. 77–92). Washington, DC: American Psychiatric Publishing.

Stern, D. N. (May, 2008). The clinical relevance of infancy: A progress report. *Infant Mental Health Journal, 29*(3), 177–188.

Stockett, K. (2009). *The help*. New York, NY: Putnam.

van der Kolk, B. (2001). Trauma and PTSD: Aftermaths of the WTC disaster—an interview with Bessel A. van der Kolk, MD. *Medscape General Medicine, 3*(4).

Watkins, J. G. (1971). The affect bridge: A hypnoanalytic technique. *International Journal of Clinical and Experimental Hypnosis, 19*, 21–27.

Watkins, J. G. (1990). Watkin's affect or somatic bridge. In D. C. Hammond (Ed.), *Handbook of hypnotic suggestions and metaphors* (pp. 523–524). New York, NY: Norton.

Watts, A. (1951). *The wisdom of insecurity: A message for an age of anxiety*. New York, NY: Pantheon Books.

Wesselmann, D., & Potter, A. (2009). Change in adult attachment status following treatment with EMDR: Three case studies. *Journal of EMDR Practice and Research, 3*(3), 190–200.

Wildwind, L. (1993, March). *Chronic depression*. Workshop presentation at the EMDR conference, Sunnyvale, CA.

Winnicott, D. W. (1971). The use of an object and relating through identifications. In *Playing and reality* (pp. 76-93). Harmondsworth, UK: Penguin.

Winnicott, D. W. (1975). *Through paediatrics to psychoanalysis*. New York, NY: Basic Books.

Wolpe, J. (1991). *The practice of behavior therapy* (4th ed.). New York, NY: Pergamon.

Zaghrout-Hodali, M., Ferdoos, A., & Dodgson, P. (2008). Building resilience and dismantling fear: EMDR group protocol with children in an area of ongoing trauma. *Journal of EMDR Practice and Research, 2*(2), 106–113.

Index

In this index, *b* denotes box and *f*
denotes figure.

Symbols
>>>>>, explanation of, xxiii

AAI. *See* Adult Attachment Interview
  (AAI)
abandonment, history of
  in "Aliyah" case example, 333–35
  in "Ken" case example, 345, 346,
    347
  in "Mary" case example, 161, 169,
    288, 289, 293–96
  See also relational trauma
Abdulbaghi, A., 13
abreactions
  eye movements (EMs) and, 147
  handholding and, 150–51
  interweaves during, 234
  movement during, 224
  support people and, 153
  tapping in during, 148
  therapist skill and, 11
  therapist talking during, 208–9
abuse. *See* childhood abuse, history of;
  relational trauma
accelerated experiential-dynamic
  psychotherapy, 119
action figures, 61
active imagination, 82
  See also guided imagery; imagination
adaptive coping efforts, 122–23
adaptive information processing (AIP)
  model, 19, 183

ADD. *See* attention-deficit disorder
  (ADD)
ADHD. *See* attention-deficit/hyper-
  activity disorder (ADHD)
adjunctive therapists, 54, 153, 160–173,
  162–64, 288–320
Adult Attachment Interview (AAI), 7,
  140
adult self
  as nurturing figure, 55
  as protector figure, 60, 61,
    62*b*–63*b*
  See also child self and adult self
    relationships
AF-EMDR. *See* attachment-focused
  EMDR (AF-EMDR)
affect bridging, 175
affect management. *See* desensitization; therapeutic containers
affect tolerance
  countertransference management
    and, 41
  distancing techniques and, 153
  importance of, 39–40
  information gathering and, 143
  interweave pitfalls and, 233–34
  therapeutic containers and, 155
  See also charge, emotional
Aibileen (*The Help*), 54, 125
AIP model. *See* adaptive information
  processing (AIP) model
alcoholism, case example concerning,
  264–271
Alexander, F., 17–18
"Aliyah" (case example), 321–340

ambivalent and preoccupied attachment, 9–10
American Psychological Task Force on Evidence-Based Practice, 12–13, 17
Amini, F., 32
angels, 54, 61, 126, 259–260, 261, 262, 349
animals
    interweave use of, 276–284
    as part of safe place, 168, 169
    as resource figures, 55, 61
    in treatment sessions, 153
    See also pets
anorexia. *See* eating disorders, case example of
anxiety
    ambivalent and preoccupied attachment and, 9, 10
    case examples of, 70–72, 256–264, 321–340
    in children, 142
art
    as a closure tool, 193–94
    pacing of treatment sessions and, 201
    progress reevaluation through, 199
    safe or peaceful place enhanced through, 47, 50–51, 51*b*
Artemis Rising Foundation, 27
attachment
    four S's of, xiii
    lack of, 124–25
    neurophysiological responses within, 107
attachment figure consolidation, 370–72
attachment figures, 140–42
    See also resources and resource figures
attachment-focused EMDR (AF-EMDR)
    definition of, 5
    principles of, 12–28, 29*f*
    See also case examples

attachment repair, therapist's, 30–31, 315–17
attachment-repair resources. *See* resources and resource figures
attachment styles, 7–11, 124–25
attention-deficit disorder (ADD), 142
attention-deficit/hyperactivity disorder (ADHD), 142
attunement
    client safety created through, 15–16, 138–39
    during desensitization waves, 207–8
    eye contact and, 152, 204
    grounded spacious, 205–6
    interweaves and, 231
    nonverbal, 31–32
    nonverbal communication, 35–36
    as a resource, 119, 122
    tapping in and, 148–49
    target creation and development and, 187
    See also various case examples
attunement capacity, 31–33, 33
August (*The Secret Life of Bees*), 56
authenticity capacity, 36
avoidant attachment, 8–9, 346

babies. *See* infants
Bargh, J., 32
behaviors, problematic, 178
beliefs. *See* blocking beliefs, checking for; blocking beliefs, resources for; negative beliefs; positive cognitions
Big Mama. *See* "Mary" (case example)
bilateral stimulations (BLS)
    avoidant attachment and, 9
    blocked processing and, 217
    bridging techniques and, 177*b*, 178*b*
    desensitization and, 204, 205, 207
    in EMDR-M, 181, 182
    exploration of issues and, 171
    forms of, xxiii, 25, 146–49
    frequency and pace for, 25–26, 75
    grief and, 111

history taking and, 141
imagination and, 22, 25
metaphor use and, 154
precautions for, 27, 207
probing statements and, 315
as resource stimulation, 19, 22
safe or peaceful place and, 47–48,
    167–68, 169
in standard EMDR protocol, 180
symbols for, xxiii
tapping in as pun for, 20
during therapeutic relationship, 119
See also right-brain activation; Tac/
    AudioScan; tapping in; *various
    case examples*
bingeing, 178
See also eating disorders, case
    example of
birth traumas, 80–92, 362–64
blocked, in processing, 216–231, 232
See also getting stuck, prevention of
blocking beliefs, checking for, 217–221
blocking beliefs, resources for, 21,
    131–34
See also negative beliefs
body experience sensitivity, 33–35, 41
body scan
    changing location of, 187
    EMDR-M and, 28, 29b, 182, 183b,
        187, 188b
    standard EMDR protocol and, 180,
        181b
    See also various case examples
body sensations
    blocked processing and, 218, 222–24
    bridging techniques and, 175–76,
        177b, 178
    disorganized and unresolved trauma
        or loss and, 10
    EMDR-M and, 29b, 181, 182
    grounded spacious attunement and,
        205
    memories of healthy relating and,
        121
    positive imagery and, 53b
    protector figures and, 64

in standard EMDR protocol, 179,
    180
SUDS and, 187
unconscious mind and, 7
validation of personal reality, as an
    interweave, and, 240–41
without target development, 186
in yoga, xix
See also body experience sensitivity;
    sensory activation
bonding, 32
books, as a resource, 125–26
See also specific titles
books, as therapeutic containers, 155
boundaries, healthy, 123–24, 318, 348
boundary-maintenance capacity, 37
Bowlby, J., xix, 16
bridging techniques, 84, 175–76, 176b–
    78b, 178–79
Brightman, H., 27
Buddha, xviii, 126
Buddhism, xviii
bulimia. *See* eating disorders, case
    example of
butterfly hug, 25, 108, 114

"Carla" (case example), 271–76
case examples
    adjunctive therapists, 160–173,
        288–320
    alcoholism, 264–271
    anxiety, 70–72, 124–25, 256–264,
        321–340
    childhood abuse history, 34–35, 54,
        95–106, 239, 242–43, 246–47,
        250–51, 271–76
    depression, 124–25, 271–76, 341–372
    developmental deficits repair,
        92–106, 321–340
    early attachment trauma, 160–173,
        288–372
    eating disorders, 321–340
    empathic resonance, 34–35, 54
    enmeshed mother, 246–47, 271–76
    ideal father, 99–106
    lack of attachment, 124–25

open-ended question, 239
panic attacks, 341–372
preparation of client for
    EMDR,160–173
PTSD, 271–76, 321–340
rejection history, 92–94, 160–173,
    288–320
split-screen interweave, 250–51
stalking behavior, 341–372
"What do you know to be true?,"
    242–43
"Cassie" (case example), 92–94
cats, 55, 281–84
censoring precautions, 177b, 181, 182
chair arrangements. *See* seating
    arrangements
challenging life situation, resources for,
    131–34
channels of association, 211, 217
    See also looping; memory networks;
    target creation and development
charge, emotional
    bridging techniques and, 177b
    distancing techniques and, 153–54
    EMDR-M benefit and, 186b
    as focus for processing, 210–11,
    213
    hand holding and, 204
    interweaves and decrease in, 231
    target creation and development and
    lack of, 9, 21, 73, 124
    therapeutic containers and, 143,
    296–97
    See also body scan; body sensations
Chartrand, T., 32
Charvat, M., 27
child development knowledge, 42, 81
childhood abuse, history of
    ADD and ADHD symptoms and,
    142
    case examples with, 34–35, 54,
    95–106, 242–43, 246–47, 250–51,
    271–76
    lack of positive memories and, 120
childhood information gathering,
    141–42

child self and adult self relationships
    assessment and development of,
    59–60
    blocked processing and, 220, 221–22
    dependent family members and,
    245–47
    ideal mother interweave and, 78–79
    interweaves and, 56, 59, 230–31, 236,
    237–38, 239, 253–54
    nurturing figures and, 172, 190
    positive cognitions and, 334–35
    protector figures and, 169–171, 190
    safe or peaceful place and, 168
    See also inner child loving-kindness
    meditations
choice/control, as a blocking belief,
    220–21
circle of inner helpers, 68–72, 69b
circle of love, 111, 112b
circle of protection, 65, 65b, 169
client-centered therapy
    as an AF-EMDR principle, 18–19
    BLS and, 147
    desensitization attunement and,
    204–6
    dual awareness and, 208–9
    EBPP in, 12–14
    EMDR-M and, 27–28
    interweave pitfalls and, 234–35,
    244–45
    pacing of treatment sessions and,
    200–202
    rigidity in EMDR protocols and, 12
    standard EMDR protocol versus,
    179
clients
    avoidance of categorizing, 7–8
    censoring precautions for, 177b, 181,
    182
    EMDR and preparation of, 139, 143,
    145–157, 160–173
    empowerment of, 67, 145, 220, 234,
    249
    experiencing feeling by, 233–34
    gay and lesbian, 83
    narrative coherence of, 140

as protector figures, 64
talking as choice of, 204–5, 208
between treatment session suggestions for, 194–96
See also case examples
client safety
during abreactions, 208–9
as an AF-EMDR principle, 14–16, 27–28, 138–39
birth trauma repair and, 83–92
blocked processing and, 225–27
BLS and, 20
distancing techniques and, 15, 153–54
dual awareness and, 208–9
eye contact and, 152, 204
eyes closed and, 147
healthy boundaries and, 123–24
incomplete sessions and, 188–89
memory chaining, prevention of, and, 156
negative memories and, 26
neglect history and, 219
nonverbal communication and, 15, 82
positive cognitions and, 191
positive neuro networks and, 23
relationship repair and creation of, 17
resource reinstallation and, 157
safe touch and, 5, 148–49, 150–52
seating arrangements and, 149
See also ego strength; safe or peaceful place; trust
closure
art as a tool for, 193–94
ending treatment sessions without, 188–89, 196b–97b
guided imagery as a tool for, 192–93
interweaves as, 189–191, 217, 235–36, 253–54
love resources as a tool for, 194
positive cognition or image installation for, 191
cognitive interweaves. *See* interweaves

co-mothers, 78
complicity, 221, 239
conception, 80–83
conflict-free images, 52, 53b
consultation, for therapists, 41
See also adjunctive therapists
containers. *See* therapeutic containers
control, within traumatic memories, 127, 153–54
See also choice/control, as a blocking belief
coping efforts, 122–23
coping skills, 122–23, 143
corrective emotional experience, 17–18, 119
countertransference management, 41–42
courage capacity, 39–40
creative expression, as homework, 196
See also art
creative potential, underutilized, case example of, 276–284
criticism. *See* self-criticism
cue words, for continuing or stopping, 149
cue words, for resource installation, 131, 134
cue words, for safe place, 48, 49b
cultural differences, 152, 185
Curran, L., 27
cutting, 178

Dalai Lama, xviii, 66
dance of attunement, 33–34
See also attunement
Darsa, K., 27
"David" (case example), 99–106
DBT. *See* dialectical behavior therapy (DBT)
debriefing, 68b, 119, 188b, 197b
depression
in children, 142
positive cognitions and, 211
positive memories and, 121–22, 123
synaptic pruning and, 23
See also case examples

desensitization
  in EMDR-M, 182
  overview of, 203–14, 212*b*, 215*b*
  in standard EMDR protocol, 180
  See also various case examples
Developing a Secure Self (Steele),
  125–26
developmental deficits repair
  case examples of, 92–106, 341–372
  interweaves and, 231
  new parent creation and, 73–94
  nonlinear processing in, 292
  See also child self and adult self
    relationships; parent-child
    relationships
*Developmental Needs Meeting
  Strategy* (Schmidt), 125
developmental stages, moving through,
  92–94
  See also various case examples
dialectical behavior therapy (DBT),
  322
DID. *See* dissociative identity disorder
  (DID)
disloyalty, 78
dismissing attachment. *See* avoidant
  attachment
disorganized and unresolved trauma
  or loss, 10–11
dissociation
  body experience sensitivity and, 34
  closed eyes and, 147
  eye contact and, 209
  floatback versus, 175
  interweaves for, 240
  memory gaps and, 140
  dissociative identity disorder (DID),
    114
  distancing techniques, 15, 153–54
  distress. *See* affect tolerance; client
    safety
dogs
  client safety and, 15, 153
  interweave use of, 277–281
  as resource figures, 55, 61, 170, 323,
    332, 337, 338, 340

Drama of the Gifted Child (Miller), xvii
drawing, 193–94, 196, 250
drinking, 178
  See also alcoholism, case example
    concerning; substance abuse
dual awareness
  in case examples, 303
  fostering, 208–9
  See also attunement
DVDs, as a therapeutic container, 193
Dyadic Resourcing (Manfield), 126
dysregulation, 10–11
  See also abreactions

early attachment trauma
  case examples of, 160–173, 288–320,
    321–340, 341–372
  feelings of manipulation and, 185
  processing stages of clients with, 228
  repair of, 93–94
  See also birth traumas
earned secure attachment, 7, 8
eating disorders, case example of,
  321–340
EBPP. *See* evidence-based practice in
  psychology (EBPP)
education interweaves, 252, 344
ego states, blocked processing and, 225,
  361–62
ego strength
  challenging life situation and, 131
  information gathering and, 143
  interweaves and, 231
  lack of safety and, 142
  pacing of treatment sessions and, 201
  positive experiences and memories
    and, 52
  resource development and installa-
    tion and, 46, 144
Einstein, A., 66
EMDR. *See* eye-movement desensitiza
  tion and reprocessing (EMDR)
EMDR (Shapiro & Silk-Forrest), 146
The EMDR Early Trauma Protocol
  (O'Shea), 126
EMDR Essentials (Maiberger), 146

EMDRIA. *See* EMDR International Association (EMDRIA)

EMDR International Association (EMDRIA), 4

EMDR in the Treatment of Adults Abused as Children (Parnell), xvii, 4, 14, 59, 139

EMDR modified protocol (EMDR-M)
as an AF-EMDR principle, 27–28, 29*b*
benefits of, 186*b*
body scan and, 28, 29*b*, 182, 183*b*, 187, 188*b*
bridging techniques and, 177*b*
as EBPP, 13–14
memory processing via, 203–4
overview of, 180–82, 183*b*, 185–87, 188*b*
rationale for, 183–85
See also case examples; treatment sessions

EMDR Solutions (Shapiro), 252

emotional abuse, history of, 146, 276–284
See also relational trauma

emotional regulation, 10, 15, 18
See also charge, emotional

emotions, 39–40, 209

empathic resonance, 34–35, 54

empathic resonance capacity, 31–33

empathy, as a resource, 119
See also attunement; therapeutic relationship

empowerment, 67, 145, 220, 234, 249
See also self advocacy

EMs. *See* eye movements (EMs)

encouragement, 204, 208–9, 222, 225
See also positive cognitions

enmeshed mothers, case examples of, 246–47, 271–76

Esalen Institute, 12, 95

essential EMDR protocol, 28

essential spiritual self, 127–29, 129*b*

evaluations, for EMDR readiness, 45–46, 118, 144*b*, 173

evaluations, of desensitization processing, 209–12

evaluations, of treatment progress, 198–200
See also Subjective Units of Distress Scale (SUDS); Validity of Cognition Scale (VoC)

evidence-based practice in psychology (EBPP), 12–14

Ewing, N., 256, 276

"Exploring the Efficacy of Parnell's Modified Eye Movement Desensitization and Reprocessing Protocol for Participants Diagnosed with Posttraumatic Stress Disorder" (Brightman, Curran, and Parnell), 27

Extending EMDR (Manfield), 140

eye contact
in AF-EMDR, 5, 152
in case examples, 311, 340, 363
desensitization and, 204, 207
dissociation and, 209
validation of personal reality and, 241
See also eyes closed, client safety and

eye-movement desensitization and reprocessing (EMDR)
evolution of, 3–5
example of session of, 157–59
phases of, 4
preparation of client for, 139, 143, 145–157, 160–173
standard EMDR protocol, 179–180, 181*b*
therapist experience of, 31
See also case examples; EMDR modified protocol (EMDR-M); treatment sessions

eye movements (EMs), 146–47

eyes closed, client safety and, 147

"false self," xx

family members, responsibility as children to, 245–47, 266

See also fathers; mothers; parents
family resources, as an interweave,
  245–47
fathers. *See* ideal father; ideal parents
fears, blocked processing and, 225–27
  See also client safety
feeder memories, 188–89, 224
feeling, capacity for. *See* affect tolerance; body experience sensitivity;
  therapeutic relationship
feelings. *See* affect tolerance; emotional
  regulation; emotions
Felder, E., 321
fight-or-flight response, 107, 309
Finch, A., 54
floatback, 175
flooding, prevention of, 139, 156, 212
forbidden impulse expression, as an
  interweave, 249–250
Forgash, C., 225
Fosha, D., 119
four S's of attachment, xiii
free-associative processing, 26, 206–7
  See also various case examples
French, T., 17
Freud, S., 17, 33
future pace, bridging techniques and,
  176, 178*b*
future templates, 129, 132, 351, 361,
  369

gay and lesbian clients, 83
A General Theory of Love (Lewis,
  Amini, and Lannon), 32
getting stuck, prevention of, 212, 214
  See also interweaves
glass wall, 15, 154
God, 56, 126, 273, 275
  See also Higher Power
goddesses, 67, 126, 325
Goldstein, J., xviii, 113
gratitude, as homework assignment, 24
grief, 78, 109*b*, 111
grounded spacious attunement, 205–6
grounding exercises, 197*b*
guided imagery

avoidant attachment and, 9
as a closure tool, 192–93
in example treatment session, 158
for ideal mother, 75
information gathering and, 141
for inner wisdom figures, 66
love resources and, 108, 110
memory chaining, prevention of,
  and, 156
pacing of treatment sessions and,
  201
to repair womb and birth experiences, 81–83
for therapeutic containers, 155
as transitional objects, 195
  See also tapping in; therapeutic
  containers

Hakomi psychotherapy, 34, 315
Hammer, E., 32
handholding
  attunement and, 149
  desensitization and, 204
  as distancing technique, 154
  intimacy capacity and, 15, 36
healing imagery, 192–93
*Healing the Heart of Dissociation with
  EMDR and Ego State Therapy*
  (Forgash), 225
health maintenance, as homework, 196
healthy relating, media sources of,
  125–26
healthy relating, memories of, 120–23,
  131–34, 150–51
  See also love resources
heart refuge, 112–13, 113*b*
Hebb's law, 22
The Help, 54, 125
Higher Power, 130, 130*b*
  See also God
higher self. *See* essential spiritual self
history taking
  bilateral stimulations (BLS) and,
  141
  EMDR preparation and, 4, 138, 139,
  140

memories of healthy relating during, 120

nurturing figures during, 53

resource development and installation during, 73, 145

See also case examples; information gathering

homework assignments

art as, 196

as containment or facilitation of processing, 196

ideal mother development, 77

negative and positive messages as, 318

resource development and installation, 166, 351

safe or peaceful place as, 169

self-criticism within, 166–67

homosexual clients. *See* gay and lesbian clients

hormones, 107, 151

Howard, R., 341

Hughes, D., 15, 31, 37, 150

hypervigilance, 23

hypnotherapy, 153

ideal father, 83, 99–106, 245, 359

See also ideal parents

ideal mother

in case examples, 310–13, 358–59

developing and tapping in an, 73–77

developmental deficits repair using, 95–98

interweave use of, 78–79, 245

roadblocks to creating an, 76–78

sensory activation and, 75, 81–82, 93

sister as, 230

validation of personal reality and, 229

See also Aibileen (*The Help*); ideal parents

ideal parents, 227–230, 330–32, 358, 359

See also ideal father; ideal mother

"If this was your child/friend" interweaves, 237–38

imagery. *See* guided imagery

images, for closure, 191

imaginary containers. *See* therapeutic containers

imagination

as freeing, 76, 92, 358

metaphor use and, 154

neural pathway creation through, 21, 74, 77, 360

tapping into, 21–23, 24–27

See also free-associative processing; guided imagery; resources and resource figures

imagination interweaves, 247–250, 253–54

"I'm confused" interweaves, 237

impulse expression, as an interweave, 249–250

Indians and Indian spirits, 168, 169

See also Native American elders

infants, 31, 32

See also child self and adult self relationships; rebirthing experiences; womb experiences

information gathering, 138, 139–143

See also history taking

inner advisors, 66–68, 67b–68b

inner child loving-kindness meditations, 116–17, 117b

inner helpers, team of, 68–72, 69b

inner wisdom figures, 65–67, 67b–68b

inquiry interweaves, 216, 236–240, 299

insecure attachment, xiv–xv

insecurity wisdom, 40

integration, importance o, xiii–xiv

internal cues. *See* body experience sensitivity; body scan; body sensations

internal working models, 7, 16

interpersonal neurobiology (IPNB), xiii, xiv–xv

intersubjectivity, 36

See also attunement; empathic resonance; therapeutic relationship

interweaves
  during abreactions, 234
  animal use in, 276–284
  in birth trauma repair, 86, 87
  blocked beliefs and matching, 218
  categories of, 236–252, 245*b*,
    254*b*–55*b*
  child development knowledge and,
    42
  closure through use of, 189–191, 217,
    235–36, 253–54
  creation of, 231–33, 232*b*
  ideal father as, 83
  ideal mother as, 78–79, 245
  inner advisors as, 68
  nuances and pitfalls of, 231–36,
    244–45
  overview of, 230–31
  playfulness and, 39
  protector figures as, 61
  resource development and installa-
    tion as, 45, 46
  Socratic, 89, 191
  See also various case examples
intimacy capacity, 15, 33–34, 36,
    148–49
  See also attunement
intuitions, 30–31
Invisible War, 27
IPNB. *See* interpersonal neurobiology
    (IPNB)

Jesus, 54, 67, 126, 127
journaling, 196, 199, 200
judgment. *See* self-criticism
Jung, C., xvii
Jung Institute, xviii

"Ken" (case example), 341–372
Kidd, S., 56
kinesthetic processing, 210
Klein, J., xviii, xix
Korn, D., 13, 131
Kornfield, J., xviii

Lannon, R., 32

"Leah" (case example), 264–271
Leeds, A., 131
left-brain information, 8, 34
lesbian clients. *See* gay and lesbian
    clients
Levine, P., xix
Lewis, T., 32
Lifespan Integration (Pace), 126
limbic resonance, 32
listening ability, 30–31
looping
  approaches to decrease, 217–225
  blocked processing and, 23, 216–17,
    221, 222
  interweaves and, 45, 59, 78–79, 212,
    234–35
  playfulness and, 39
  therapist's sense of, 33
love, neurophysiological responses of,
    107
loved ones, 108, 109*b*, 110, 116*b*
  See also ideal mother; ideal parents;
    pets; those who love you
love resources
  as a closure tool, 194
  overview of, 107–17, 109*b*, 110*b*–11*b*,
    112*b*, 113*b*
  See also attunement; memories of
    healthy relating
loving-kindness meditations, 113–14,
    114*b*–15*b*, 116–17, 116*b*, 117*b*

Mahler, M., xix
Maiberger, B., 146
Main, M., 7, 8
maladaptive schema, resources for,
    131–34
Manfield, P., 126, 140
manipulation, feelings of, 185
Marich, J., 146
Martinez, R., 249
"Mary" (case example), 160–173,
    288–320
Mary (mother of Jesus), 54, 126
media sources of healthy relating,
    125–26

medical procedures, history of, 221
medication, need for, 143, 196
meditations, xviii–xix
  See also loving-kindness meditations;
    mindfulness meditation
Mednick, J., 27
memories
  gaps in, 140
  tapping in resources and negative, 26
  target refocus on earlier stronger,
    213
  therapeutic containers for, 155
  See also positive memories
memories of healthy relating, 120–23,
  131–34
memory chaining, prevention of, 156
memory network activation, 28
memory networks
  bridging techniques and, 177*b*, 178
  EMDR-M and, 182
  interweaves and, 230, 236
  positive cognitions and, 184
  processing and activation of, 203
  Resource Tapping and, 22
  standard EMDR protocol versus,
    179
  See also trauma networks
mental illness, case examples concerning, 271–76
metaphors, as a resource, 352–56
metaphor use, as distancing technique,
  154
metta, 113
Miller, A., xvii–xviii, xix–xx, 40, 41–42
Milstein, P., 95
mind-body circuitry, 22
  See also neuro networks and neural
    pathways
mindfulness meditation, xix, 31, 206
"Mirium" (case example), 69–72,
  70–72, 256–264
mirroring, 241
mirror neuron system, 32, 108
Mobely, M., 125
"Monica" (case example), 34–35, 54
Moses, 54, 71, 126

mothers
  dependence on children by their,
    245–47
  empathic resonance in, 32
  enmeshed, 246–47, 271–76
  issues affecting attachment capacity
    in, 141–42
  See also co-mothers; ideal mother
movement. *See* physical act, with
  resource development and
  installation
movement, during abreactions, 224
movement, in assessing body sensations, 223
movies
  as a distancing technique, 15,
    153–54, 156
  as a processing measure, 213
  as a resource, 125–26
  as a therapeutic container, 193

narrative coherence, 140
Native American elders, 54, 67
negative beliefs, 161, 166, 354
  See also blocking beliefs, checking
    for; *various case examples*
negative cognitions, 179, 181, 182, 344
negative memories, 26, 155
  See also various case examples
neglect, history of
  avoidant attachment and, 8
  in case examples, 99–106, 160–173,
    276–284, 287–320, 306–7
  choice/control and, 220–21
  client safety and, 219
  interweaves and, 234–35, 236, 245,
    252, 253–54
  looping and, 216
  loving-kindness meditations and, 116
  narrative coherence and, 140
  pacing of treatment sessions and,
    201–2, 228
  positive cognitions and, 211
  positive memories and, 52
  resource development and installa-
    tion and, 46, 54, 55, 73, 201

safe or peaceful place and, 46
safe touch and, 150
targets and severity of, 21
therapeutic relationship and, 16
See also relational trauma
neuro networks and neural pathways
attachment styles and, 7, 9
corrective emotional experience and,
18
disorganized and unresolved trauma
or loss, 11
handholding and, 151
imagination and creation of, 21, 74,
77, 360
positive imagery and, 52
relationship repair and creation of,
16
Resource Tapping and, 4, 19–27, 23
See also right-brain to right-brain
connections; sympathetic nervous
system
neurophysiological responses, 107, 151
nondirective questions, during desensitization, 207–8
nondual interweaves, 243–44
nonlinear processing, of symptoms,
292
nonverbal attunement, 31–32
nonverbal communication
avoidant attachment and, 8
body experience sensitivity and, 34
client safety created through, 15, 82
during desensitization, 207
grounded spacious attunement and,
206
See also eye contact
nonverbal communication attunement,
35–36
nurturing figures, 35, 52–60, 53*b*, 58*b*,
171–73
See also ideal father; ideal mother;
ideal parents; love resources;
various case examples

Oakley, A., 311, 313
Omaha, J., 155

open-ended questions, as interweaves,
238–39
See also Socratic interweaves
Oprah, 133, 134
orbital frontal cortex, 22
O'Shea, K., 126
outcome-focused interweaves,
239–240
overeating, 178

Pace, P., 126
PACE capacity, 37–39
pacing, of treatment sessions, 200–202,
227, 228, 233–34
panic attacks, in case examples,
341–372
parasympathetic nervous system, 151
parent-child relationships, 31, 32, 107,
252
See also mothers; relational trauma;
various case examples
parents
issues affecting attachment capacity
in, 141–42
as nurturing figures, 54
See also ideal father; ideal mother;
ideal parents; mothers
Parnell, L., 311, 314, 321, 339, 341, *See*
"Patty" (case example), 246–47
peaceful place. *See* safe or peaceful
place
peptides, 107
perspective broadening, as an interweave, 243
pets
ideal mother development and, 75
as nurturing figures, 55
in treatment sessions, 153, 323, 332,
337, 338, 340
See also cats; dogs
pets, case examples with, 277–284
Phillips, M., xix, 52, 128
physical abuse, history of
bilateral stimulations (BLS) and, 148
in case examples, 34–35, 95–98, 242,
271–76, 321–340

seating arrangements and, 152
therapeutic relationship and, 16
See also Invisible War; relational
trauma
physical act, with resource development and installation, 134
playfulness, acceptance, empathy, and
curiosity (PACE), 37–39
poetry writing, 196, 199
polyvagal theory, 309
Porges, S., 309
positive cognitions
child self and adult self relationships
and, 334–35
for closure, 191
during desensitization, 211
EMDR-M and, 28, 181, 183–84
in standard EMDR protocol,
179–180
target nuances and, 214
See also various case examples
positive experiences, 23–24, 38, 122–23,
143
positive memories, 52, 53*b*, 155
See also memories of healthy
relating
positive statements, 204
See also positive cognitions
post-traumatic stress disorder (PTSD)
case examples of, 321–340
EMDR and, 3, 4
EMDR-M and, 13, 27
synaptic pruning and, 23
Potter, A., 13
preoccupied attachment, 9–10
preparation of client for EMDR,
160–173
presence ability, 31, 36
Prichard, H., 160, 200, 202, 287
primary therapists, 54, 153, 162–63,
171
probing statements, 315
processing. *See* adaptive information
processing (AIP) model; case
examples; desensitization; free-
associative processing

process-oriented positive cognition,
191
See also positive cognitions
procrastination, 178, 371
progress reevaluation, 198–200
protection, circle of, 65, 65*b*
protector figures, 60–62, 62*b*–63*b*,
64–65, 65*b*
See also various case examples
psychological abuse. *See* relational
trauma
PTSD. *See* post-traumatic stress
disorder (PTSD)
pulsers, 25, 93, 147, 150, 166
See also Tac/AudioScan; tappers

questioning, 19, 207–8
See also open-ended questions, as
interweaves

rapid eye movement (REM) sleep,
146
rapport. *See* attunement; client safety;
therapeutic relationship
readiness assessment, for EMDR,
144*b*, 173
reality, validation of, 240–43
rebirthing experiences, 239–240,
310–13, 349–350
reflective listening, avoiding, 210
rejection history, case examples of,
160–173, 288–320
relating, media sources of healthy,
125–26
relating, memories of healthy, 120–23
See also love resources
relational trauma
definition of, 6
disorganized and unresolved, 10–11
EMDR-M and, 27
examples of, xix
lack of positive memories and, 120
shame and, 185
standard EMDR protocol and,
179
synaptic pruning and, 22–23

See also abandonment, history of; case examples; childhood abuse, history of; rejection history, case examples of

relationship repair, 16, 17
See also various case examples

relaxation, 46, 47, 49*b*, 52

release, in desensitization, 207

REM. *See* rapid eye movement (REM) sleep

resistance, 38

resonance. *See* attunement; empathic resonance; right-brain to right-brain connections

resource development and installation

  in case examples, 69–72, 166–67, 168, 335–36, 347–361

  for current life situation, blocking belief, or maladaptive schema, 131–34

  ego strength and, 46, 144

  in first session, 145, 146

  during history taking, 73, 145

  homework assignment of, 166, 351

  physical act with, 134

  readiness assessment for EMDR and, 45–46, 118, 144*b*, 173

  sensory activation and, 24, 26, 170

  See also resources and resource figures; Resource Tapping; tapping in

resource interweaves, 234, 244–47, 245*b*, 295, 328, 334

resource reinstallation, 157

resources and resource figures

  animals as, 55, 61, 170, 323, 332, 337, 338, 340

  for different attachment styles, 124–25

  for family members, 245–47

  healthy boundaries, 123–24

  ideal father, 83, 99–106, 245, 359

  ideal parents, 227–230, 330–32, 358, 359

love, 107–17, 110*b*–11*b*, 112*b*, 113*b*, 194

media sources of healthy relating, 125–26

memories of healthy relating, 120–23, 131–34

metaphors as, 352–56

overview of, 45–72

spiritual, 54, 56, 61, 126–130, 129*b*, 130*b*

support people in treatment sessions, 152, 153

See also ideal mother; right-brain to right-brain connections; therapeutic relationship

Resource Tapping

  as an AF-EMDR principle, 19–27

  avoidant attachment and, 9

  Buddhism and, xviii

  in case examples, 329, 347

  definition of, 6–7

  disorganized and unresolved trauma or loss, 11

  instructions for, 24–27

  introduction and foundation of, 45–46, 145, 146

  memory networks and neural pathways and, 22, 23

  pacing of treatment sessions and, 201

  positive focus with, 21

  precautions for, 27, 148

  results using, xxi, 38

  symptom alleviation through, 20

  techniques for, 148–49

  Tibetan influence in, xviii

  See also resource development and installation; resources and resource figures; tapping in

resource toolkit, 24

responsibility, as a blocking belief, 219–220

responsibility, to family members, 245–47, 266

rewriting the scene, as an interweave, 249

right-brain activation, 74, 75, 175, 205–6
    See also bilateral stimulations (BLS); guided imagery; sensory activation
right-brain integration, 8–9
right-brain organization. *See* neuro networks and neural pathways
right-brain to right-brain connections
    attachment repair and, 30–31
    dance of attunement and, 34
    empathic resonance and, 32
    eye contact and, 152, 204
    See also attunement; therapeutic relationship
Ross, C., xix, 228
Russell, M., 13

sacred place, 51
"safe island," 50–51
safe objects, 153
safe or peaceful place
    in case examples, 167–69, 358
    desensitization and, 209
    heart refuge as, 112–13, 113*b*
    overview of, 46–52, 49*b*, 51*b*
    See also boundaries, healthy
safe touch, 5, 148–49, 150–52
safety. *See* client safety
safety, as a blocked belief, 218–19
Salzberg, S., 113
sand tray, 201
Schmidt, S., 55, 61–62, 125
Schore, A.
    corrective emotional experience and, 18
    emotional regulation, 15
    as influence on author, xix
    nonverbal communication, 35
    relational trauma, 6
    right-brain to right-brain connection, 206
Schore, J., 35
Scully, R., 27
sculpting, 193, 196
seating arrangements, 148, 149–150, 152

secondary gains, 226
The Secret Life of Bees (Kidd), 56
secure attachment, xiii, 8
self advocacy, 202
    See also empowerment
self-criticism, 166–67
self-esteem, 142
sensory activation
    challenging life situation and, 131
    ideal mother and, 75, 81–82, 93
    memories of healthy relating and, 121
    positive imagery and, 52
    resource development and installation and, 24, 26, 170
    safe or peaceful place and, 47, 52
    spiritual figures and, 126
    therapeutic relationship and, 105
    those who love you and, 110
    See also bilateral stimulations (BLS); body sensations; guided imagery; safe touch
sexual abuse, history of
    in case examples, 34–35, 95–98, 239, 242–43, 271–76, 321–340
    ideal mother and, 79
    loving-kindness meditations and, 114
    seating arrangements and, 152
    self advocacy and, 202
    sexual arousal and, 252
    split-screen interweaves and, 250
    therapeutic containers and, 194
    therapeutic relationship and, 16
    touch and, 148
    See also relational trauma
sexual arousal, 218, 221, 223, 239, 252
shame, 9, 10, 108, 185, 221
    See also sexual arousal
Shapiro, F.
    adaptive information processing (AIP) model, 18–19
    assessing progress, 198
    cognitive interweaves, 231, 236
    EMDR origins, 3, 4
    floatback, 175
    innovator, xiv, xv

modification of EMDR protocols, 14
neuro networks, xix*n*1
positive cognitions, 183
safe place, 48
Validity of Cognition Scale (VoC), 180, 184
Shapiro, R., 251
Siegel, D., xiii–xv, xix, xx, 12, 151
silent witness. *See* essential spiritual self
sister, as ideal mother, 230
social anxiety, case examples of, 70–72, 256–264
Socratic interweaves, 89, 191, 220, 237
    See also open-ended questions, as interweaves
soldiers, female, 27
Somatic Experiencing, 34, 201
somatic reactions. *See* body scan; body sensations; sensory activation
somatic resources. *See* safe touch
sorting interweaves, 250–52
sounds, disturbing, 155
spiritual figures and resources, 54, 56, 61, 126–130, 129*b*, 130*b*
split-screen interweaves, 250–51
stalking behavior, case examples of, 341–372
standard EMDR protocol, 179–180, 181*b*, 187
    See also EMDR modified protocol (EMDR-M); eye-movement desensitization and reprocessing (EMDR)
Steele, A., 125
story-telling ability, 140
Streep, M., 56, 93
Subjective Units of Distress Scale (SUDS)
    blocked processing and, 217
    body scan location and, 187
    in EMDR-M, 28, 181–82, 185
    incomplete sessions and, 189
    interweaves to close sessions and, 253
    in standard EMDR protocol, 180

target nuances and, 214
suboptimal regulation, xiv
substance abuse, 10
    See also alcoholism, case example concerning; drinking
successes, tapping in, 200
SUDS. *See* Subjective Units of Distress Scale (SUDS)
Sundelin-Wahlsten, V., 13
support people, in treatment sessions, 152, 153
"Susan" (case example), 95–98
sympathetic nervous system, 107, 113, 142
sympathetic–parasympathetic system, 23
symptom-focused approach, 174, 174–75, 199–200
symptoms
    nonlinear processing of, 292
    as part of information gathering, 138, 139
    progress reevaluation through improvement in, 198, 199–200
    Resource Tapping and alleviation of, 20
    See also anxiety; body sensations; depression; dissociation; post-traumatic stress disorder (PTSD)
synaptic pruning, 22–23

Tac/AudioScan
    as bilateral stimulation (BLS), xxiii, 25
    in case examples, 96, 166
    client-centered therapy and, 147–48
    See also pulsers; tappers
talking, as an interweave pitfall, 234
talking, during desensitization, 204–5, 208–9, 210
talking, in assessing body sensations, 223–24
talk therapy
    EMDR and, 4, 5
    pacing of treatment sessions and, 201–2, 210, 228

pitfalls of, 234
therapeutic relationship and, 119
tapes, of relaxation exercises and safe
    place resources, 195
tappers, 352, 357
    See also pulsers
tapping in
    attunement and, 148–49
    circle of inner helpers, 69b
    the circle of love, 112b
    circle of protection, 65b
    the essential spiritual self, 128–29,
        129b
    the heart refuge, 113b
    your Higher Power, 130b
    an ideal father, 83
    an ideal mother, 73–77
    to imagination, 21–23, 24–27
    inner advisors, 67b–68b
    loved ones, 109b
    nurturing figures, 58b
    as preferred term, 20
    protector figures, 62b–63b, 63b
    safe or peaceful place, 49b, 51b
    of therapeutic relationship, 119
    therapist's attachment repair,
        315–17
    those who love you, 110b–11b
    See also resource development and
        installation; resources and resource
        figures; Resource Tapping; various
        case examples
Tapping In (Parnell), xvii, 21
    target creation and development
    earlier stronger memories and, 213
    in EMDR-M, 187
    lack of emotional charge and, 9, 21,
        73, 124
    overview of, 174–76, 176b–78b,
        178–79
    in standard EMDR protocol, 179
    See also bridging techniques; chan-
        nels of association; charge,
        emotional
targets, 198, 199–200, 213–14, 235
television, as a resource, 125–26

therapeutic containers
    in case examples, 296–97, 351
    courage capacity as, 40
    creation of, 143–44, 144f, 151,
        155–56
    drawing of, 194
    grief and sadness and, 109b
    handholding and, 151
    negative memories and, 26
    resource development and installa-
        tion and, 46
    resource installation and, 56
    for unfinished material, 193, 197b
    See also affect tolerance; ego
        strength
therapeutic relationship
    as an AF-EMDR principle, 16–18,
        118–120, 137–38
    ambivalent and preoccupied attach-
        ment and, 9
    avoidance of categorizing clients
        within, 7–8
    blocked beliefs and, 218
    bridging techniques and, 178
    in case examples, 319, 331, 332
    client fears within, 226
    disorganized and unresolved trauma
        or loss, 11
    emotional regulation through, 15
    facilitation within, 19
    healthy boundaries within, 123
    pacing of treatment sessions and,
        202
    as safe or peaceful place, 47
    sensory activation and, 105
    staying out of the way in, 208, 209
    SUDS and VoC and, 185
    treatment structure clarification
        within, 164
    VoC and, 184
    See also attunement; client-centered
        therapy; client safety; nonverbal
        communication
therapeutic shifts, in case examples,
    313–14
therapists

attunement by, 205–6, 207
characteristics and skills for, 30–42
EMDR experience for, 31
lack of interweave use among, 217
progress reevaluation as feedback
    for, 200
as support people in treatment
    sessions, 153
See also adjunctive therapists;
    primary therapists
A Therapist's Guide to EMDR (Parnell)
attunement, 33
child self and adult self relation-
    ships, 59
client safety and, 15
EMDR client preparation, 139
EMDR protocol, 4, 28
essential spiritual self, 127
as evolution of author's techniques,
    xvii
information gathering, 139
interweave pitfalls, 233
target creation and development,
    174, 179
user-friendliness of, xx
those who love you, 110, 110b–11b
See also loved ones
Tibetan meditations, xviii
"Tina" (case example), 276–284
To Kill a Mockingbird, 54
touch, safe, 148–49, 150–52
transference, 178, 314–15, 332
See also countertransference
    management
Transforming Trauma: EMDR
    (Parnell), xvii, 145–46
transitional objects, 195
trauma. *See* relational trauma
trauma networks
in EMDR-M, 28, 182, 183
parent as nurturing figure and, 54
Resource Tapping and, 5, 21
VoC and, 184
See also memory networks

treatment sessions
animals and pets in, 153, 323, 332,
    337, 338, 340
assessing progress of, 198–200
clarification of structure of, 164
closure for, 188–194, 188b, 196b–97b,
    253–54
EMDR-M for, 180–87, 183b, 186b
management of desensitization in,
    211–13, 212b, 215b
pacing of, 200–202, 227, 228, 233–34
review of, as positive cognition, 191,
    192, 200
standard EMDR protocol for,
    179–180, 181b
suggestions for clients between,
    194–96
See also various case examples
triggers
body experience sensitivity and, 33
countertransference management
    and, 41
early attachment trauma and, 185
loving-kindness meditations and, 116
relationship repair and, 178
safe or peaceful place and, 47
seating arrangements and, 149
target creation and development
    and, 174–75
touch and, 148
"true self," xix–xx
trust, 241, 242–43, 335–36
See also therapeutic relationship
truth interweaves, 240–44
two-handed interweaves, 251–52

unconscious mind, 7, 176, 182, 183,
    218
unfinished material, therapeutic
    containers for, 193
unresolved trauma or loss. *See*
    disorganized and unresolved
    trauma or loss

validation of personal reality, 57, 228,
    229, 240–43
Validity of Cognition Scale (VoC)
    in EMDR-M, 13, 28, 181, 182, 183,
        184–85
    in standard EMDR protocol, 180
van der Kolk, B., 23
visualization. *See* guided imagery;
    imagination
VoC. *See* Validity of Cognition Scale
    (VoC)

Watts, A., 40
waves, during desensitization, 207, 208
weirdness factor, 147
Wesselmann, D., 13
"What do you know to be true?" case
    example, 242–43
"What do you see" interweaves, 243
Winfrey, O., 133, 134
Winnicott, D., xix, xx, 195
wisdom of insecurity, 40
witness, silent. *See* essential spiritual
    self
Wolpe, J., 180
womb experiences, 80–83, 85–89, 93,
    311–12

Yeshe, T., xviii, 113
yoga, xix